KNIGHT

RAYEARTH

Volume 2 (of 3)

ALSO AVAILABLE FROM TOKYOPOP®

**For more
information visit
www.TOKYOPOP.com**

02.03.04T

ALSO AVAILABLE FROM TOKYOPOP

MANGA

02.03.04T

Translator - Anita Sengupta
English Adaption - Jamie S. Rich
Copy Editors - Bryce Coleman, Carol Fox
Retouch - Paul Morrissey
Lettering - Monalisa de Asis
Cover Layout - Patrick Hook

Editor - Jake Forbes
Digital Imaging Manager - Chris Buford
Pre-Press Manager - Antonio DePietro
Production Managers - Jennifer Miller, Mutsumi Miyazaki
Art Director - Matt Alford
Managing Editor - Jill Freshney
VP of Production - Ron Klamert
President & C.O.O. - John Parker
Publisher & C.E.O. - Stuart Levy

E-mail: info@TOKYOPOP.com
Come visit us online at www.TOKYOPOP.com

A  Manga

TOKYOPOP Inc.
5900 Wilshire Blvd. Suite 2000
Los Angeles, CA 90036

Magic Knights Rayearth II Vol. 2

Magic Knight Rayearth II Vol. 2 ©1995 CLAMP.
First published in 1995 by Kodansha Ltd., Tokyo.
English publication rights arranged through Kodansha Ltd.

ISBN: 1-59182-267-X

First TOKYOPOP® printing: April 2003

10 9 8 7 6 5 4 3 2

Printed in the USA

The Story So Far...

The magical land of Cephiro is under attack! After the Magic Knights eliminated Princess Emeraude, they left the land without its "Pillar." Now the land is crumbling and three foreign nations lead invasion forces to claim Cephiro as their own. Each of the three countries has sent out an enchanted "road" in order to penetrate Cephiro's border. In order to become the new Pillar, however, they must find the one hidden road which leads to Cephiro's heart.

Hikaru, Umi and Fuu, three ordinary Tokyo schoolgirls who became the Magic Knights, are summoned back to Cephiro, just in time. What's strange is that no one knows who summoned them. The people of Cephiro are happy to see the girls, nonetheless. All of their old friends are there: Presea the blacksmith, Clef the magician and Ferio the swordsman, who reveals himself to be the prince! Oh, and we can't forget Mokona, the little white puffball. The girls meet a few new citizens of Cephiro as well: Lantis, Zagato's brother and a powerful warrior, and Primera, the pixie who's infatuated with him.

There isn't much time for introductions, however, as the first of the three countries begins its assault. Autozam, a land of machines, sends a giant "mech" to attack. It's piloted by the noble Eagle Vision, a former friend of Lantis, and Autozam's leader. The three girls don the "Mashin," or Spirits, in order to fight off Eagle's mech, but you can be sure he will return.

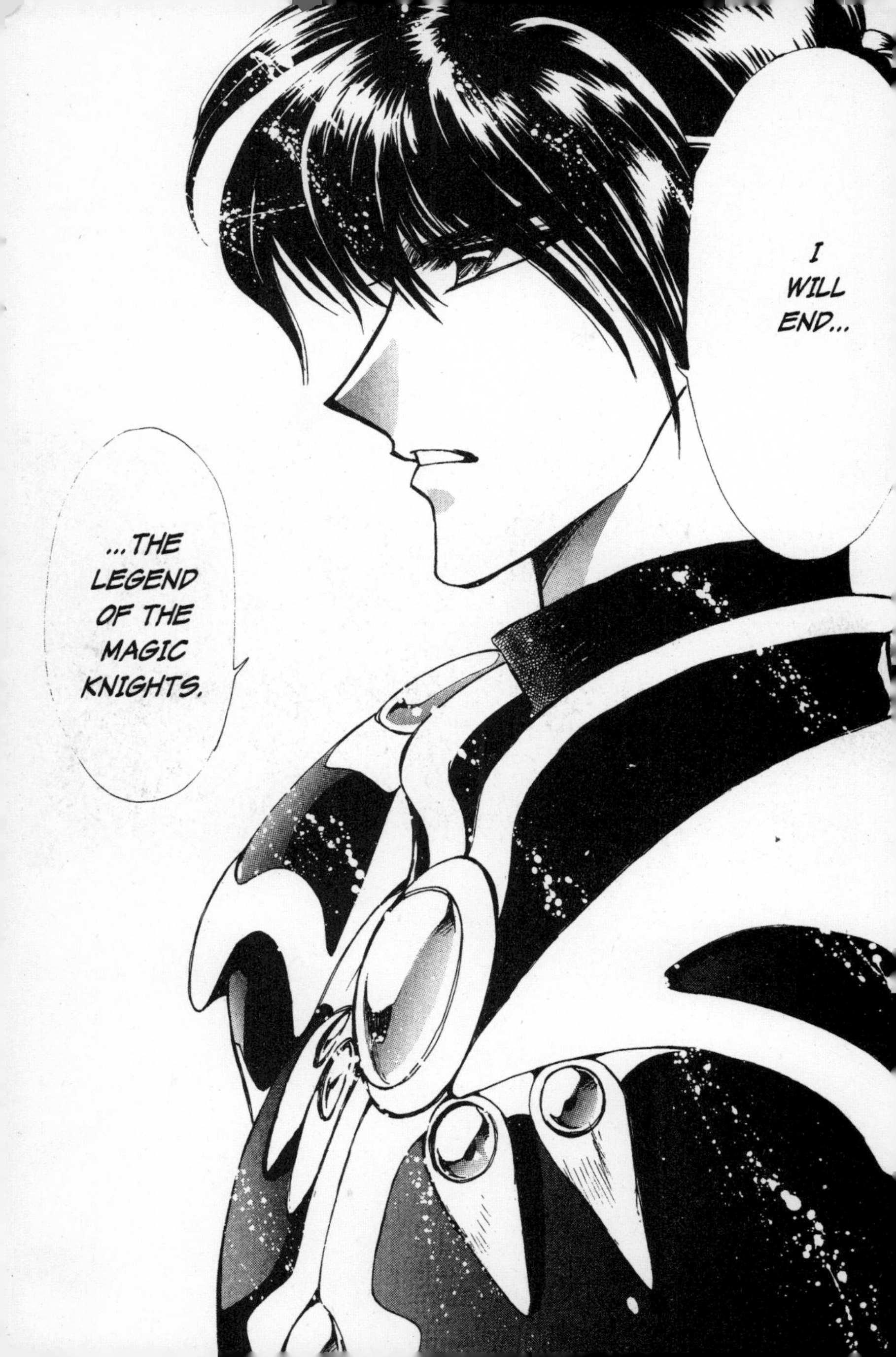
I WILL END...
...THE LEGEND OF THE MAGIC KNIGHTS.

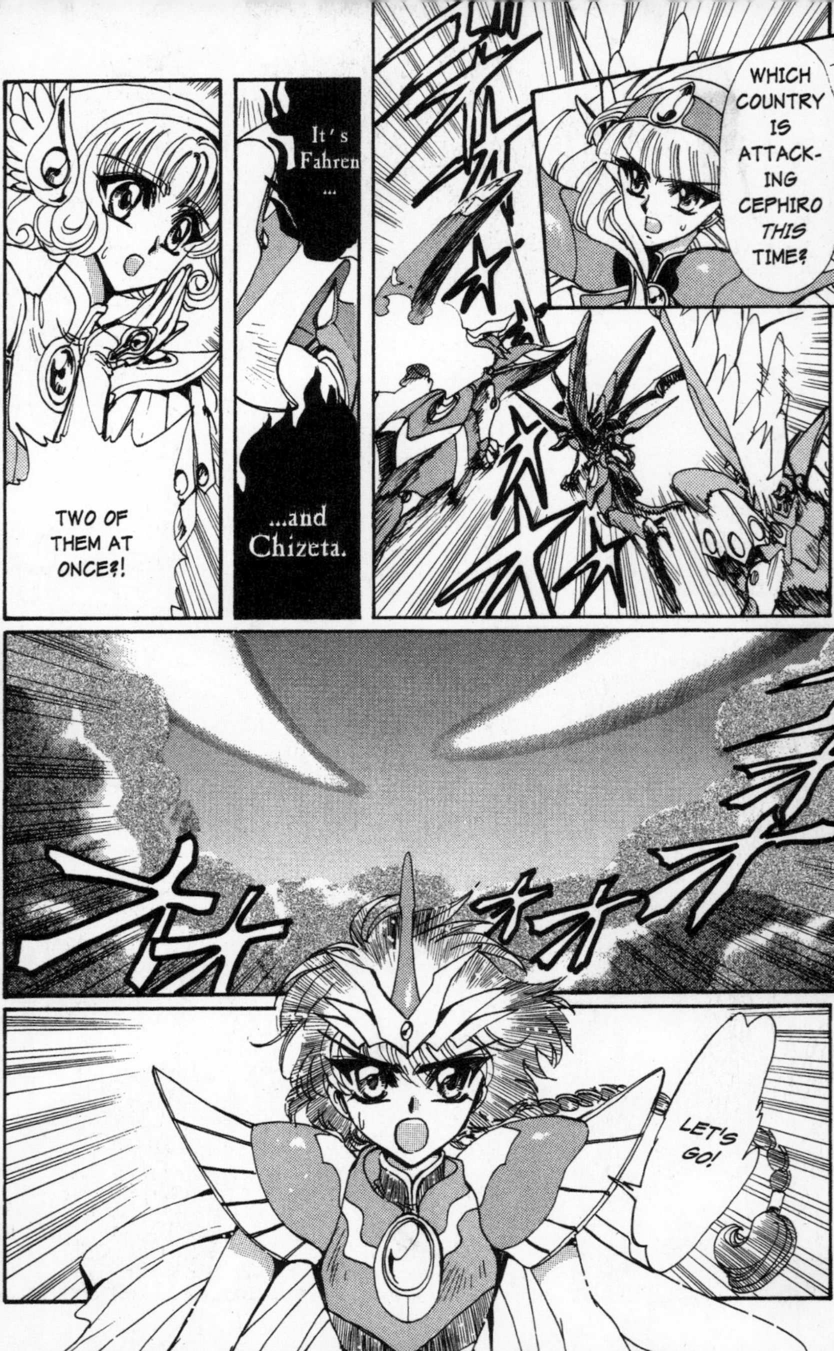
WHICH COUNTRY IS ATTACKING CEPHIRO THIS TIME?
It's Fahren ...
...and Chizeta.
TWO OF THEM AT ONCE?!
LET'S GO!

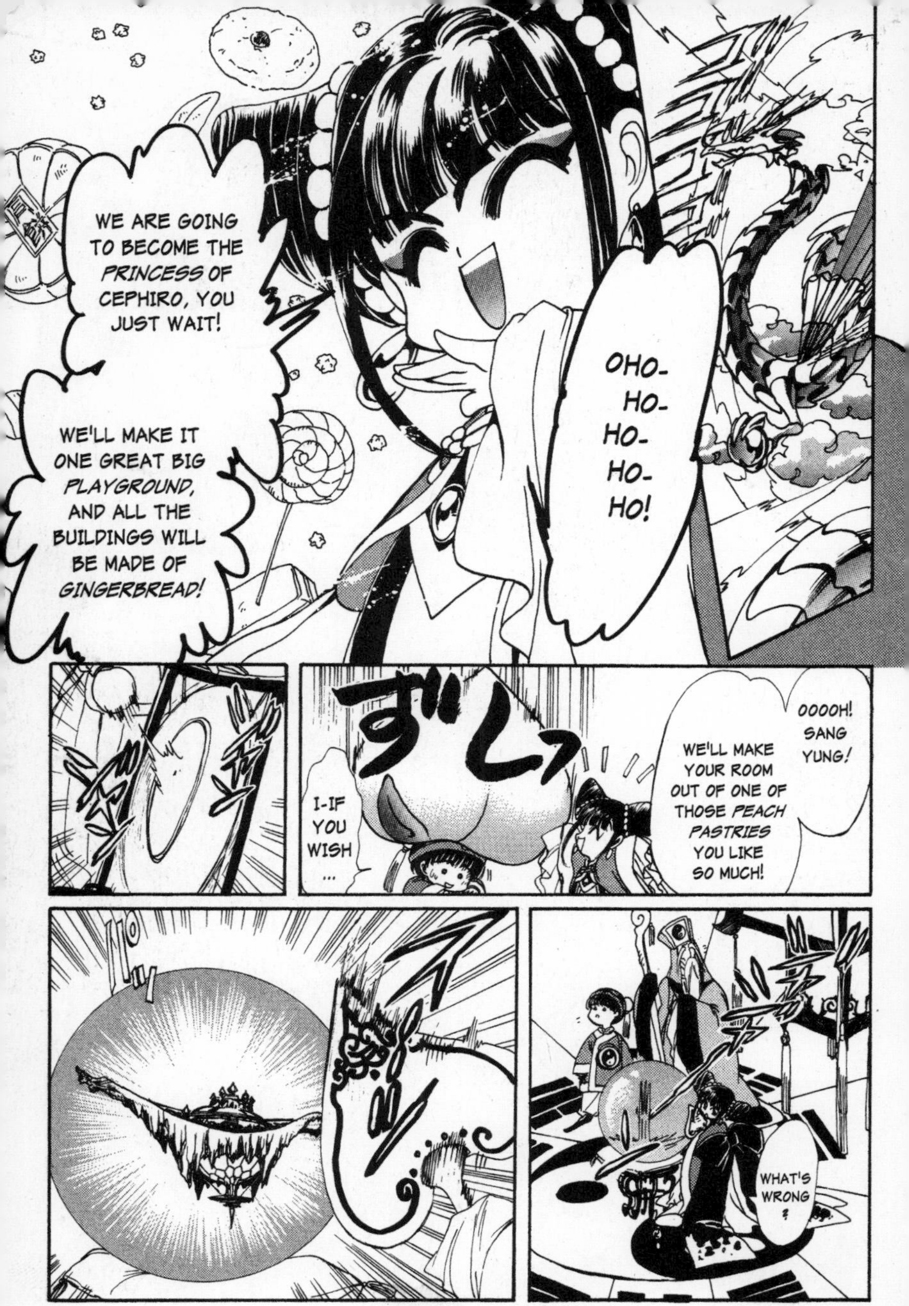

OHO-HO-HO-HO-HO!
WE ARE GOING TO BECOME THE *PRINCESS* OF CEPHIRO, YOU JUST WAIT!
WE'LL MAKE IT ONE GREAT BIG *PLAYGROUND*, AND ALL THE BUILDINGS WILL BE MADE OF *GINGERBREAD*!
OOOOH! SANG YUNG!
WE'LL MAKE YOUR ROOM OUT OF ONE OF THOSE *PEACH PASTRIES* YOU LIKE SO MUCH!
ずしっ
I-IF YOU WISH ...
WHAT'S WRONG?

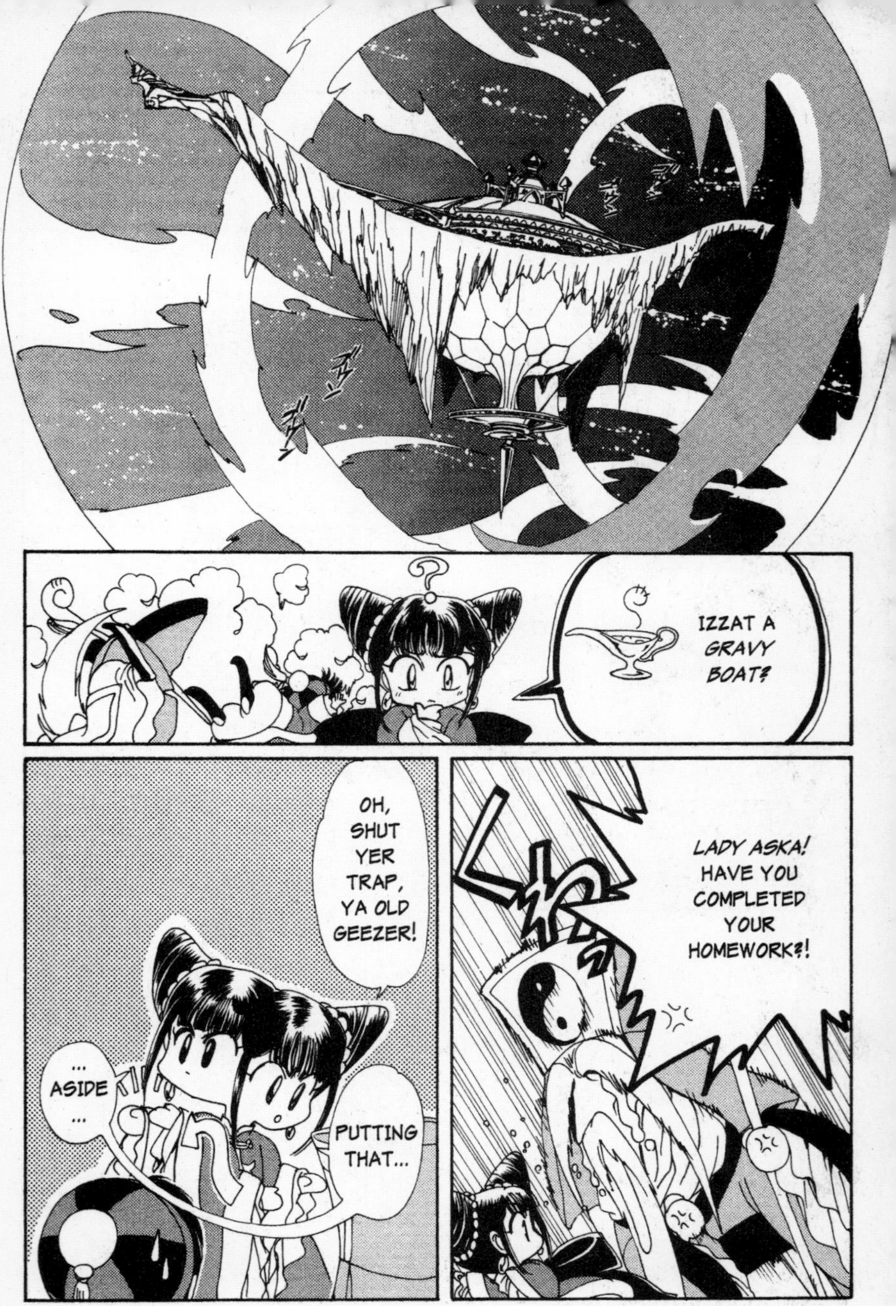
IZZAT A GRAVY BOAT?!
LADY ASKA! HAVE YOU COMPLETED YOUR HOMEWORK?!
OH, SHUT YER TRAP, YA OLD GEEZER!
PUTTING THAT...
... ASIDE ...

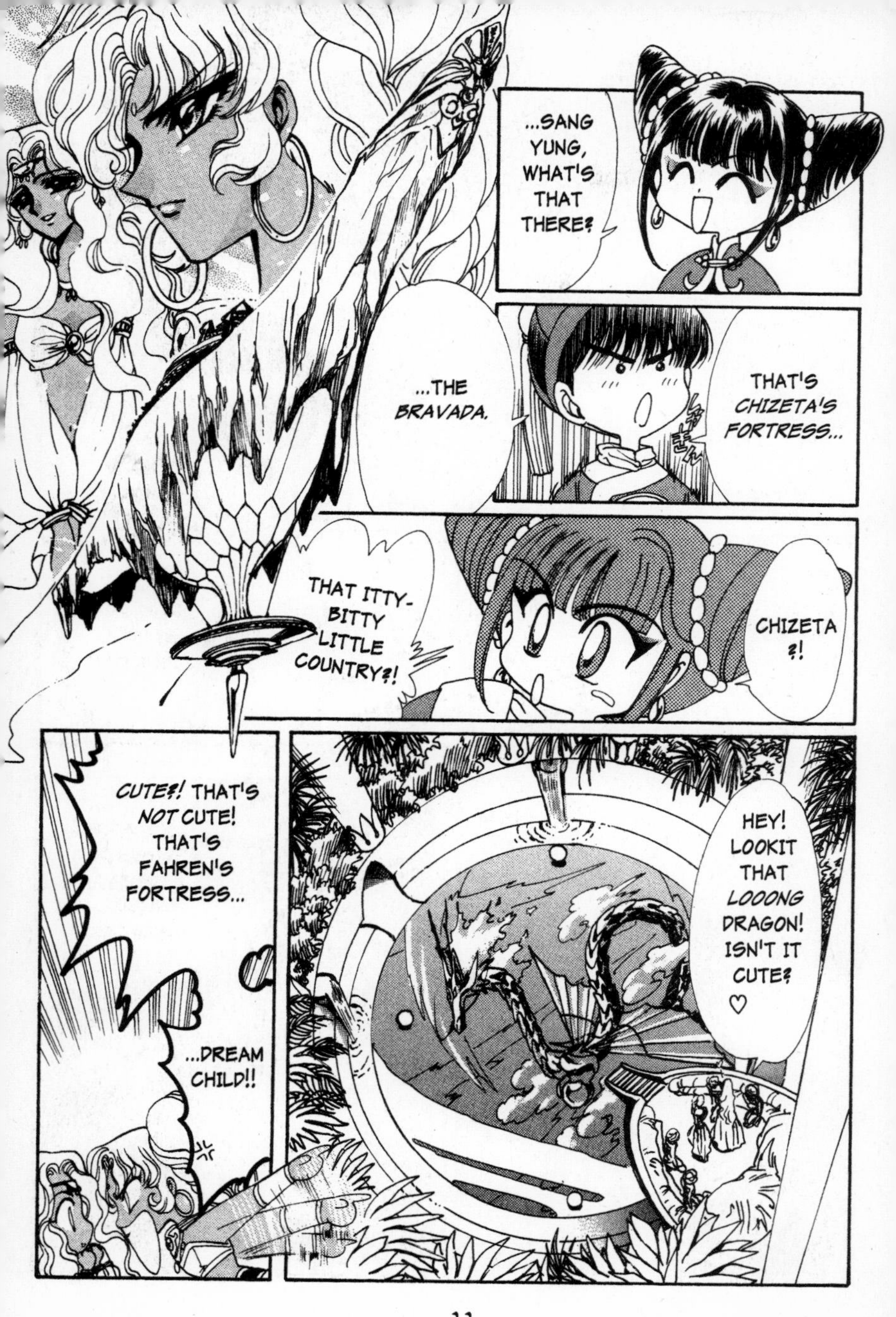
...SANG YUNG, WHAT'S THAT THERE?
THAT'S CHIZETA'S FORTRESS...
...THE BRAVADA.
CHIZETA?!
THAT ITTY-BITTY LITTLE COUNTRY?!
HEY! LOOKIT THAT LOOONG DRAGON! ISN'T IT CUTE? ♡
CUTE?! THAT'S NOT CUTE! THAT'S FAHREN'S FORTRESS...
...DREAM CHILD!!

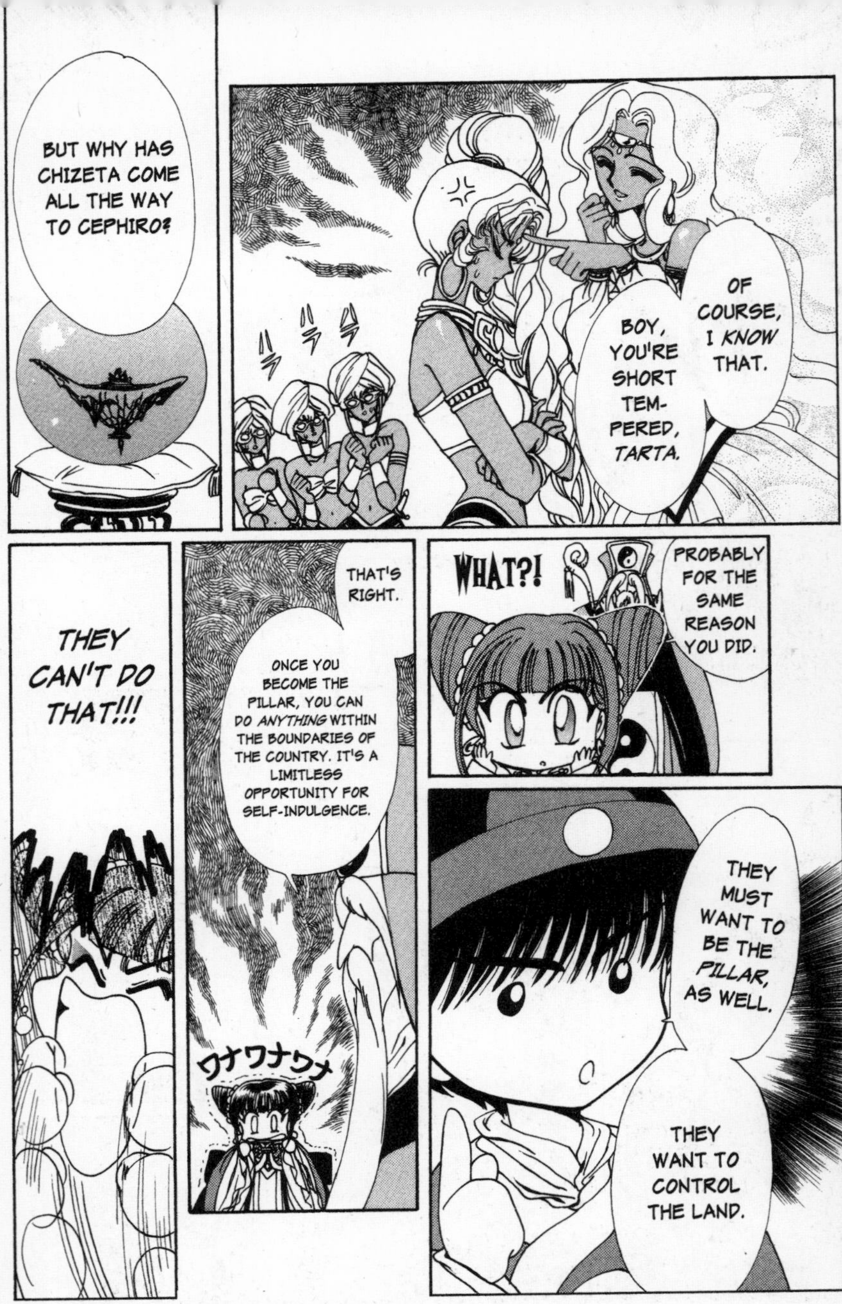

OF COURSE, I KNOW THAT.
BOY, YOU'RE SHORT TEMPERED, TARTA.
ハラ ハラ ハラ
BUT WHY HAS CHIZETA COME ALL THE WAY TO CEPHIRO?
PROBABLY FOR THE SAME REASON YOU DID.
WHAT?!
THEY MUST WANT TO BE THE PILLAR, AS WELL.
THEY WANT TO CONTROL THE LAND.
THAT'S RIGHT.
ONCE YOU BECOME THE PILLAR, YOU CAN DO ANYTHING WITHIN THE BOUNDARIES OF THE COUNTRY. IT'S A LIMITLESS OPPORTUNITY FOR SELF-INDULGENCE.
ワナワナワナ
THEY CAN'T DO THAT!!!

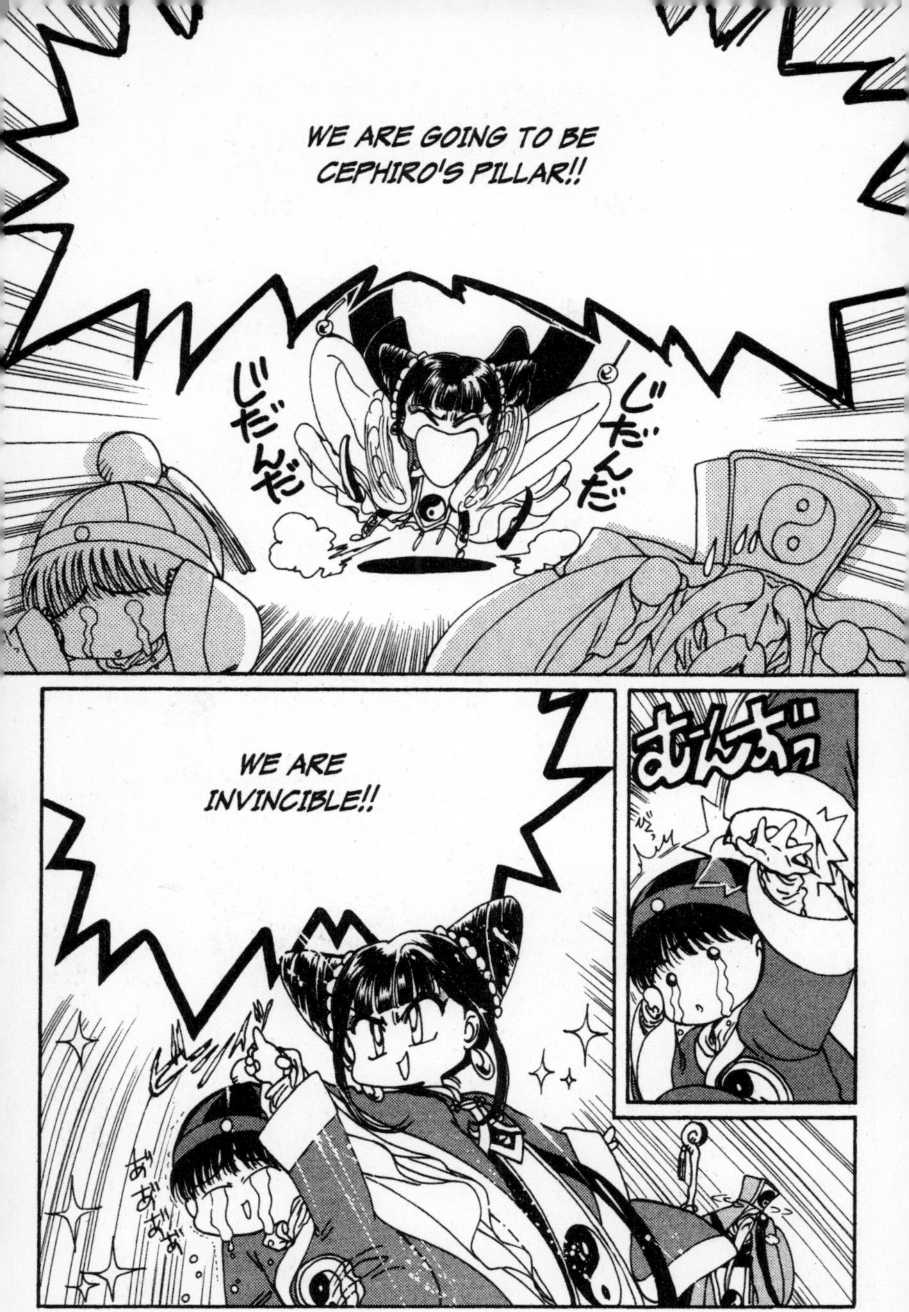
WE ARE GOING TO BE
CEPHIRO'S PILLAR!!
じだんだ
じだんだ
むんずっ
WE ARE
INVINCIBLE!!

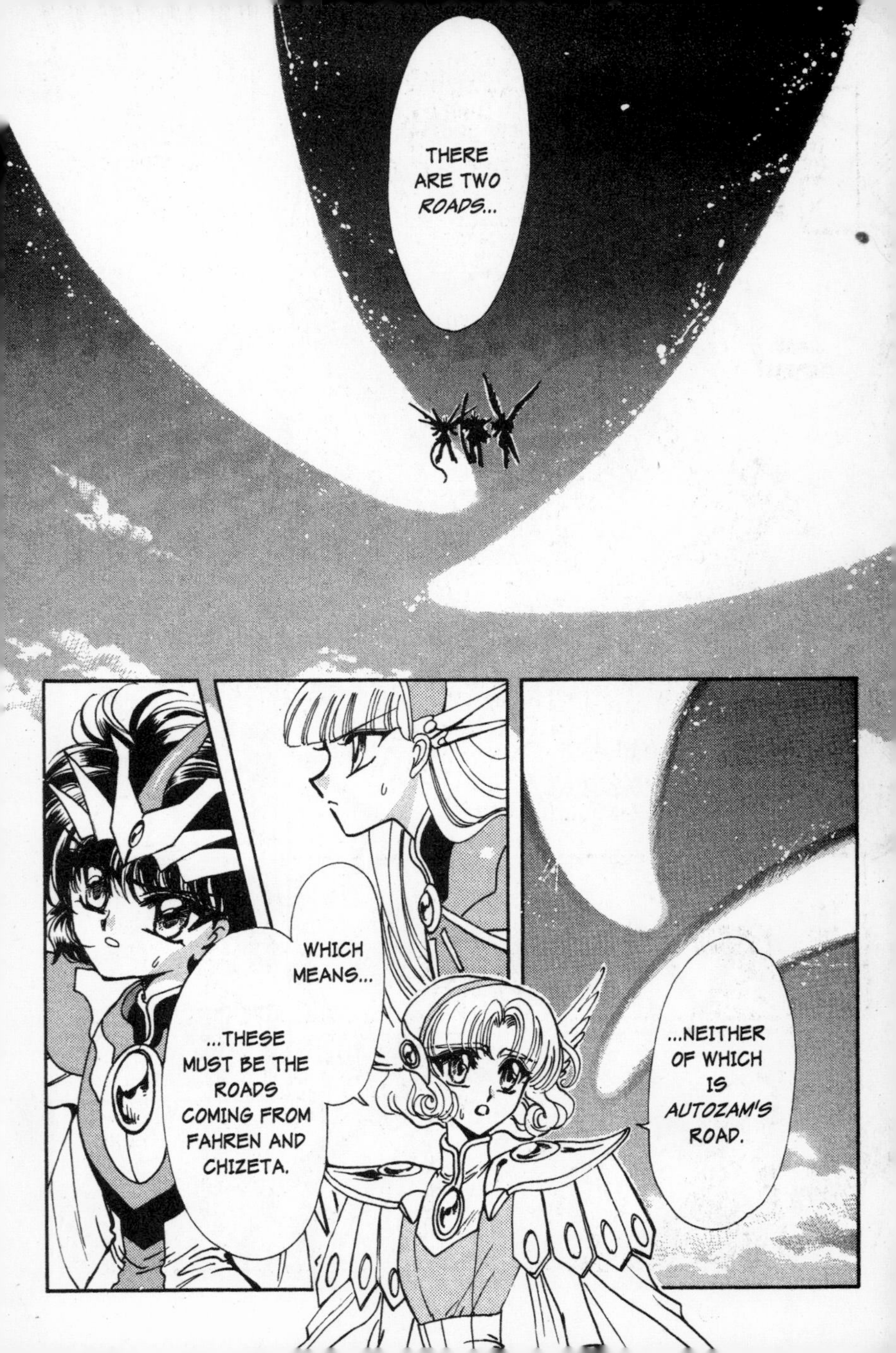
THERE ARE TWO ROADS...
WHICH MEANS...
...THESE MUST BE THE ROADS COMING FROM FAHREN AND CHIZETA.
...NEITHER OF WHICH IS AUTOZAM'S ROAD.

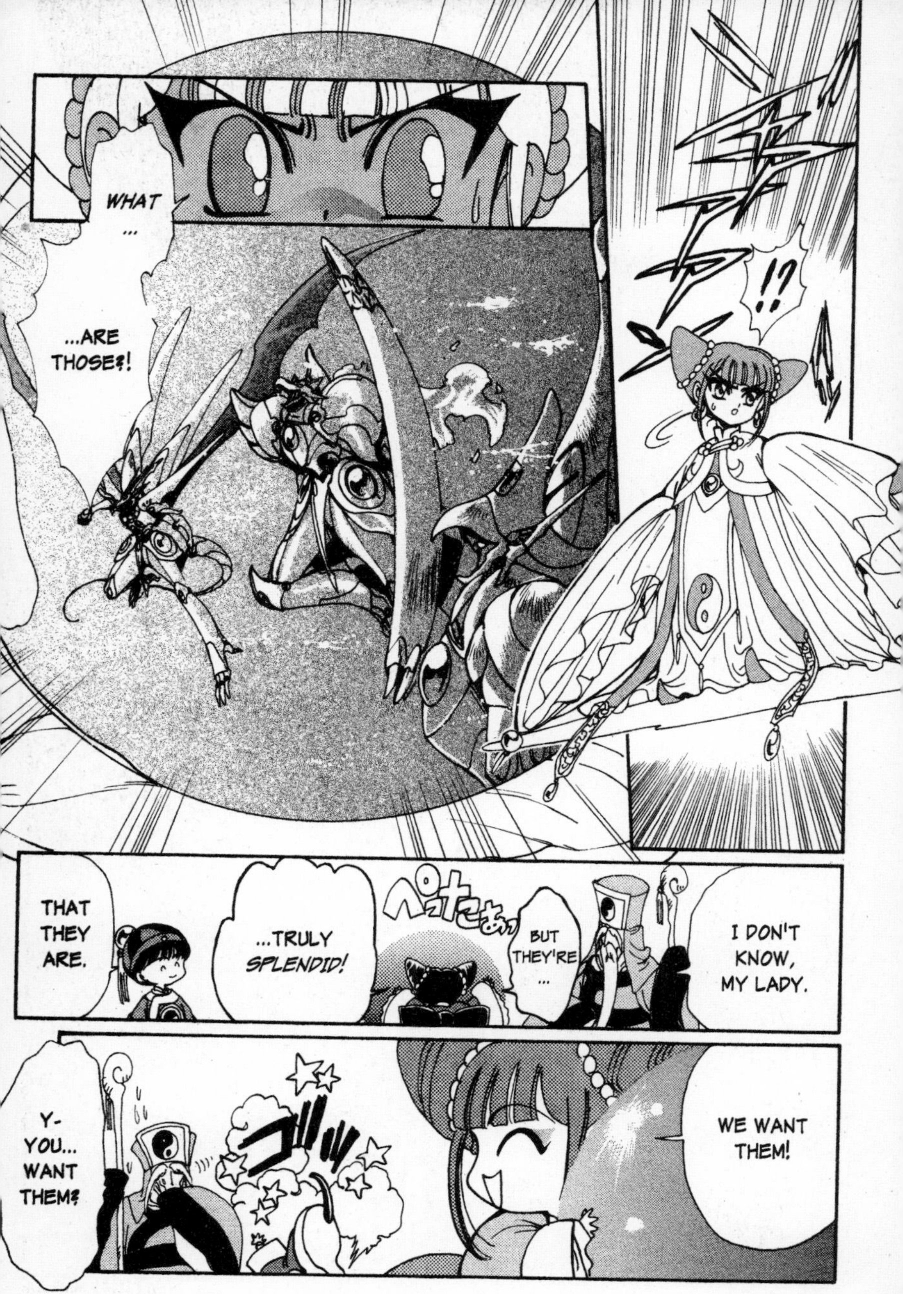
!?
WHAT ...
...ARE THOSE?!
I DON'T KNOW, MY LADY.
BUT THEY'RE ...
...TRULY SPLENDID!
THAT THEY ARE.
WE WANT THEM!
Y- YOU... WANT THEM?

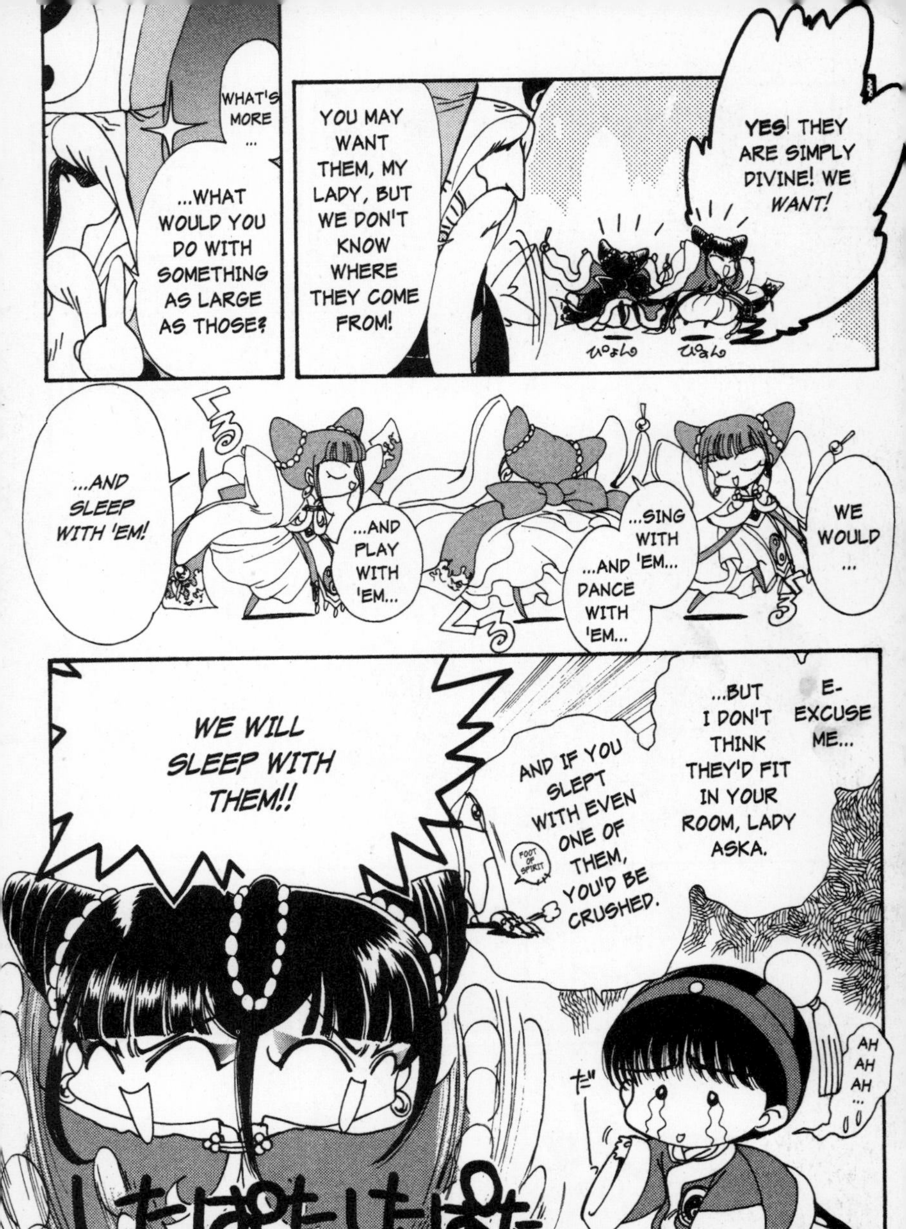
YES! THEY ARE SIMPLY DIVINE! WE WANT!
ぴょん
ぴょん
YOU MAY WANT THEM, MY LADY, BUT WE DON'T KNOW WHERE THEY COME FROM!
WHAT'S MORE ...
...WHAT WOULD YOU DO WITH SOMETHING AS LARGE AS THOSE?
WE WOULD ...
...SING WITH 'EM...
...AND DANCE WITH 'EM...
...AND PLAY WITH 'EM...
...AND SLEEP WITH 'EM!
E- EXCUSE ME...
...BUT I DON'T THINK THEY'D FIT IN YOUR ROOM, LADY ASKA.
AND IF YOU SLEPT WITH EVEN ONE OF THEM, YOU'D BE CRUSHED.
FOOT OF SPIRIT
WE WILL SLEEP WITH THEM!!
AH AH AH ...
だ
したぱたしたぱた

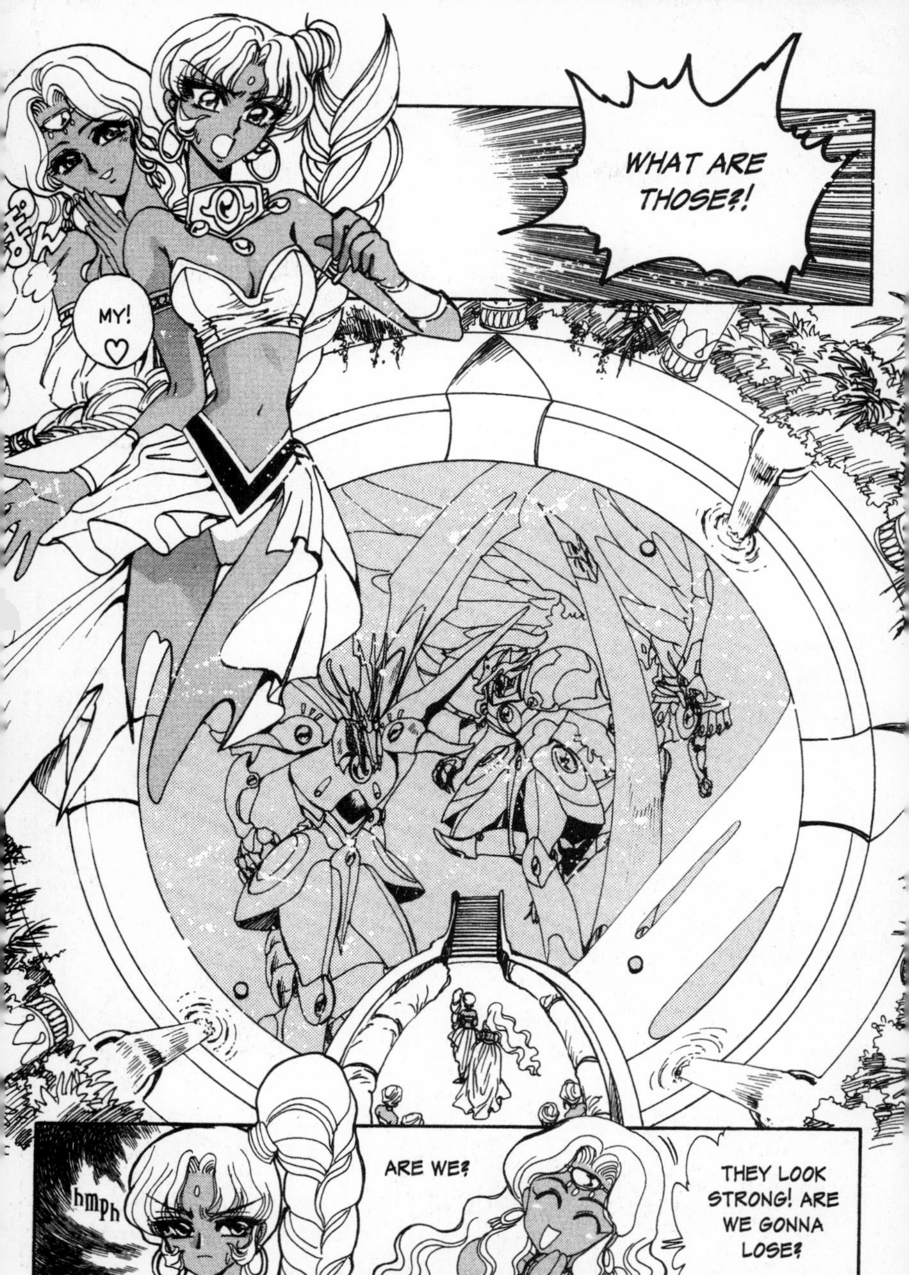
WHAT ARE THOSE?!
MY! ♡
THEY LOOK STRONG! ARE WE GONNA LOSE?
ARE WE?
hmph

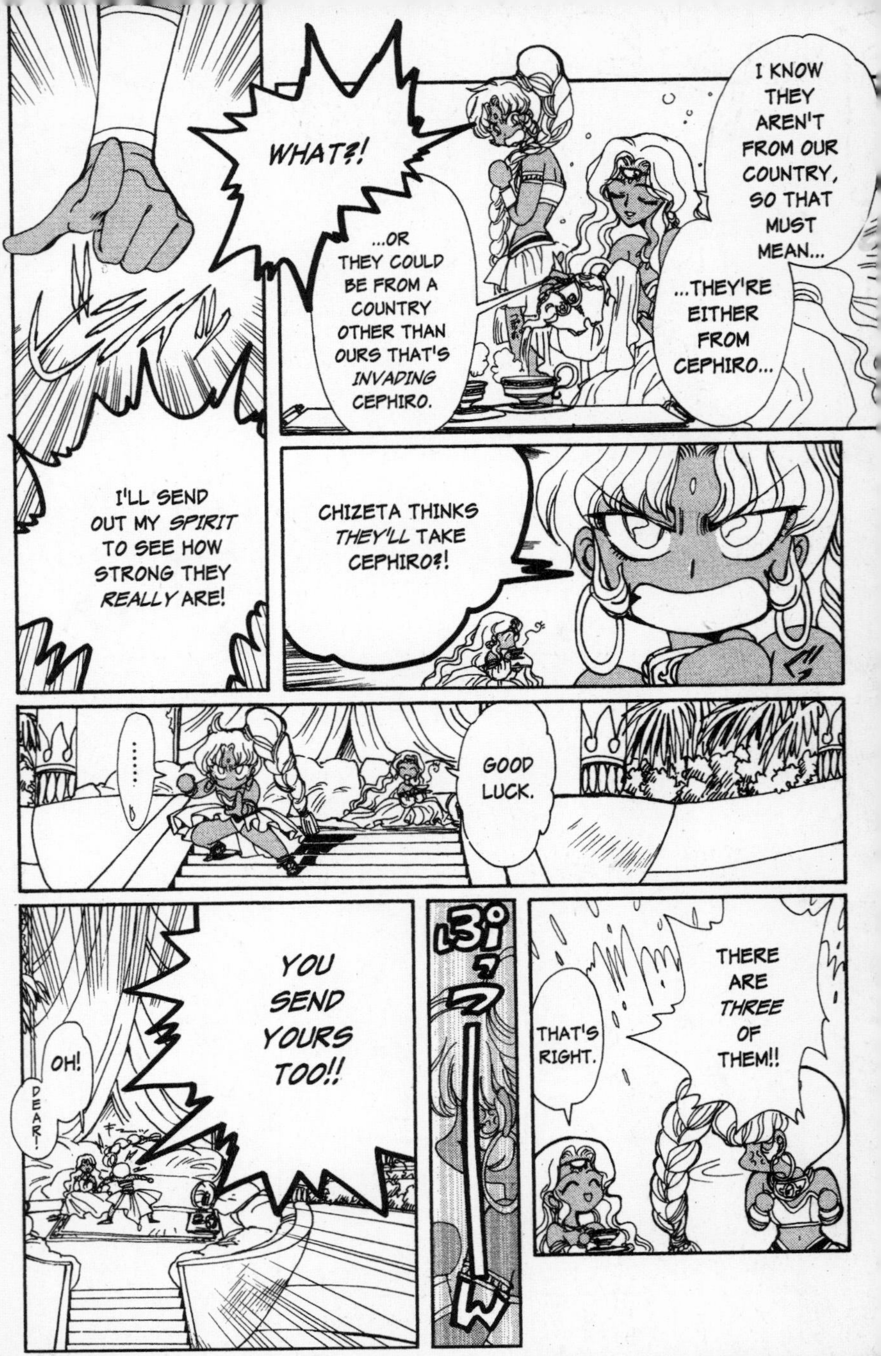
I KNOW THEY AREN'T FROM OUR COUNTRY, SO THAT MUST MEAN...
...THEY'RE EITHER FROM CEPHIRO...
...OR THEY COULD BE FROM A COUNTRY OTHER THAN OURS THAT'S *INVADING* CEPHIRO.
WHAT?!
CHIZETA THINKS *THEY'LL* TAKE CEPHIRO?!
I'LL SEND OUT MY *SPIRIT* TO SEE HOW STRONG THEY *REALLY* ARE!
GOOD LUCK.
......
THERE ARE *THREE* OF THEM!!
THAT'S RIGHT.
YOU SEND YOURS TOO!!
OH!
DEAR!

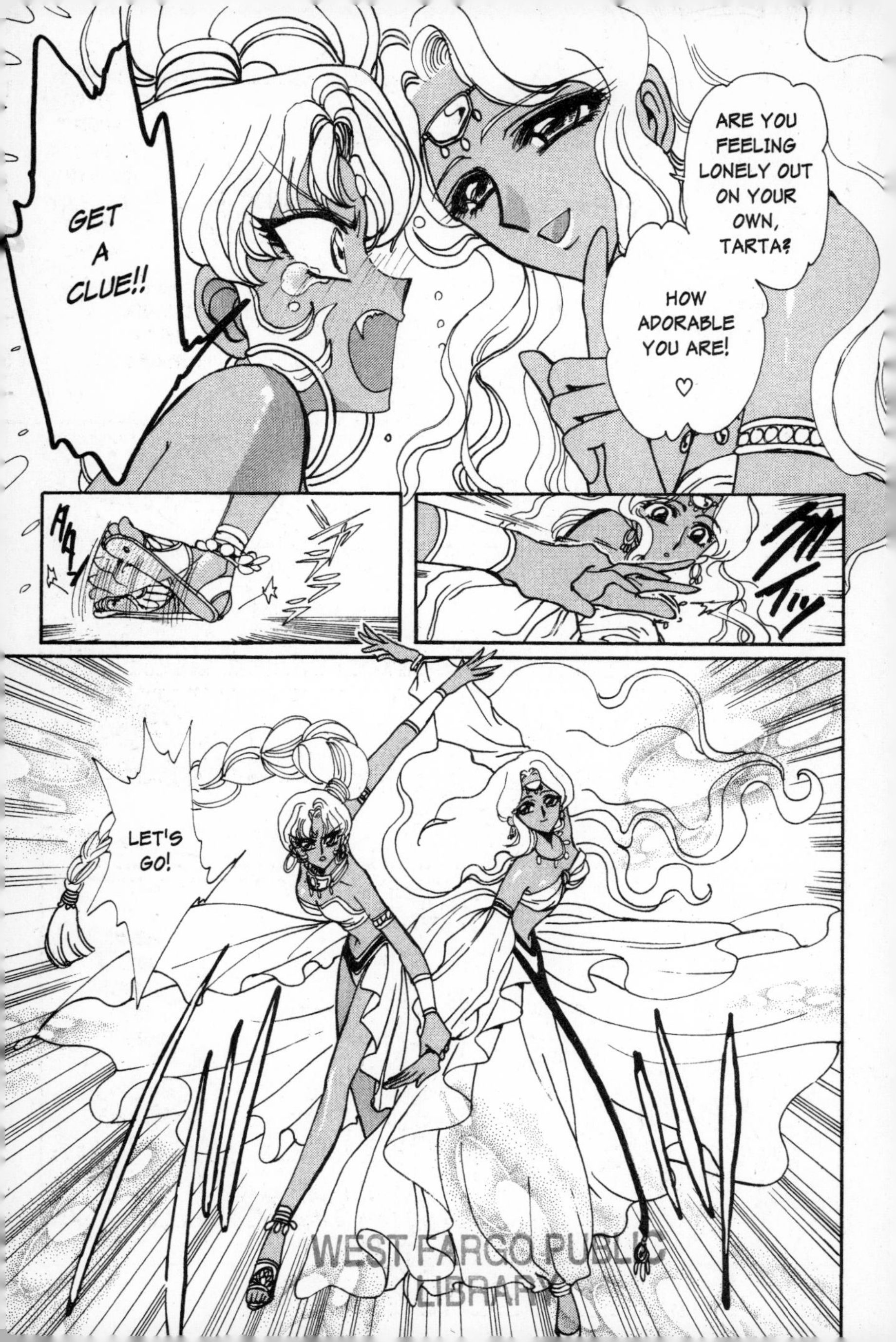
ARE YOU FEELING LONELY OUT ON YOUR OWN, TARTA?
HOW ADORABLE YOU ARE! ♡
GET A CLUE!!
LET'S GO!

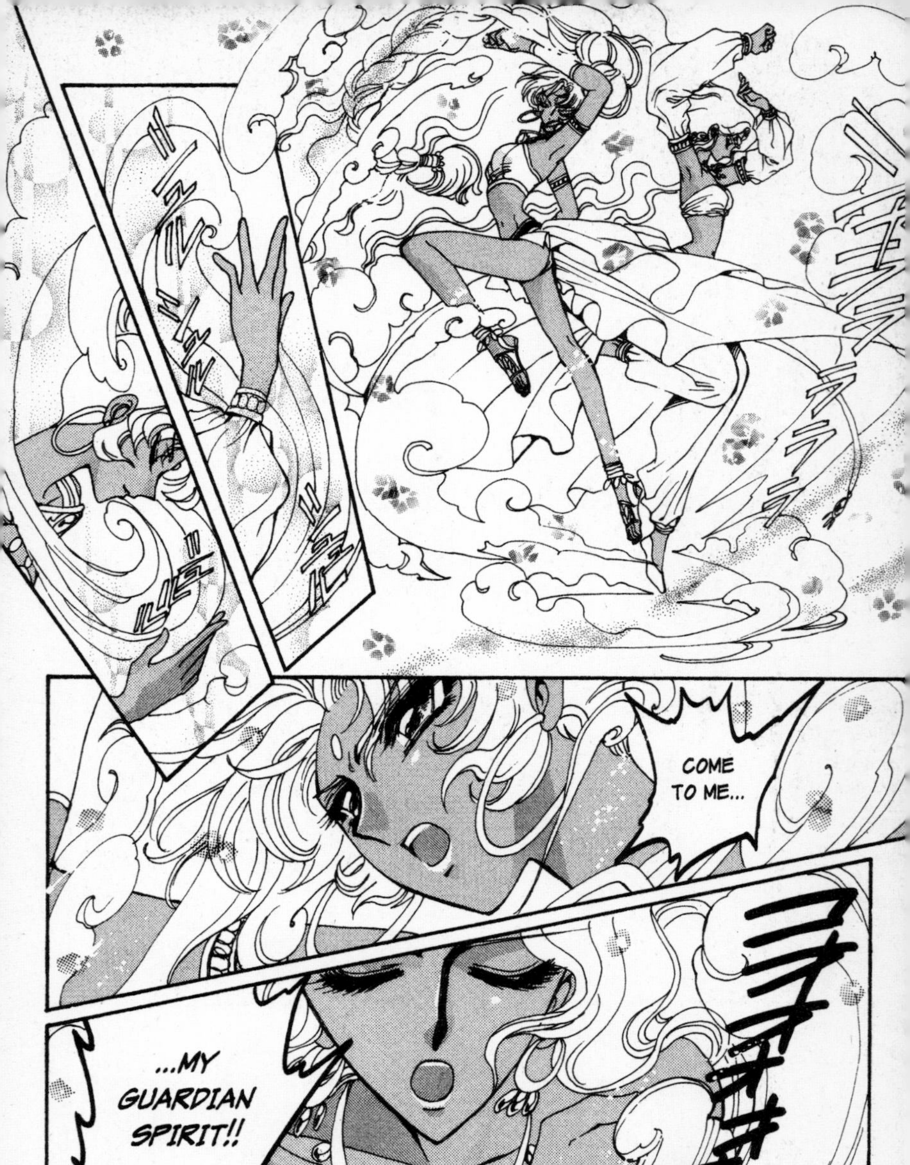
COME TO ME...
...MY GUARDIAN SPIRIT!!

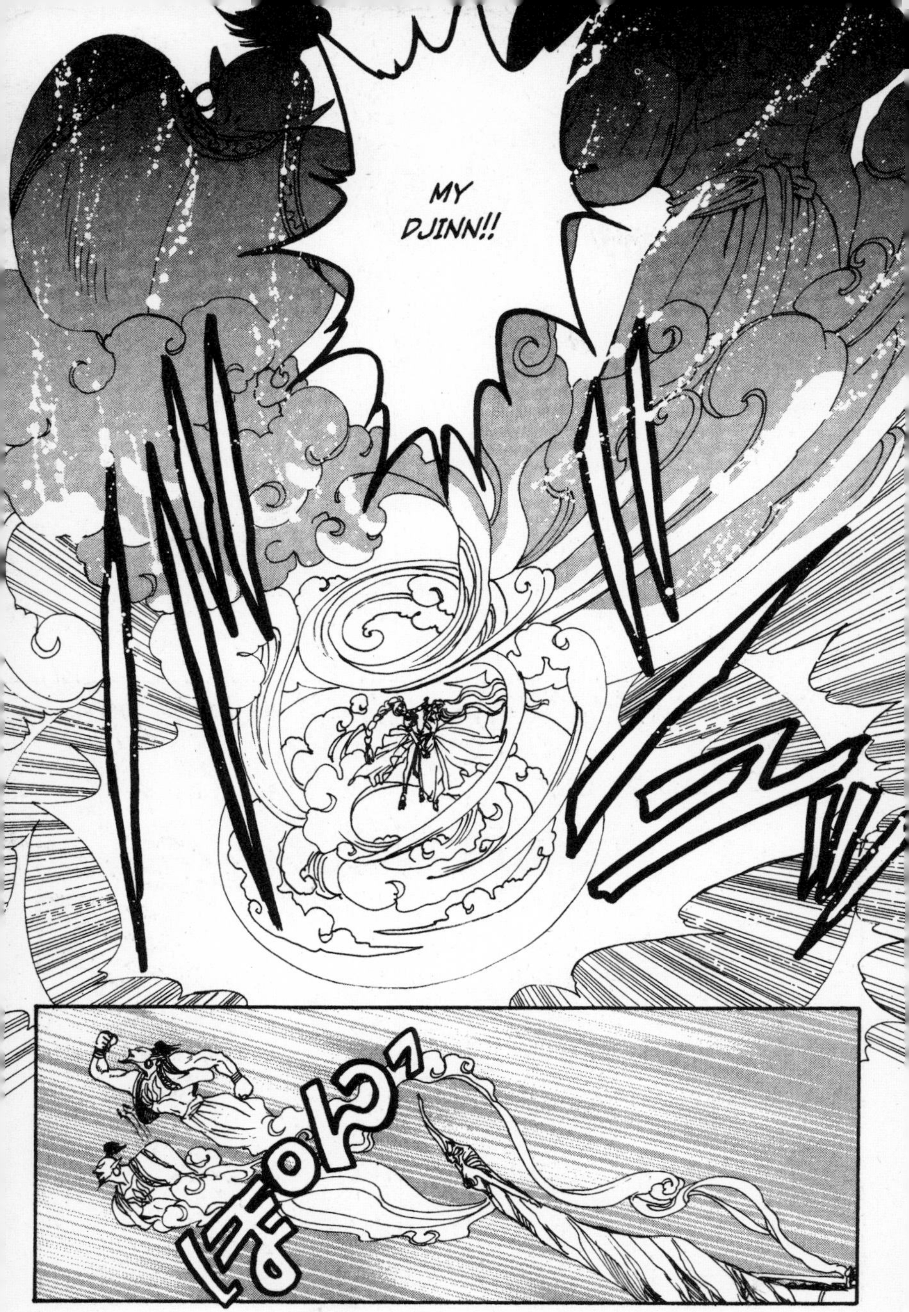
MY DJINN!!

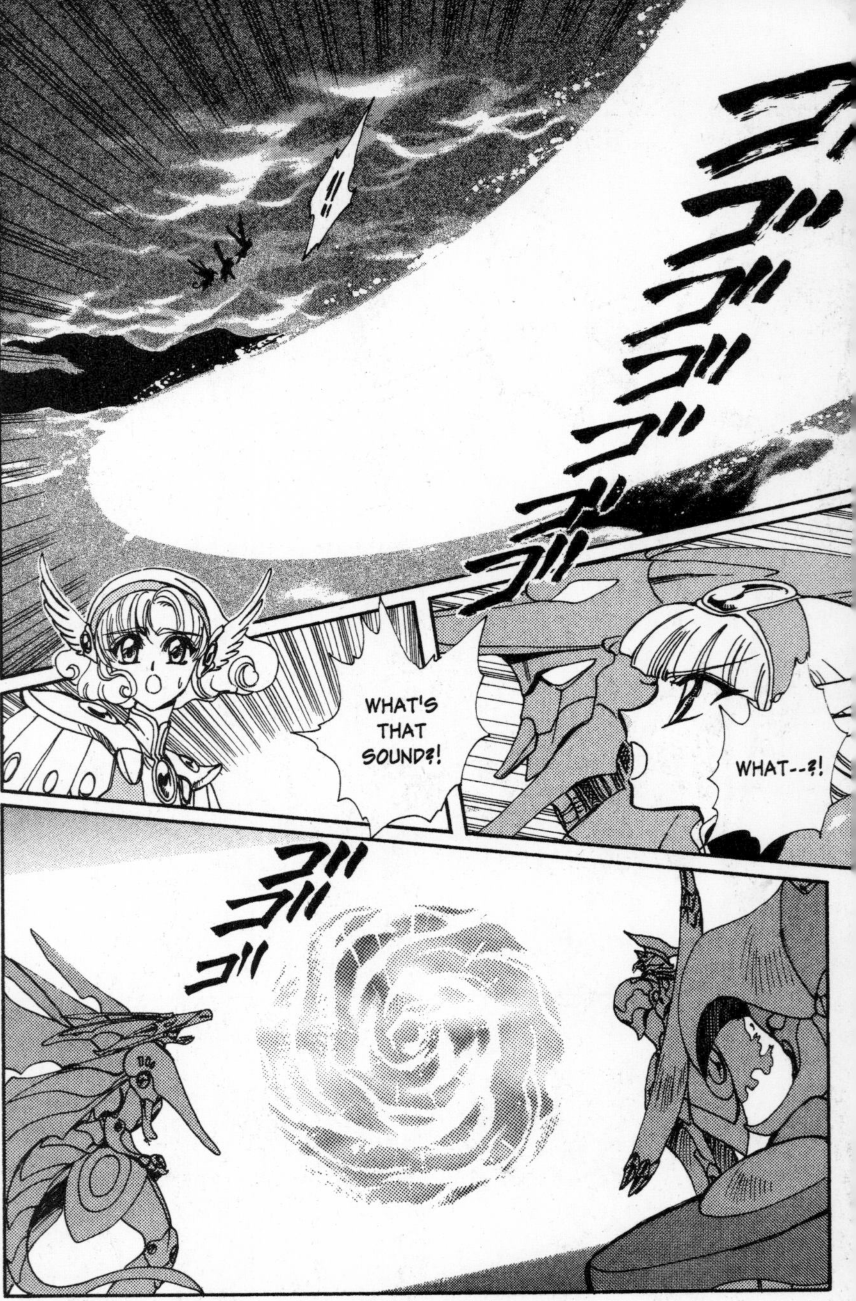
ゴゴゴゴゴ
!!
WHAT--?!
WHAT'S THAT SOUND?!
ゴゴゴ

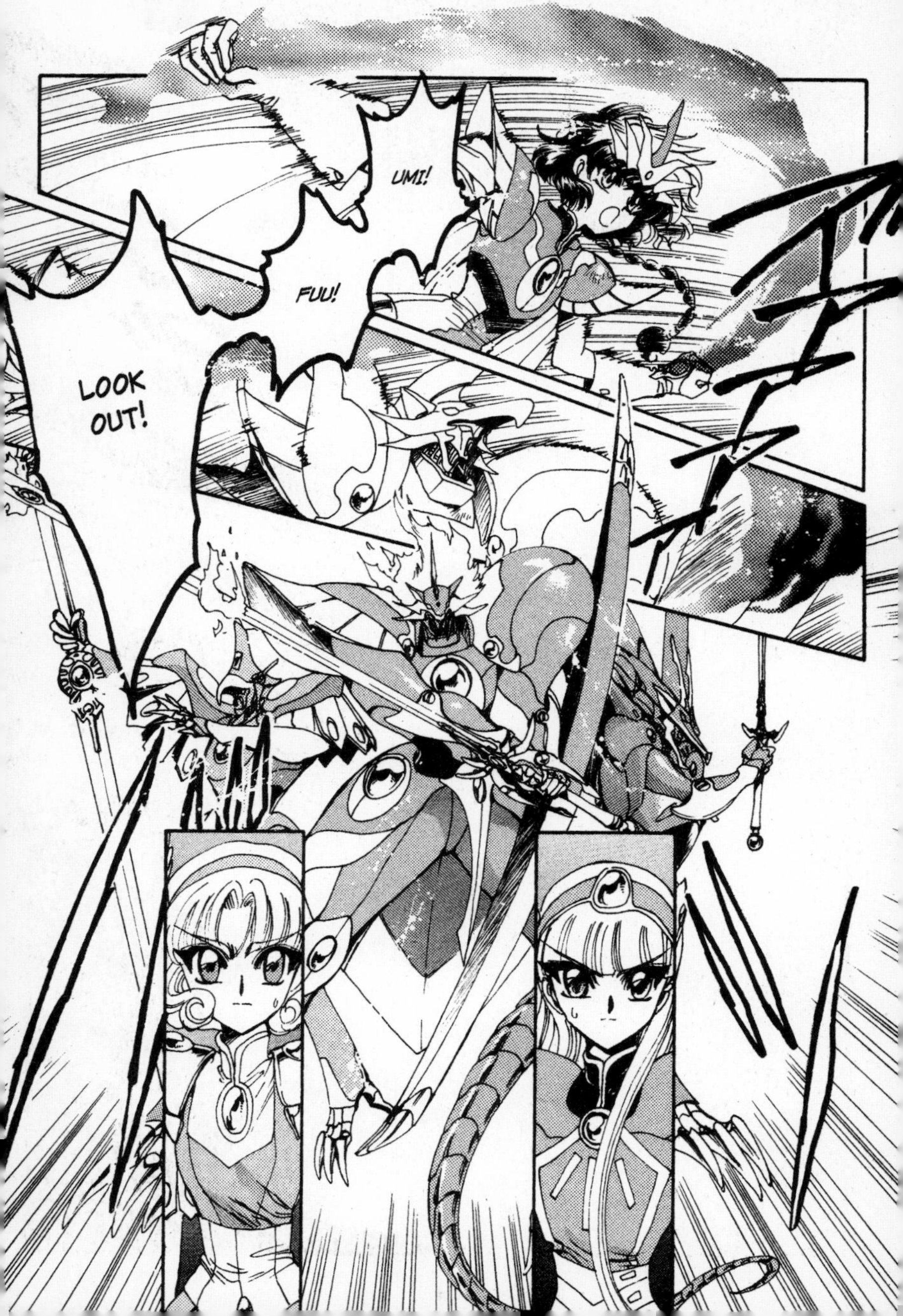
UMI!
FUU!
LOOK OUT!

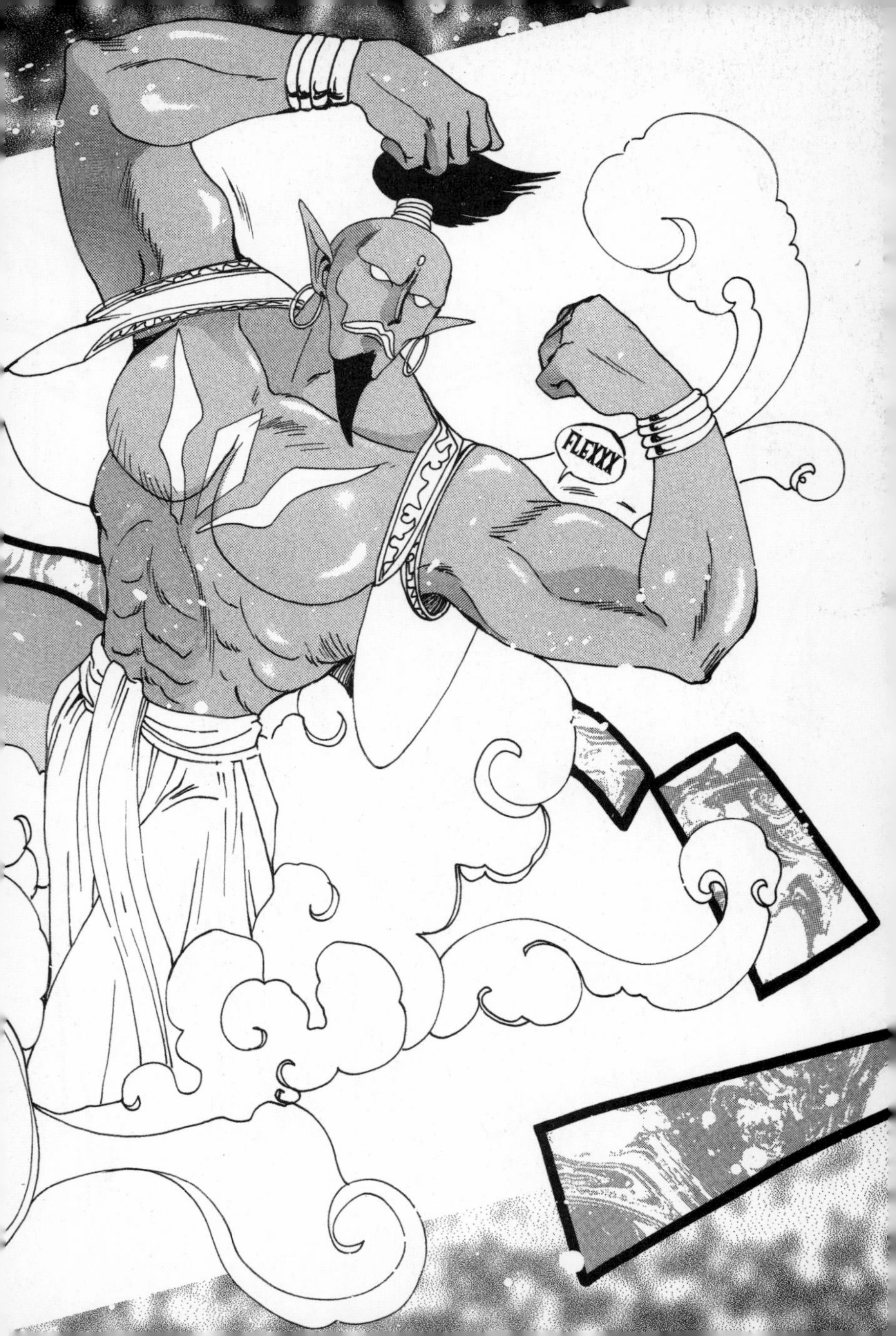
FLEXX

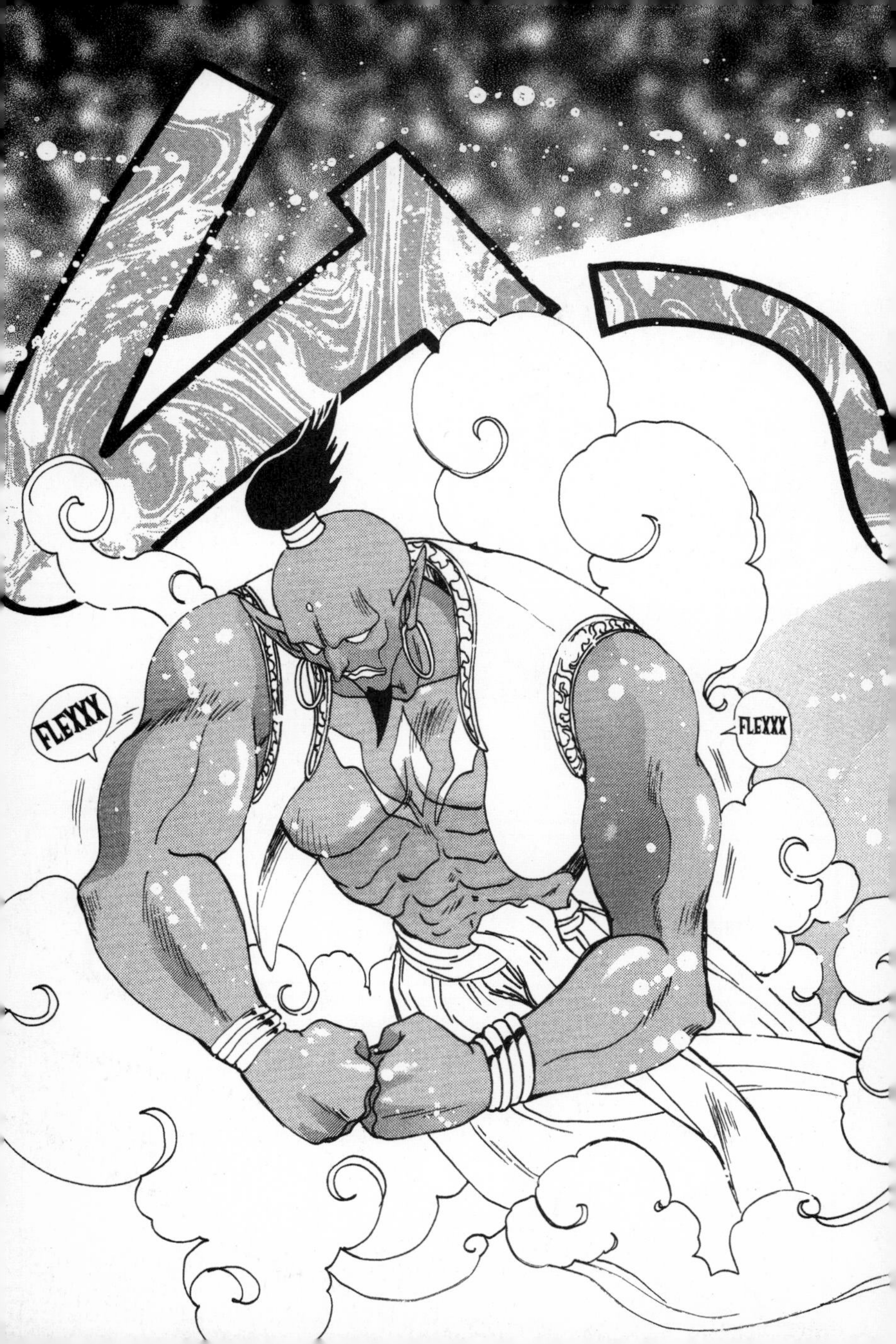
FLEXXX
FLEXXX

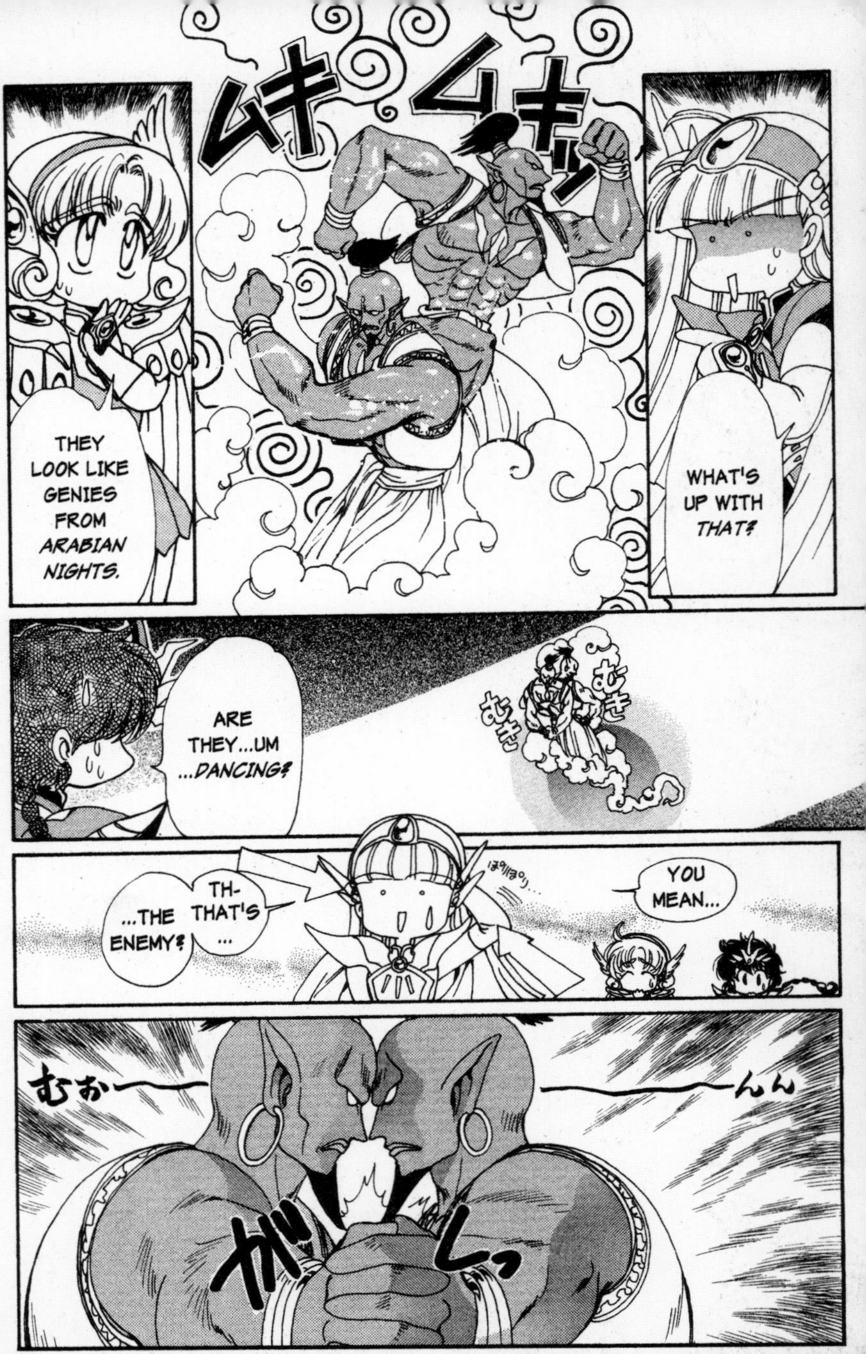
WHAT'S UP WITH THAT?
ムキムキッ
THEY LOOK LIKE GENIES FROM ARABIAN NIGHTS.
むきむき
ARE THEY...UM ...DANCING?
YOU MEAN...
TH- THAT'S ...
...THE ENEMY?
むぉー
ーんん
がしっ

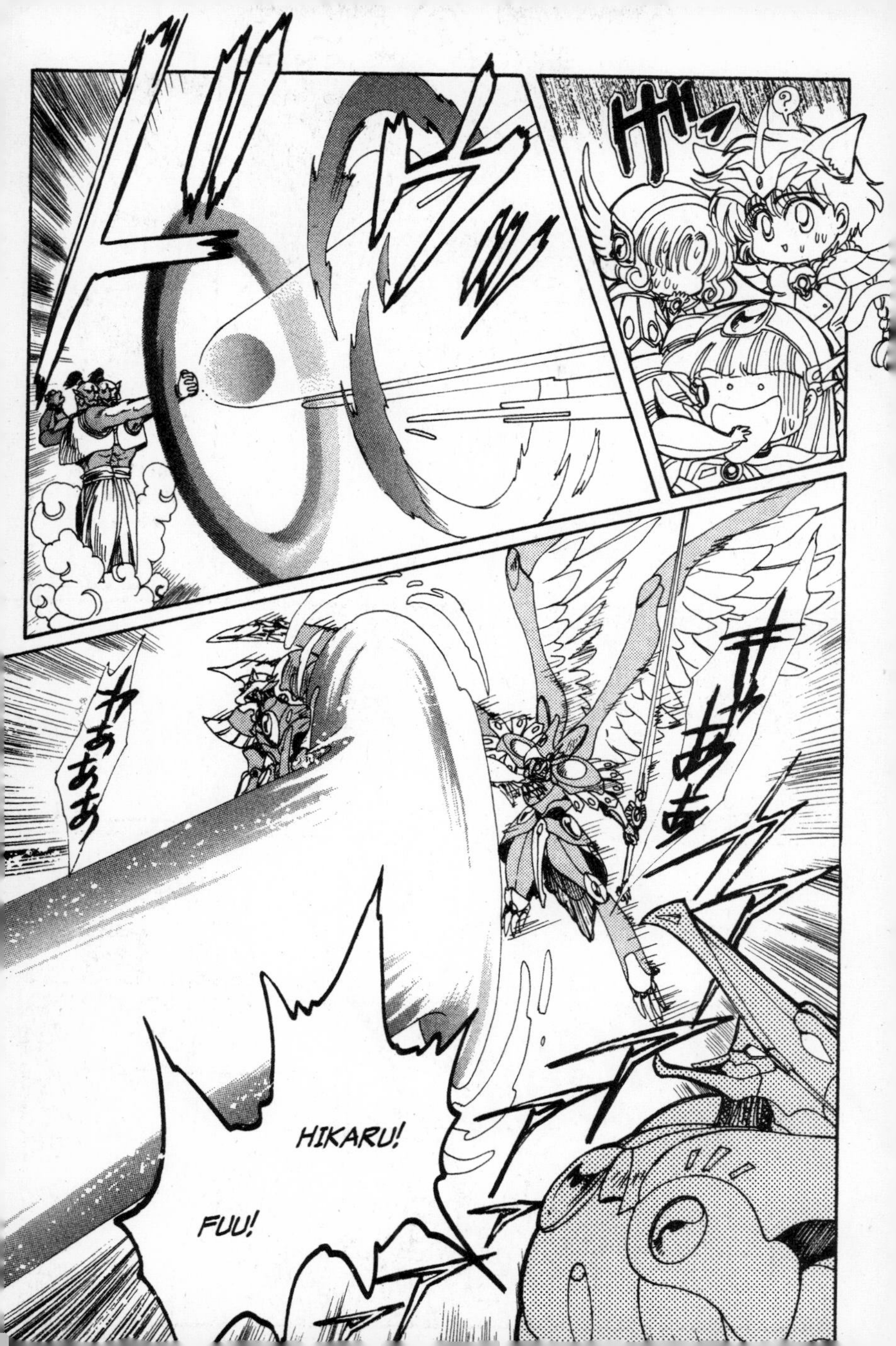
わあああ
HIKARU!
FUU!

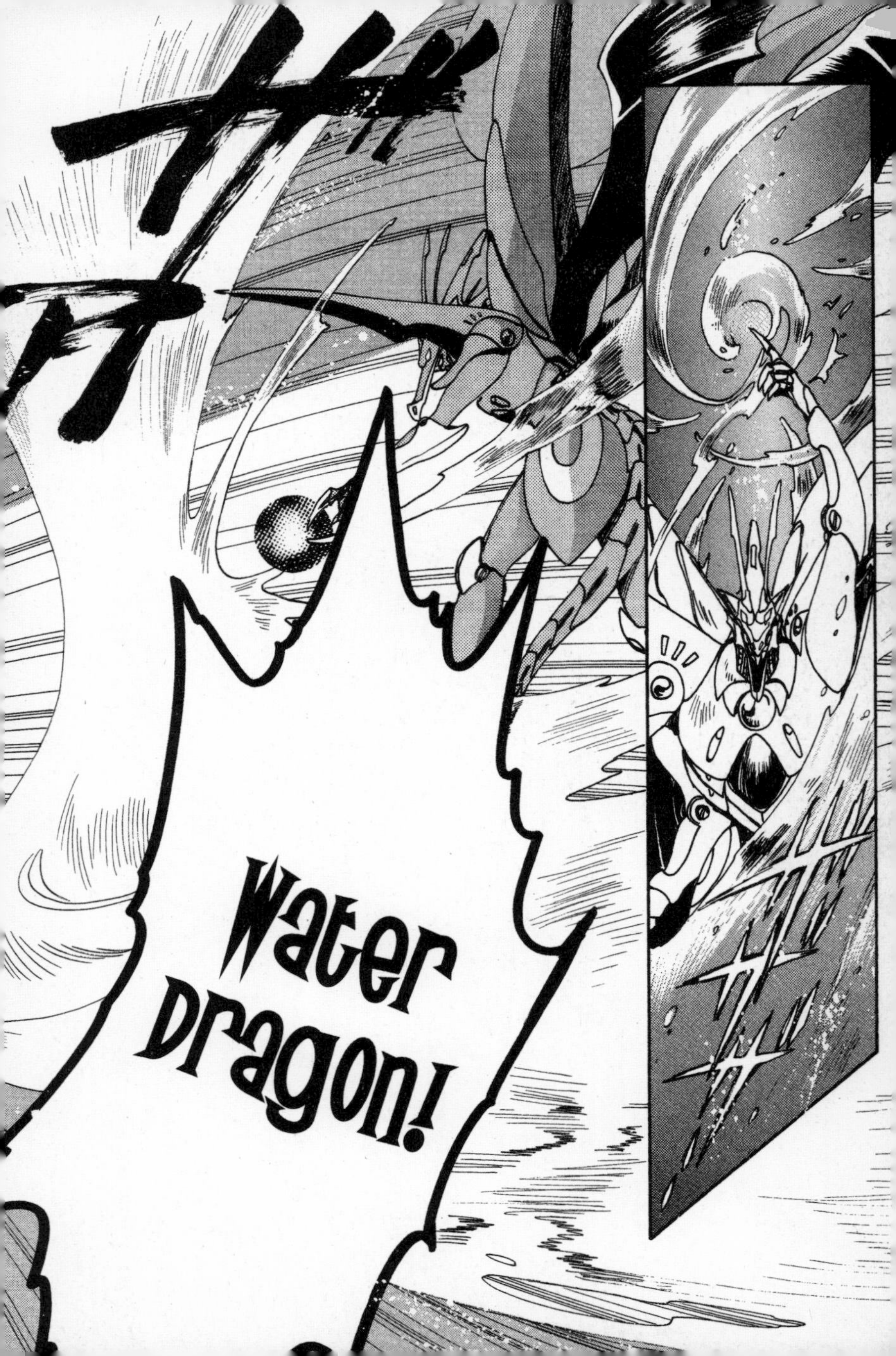
Water Dragon!

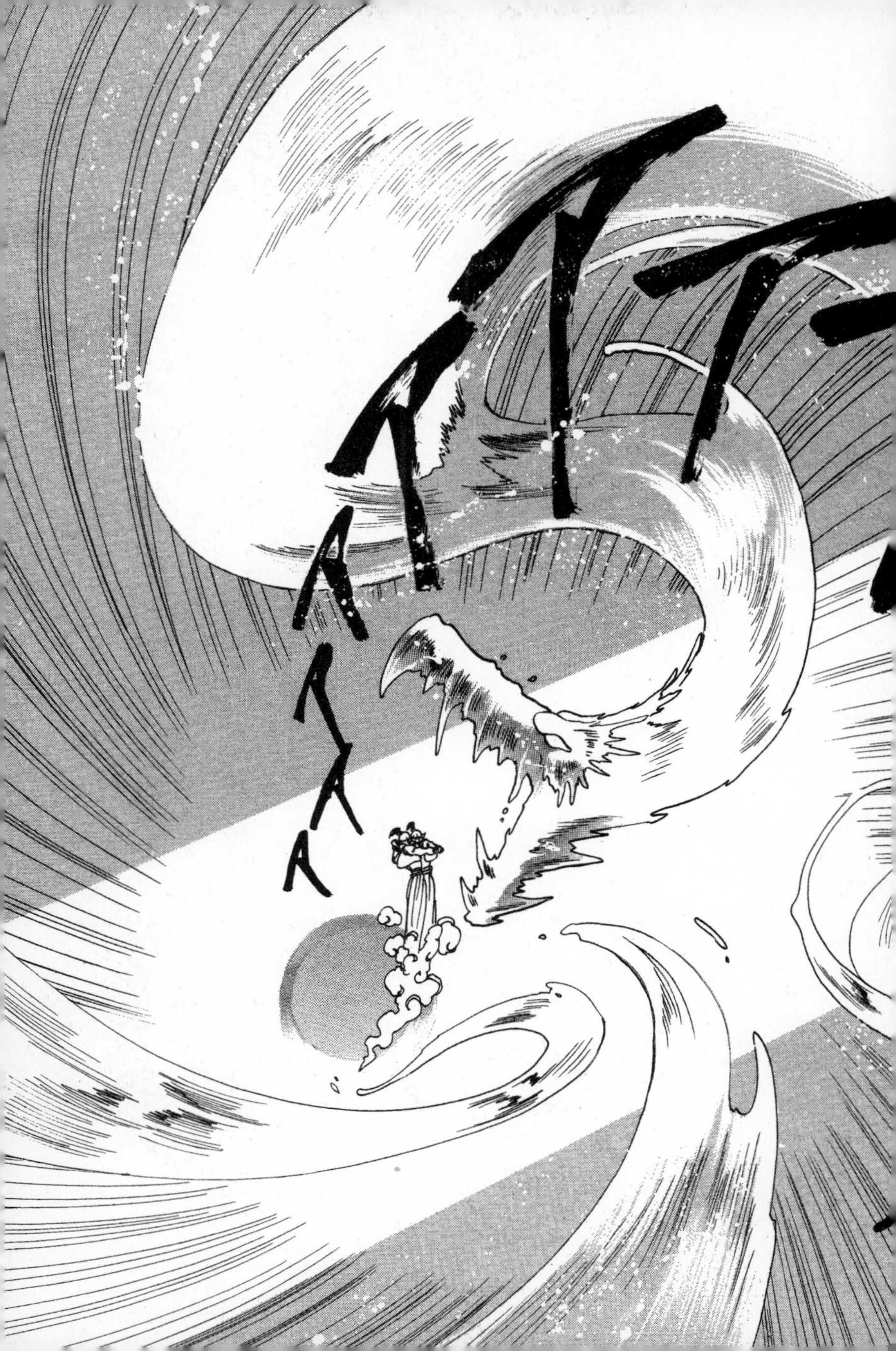

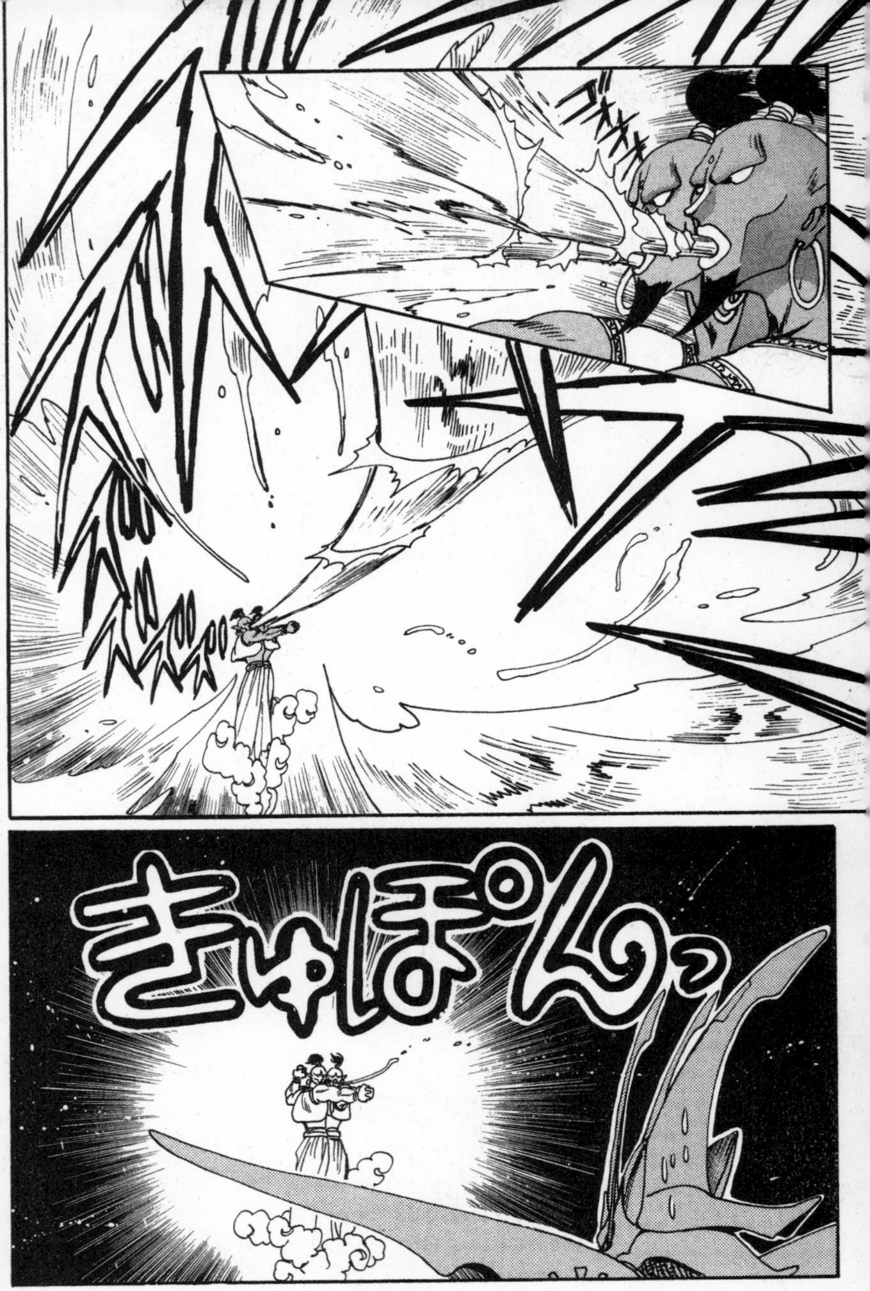
ゴオオオ
きゅぽんっ

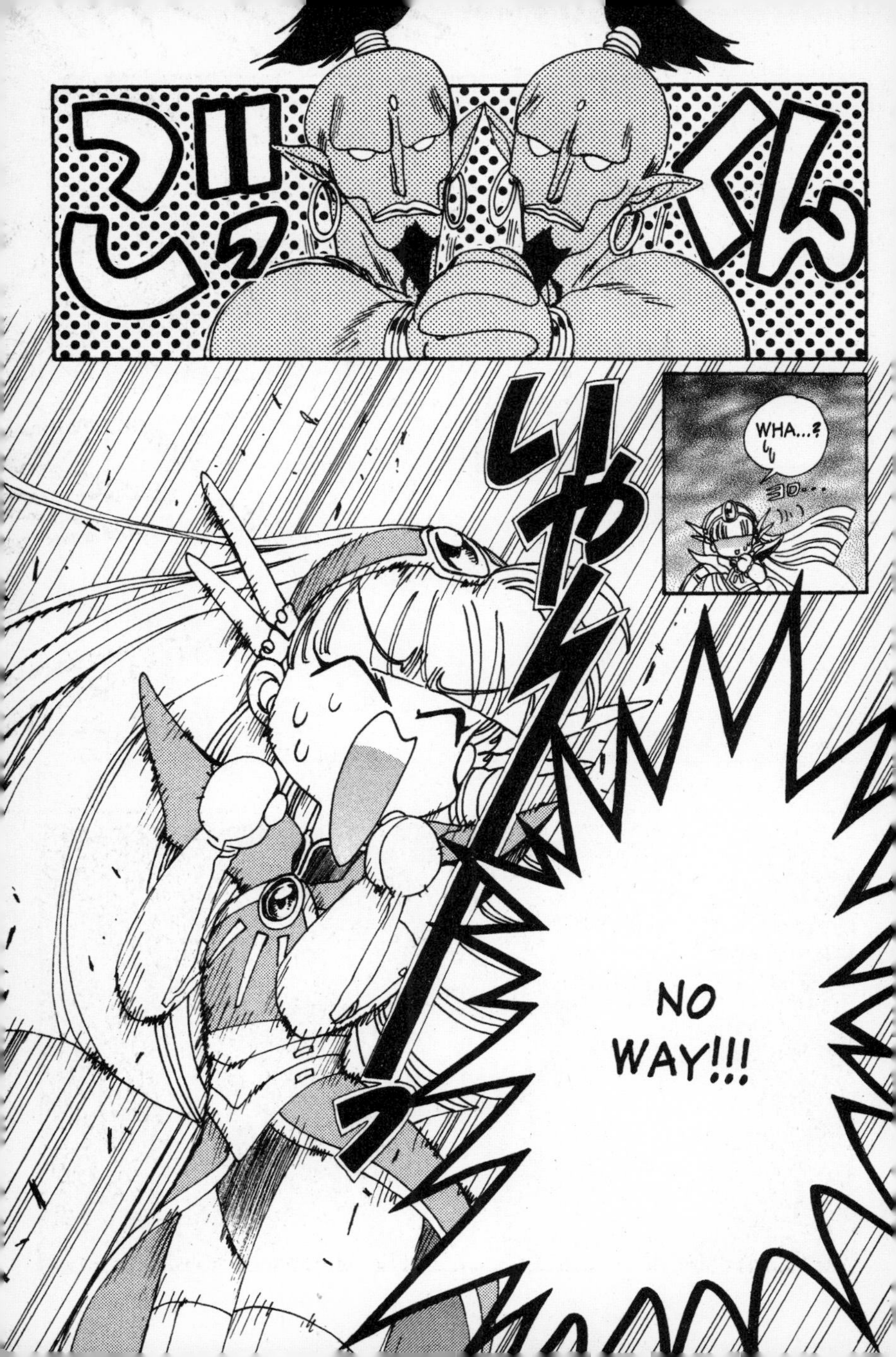

ごっくん
WHA...?
ヨロ...
しゃーーっ
NO WAY!!!

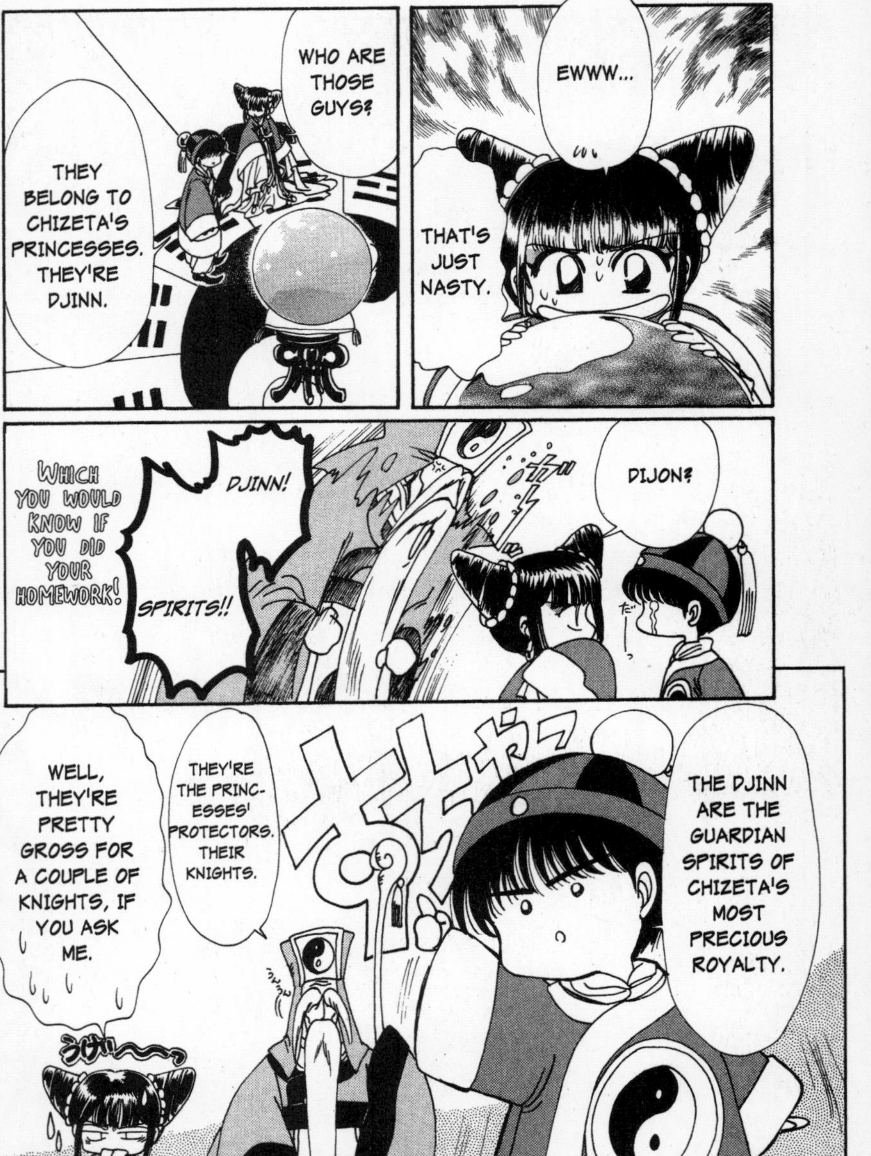
EWWW...
THAT'S JUST NASTY.
WHO ARE THOSE GUYS?
THEY BELONG TO CHIZETA'S PRINCESSES. THEY'RE DJINN.
DIJON?
DJINN!
SPIRITS!!
WHICH YOU WOULD KNOW IF YOU DID YOUR HOMEWORK!
THE DJINN ARE THE GUARDIAN SPIRITS OF CHIZETA'S MOST PRECIOUS ROYALTY.
THEY'RE THE PRINC-ESSES' PROTECTORS. THEIR KNIGHTS.
WELL, THEY'RE PRETTY GROSS FOR A COUPLE OF KNIGHTS, IF YOU ASK ME.

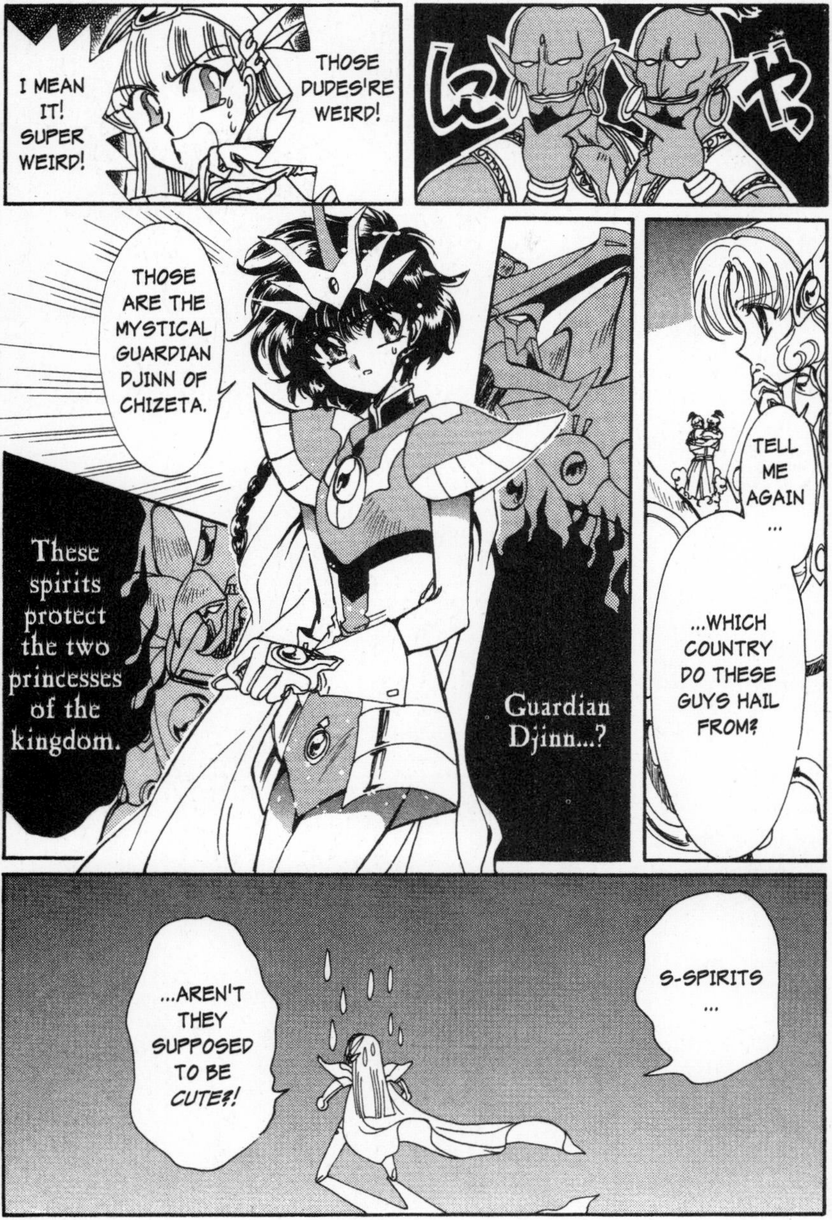
に
や
THOSE DUDES'RE WEIRD!
I MEAN IT! SUPER WEIRD!
TELL ME AGAIN ...
...WHICH COUNTRY DO THESE GUYS HAIL FROM?
Guardian Djinn...?
THOSE ARE THE MYSTICAL GUARDIAN DJINN OF CHIZETA.
These spirits protect the two princesses of the kingdom.
S-SPIRITS ...
...AREN'T THEY SUPPOSED TO BE CUTE?!

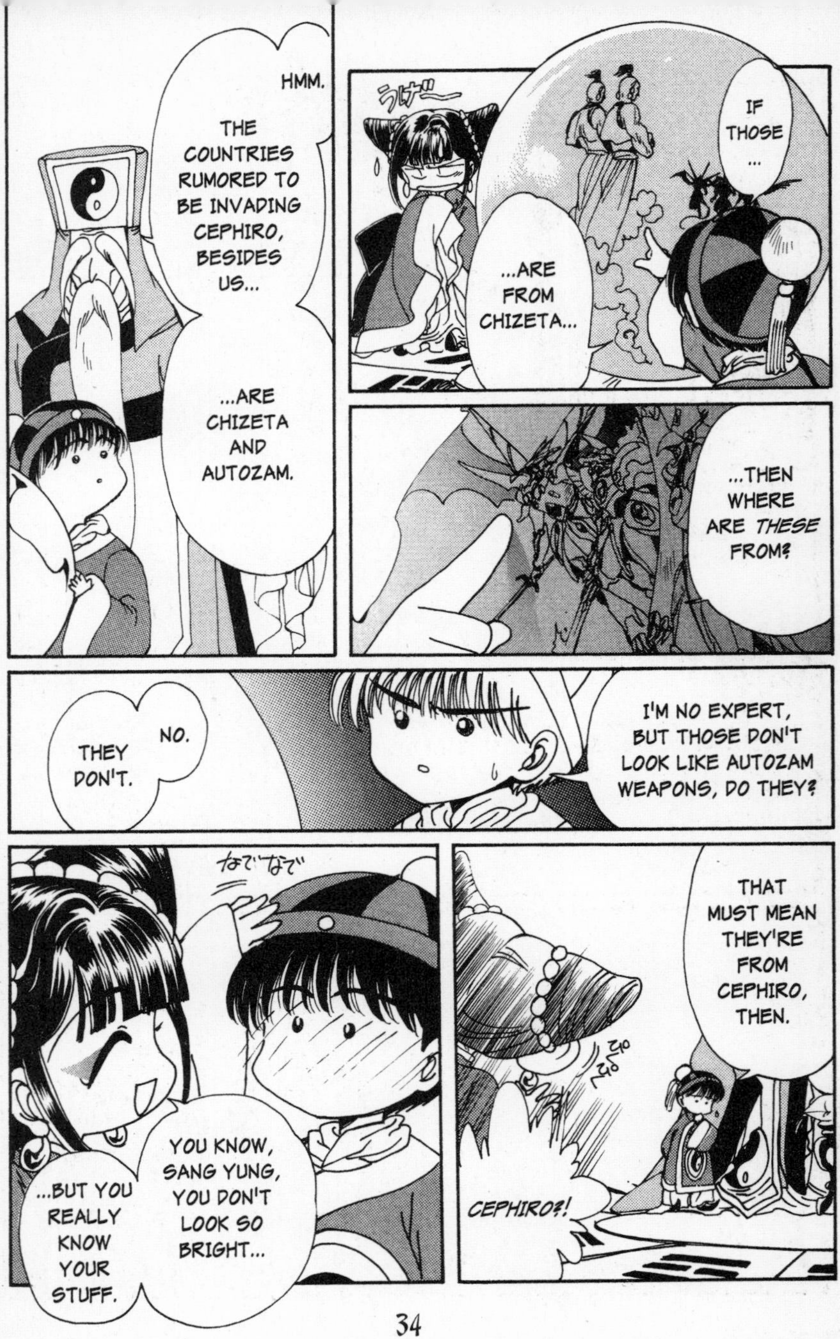
うげ~
IF THOSE ...
...ARE FROM CHIZETA...
...THEN WHERE ARE *THESE* FROM?
HMM.
THE COUNTRIES RUMORED TO BE INVADING CEPHIRO, BESIDES US...
...ARE CHIZETA AND AUTOZAM.
I'M NO EXPERT, BUT THOSE DON'T LOOK LIKE AUTOZAM WEAPONS, DO THEY?
NO.
THEY DON'T.
THAT MUST MEAN THEY'RE FROM CEPHIRO, THEN.
CEPHIRO?!
なでなで
YOU KNOW, SANG YUNG, YOU DON'T LOOK SO BRIGHT...
...BUT YOU REALLY KNOW YOUR STUFF.

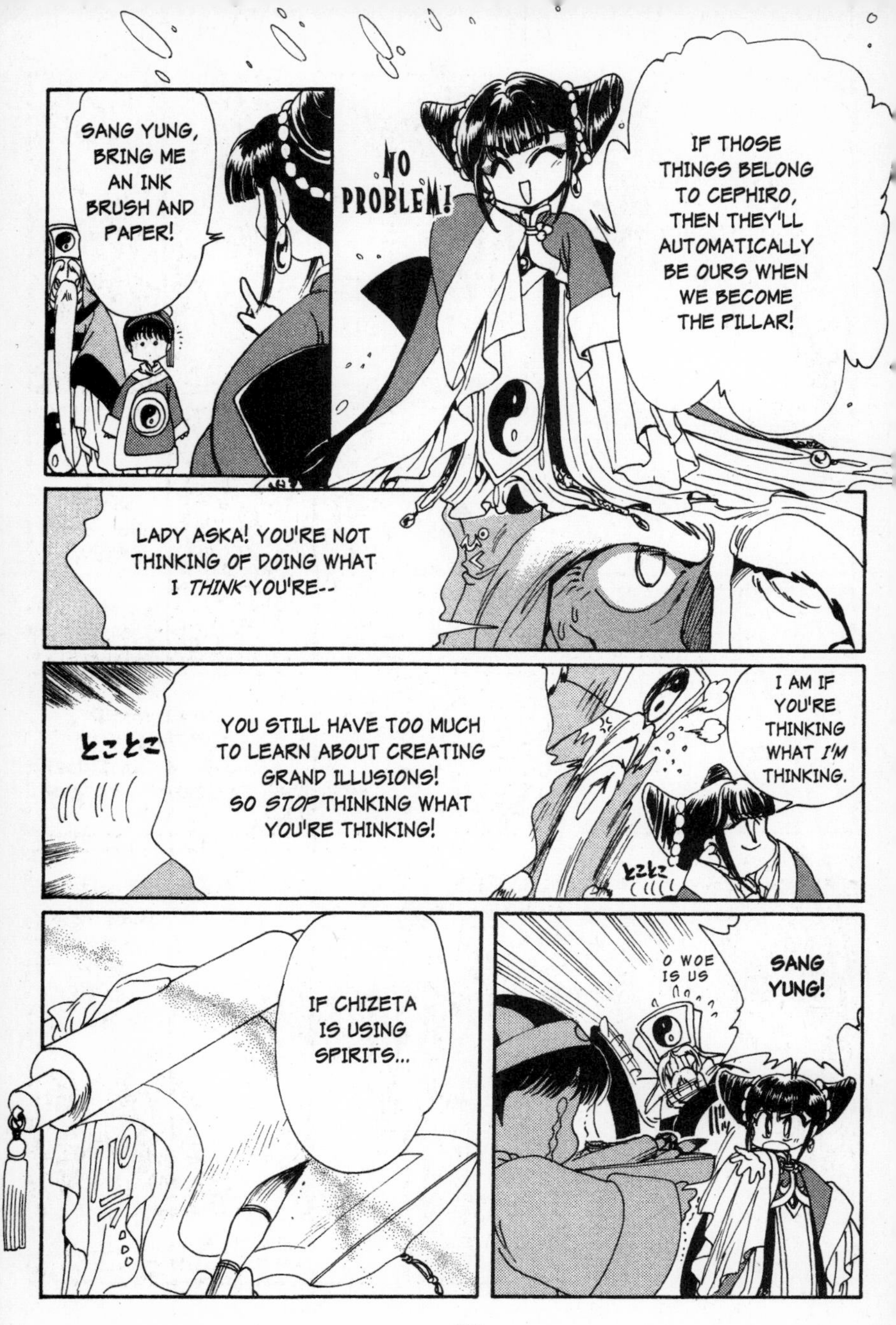

IF THOSE THINGS BELONG TO CEPHIRO, THEN THEY'LL AUTOMATICALLY BE OURS WHEN WE BECOME THE PILLAR!
SANG YUNG, BRING ME AN INK BRUSH AND PAPER!
NO PROBLEM!
LADY ASKA! YOU'RE NOT THINKING OF DOING WHAT I *THINK* YOU'RE--
I AM IF YOU'RE THINKING WHAT *I'M* THINKING.
とことこ
YOU STILL HAVE TOO MUCH TO LEARN ABOUT CREATING GRAND ILLUSIONS! SO *STOP* THINKING WHAT YOU'RE THINKING!
とことこ
SANG YUNG!
O WOE IS US
IF CHIZETA IS USING SPIRITS...

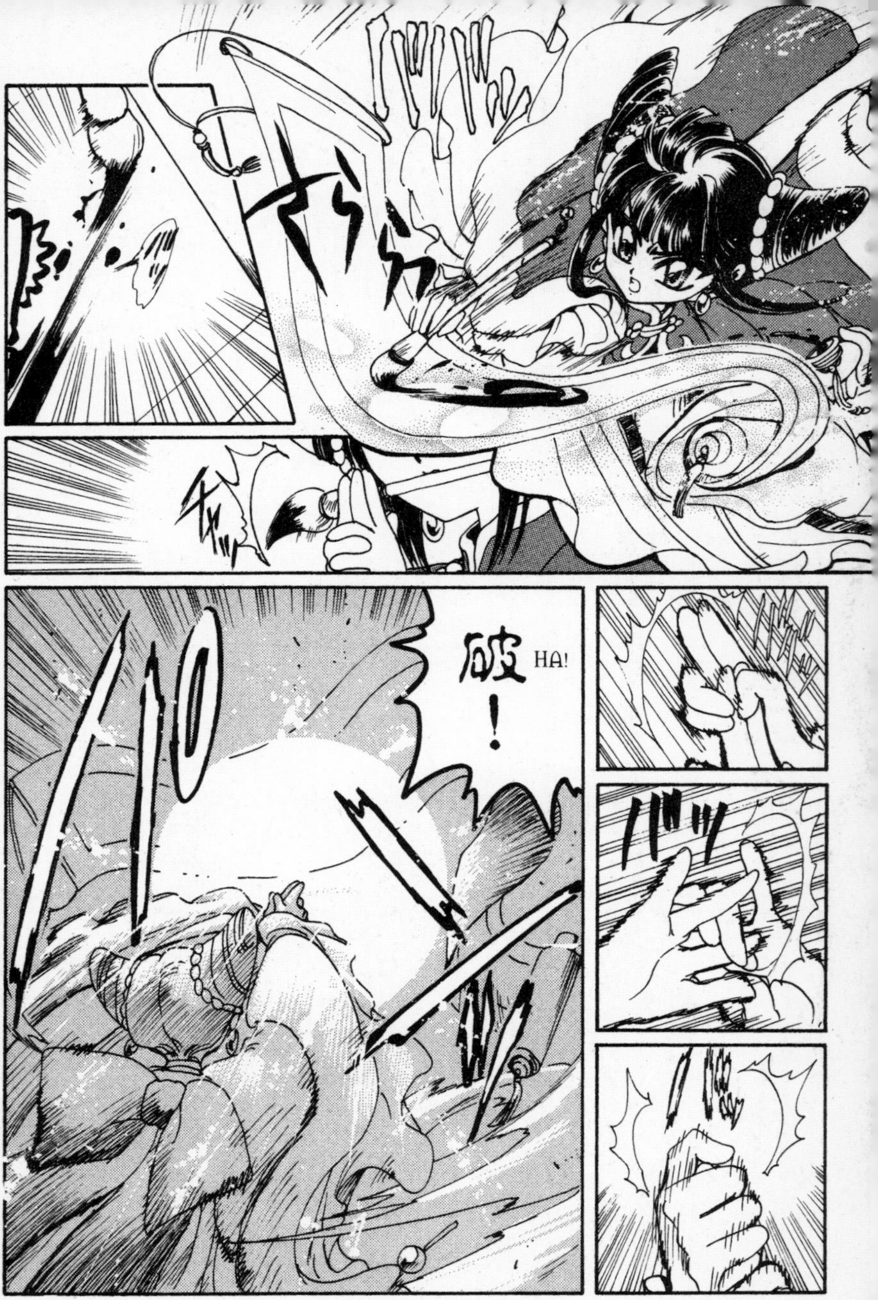
ガシッ
バッ
破 HA!
!

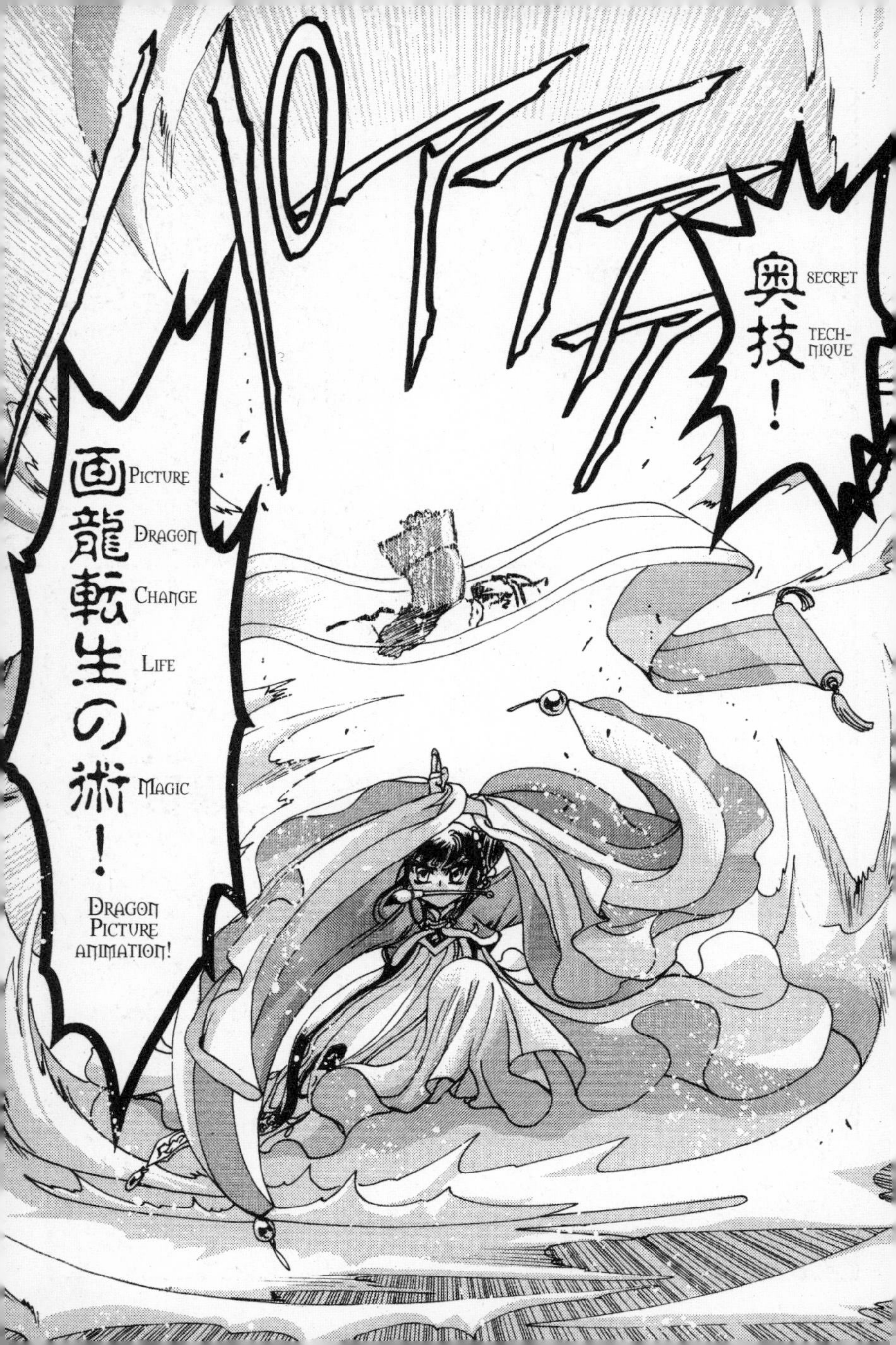
奥技！
SECRET TECH-NIQUE
画龍転生の術！
PICTURE DRAGON CHANGE LIFE MAGIC
DRAGON PICTURE ANIMATION!

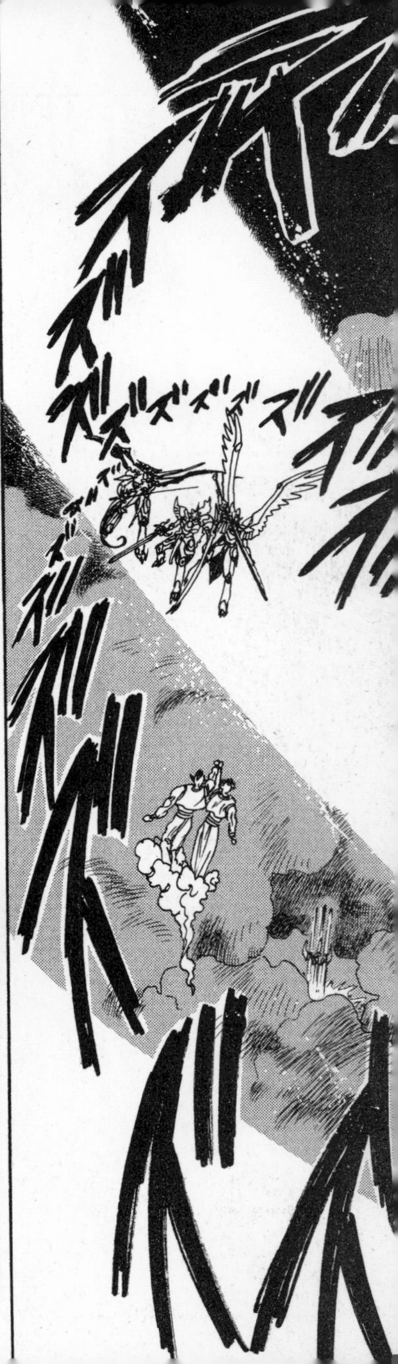

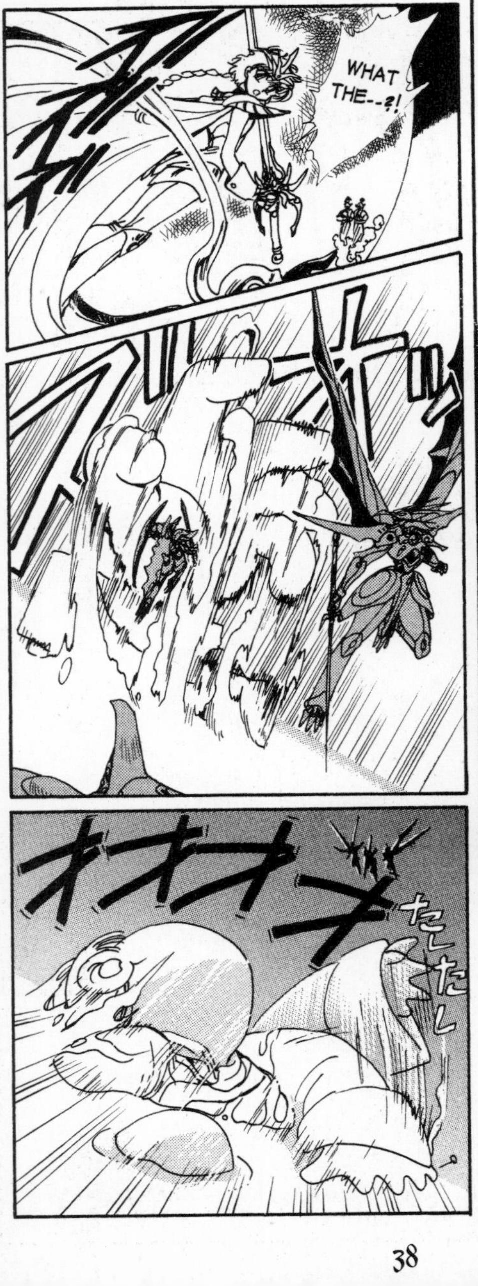
WHAT THE--?!

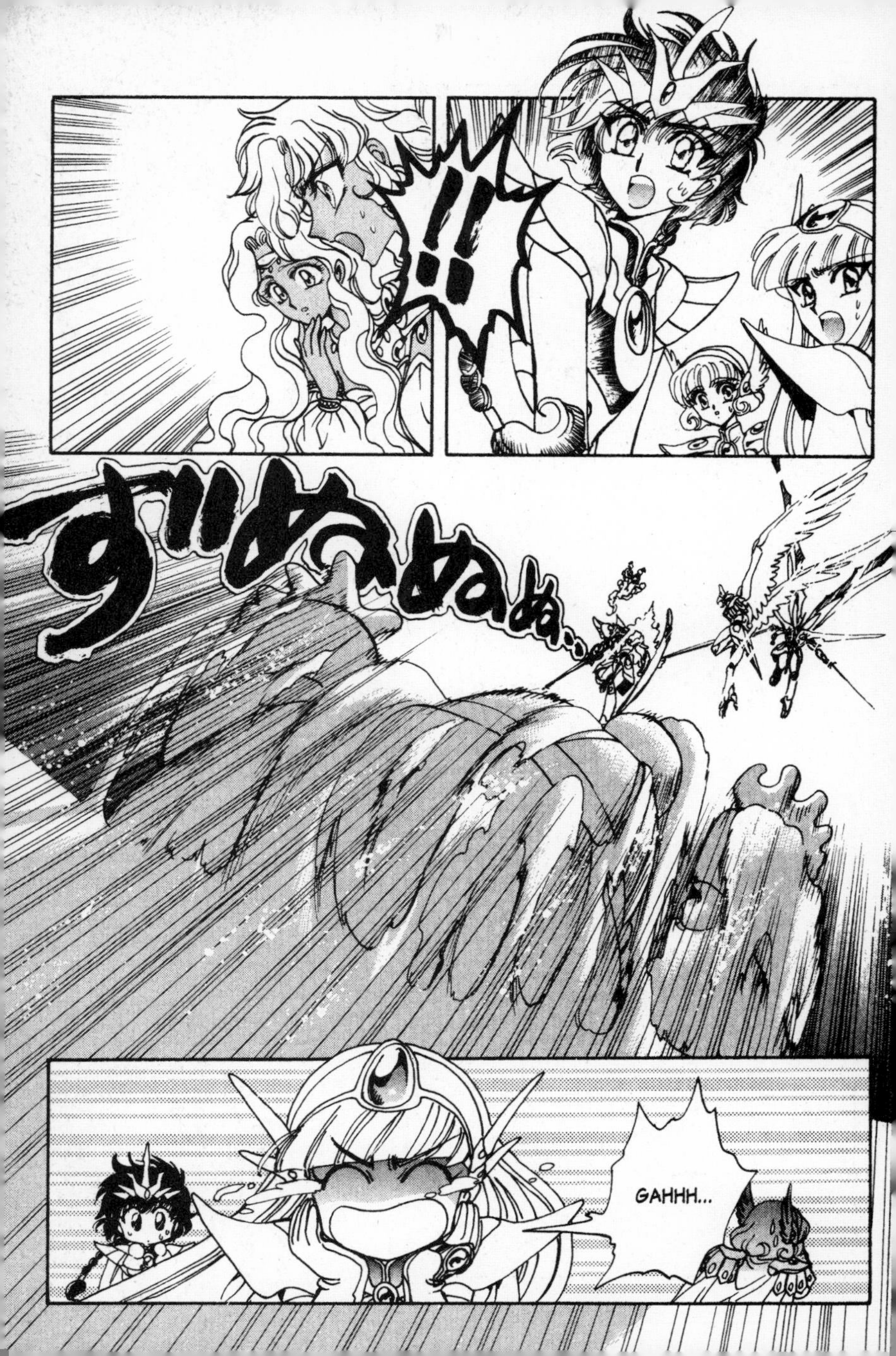
!!
GAHHH...

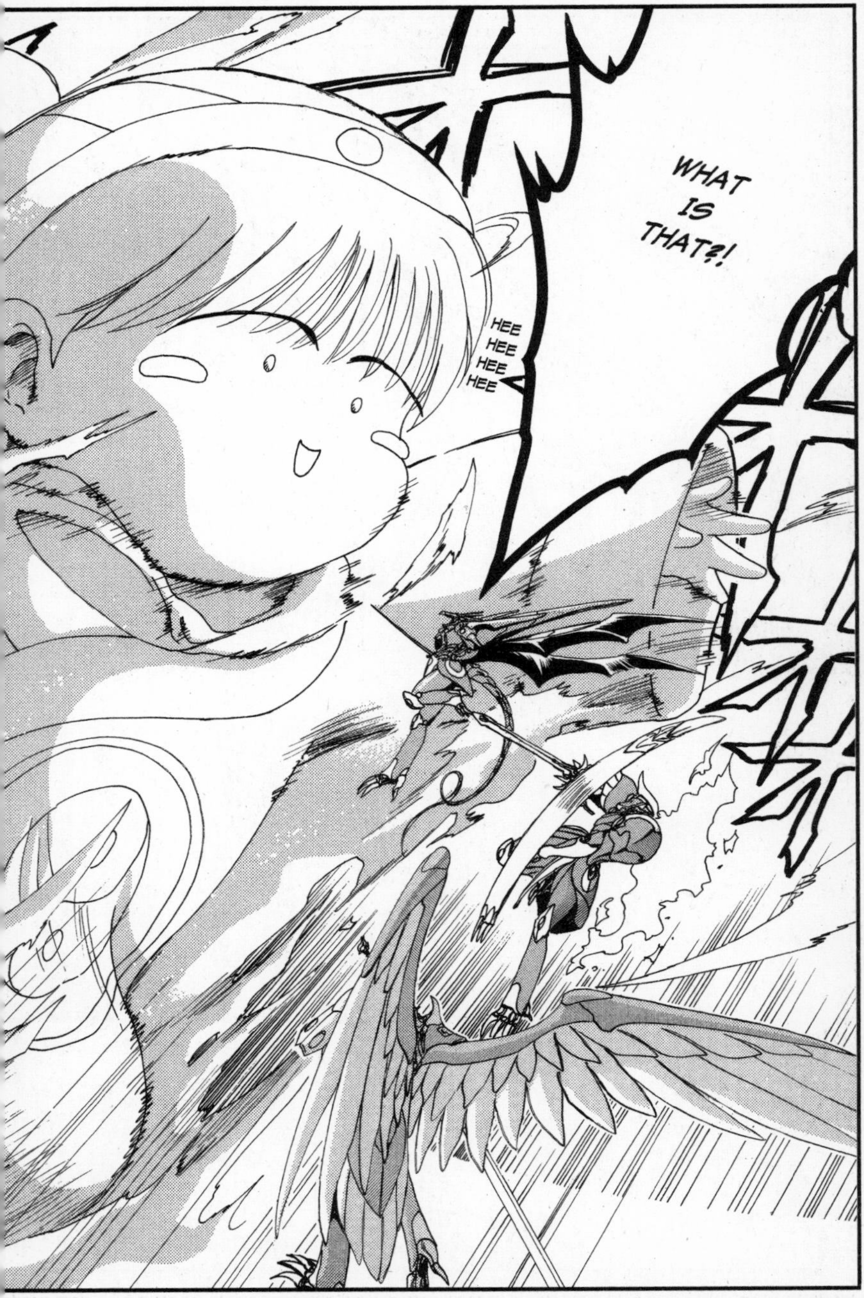
WHAT IS THAT?!
HEE HEE HEE HEE

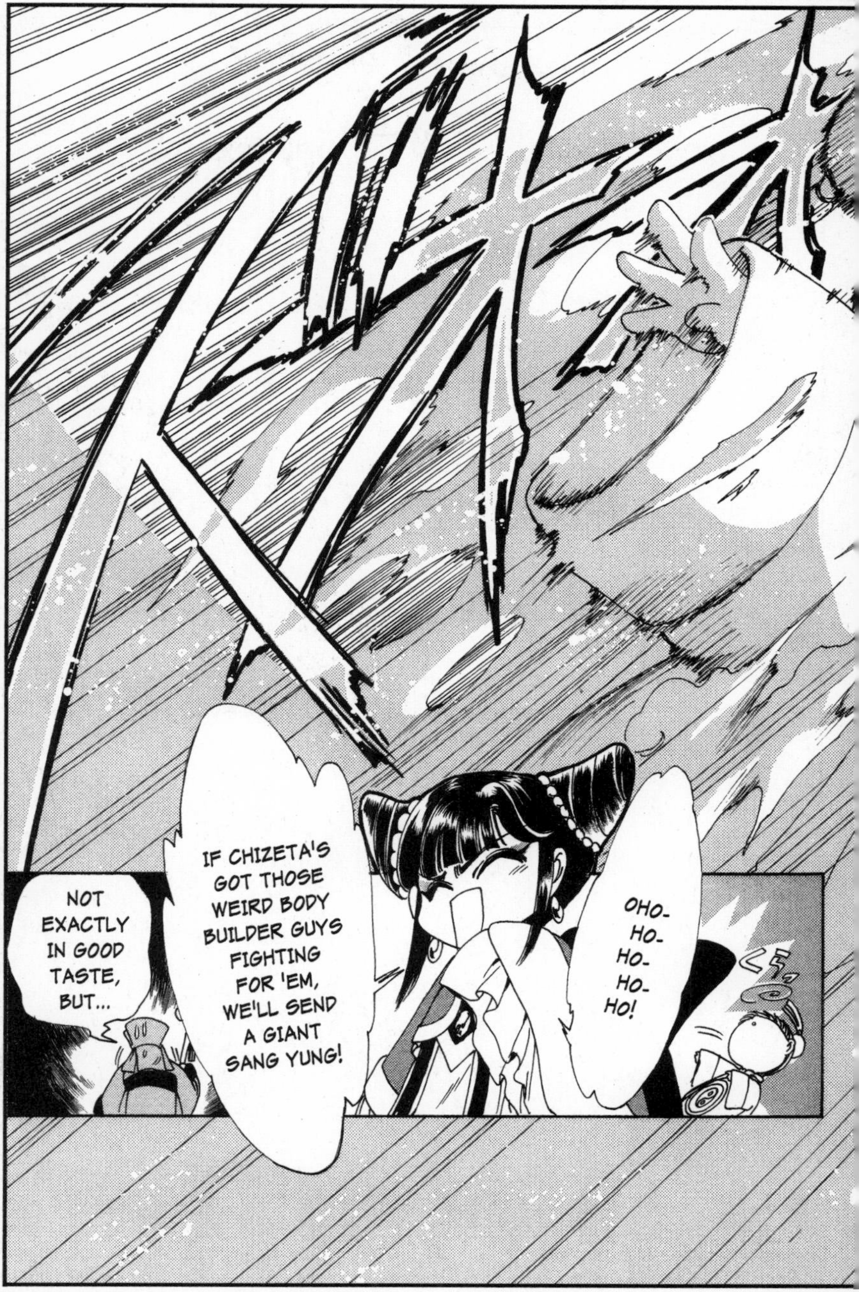

OHO-HO-HO-HO-HO!
IF CHIZETA'S GOT THOSE WEIRD BODY BUILDER GUYS FIGHTING FOR 'EM, WE'LL SEND A GIANT SANG YUNG!
NOT EXACTLY IN GOOD TASTE, BUT...

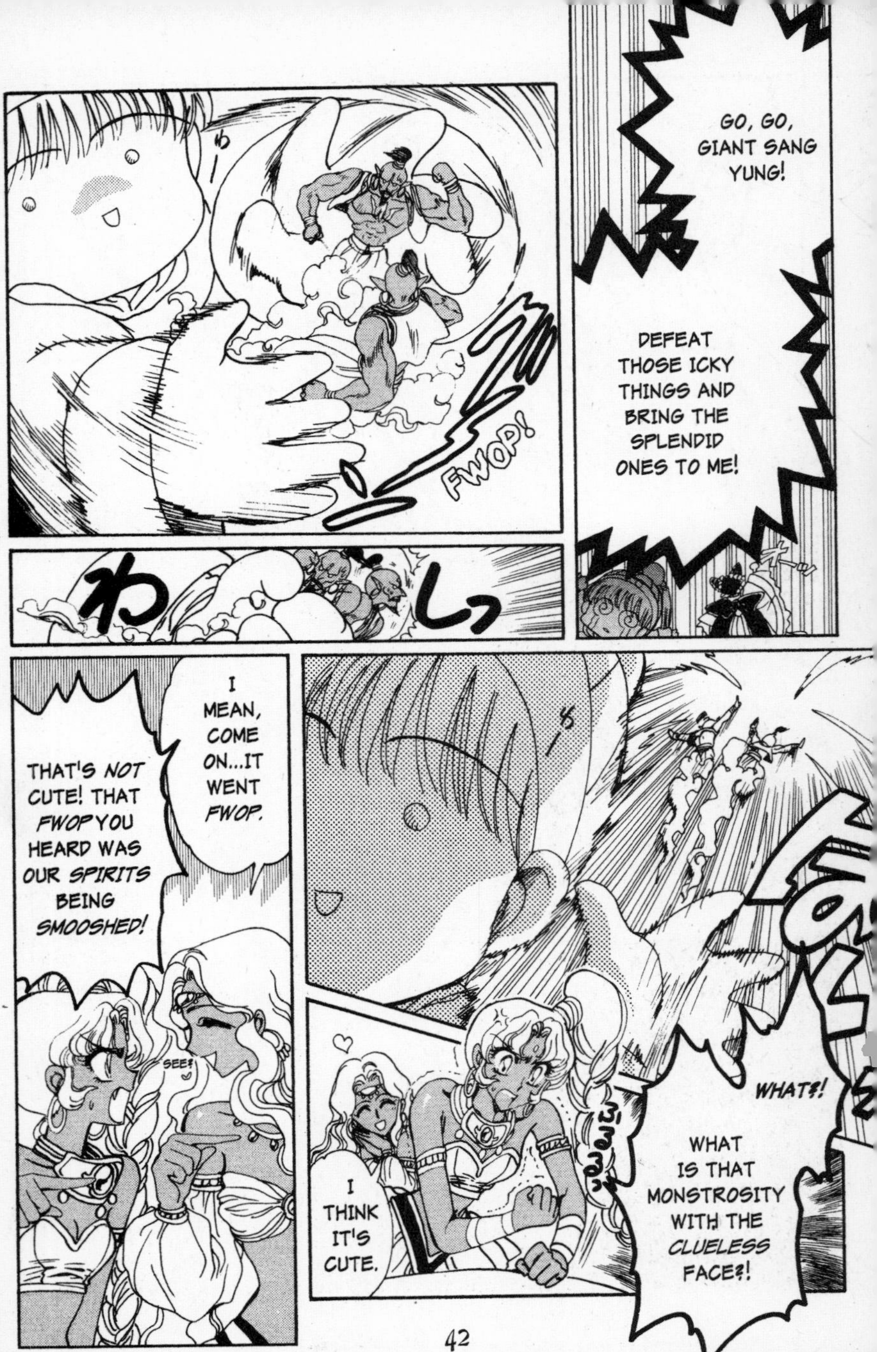
GO, GO, GIANT SANG YUNG!
DEFEAT THOSE ICKY THINGS AND BRING THE SPLENDID ONES TO ME!
FWOP!
わしっ
WHAT?!
WHAT IS THAT MONSTROSITY WITH THE *CLUELESS* FACE?!
I THINK IT'S CUTE.
I MEAN, COME ON...IT WENT *FWOP.*
THAT'S *NOT* CUTE! THAT *FWOP* YOU HEARD WAS OUR *SPIRITS* BEING *SMOOSHED!*
SEE?

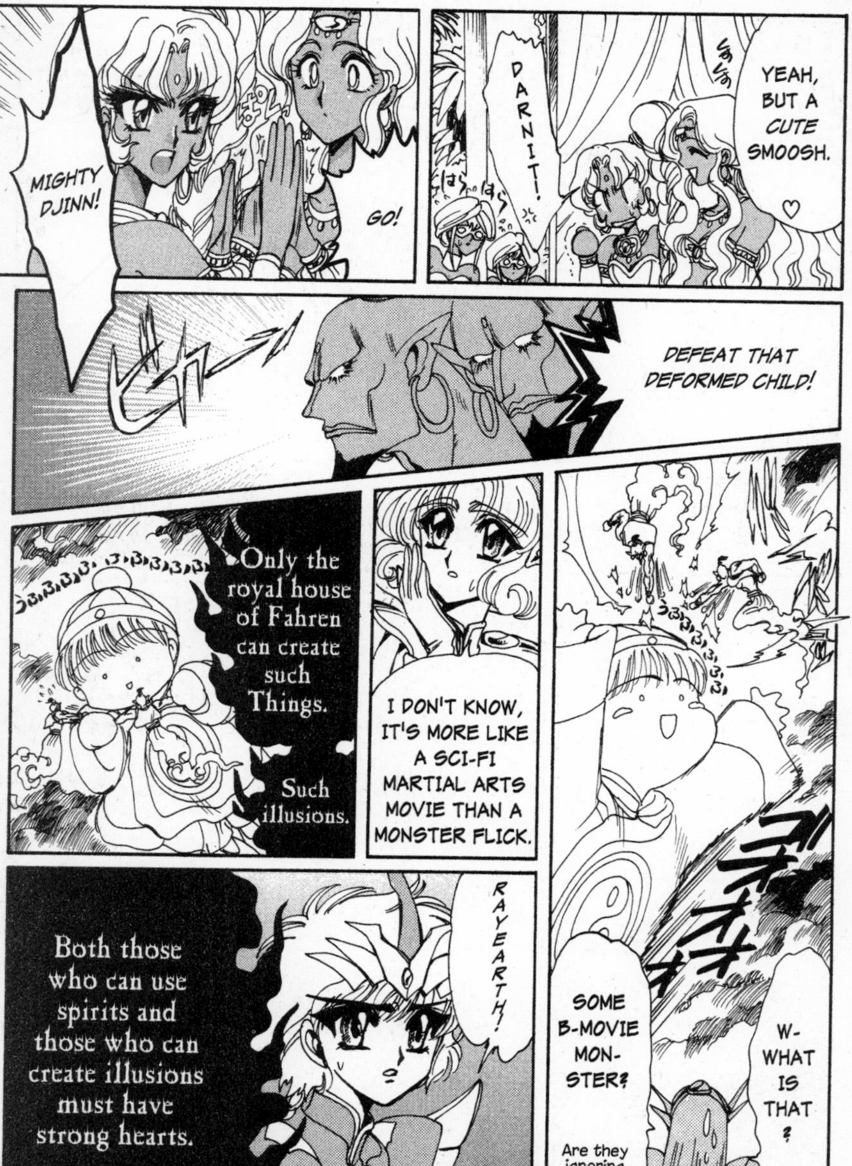
YEAH, BUT A CUTE SMOOSH. ♡
DARNIT!
MIGHTY DJINN!
GO!
DEFEAT THAT DEFORMED CHILD!
W-WHAT IS THAT?
SOME B-MOVIE MON-STER?
Are they ignoring us?
I DON'T KNOW, IT'S MORE LIKE A SCI-FI MARTIAL ARTS MOVIE THAN A MONSTER FLICK.
Only the royal house of Fahren can create such Things.
Such illusions.
RAYEARTH!
Both those who can use spirits and those who can create illusions must have strong hearts.

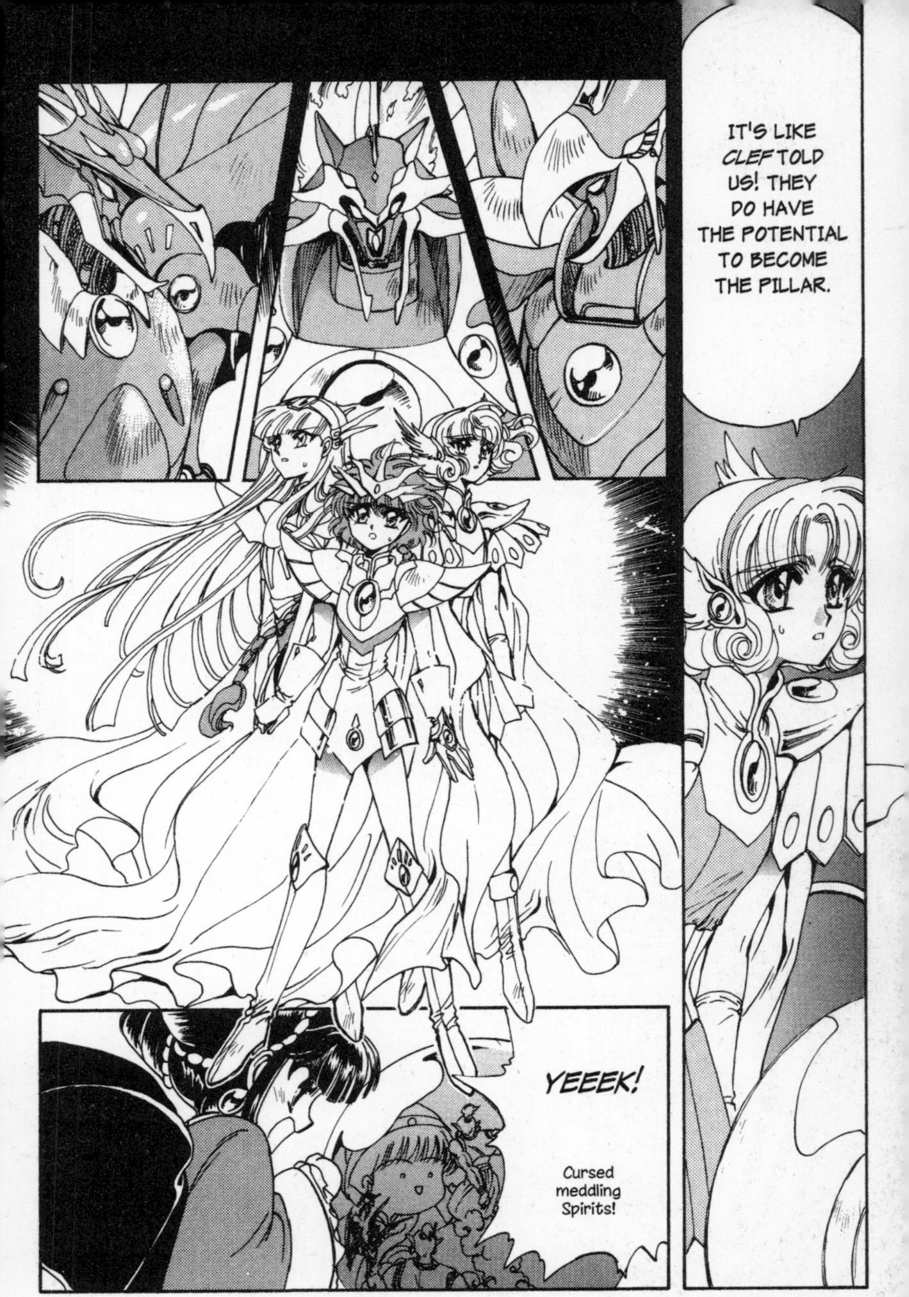
IT'S LIKE *CLEF* TOLD US! THEY DO HAVE THE POTENTIAL TO BECOME THE PILLAR.
YEEEK!
Cursed meddling Spirits!

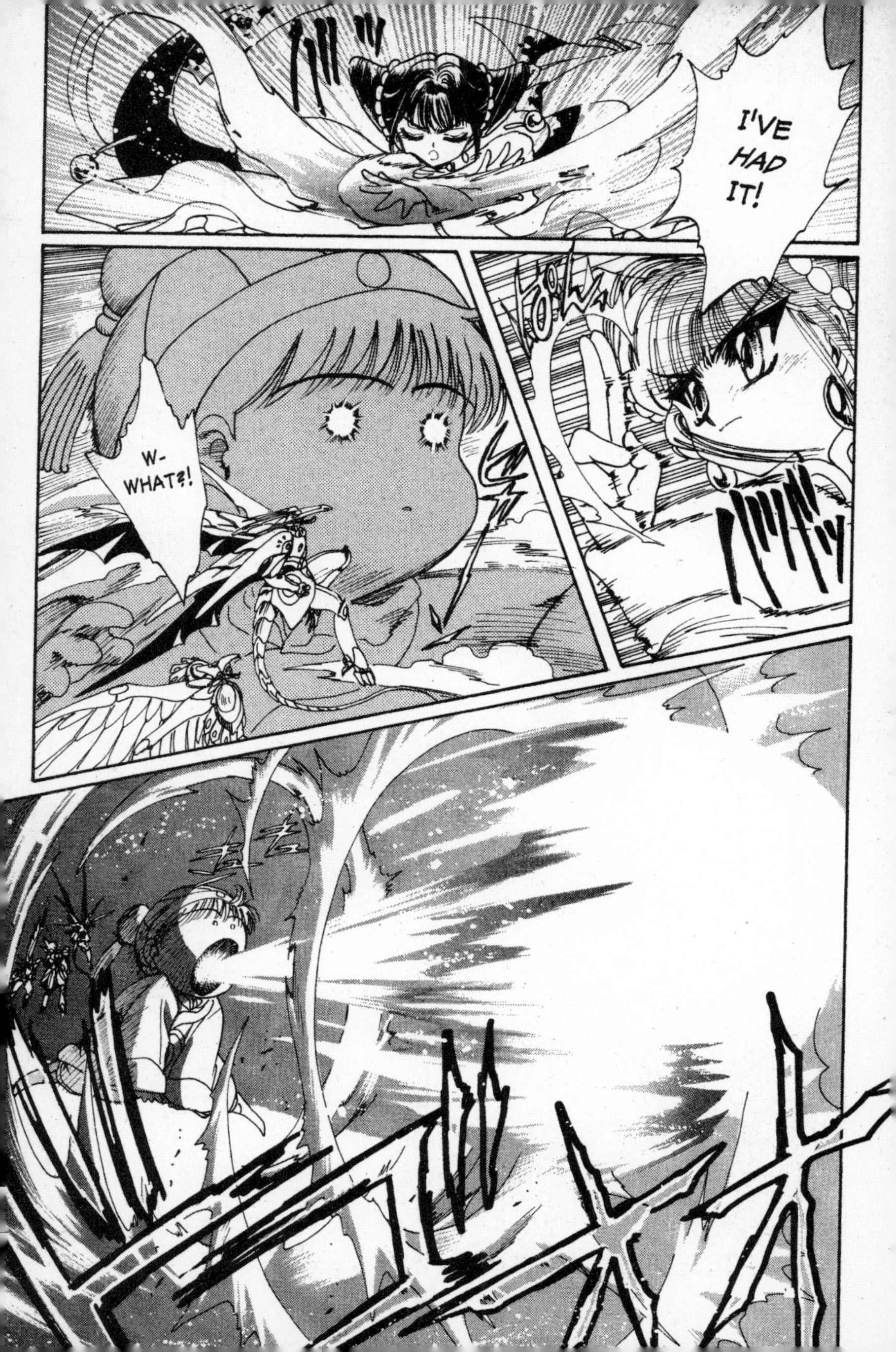
I'VE HAD IT!
W-WHAT?!

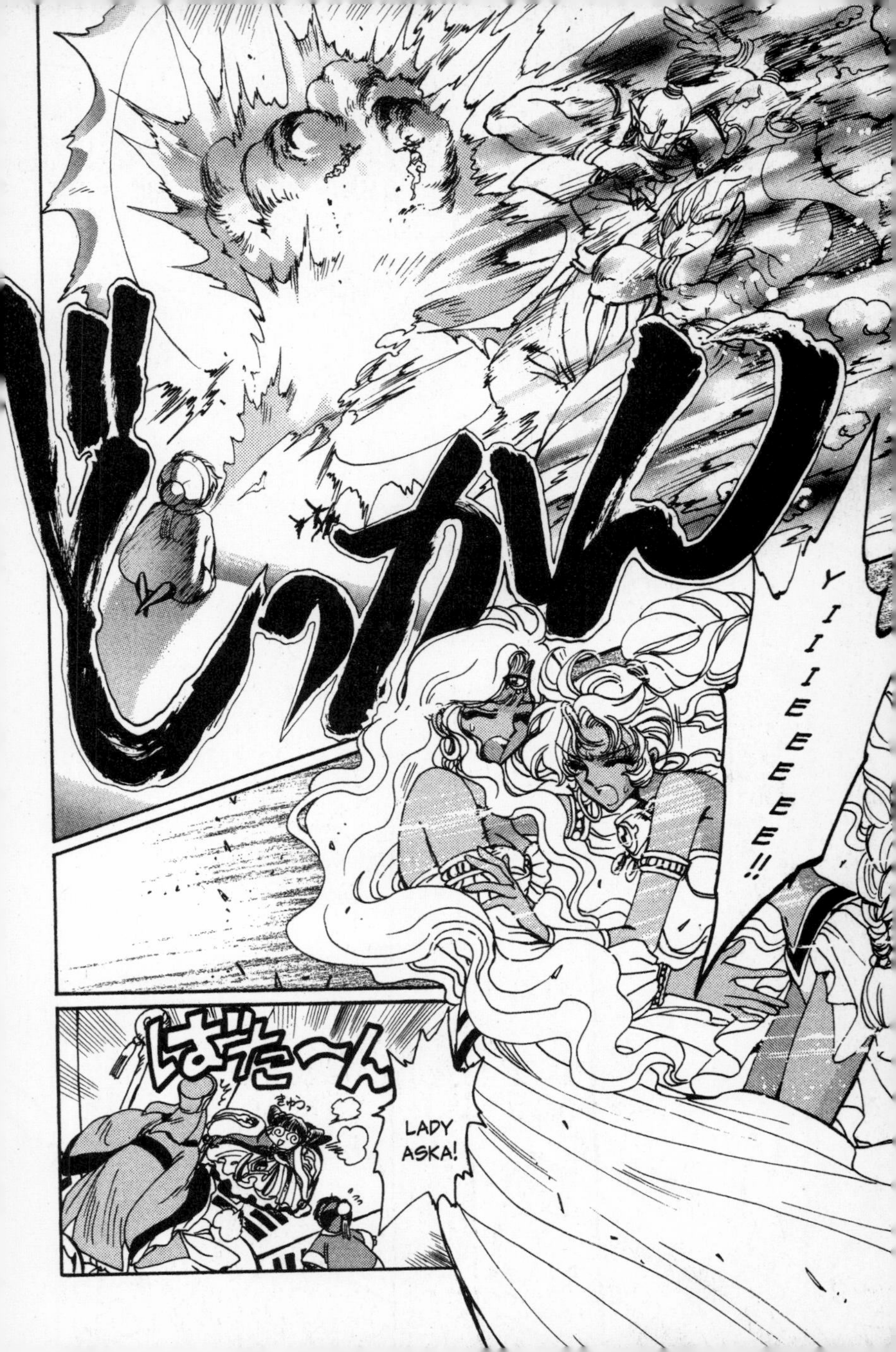
どっかん
YIIIEEEEE!!
ばったーん
きゅうっ
LADY ASKA!

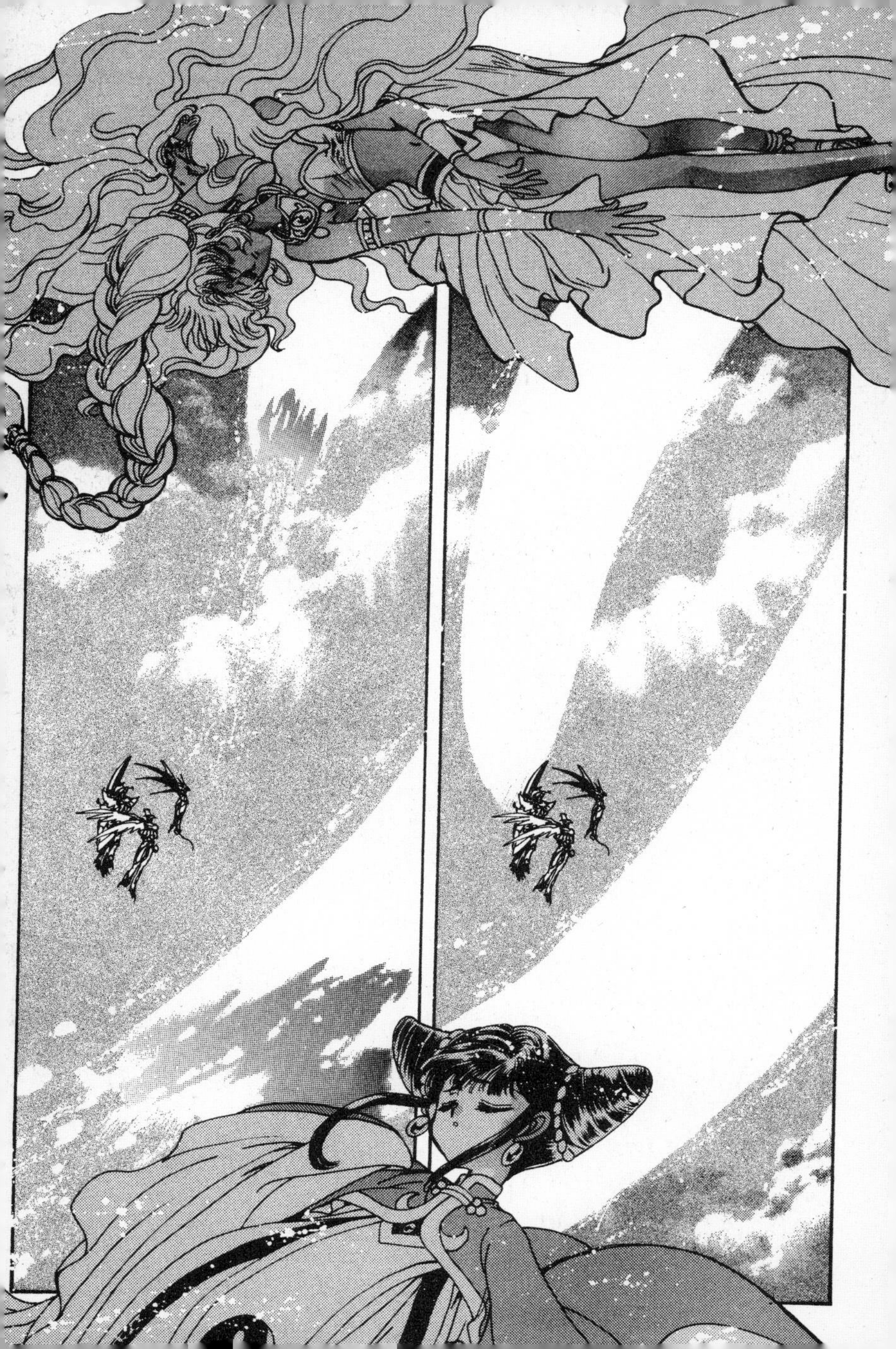

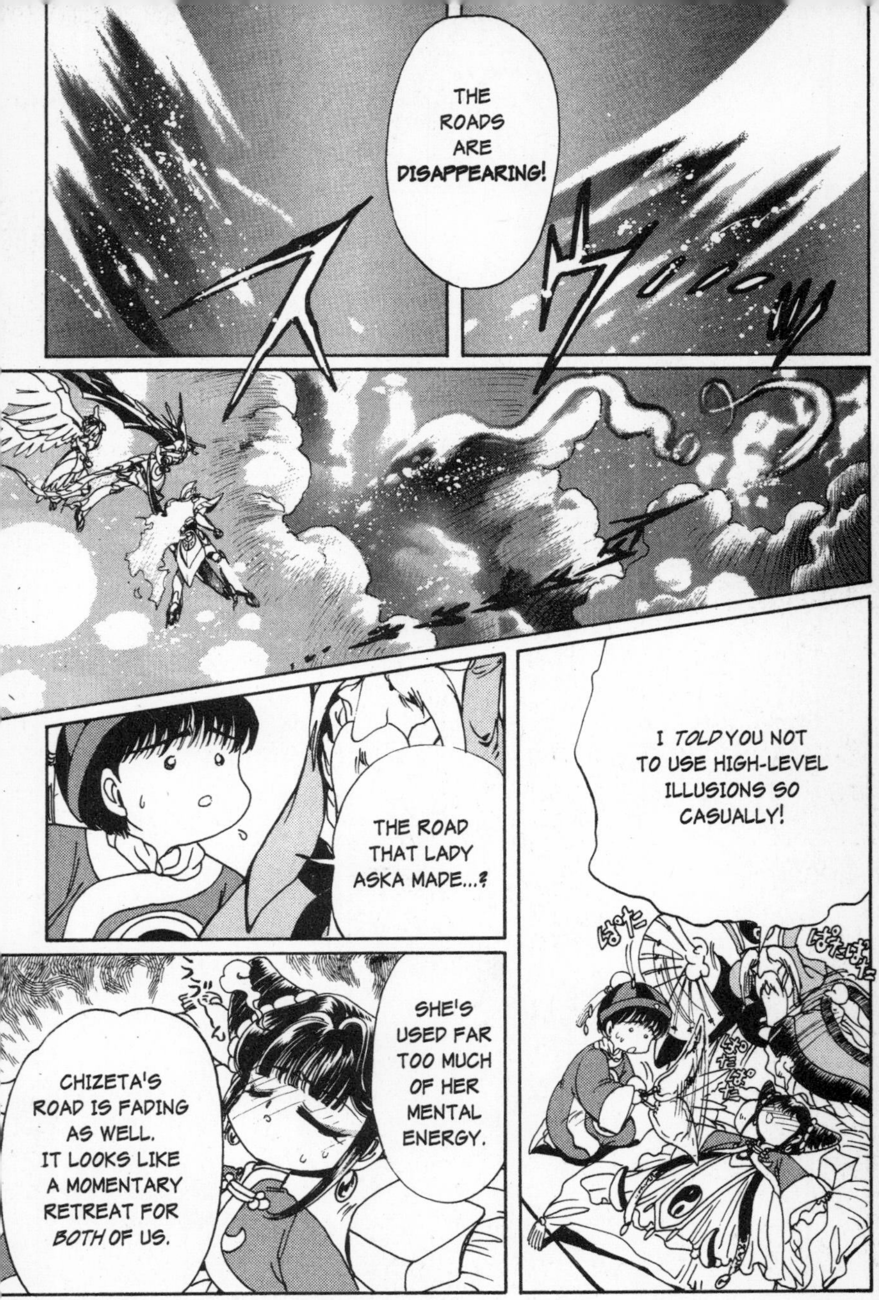
THE ROADS ARE DISAPPEARING!
I *TOLD* YOU NOT TO USE HIGH-LEVEL ILLUSIONS SO CASUALLY!
THE ROAD THAT LADY ASKA MADE...?
SHE'S USED FAR TOO MUCH OF HER MENTAL ENERGY.
CHIZETA'S ROAD IS FADING AS WELL. IT LOOKS LIKE A MOMENTARY RETREAT FOR *BOTH* OF US.

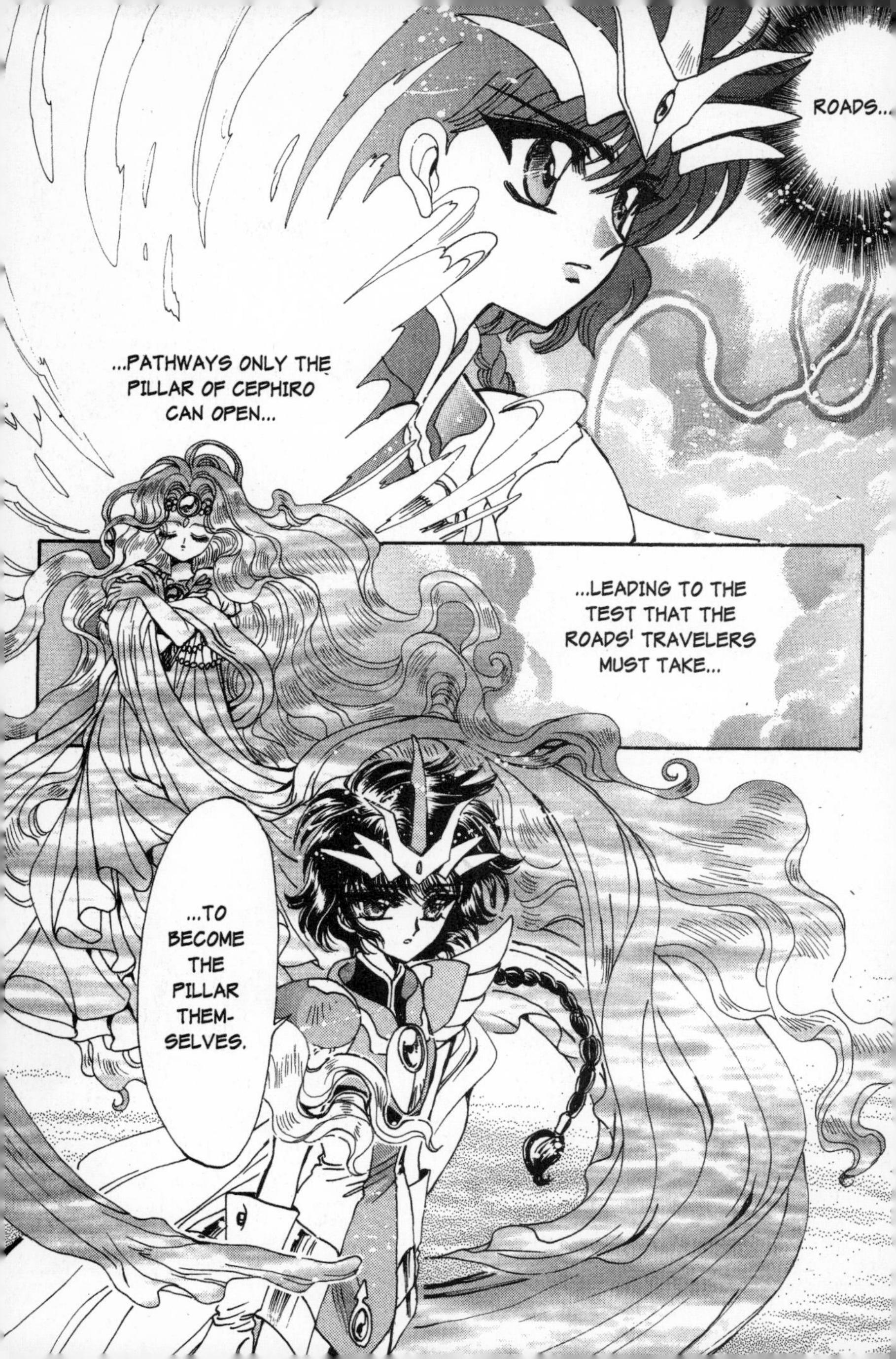
ROADS...
...PATHWAYS ONLY THE PILLAR OF CEPHIRO CAN OPEN...
...LEADING TO THE TEST THAT THE ROADS' TRAVELERS MUST TAKE...
...TO BECOME THE PILLAR THEM-SELVES.

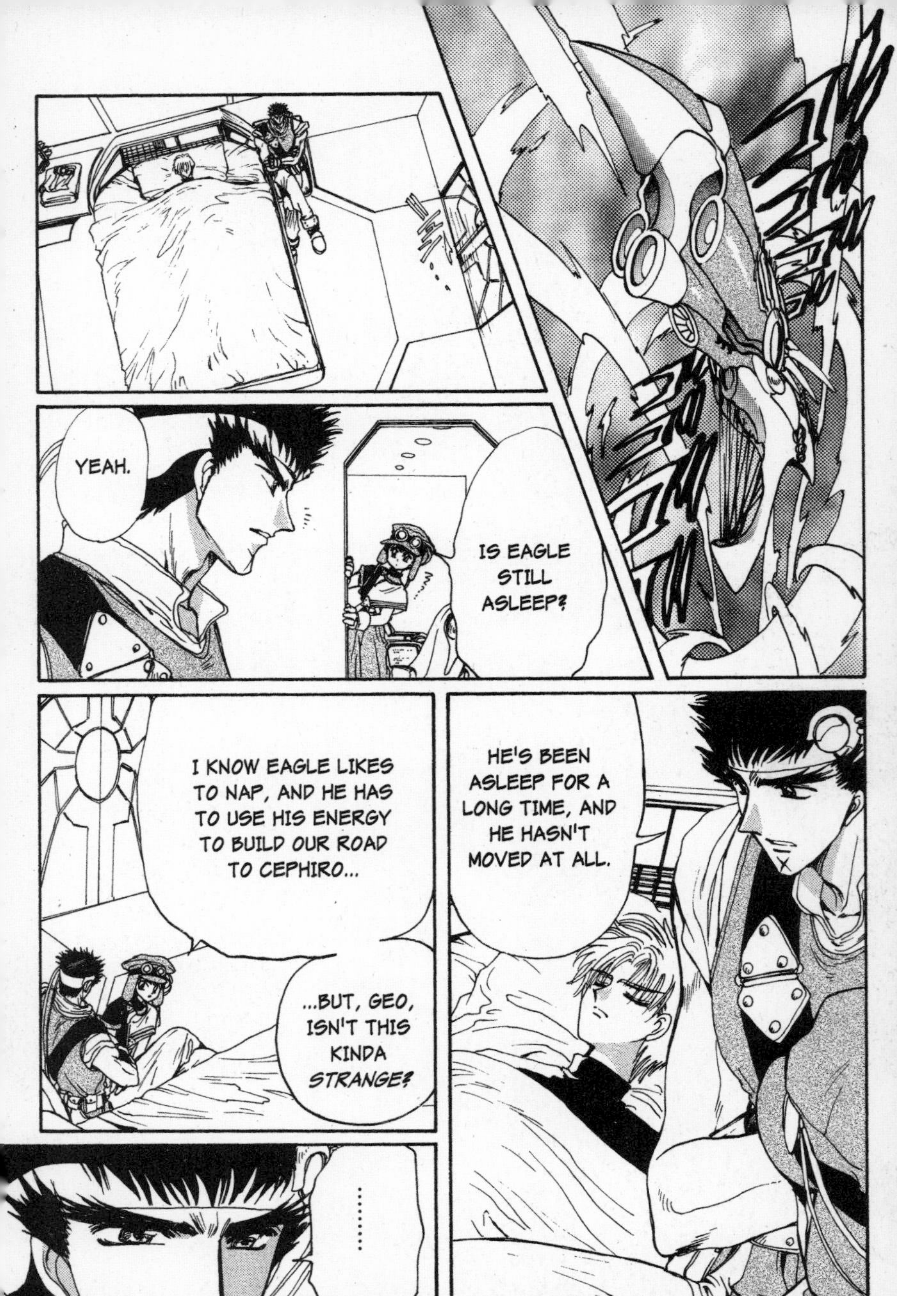
IS EAGLE STILL ASLEEP?
YEAH.
HE'S BEEN ASLEEP FOR A LONG TIME, AND HE HASN'T MOVED AT ALL.
I KNOW EAGLE LIKES TO NAP, AND HE HAS TO USE HIS ENERGY TO BUILD OUR ROAD TO CEPHIRO...
...BUT, GEO, ISN'T THIS KINDA *STRANGE?*
......

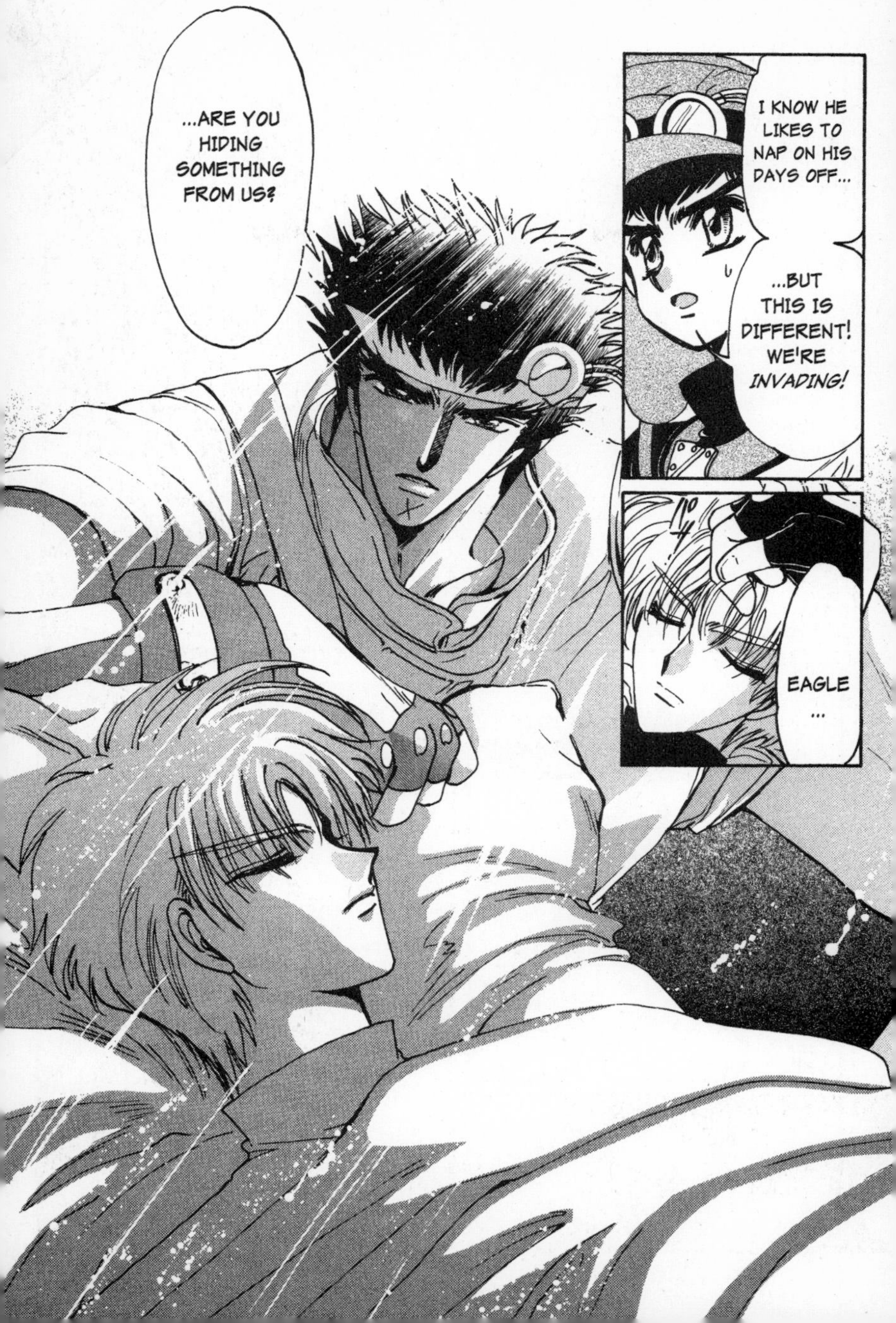
I KNOW HE LIKES TO NAP ON HIS DAYS OFF...
...BUT THIS IS DIFFERENT! WE'RE *INVADING!*
EAGLE ...
...ARE YOU HIDING SOMETHING FROM US?

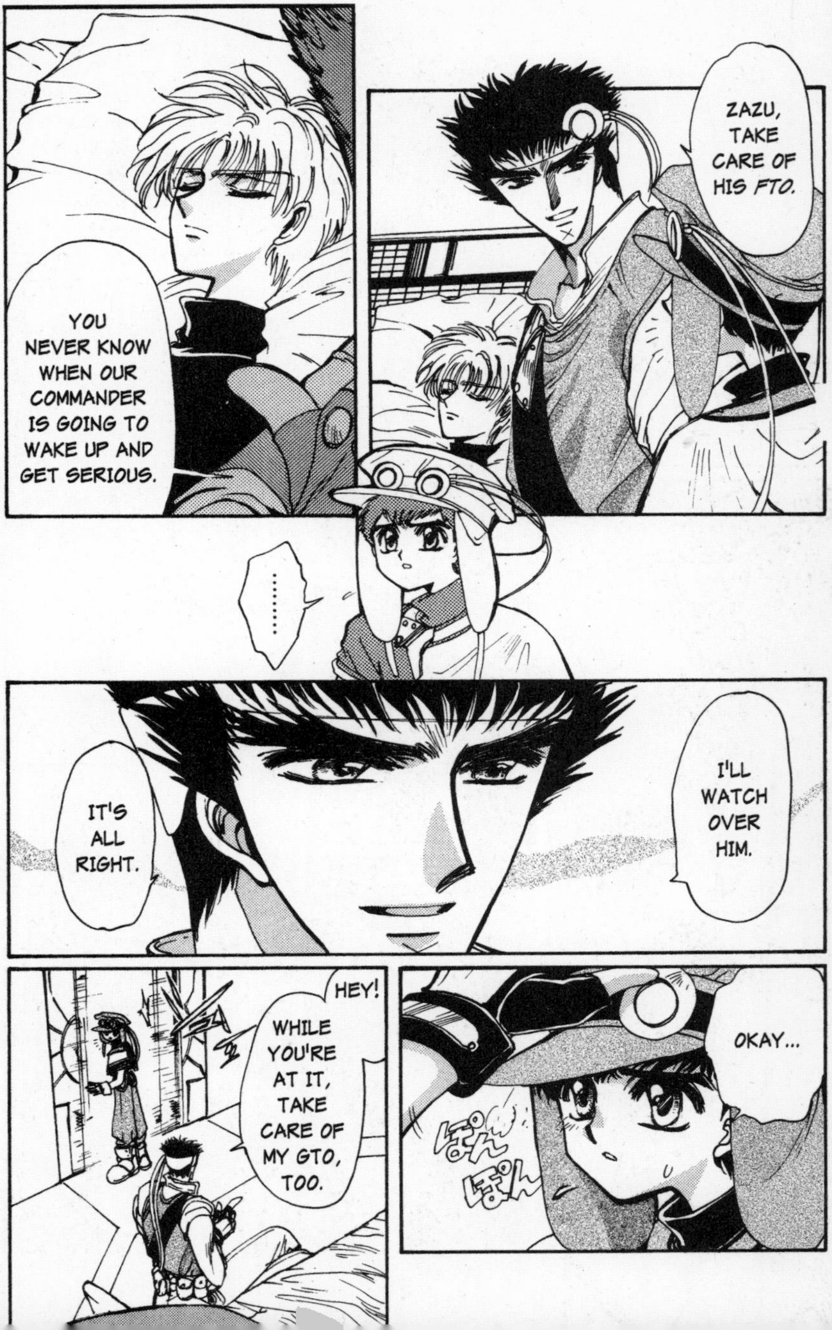
ZAZU, TAKE CARE OF HIS *FTO.*
YOU NEVER KNOW WHEN OUR COMMANDER IS GOING TO WAKE UP AND GET SERIOUS.
......
I'LL WATCH OVER HIM.
IT'S ALL RIGHT.
OKAY...
ぽんぽん
HEY!
WHILE YOU'RE AT IT, TAKE CARE OF MY GTO, TOO.

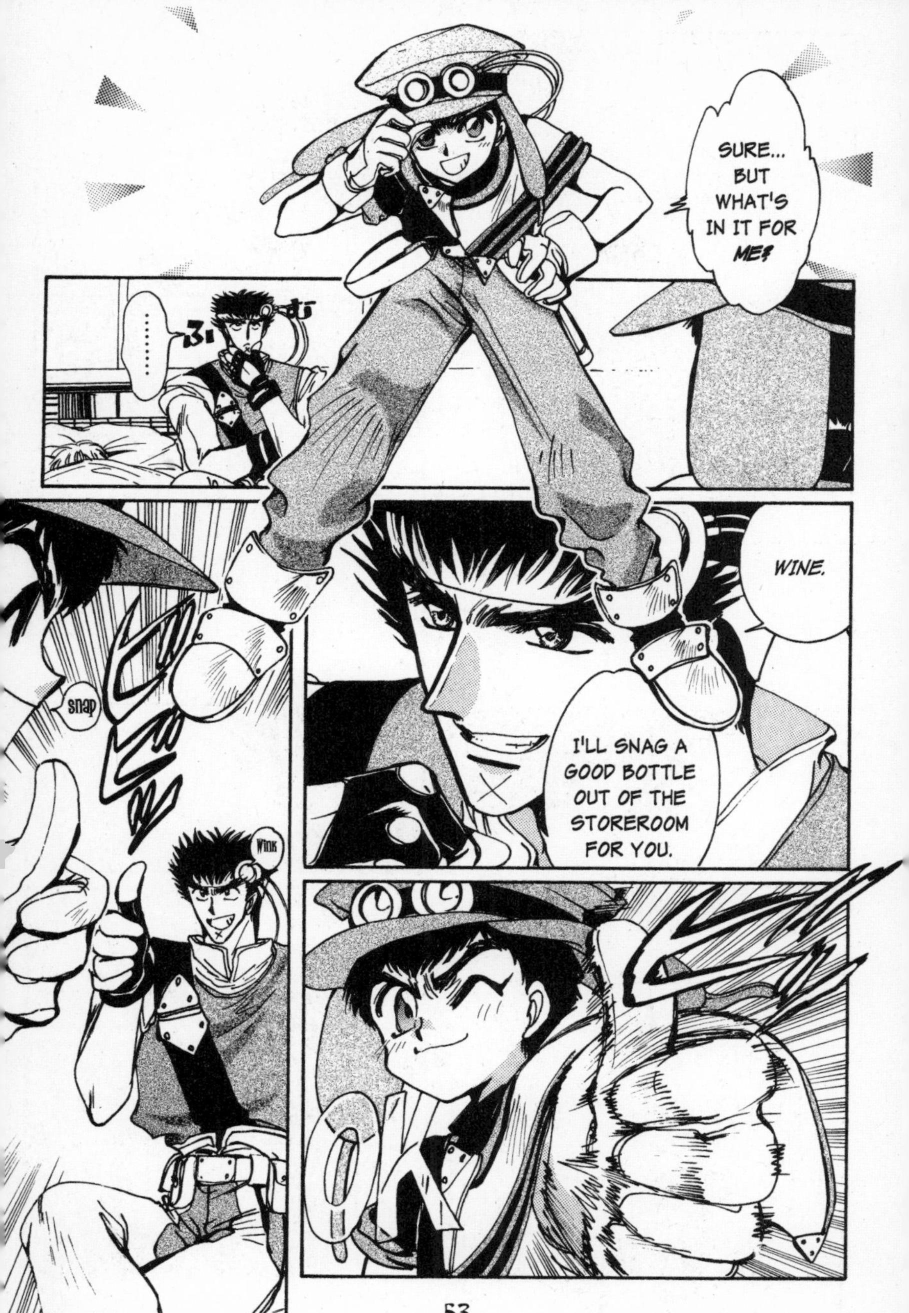
SURE... BUT WHAT'S IN IT FOR ME?
......
WINE.
I'LL SNAG A GOOD BOTTLE OUT OF THE STOREROOM FOR YOU.
snap
Wink

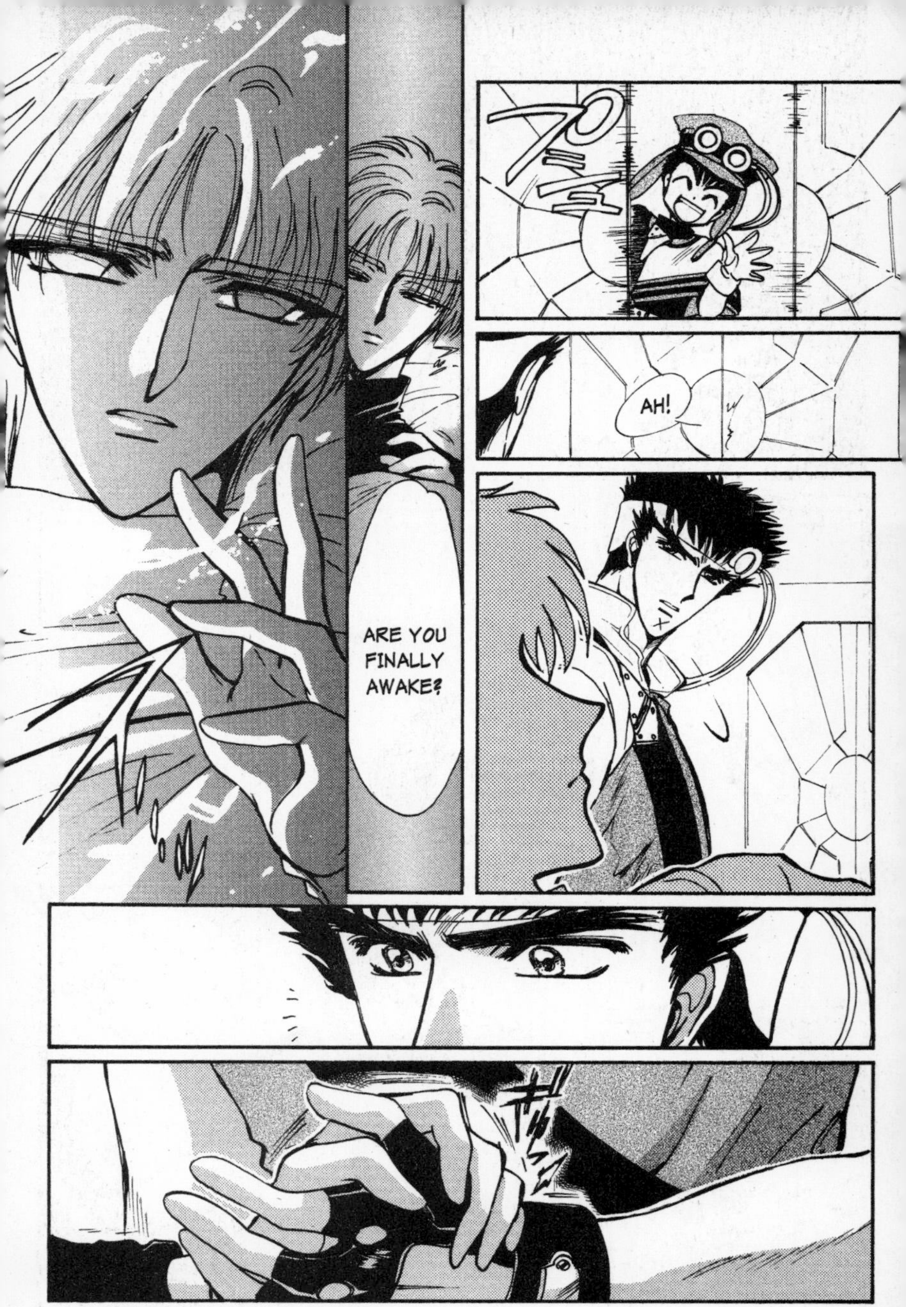
AH!
ARE YOU FINALLY AWAKE?

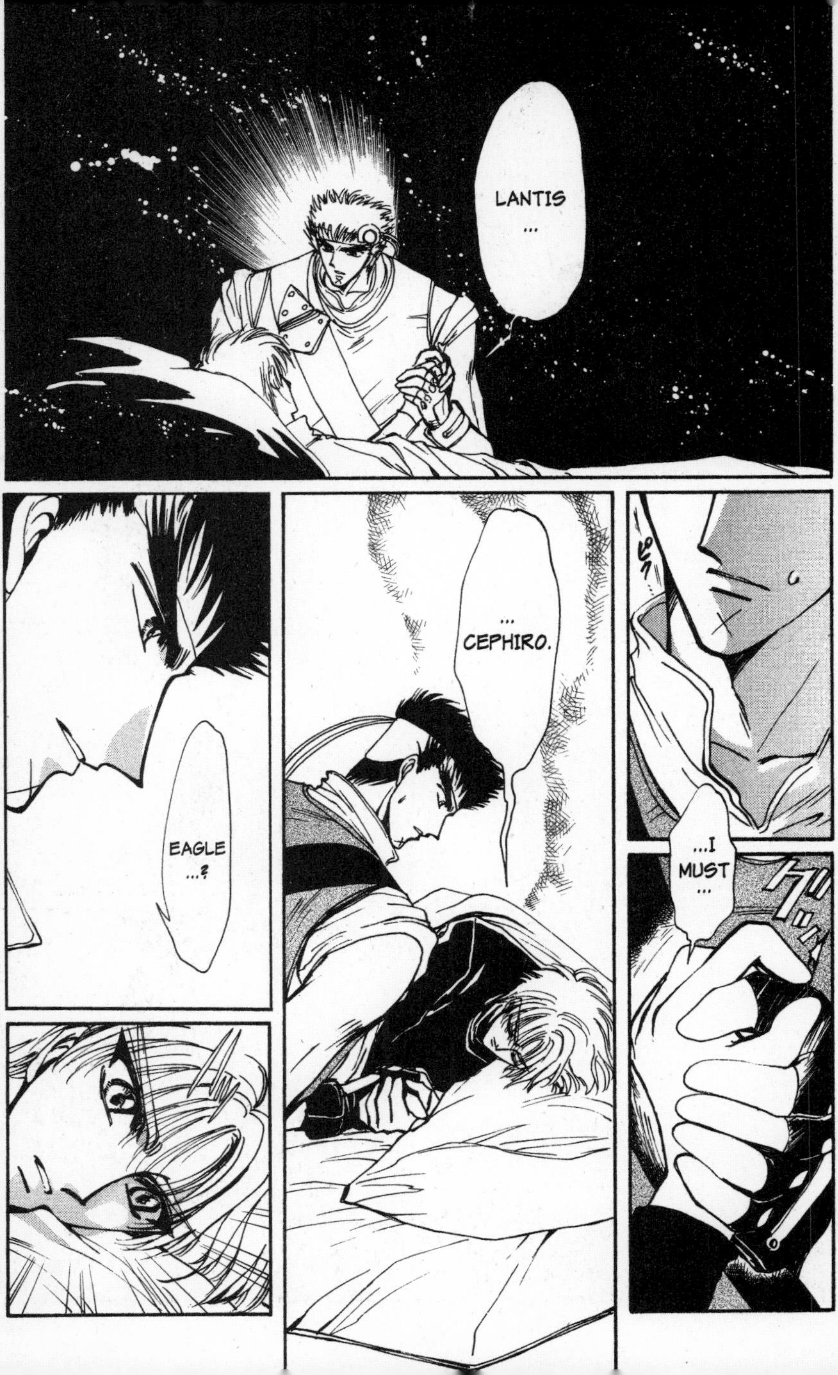
LANTIS ...
ピク
...I MUST ...
グッ
... CEPHIRO.
EAGLE ...?

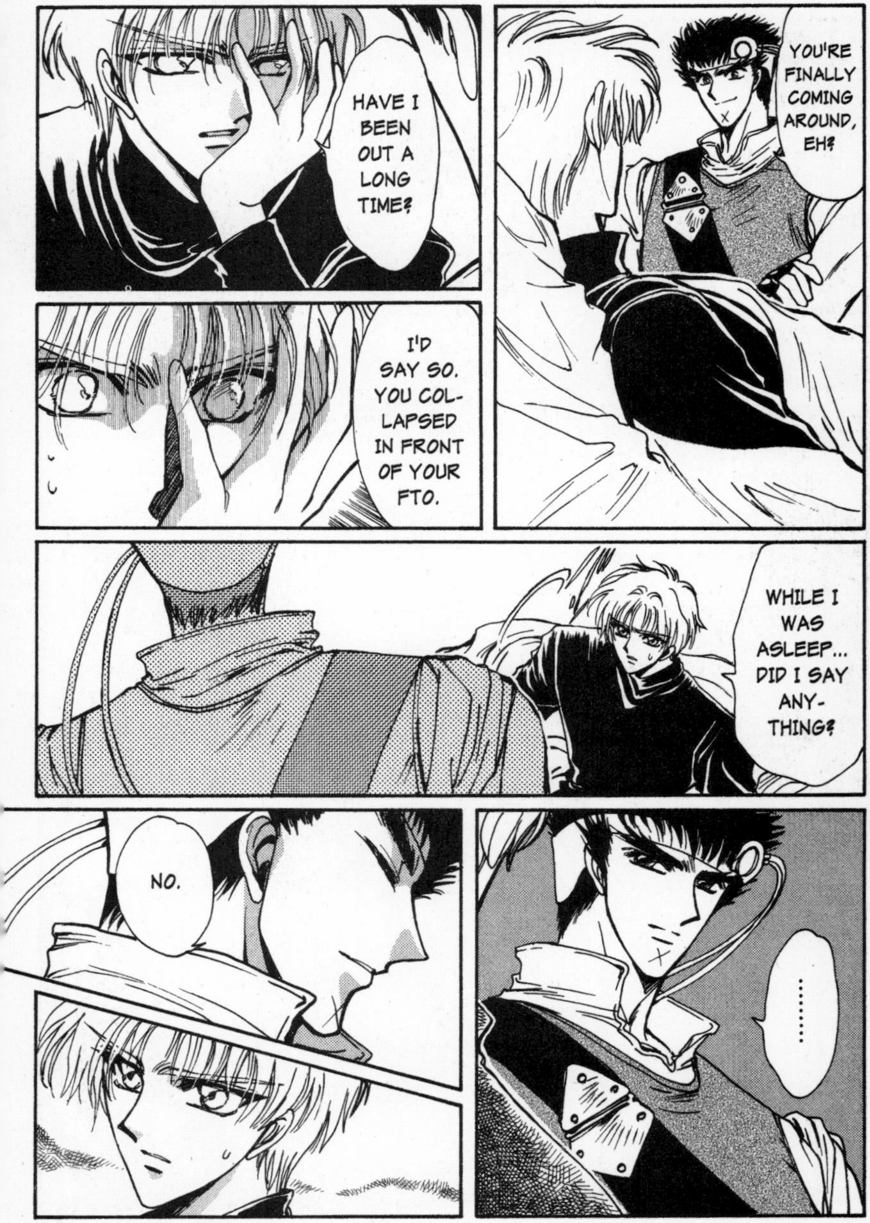
YOU'RE FINALLY COMING AROUND, EH?
HAVE I BEEN OUT A LONG TIME?
I'D SAY SO. YOU COL-LAPSED IN FRONT OF YOUR FTO.
WHILE I WAS ASLEEP... DID I SAY ANY-THING?
NO.
......

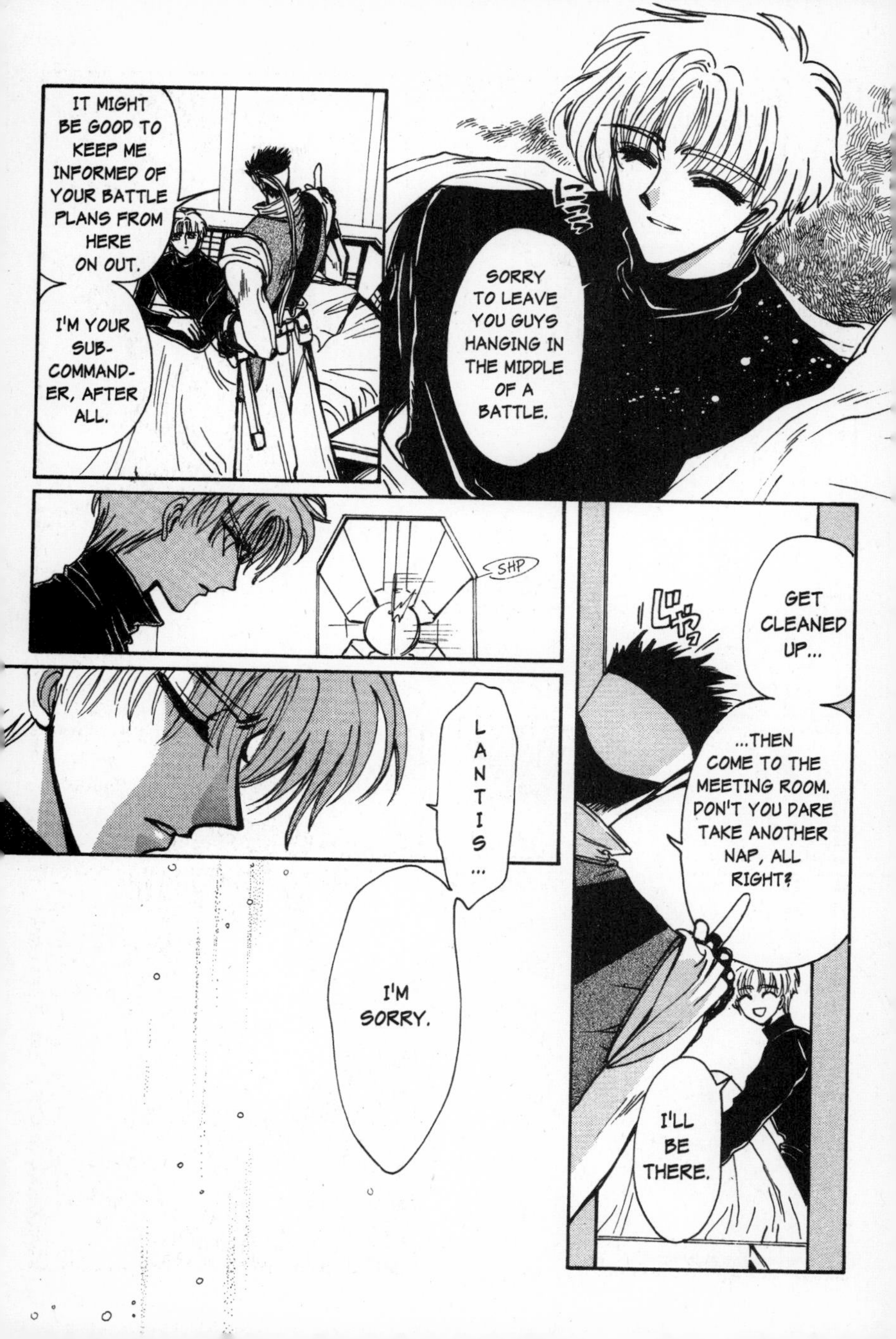
SORRY TO LEAVE YOU GUYS HANGING IN THE MIDDLE OF A BATTLE.
IT MIGHT BE GOOD TO KEEP ME INFORMED OF YOUR BATTLE PLANS FROM HERE ON OUT.
I'M YOUR SUB-COMMANDER, AFTER ALL.
GET CLEANED UP...
...THEN COME TO THE MEETING ROOM. DON'T YOU DARE TAKE ANOTHER NAP, ALL RIGHT?
I'LL BE THERE.
SHP
LANTIS...
I'M SORRY.

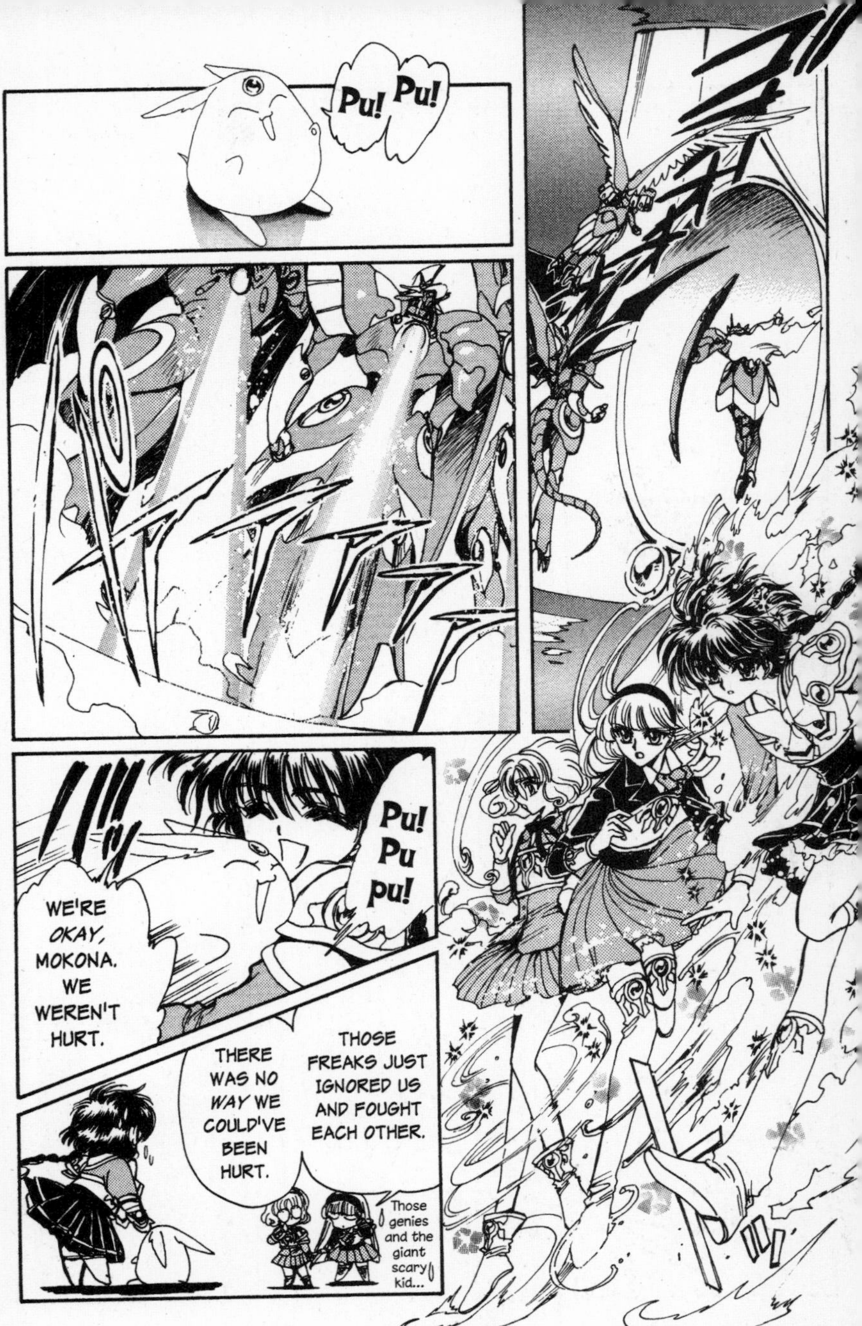
Pu! Pu!
Pu! Pu pu!
WE'RE *OKAY*, MOKONA. WE WEREN'T HURT.
THOSE FREAKS JUST IGNORED US AND FOUGHT EACH OTHER.
THERE WAS NO *WAY* WE COULD'VE BEEN HURT.
Those genies and the giant scary kid...

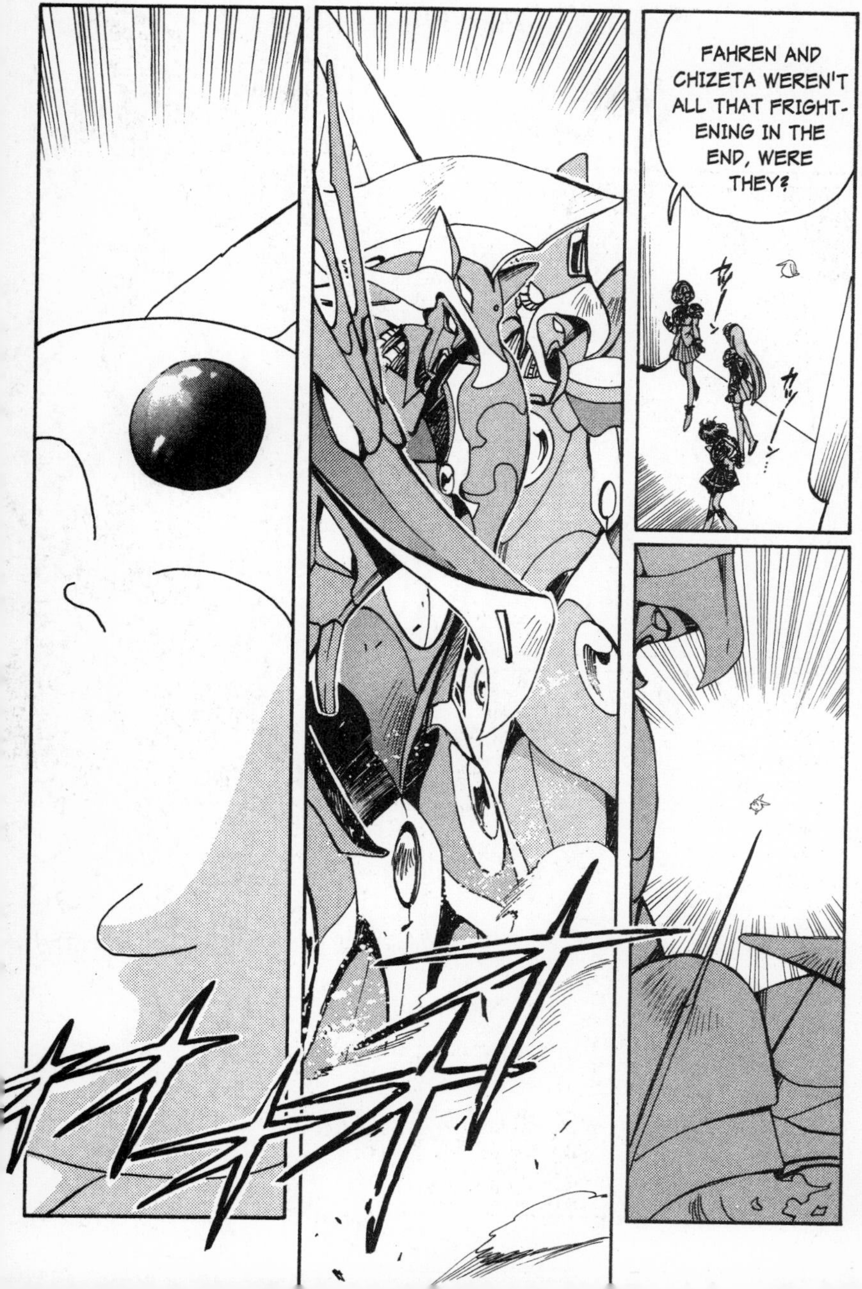
FAHREN AND CHIZETA WEREN'T ALL THAT FRIGHT-ENING IN THE END, WERE THEY?

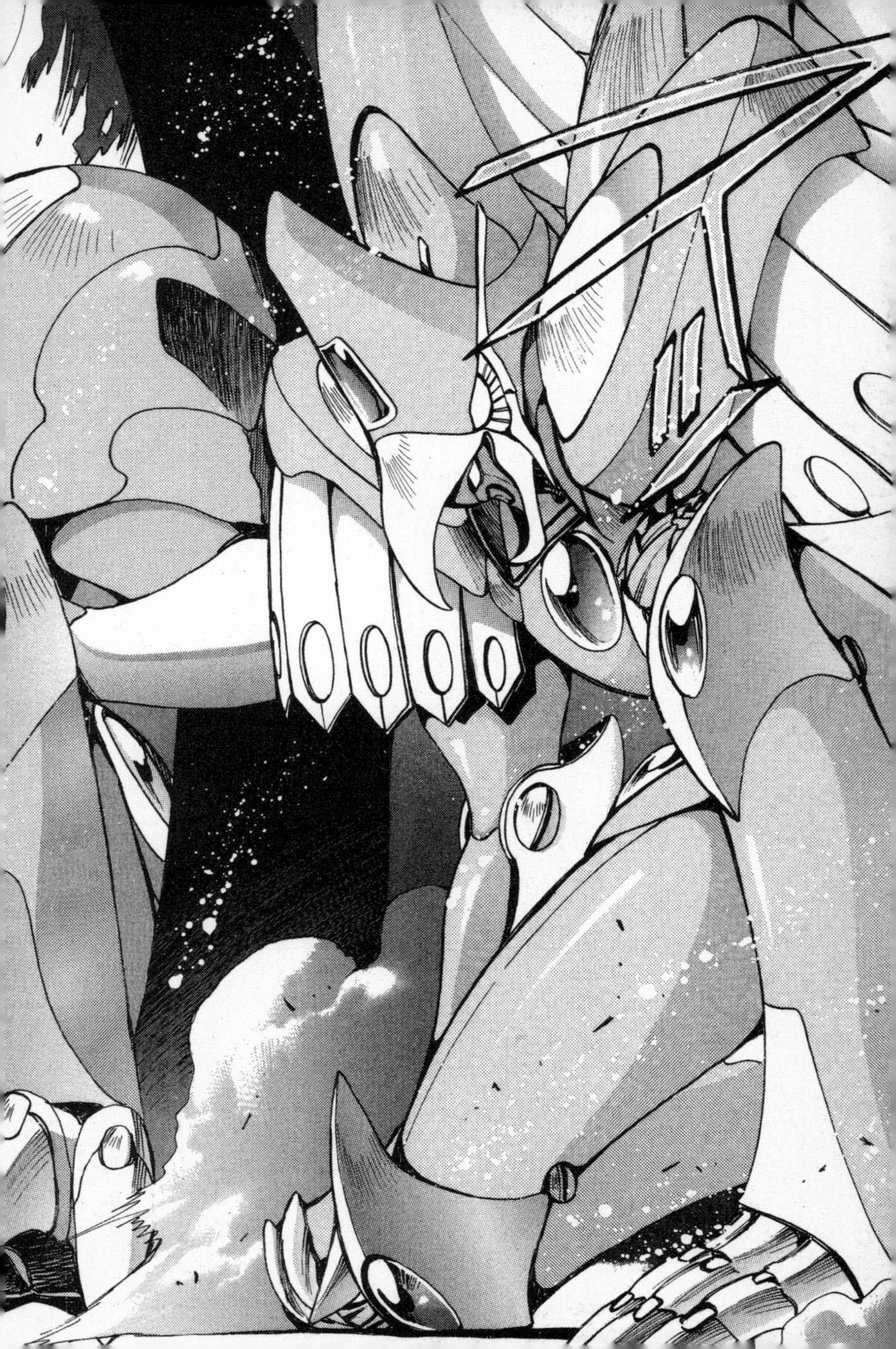

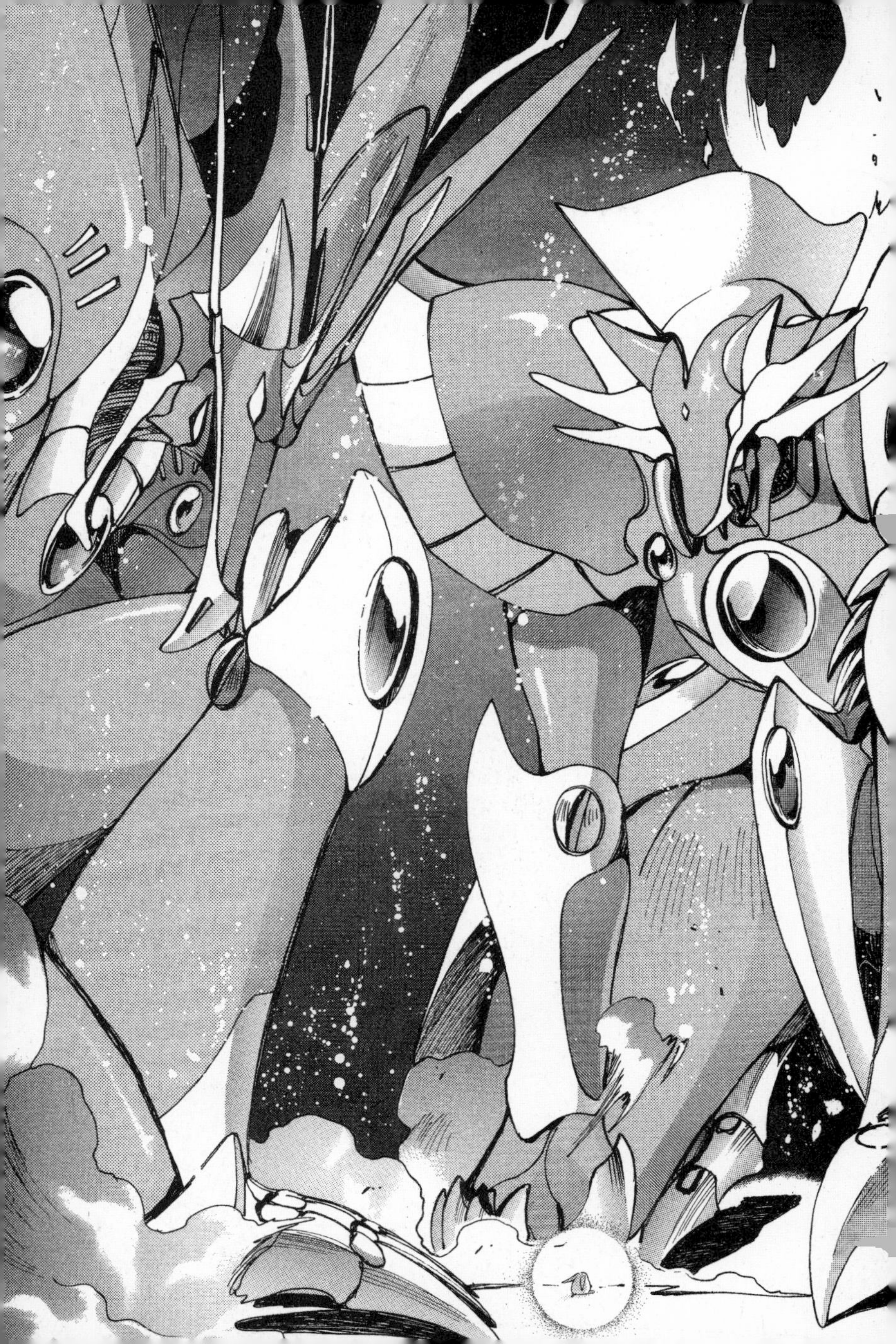

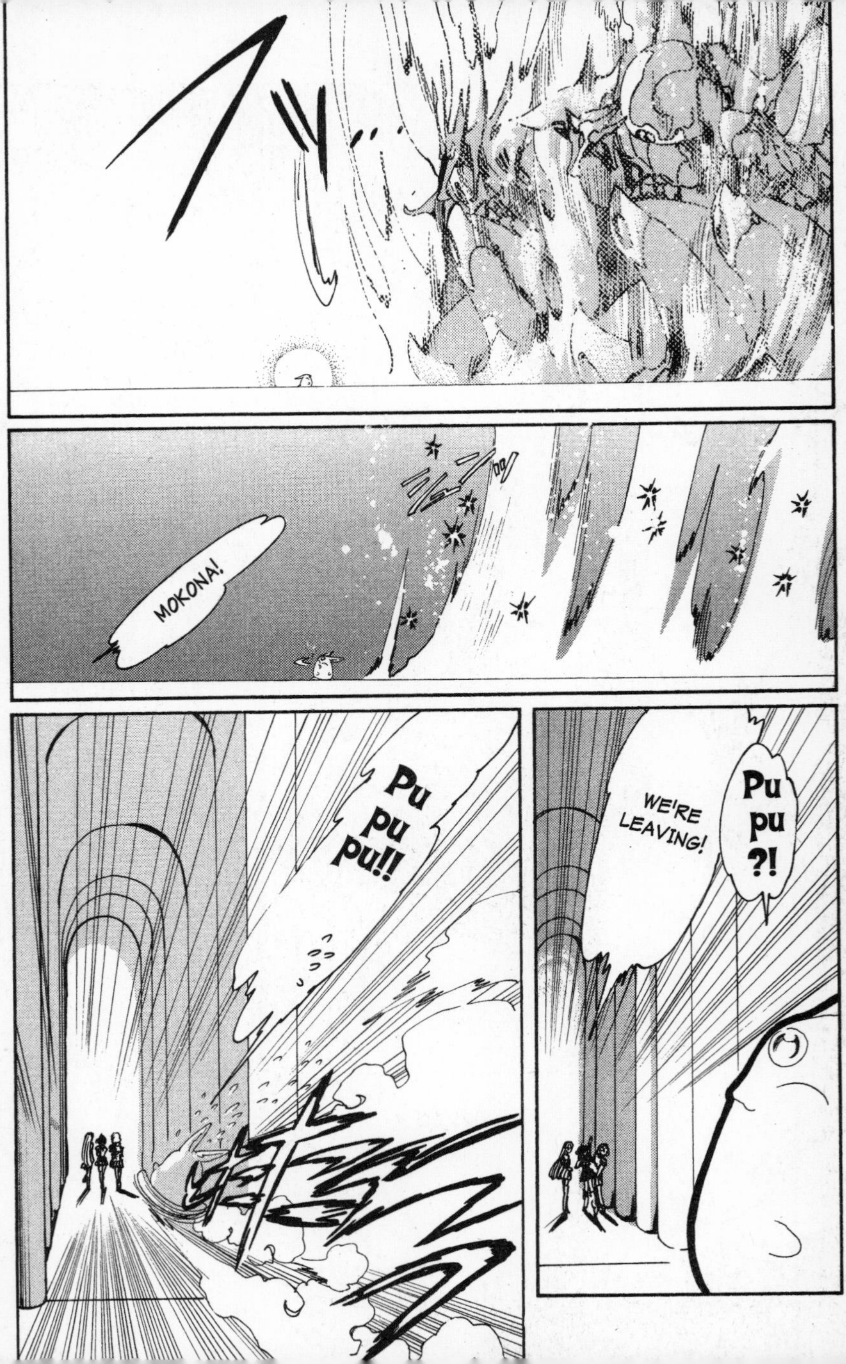
MOKONA!
Pu pu ?!
WE'RE LEAVING!
Pu pu pu!!

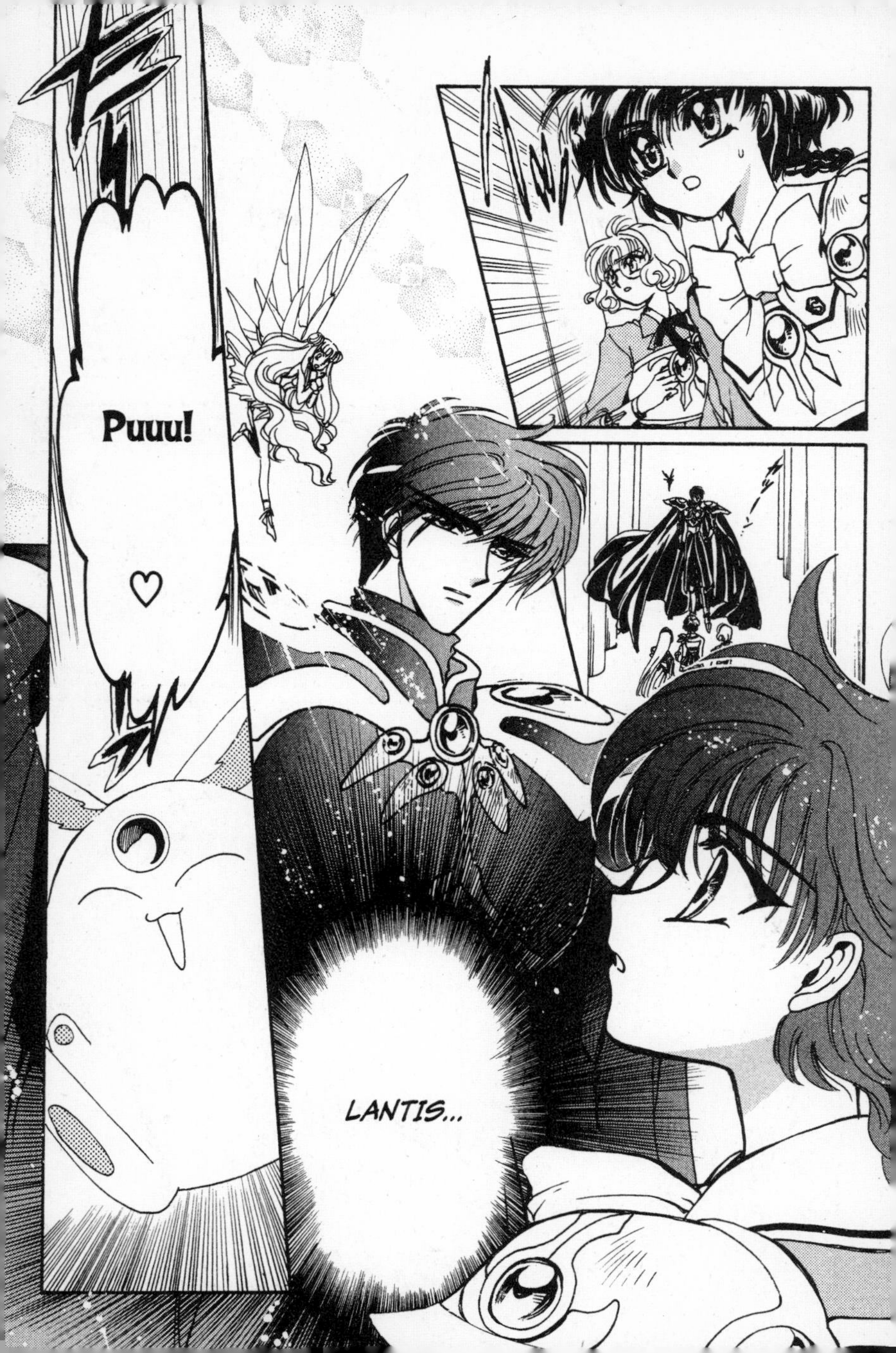

LANTIS...
Puuu! ♡

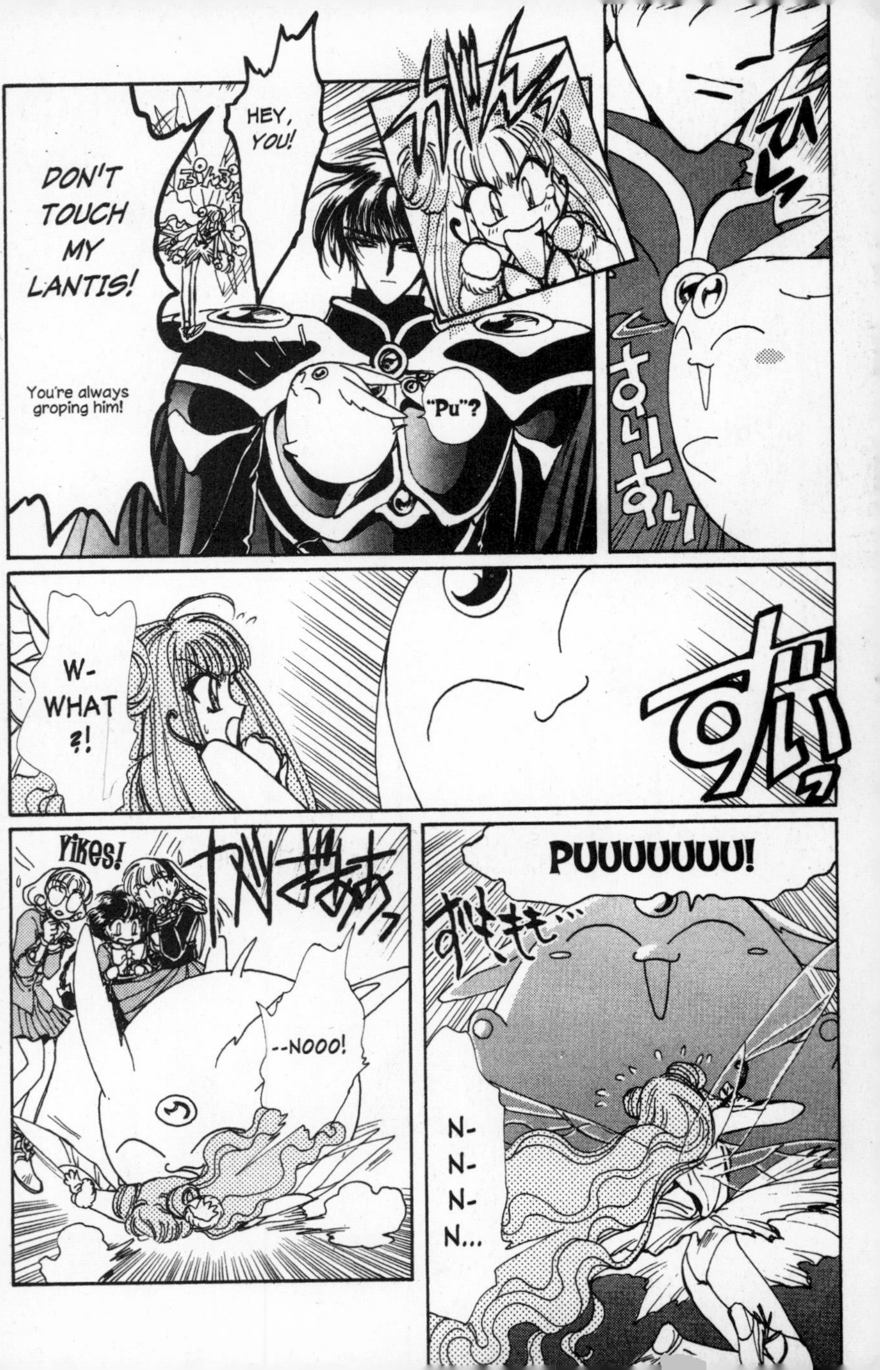

すりすり
HEY, YOU!
DON'T TOUCH MY LANTIS!
"Pu"?
You're always groping him!
W-WHAT?!
PUUUUUUU!
N-N-N-N...
Yikes!
--NOOO!

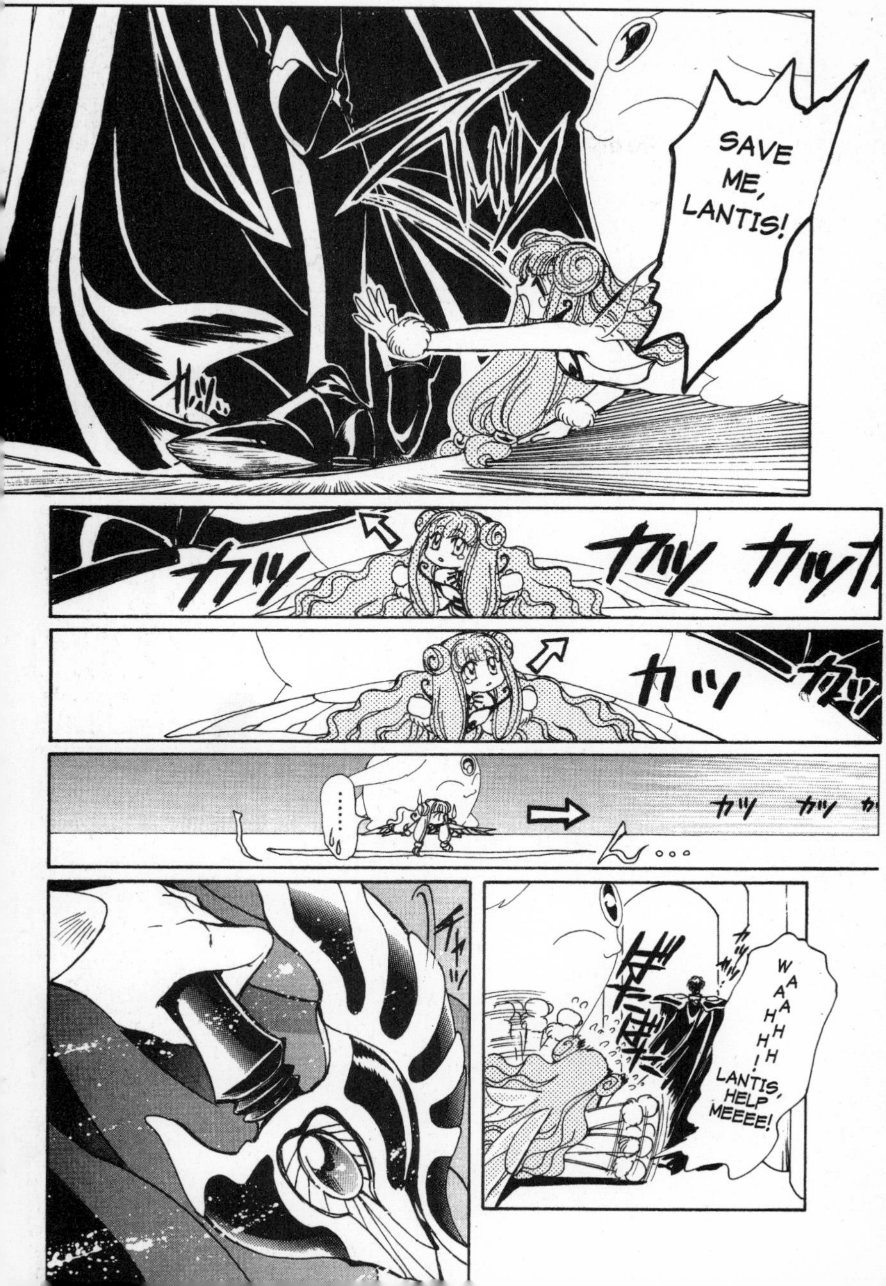
SAVE ME, LANTIS!
カツ
カツ
カツ
カツ
WAAAHHHHH! LANTIS, HELP MEEEE!

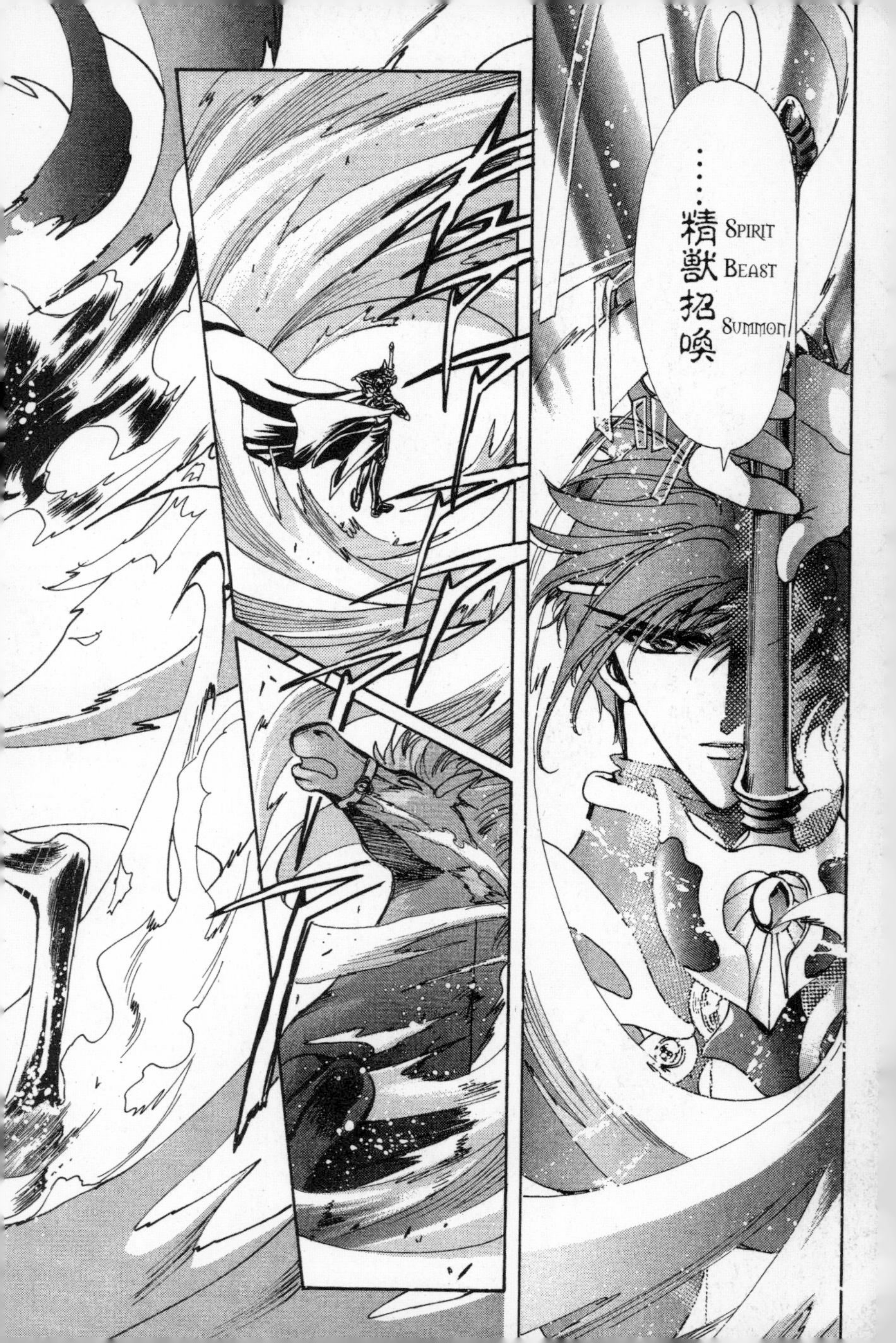
……精獸招喚 Spirit Beast Summon

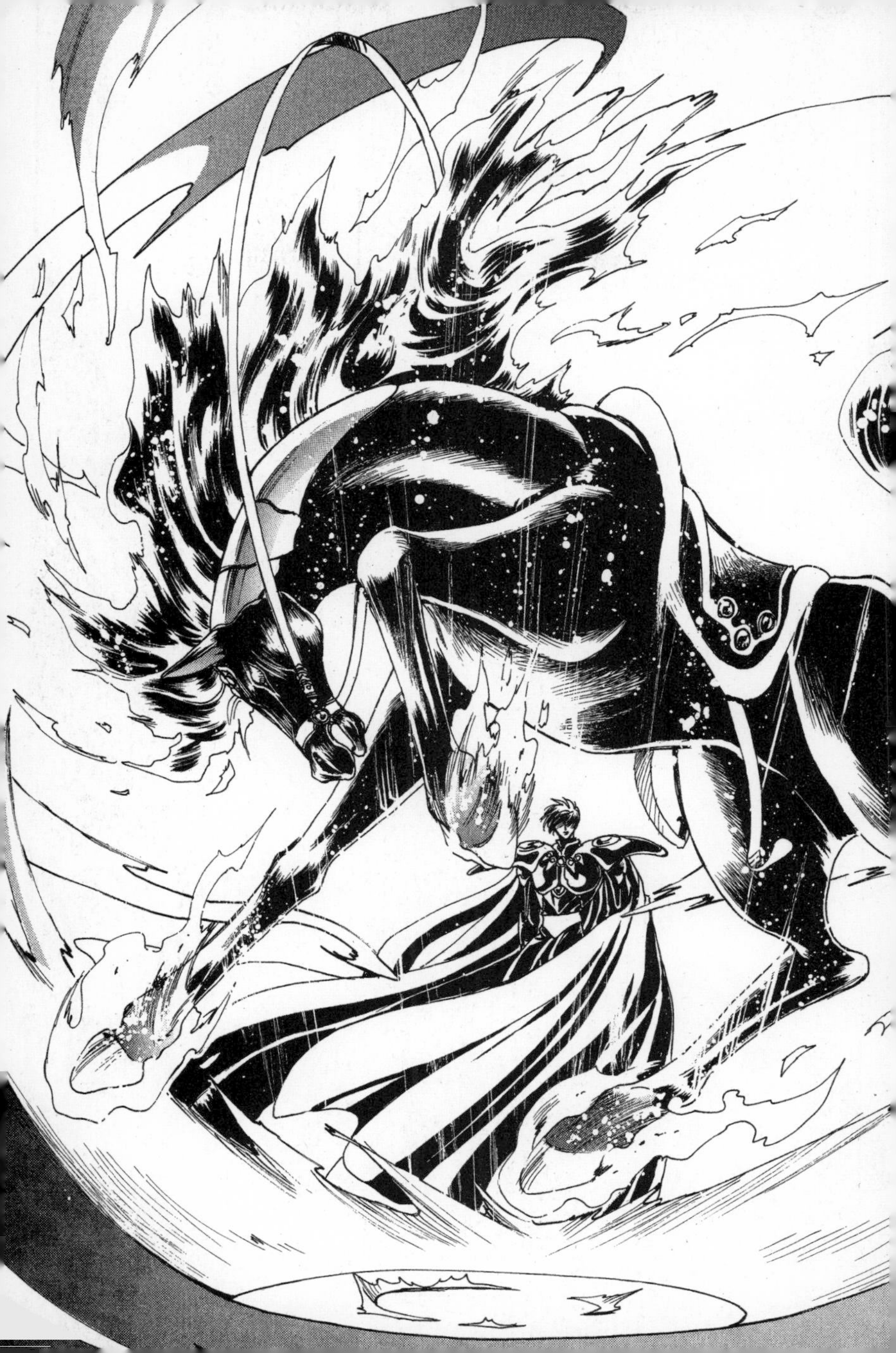

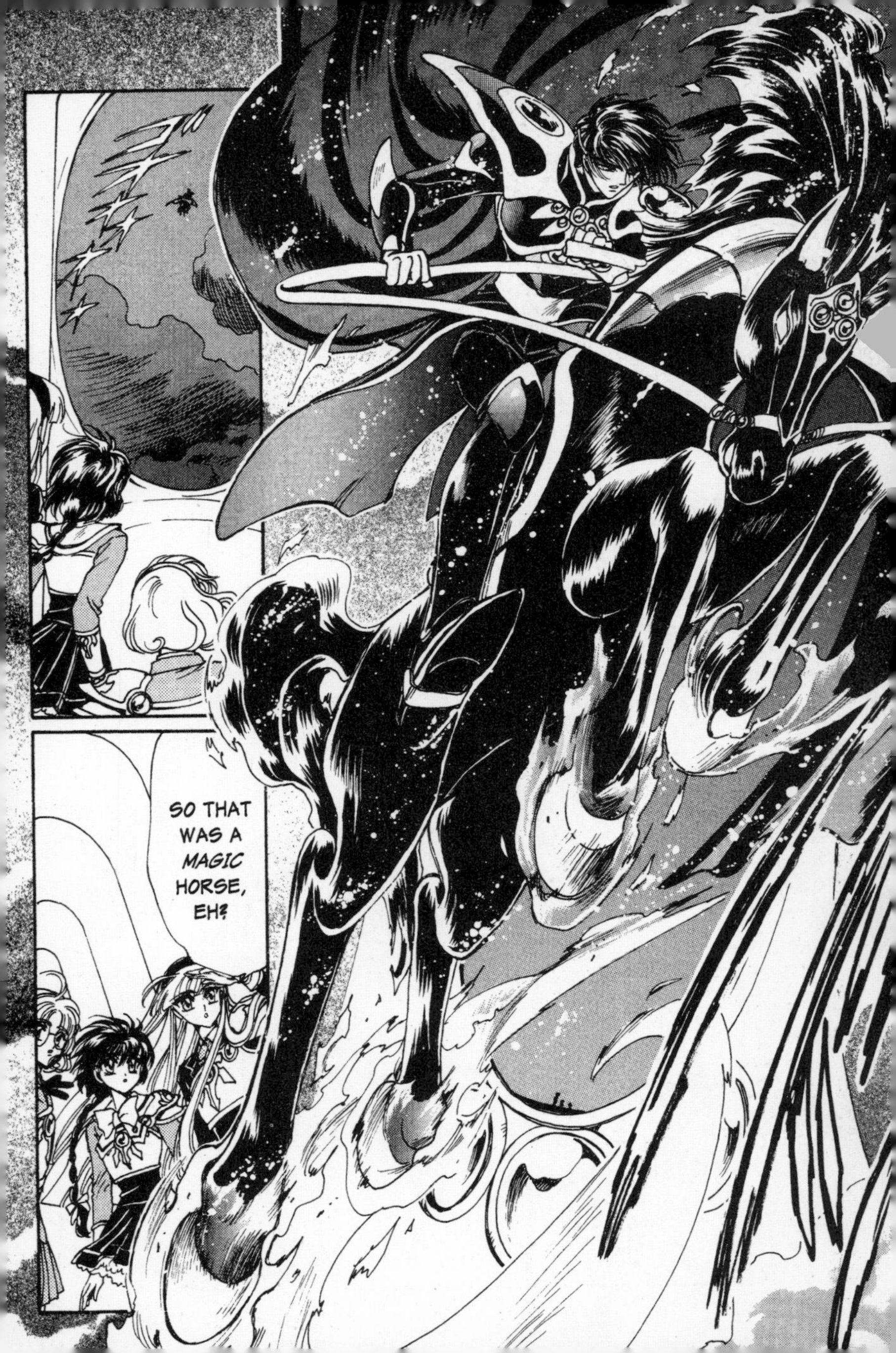
SO THAT WAS A MAGIC HORSE, EH?

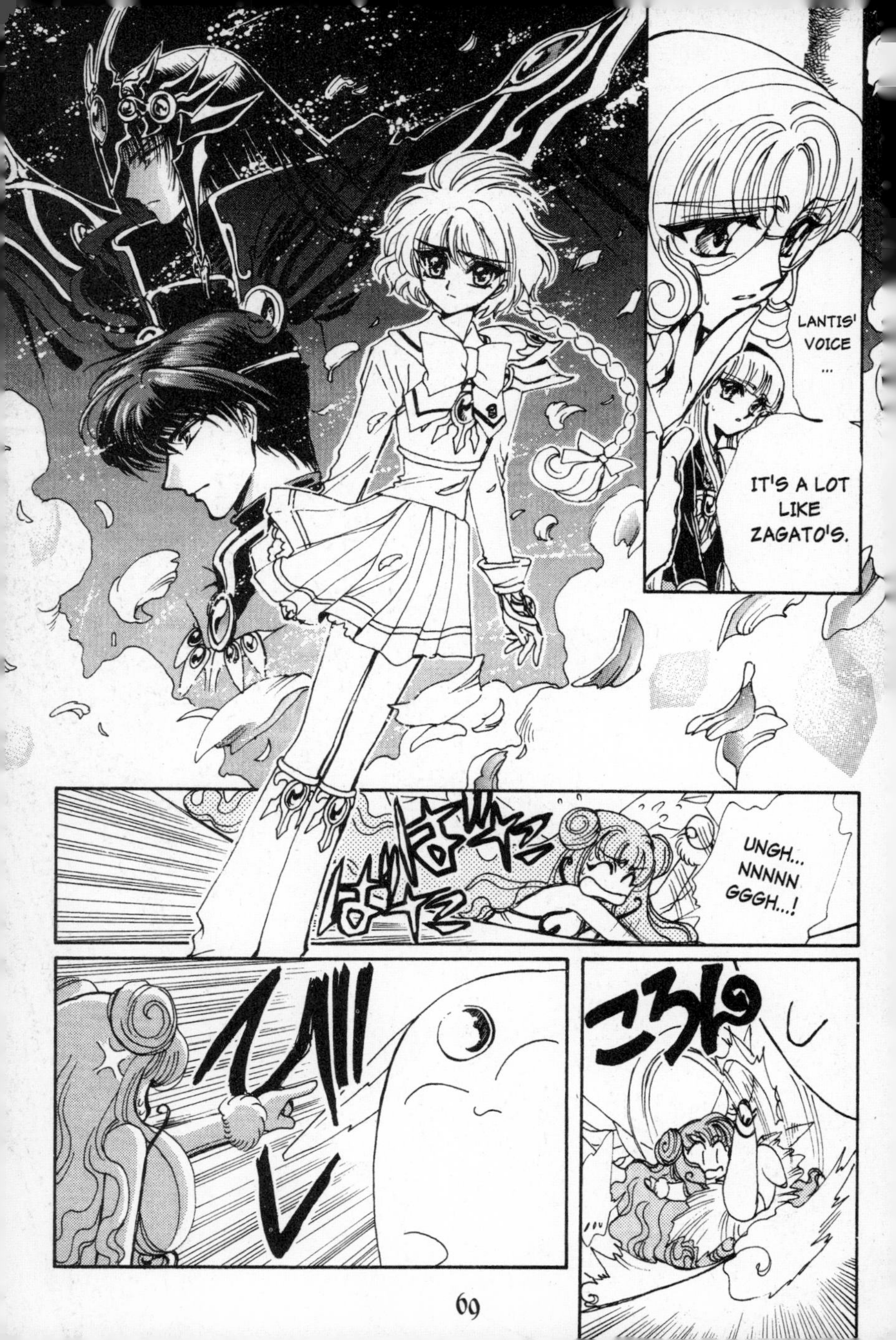
LANTIS' VOICE ...
IT'S A LOT LIKE ZAGATO'S.
UNGH... NNNNN GGGH...!

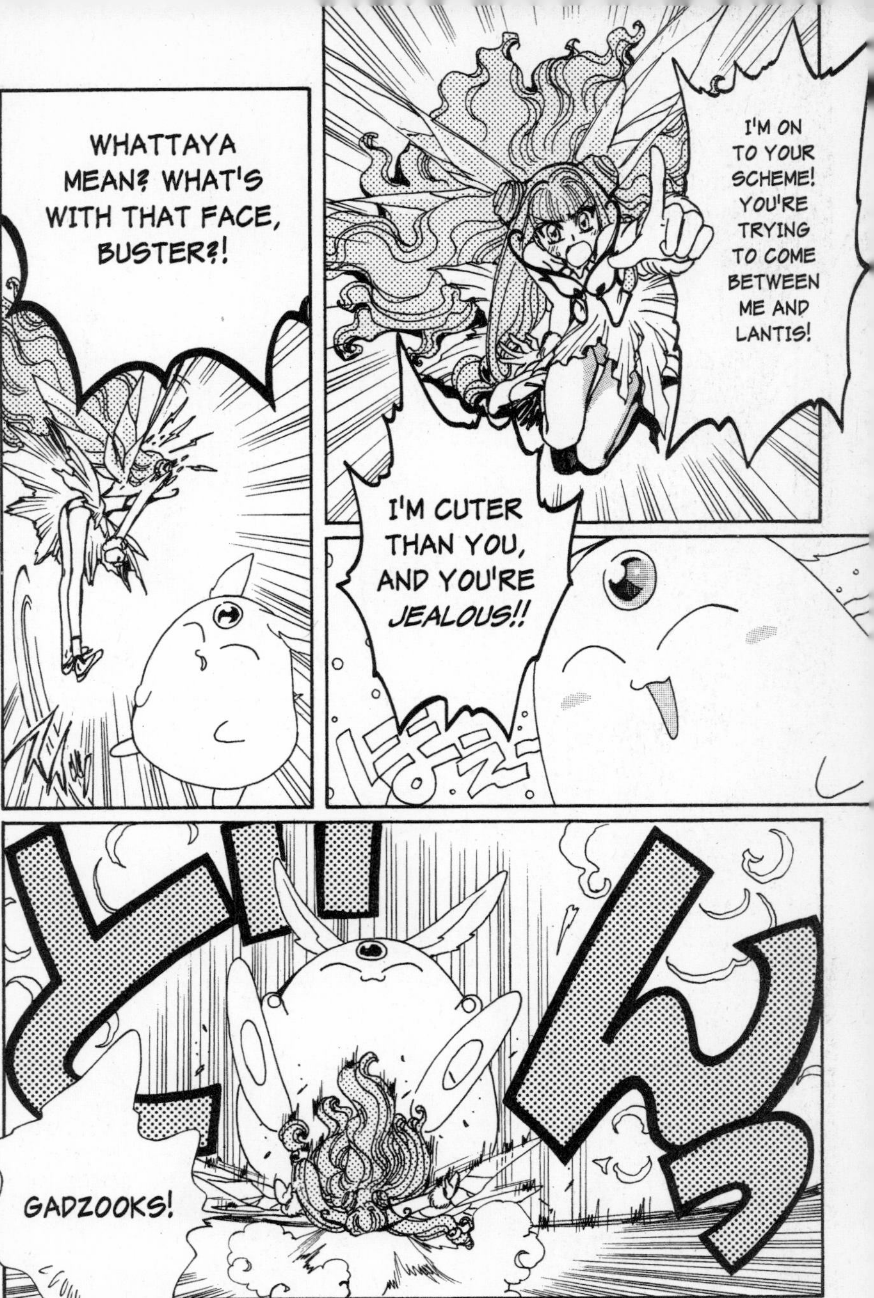
I'M ON TO YOUR SCHEME! YOU'RE TRYING TO COME BETWEEN ME AND LANTIS!
I'M CUTER THAN YOU, AND YOU'RE *JEALOUS*!!
WHATTAYA MEAN? WHAT'S WITH THAT FACE, BUSTER?!
GADZOOKS!

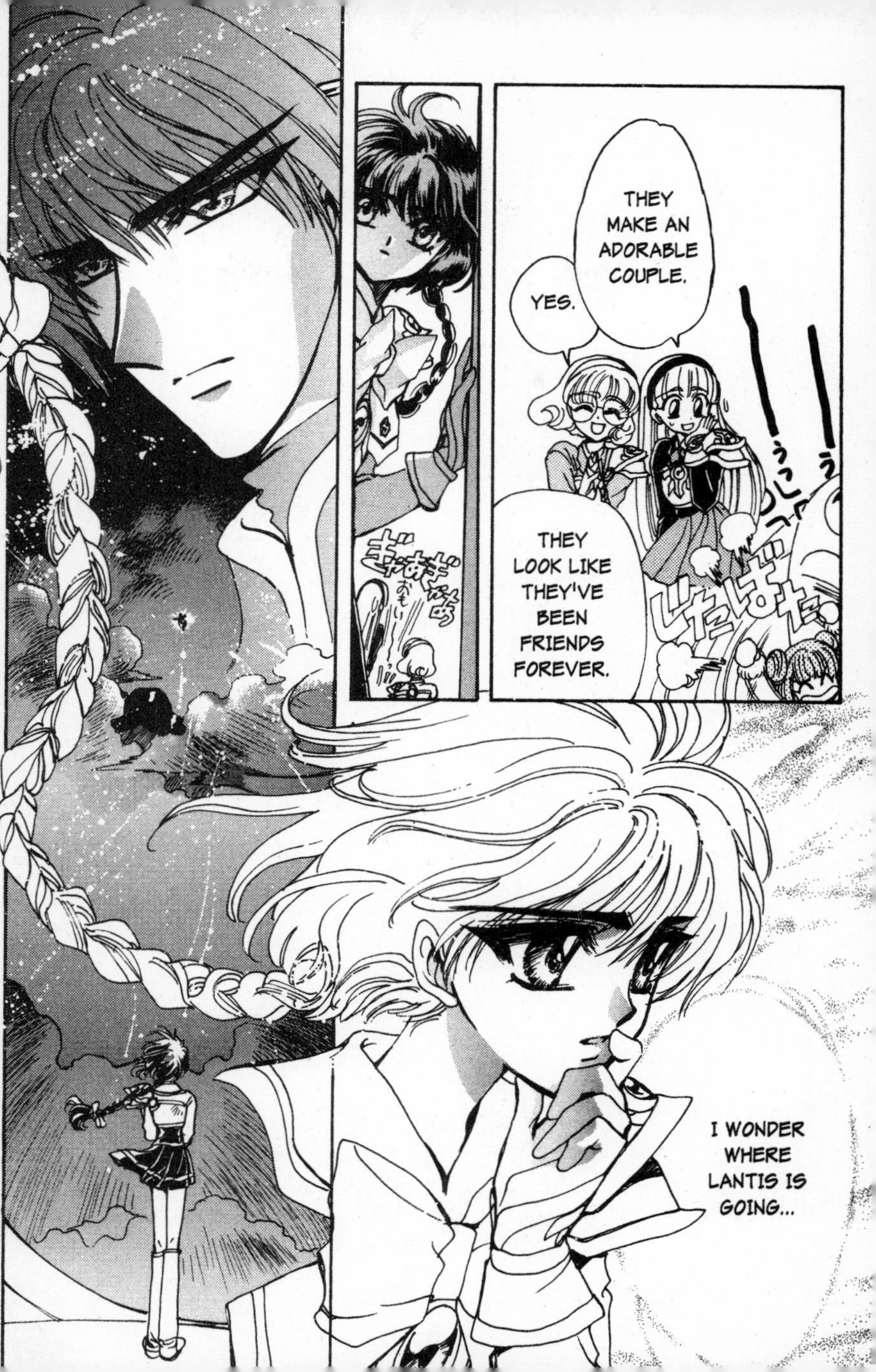
THEY MAKE AN ADORABLE COUPLE.
YES.
THEY LOOK LIKE THEY'VE BEEN FRIENDS FOREVER.
じたばた
I WONDER WHERE LANTIS IS GOING...

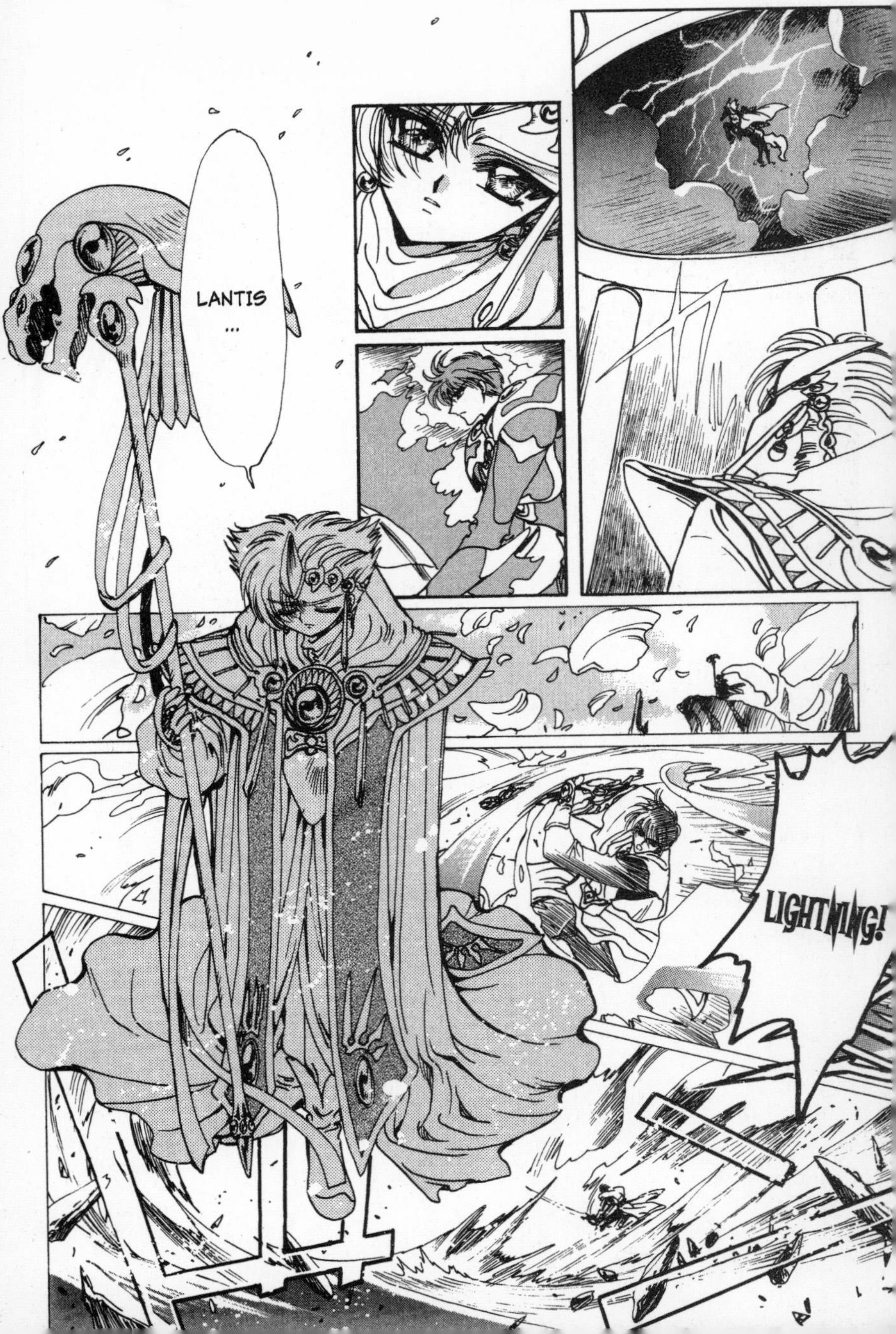
LANTIS
...
LIGHTNING!

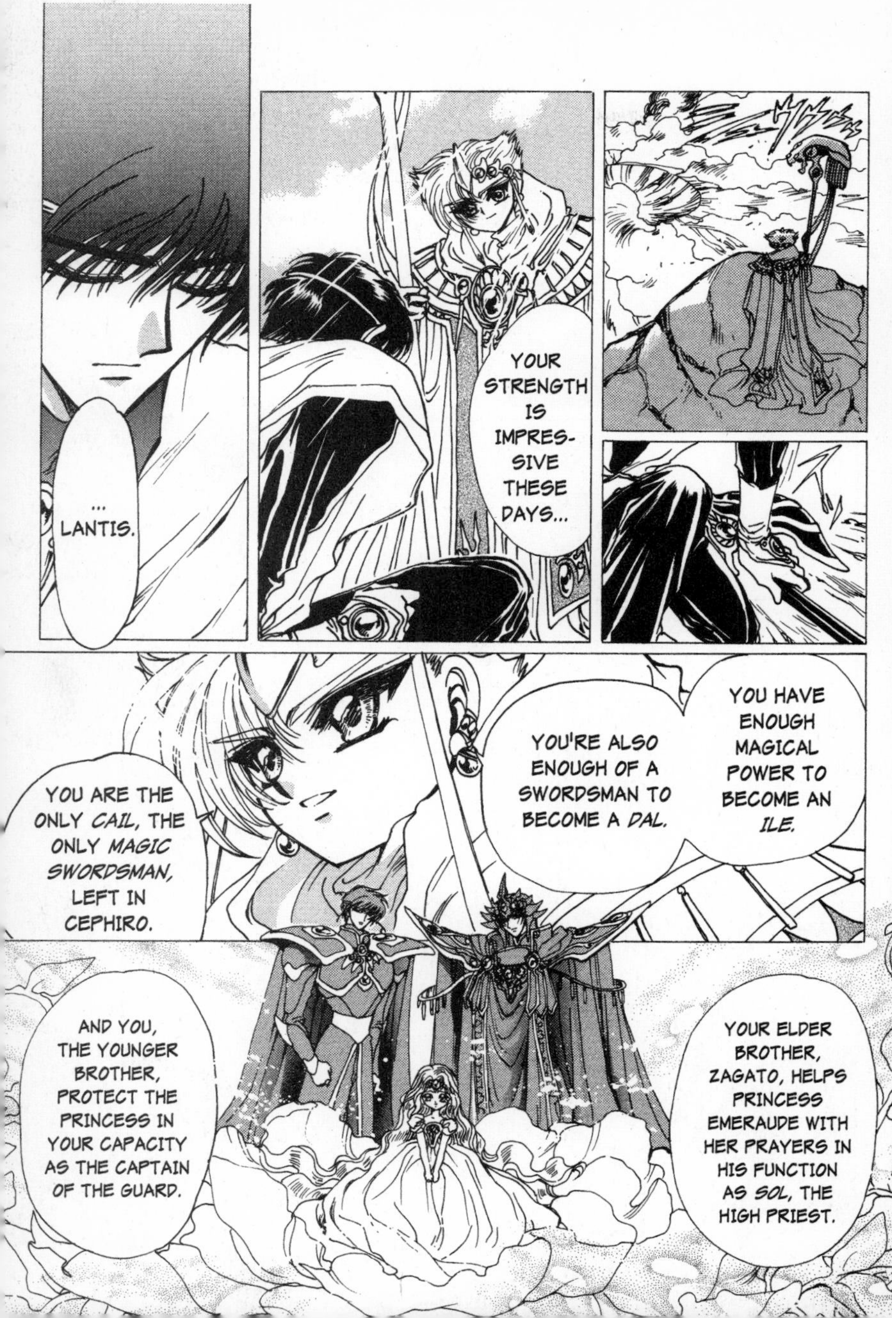
YOUR STRENGTH IS IMPRES- SIVE THESE DAYS...
... LANTIS.
YOU HAVE ENOUGH MAGICAL POWER TO BECOME AN *ILE.*
YOU'RE ALSO ENOUGH OF A SWORDSMAN TO BECOME A *DAL.*
YOU ARE THE ONLY *CAIL*, THE ONLY *MAGIC SWORDSMAN,* LEFT IN CEPHIRO.
YOUR ELDER BROTHER, ZAGATO, HELPS PRINCESS EMERAUDE WITH HER PRAYERS IN HIS FUNCTION AS *SOL*, THE HIGH PRIEST.
AND YOU, THE YOUNGER BROTHER, PROTECT THE PRINCESS IN YOUR CAPACITY AS THE CAPTAIN OF THE GUARD.

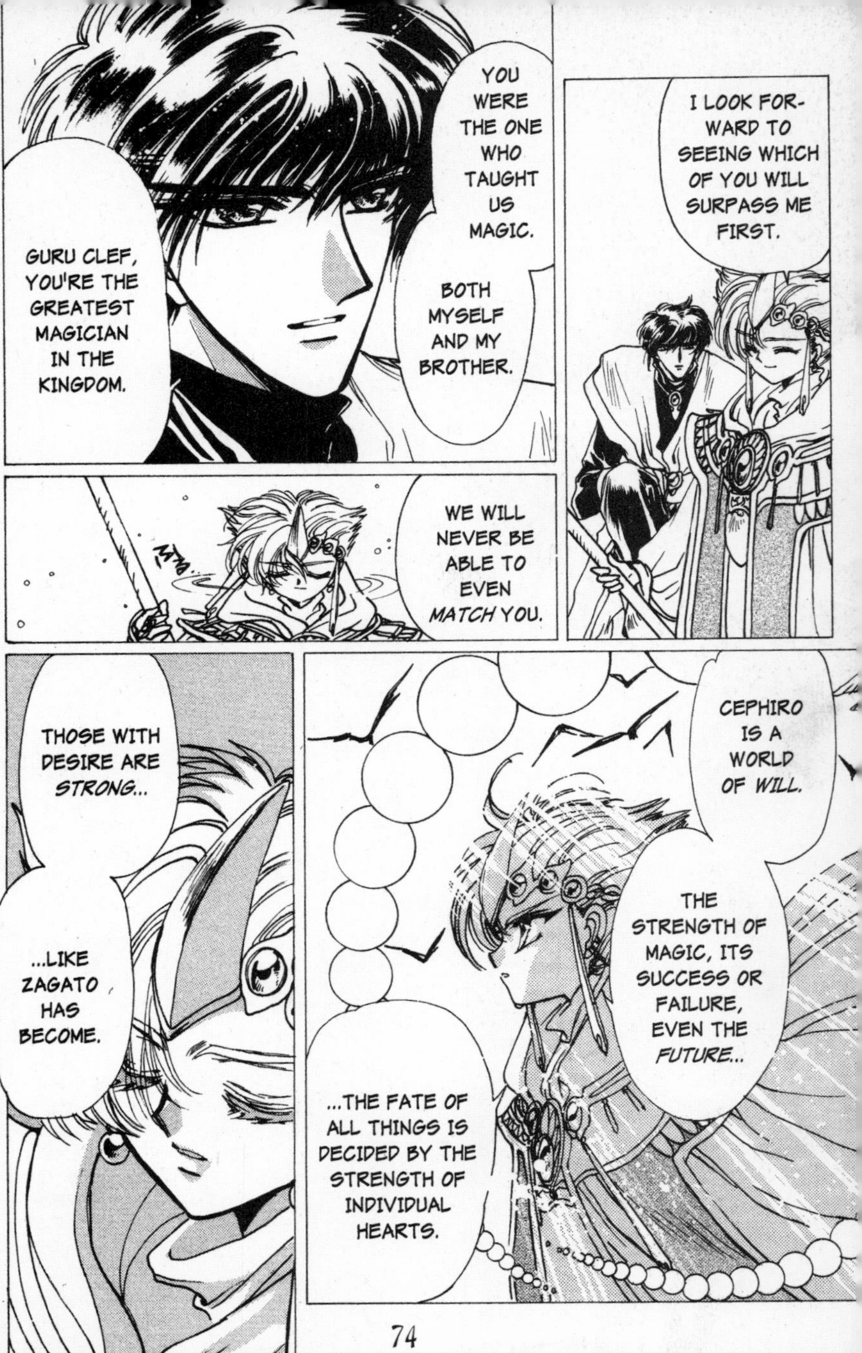
I LOOK FORWARD TO SEEING WHICH OF YOU WILL SURPASS ME FIRST.
YOU WERE THE ONE WHO TAUGHT US MAGIC.
BOTH MYSELF AND MY BROTHER.
GURU CLEF, YOU'RE THE GREATEST MAGICIAN IN THE KINGDOM.
WE WILL NEVER BE ABLE TO EVEN *MATCH* YOU.
CEPHIRO IS A WORLD OF *WILL*.
THE STRENGTH OF MAGIC, ITS SUCCESS OR FAILURE, EVEN THE *FUTURE*...
...THE FATE OF ALL THINGS IS DECIDED BY THE STRENGTH OF INDIVIDUAL HEARTS.
THOSE WITH DESIRE ARE *STRONG*...
...LIKE ZAGATO HAS BECOME.

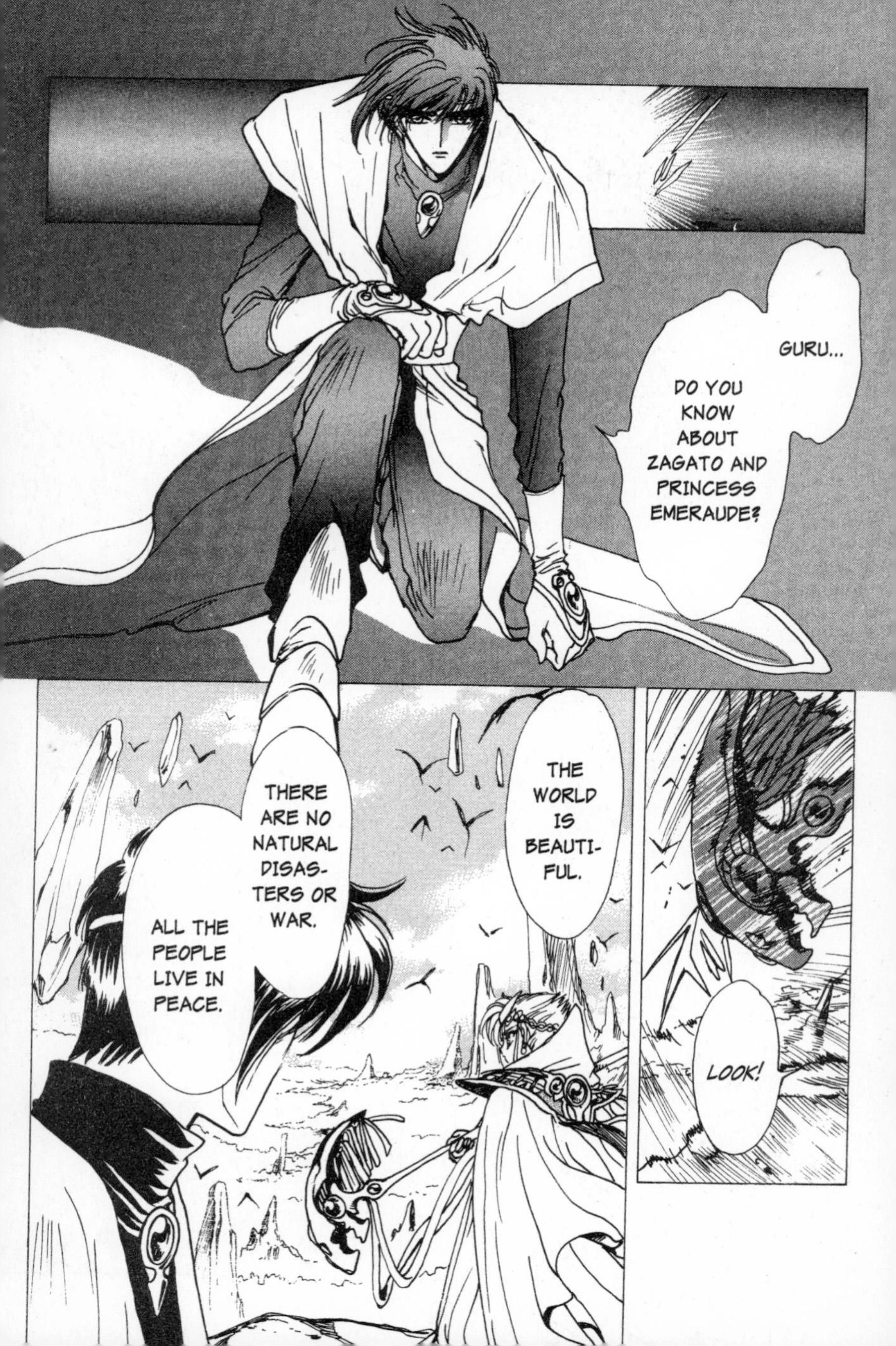
GURU...
DO YOU KNOW ABOUT ZAGATO AND PRINCESS EMERAUDE?
LOOK!
THE WORLD IS BEAUTI-FUL.
THERE ARE NO NATURAL DISAS-TERS OR WAR.
ALL THE PEOPLE LIVE IN PEACE.

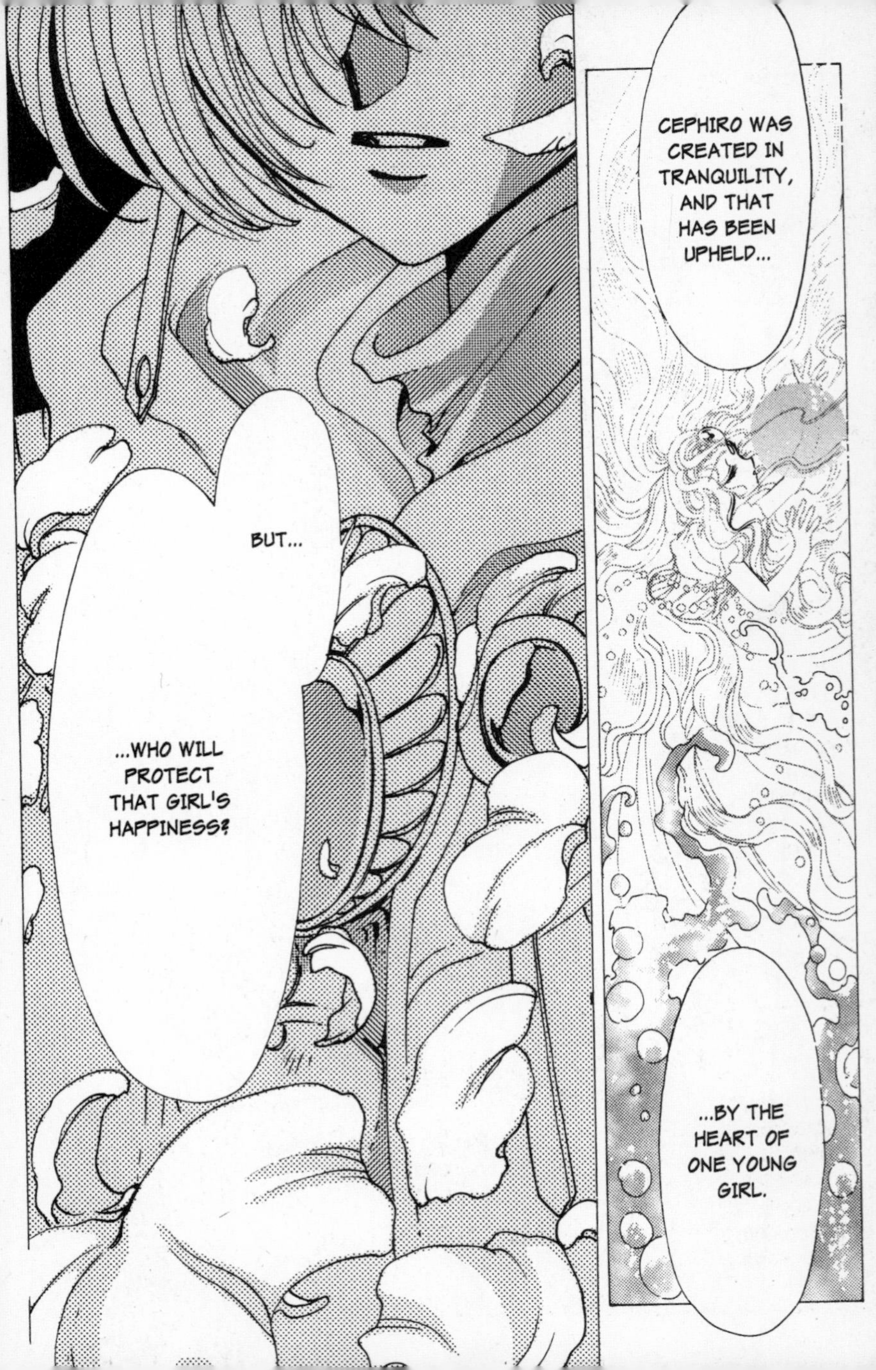
CEPHIRO WAS CREATED IN TRANQUILITY, AND THAT HAS BEEN UPHELD...
...BY THE HEART OF ONE YOUNG GIRL.
BUT...
...WHO WILL PROTECT THAT GIRL'S HAPPINESS?

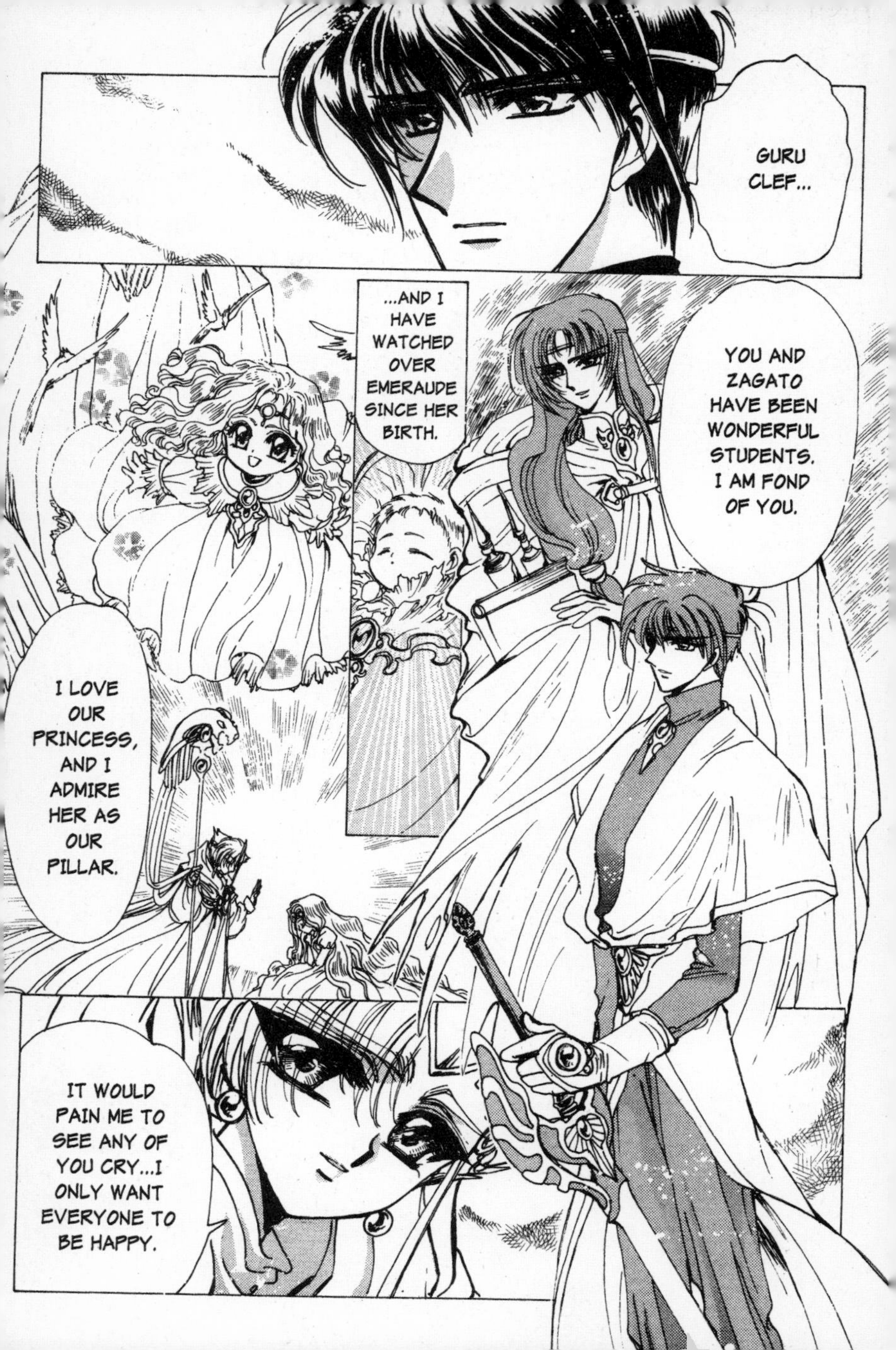
GURU CLEF...
YOU AND ZAGATO HAVE BEEN WONDERFUL STUDENTS. I AM FOND OF YOU.
...AND I HAVE WATCHED OVER EMERAUDE SINCE HER BIRTH.
I LOVE OUR PRINCESS, AND I ADMIRE HER AS OUR PILLAR.
IT WOULD PAIN ME TO SEE ANY OF YOU CRY...I ONLY WANT EVERYONE TO BE HAPPY.

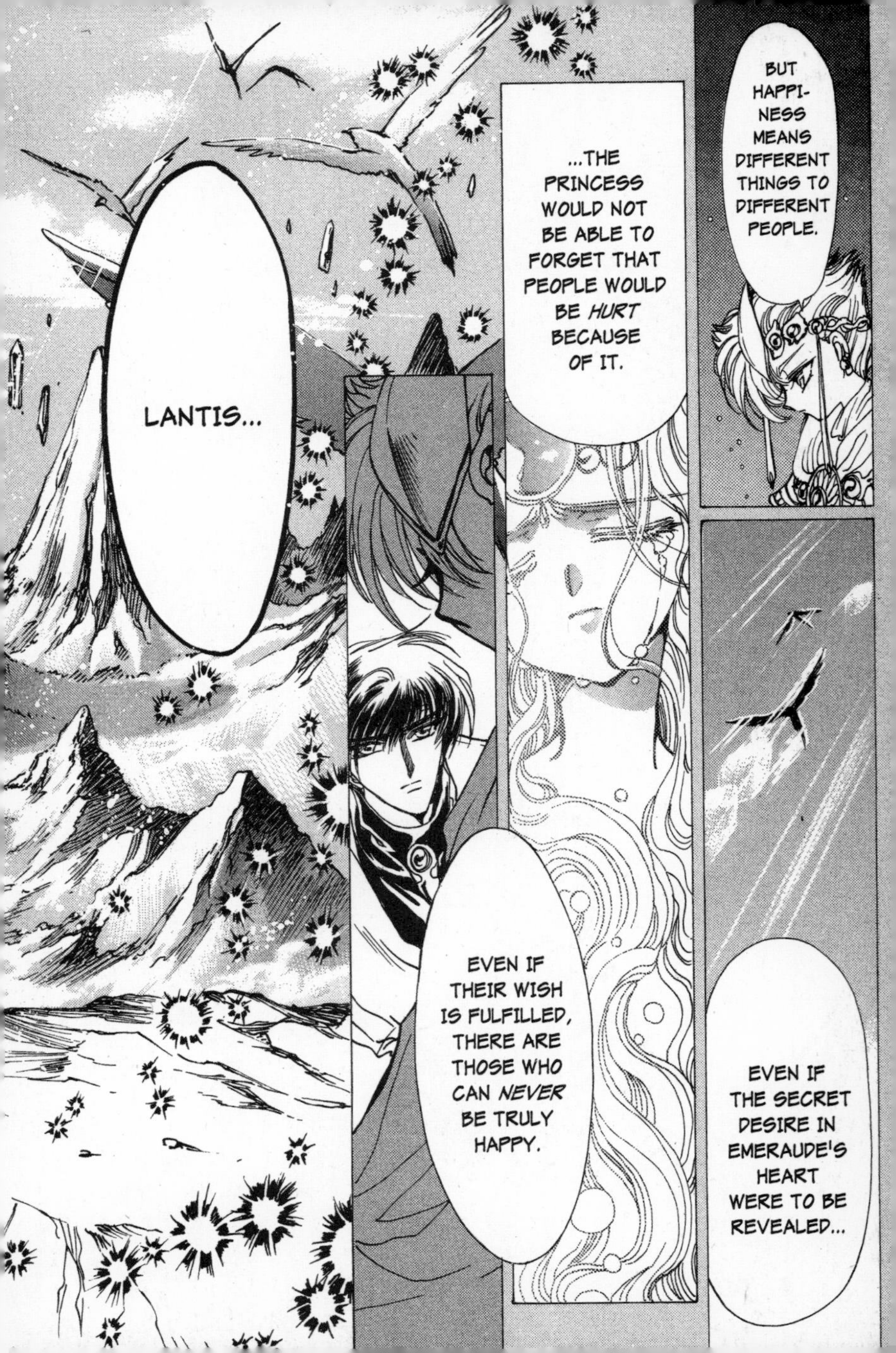
BUT HAPPINESS MEANS DIFFERENT THINGS TO DIFFERENT PEOPLE.
EVEN IF THE SECRET DESIRE IN EMERAUDE'S HEART WERE TO BE REVEALED...
...THE PRINCESS WOULD NOT BE ABLE TO FORGET THAT PEOPLE WOULD BE *HURT* BECAUSE OF IT.
EVEN IF THEIR WISH IS FULFILLED, THERE ARE THOSE WHO CAN *NEVER* BE TRULY HAPPY.
LANTIS...

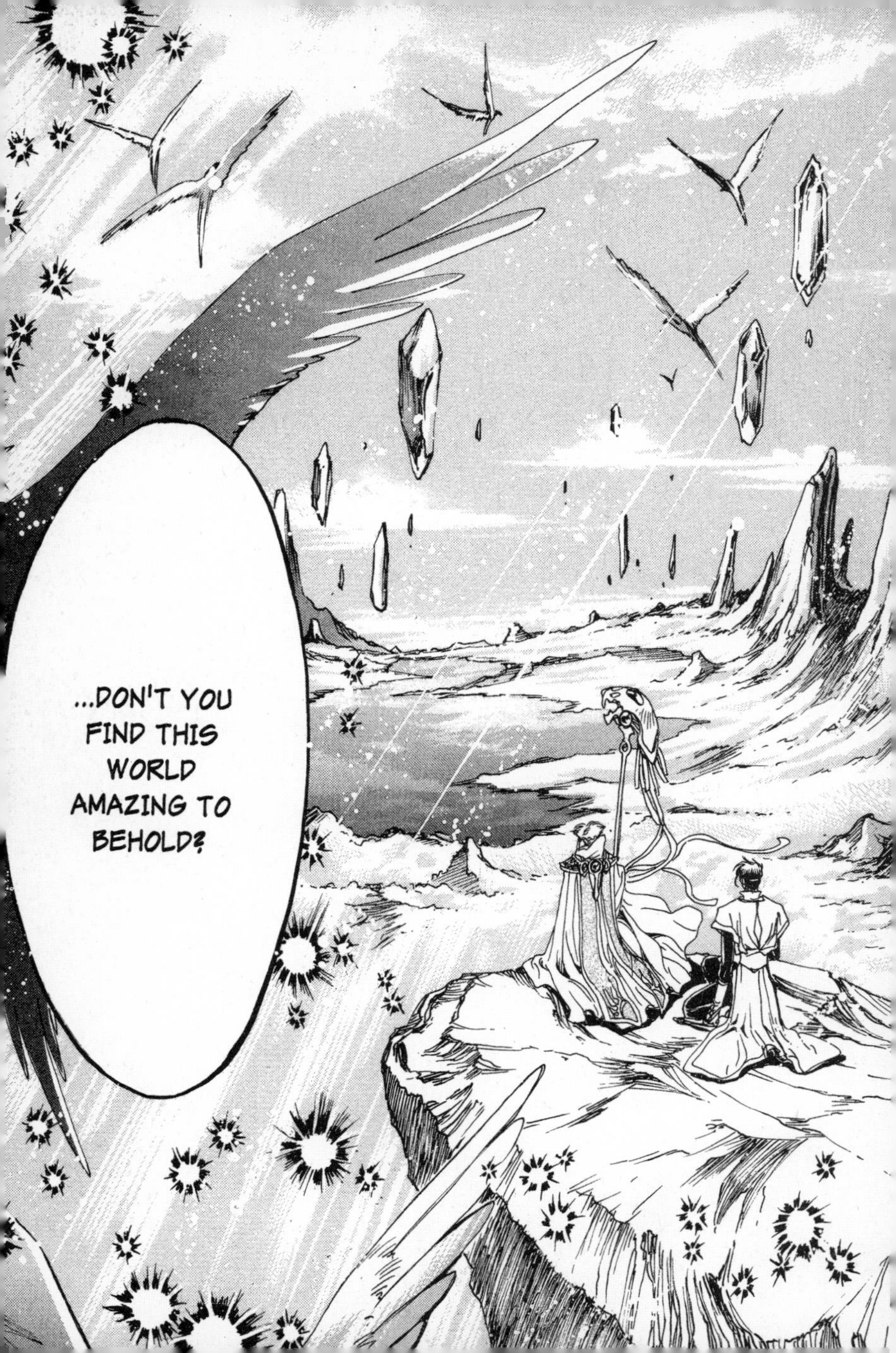
...DON'T YOU FIND THIS WORLD AMAZING TO BEHOLD?

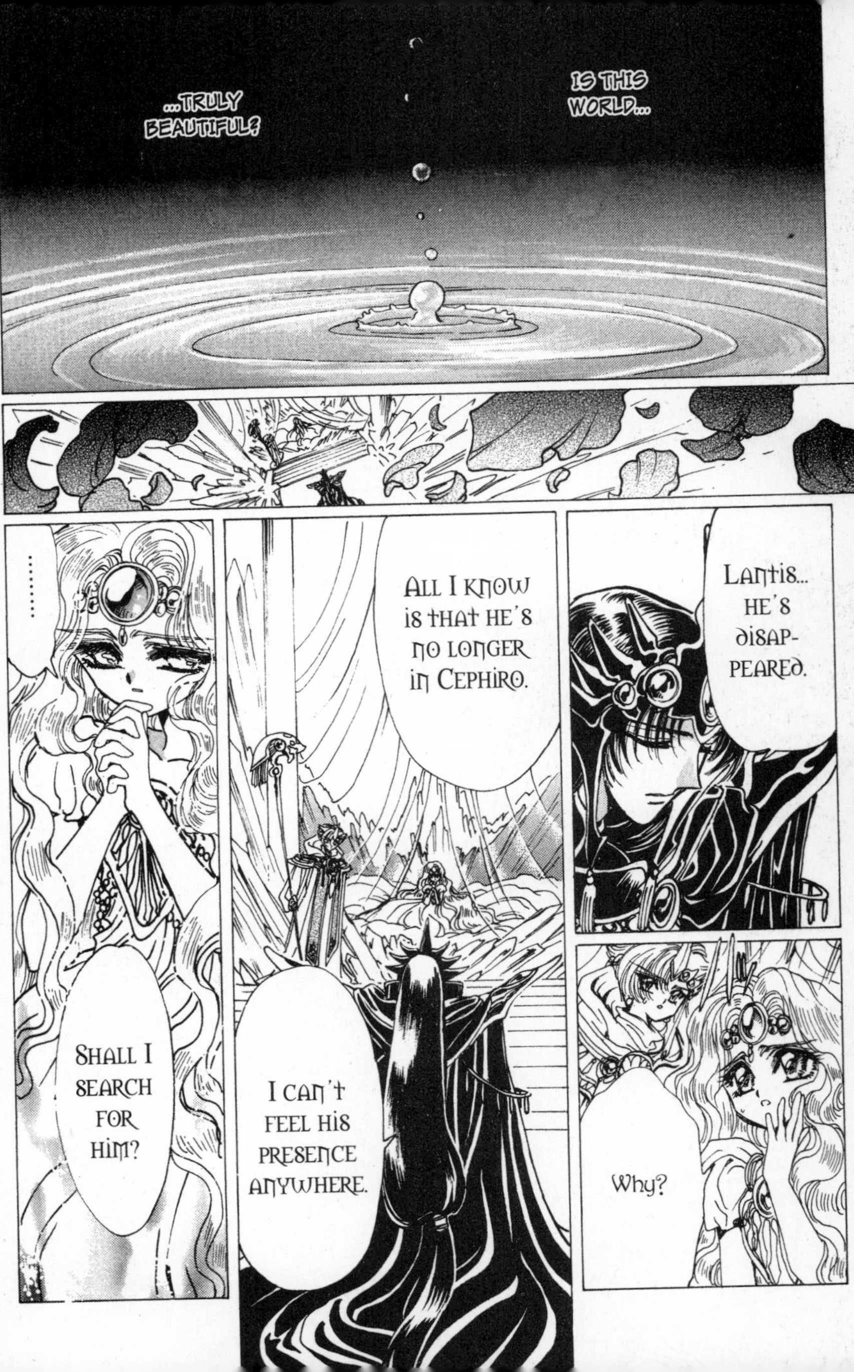
IS THIS WORLD...
...TRULY BEAUTIFUL?
LANTIS... HE'S DISAPPEARED.
WHY?
ALL I KNOW IS THAT HE'S NO LONGER IN CEPHIRO.
I CAN'T FEEL HIS PRESENCE ANYWHERE.
......
SHALL I SEARCH FOR HIM?

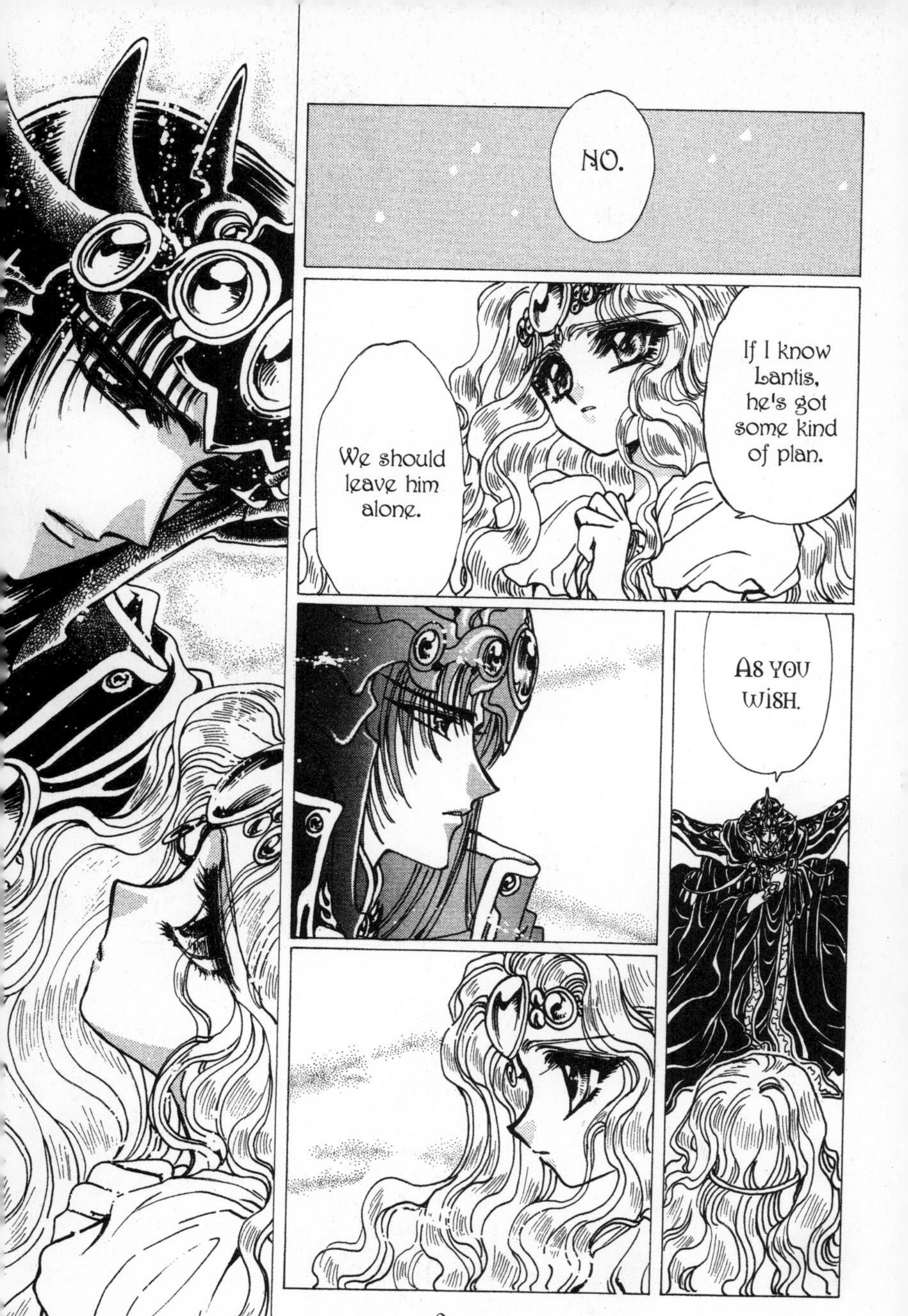
NO.
If I know Lantis, he's got some kind of plan.
We should leave him alone.
As you wish.

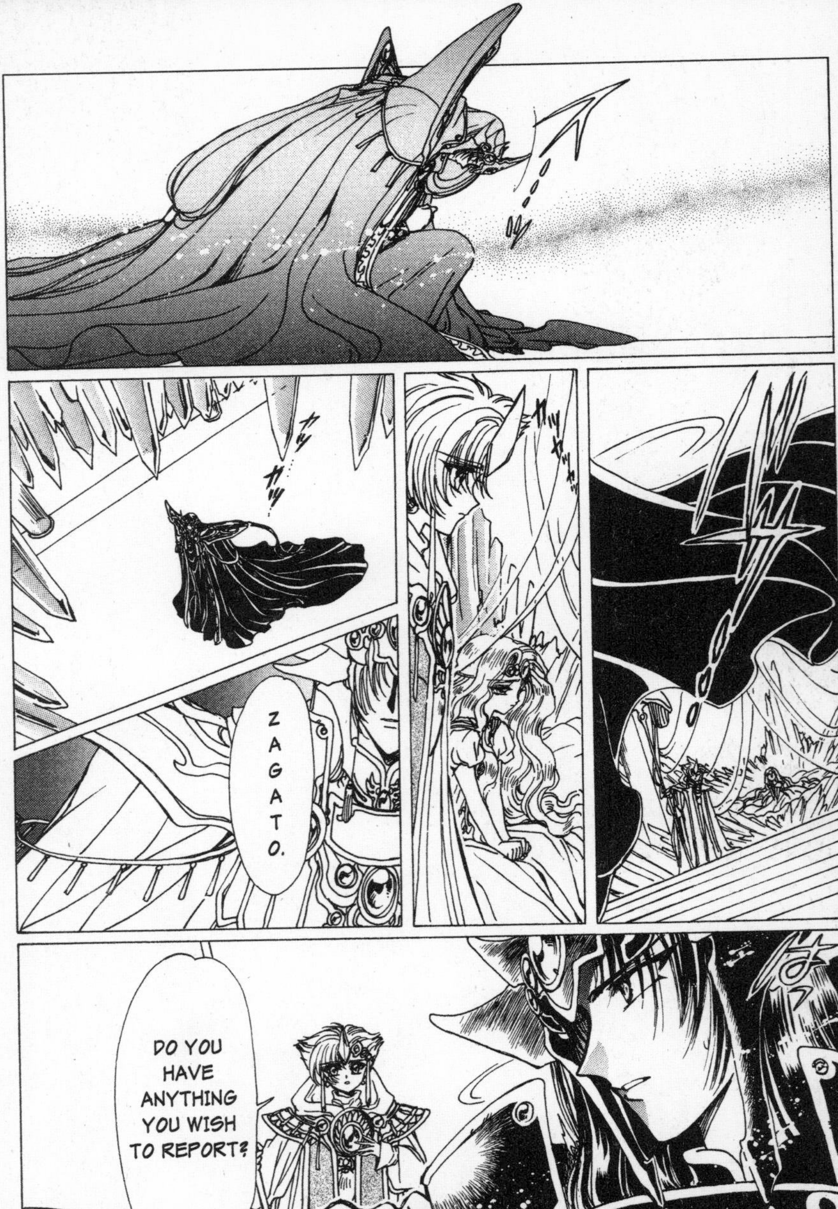
ZAGATO.
DO YOU HAVE ANYTHING YOU WISH TO REPORT?

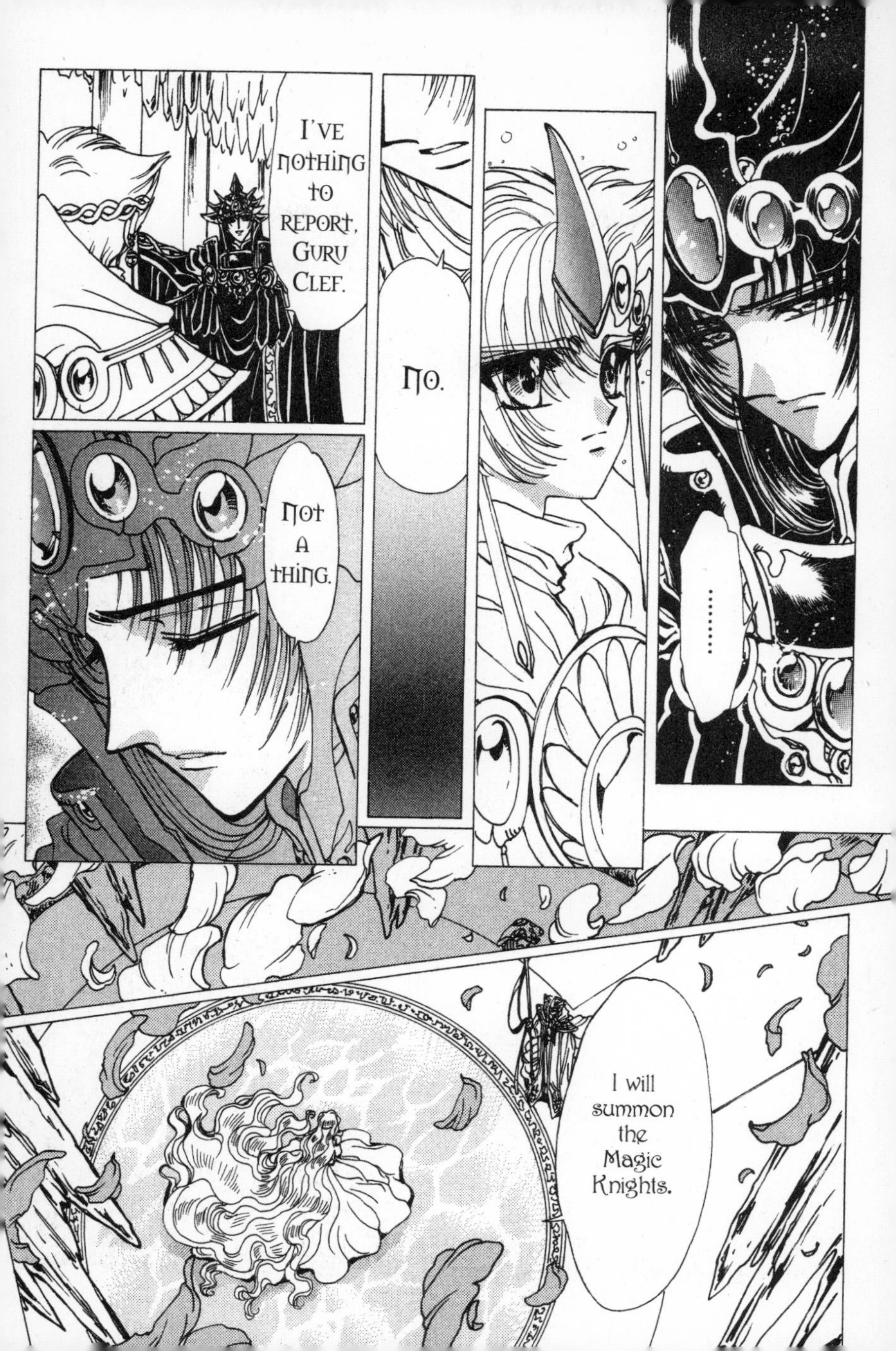

......
No.
I've nothing to report, Guru Clef.
Not a thing.
I will summon the Magic Knights.

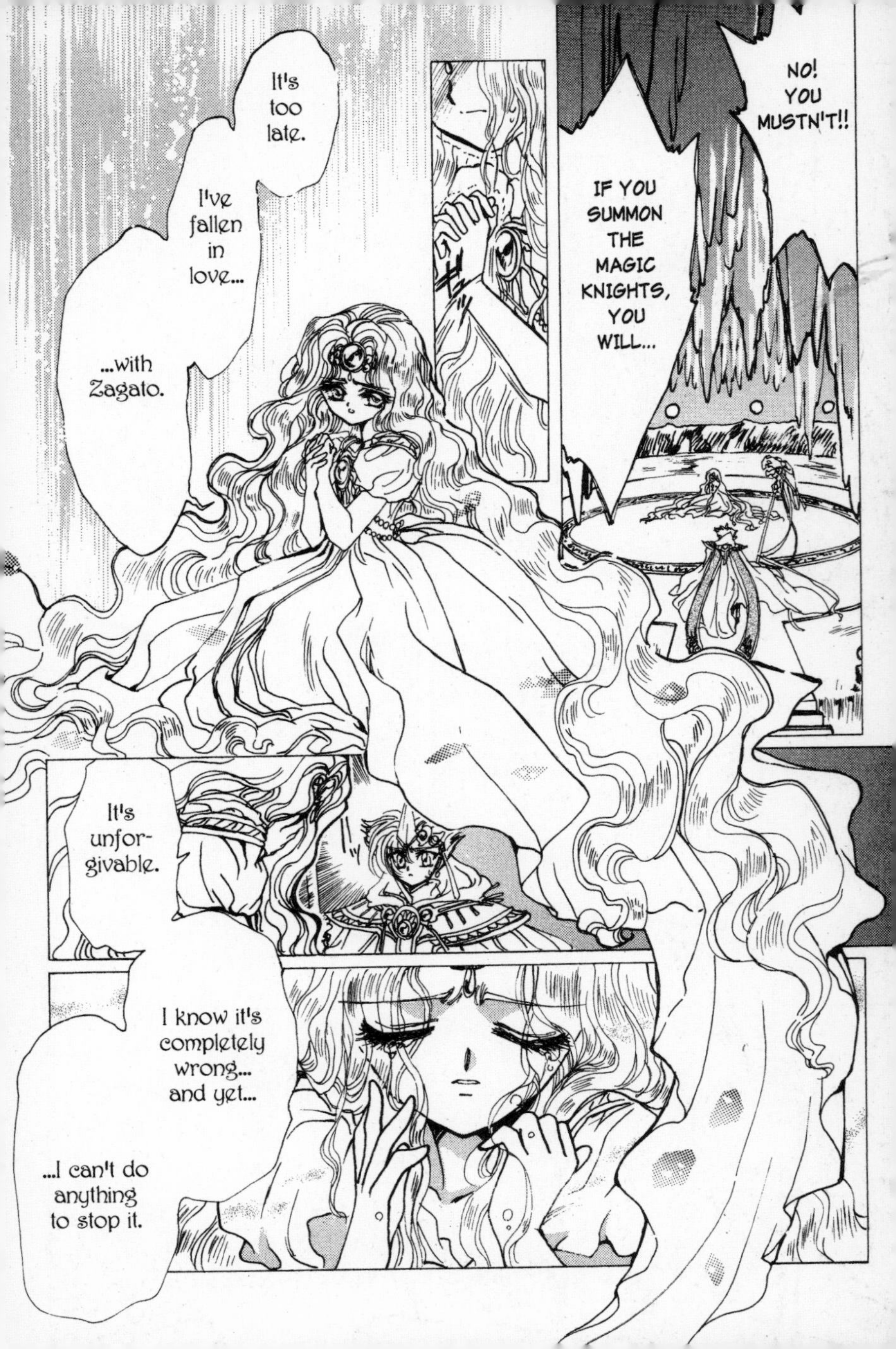
NO! YOU MUSTN'T!!
IF YOU SUMMON THE MAGIC KNIGHTS, YOU WILL...
It's too late.
I've fallen in love...
...with Zagato.
It's unforgivable.
I know it's completely wrong... and yet...
...I can't do anything to stop it.

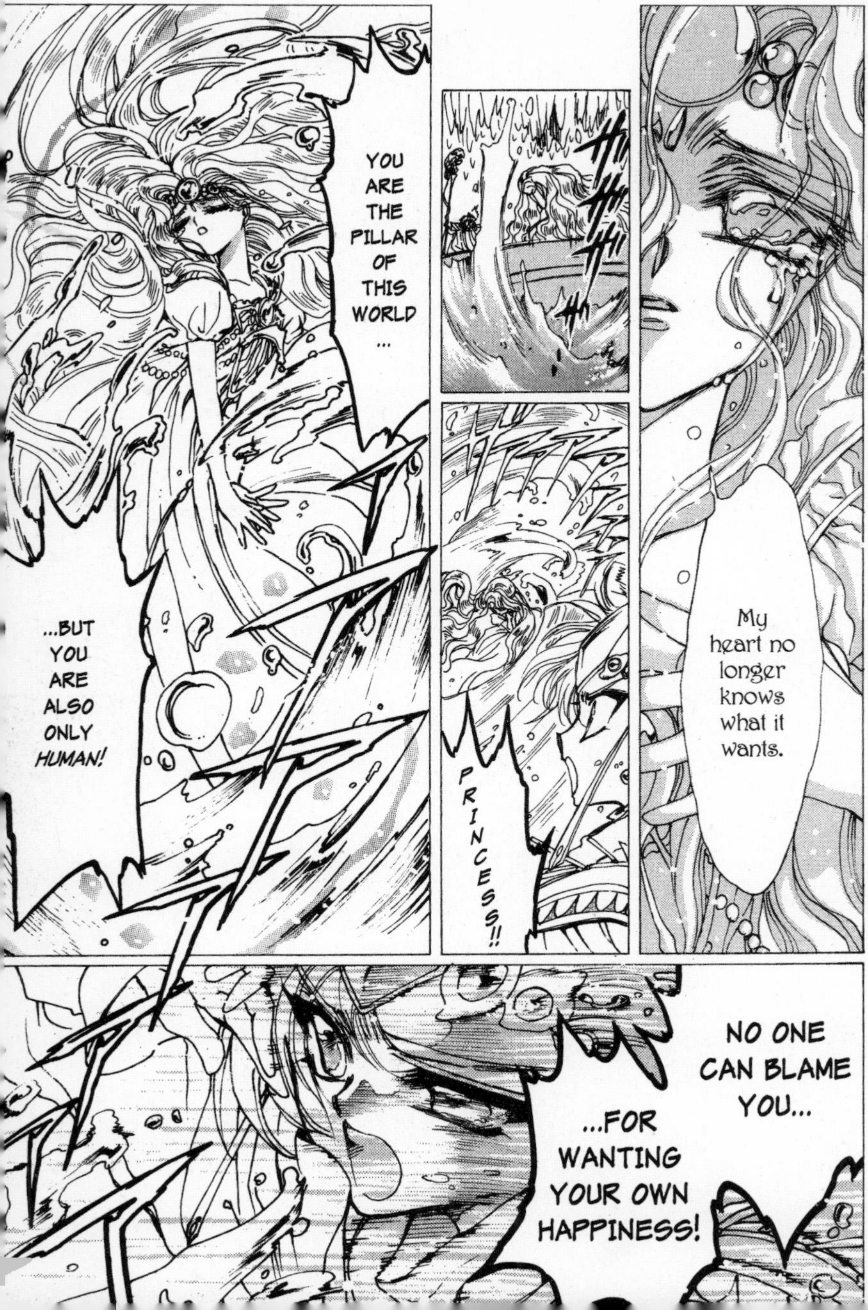
My heart no longer knows what it wants.
PRINCESS!!
YOU ARE THE PILLAR OF THIS WORLD...
...BUT YOU ARE ALSO ONLY HUMAN!
NO ONE CAN BLAME YOU...
...FOR WANTING YOUR OWN HAPPINESS!

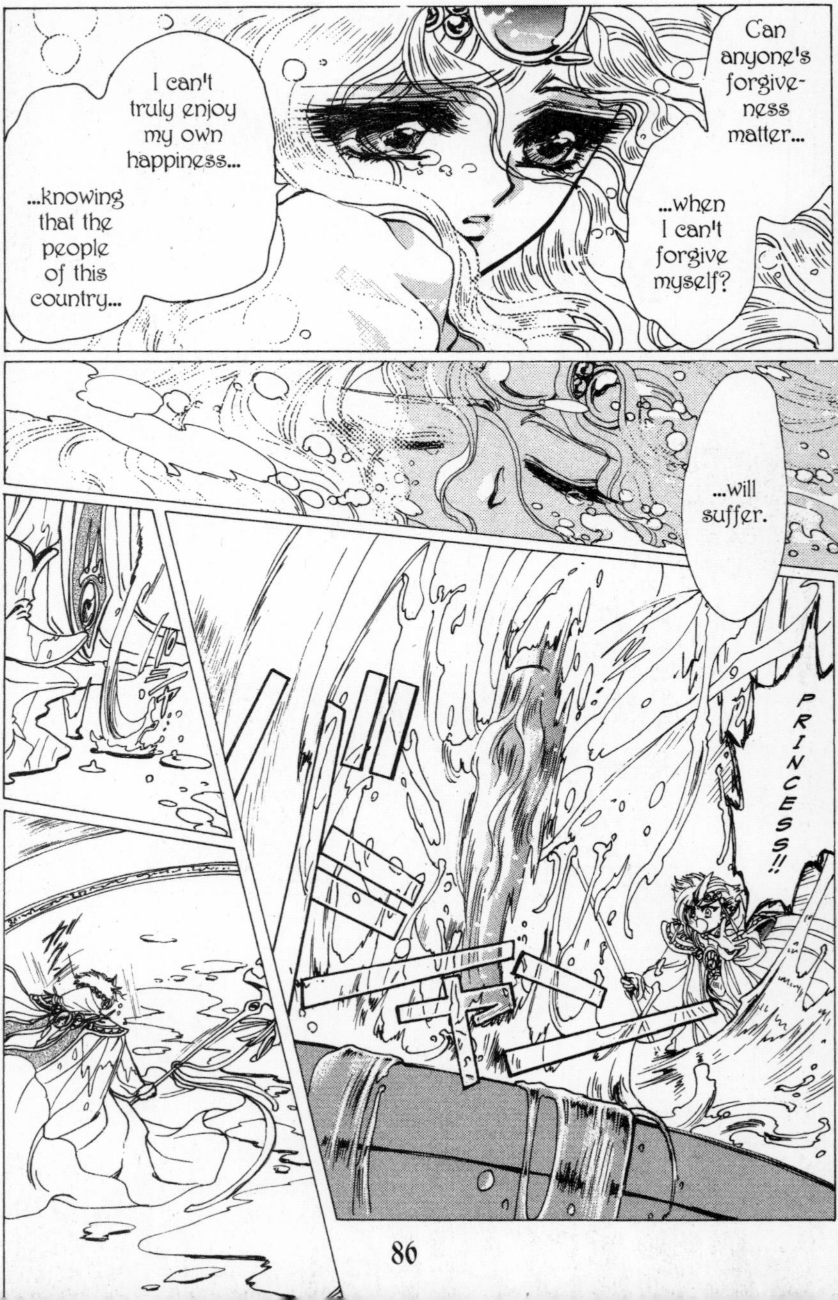
Can anyone's forgive-ness matter...
...when I can't forgive myself?
I can't truly enjoy my own happiness...
...knowing that the people of this country...
...will suffer.
PRINCESS!!

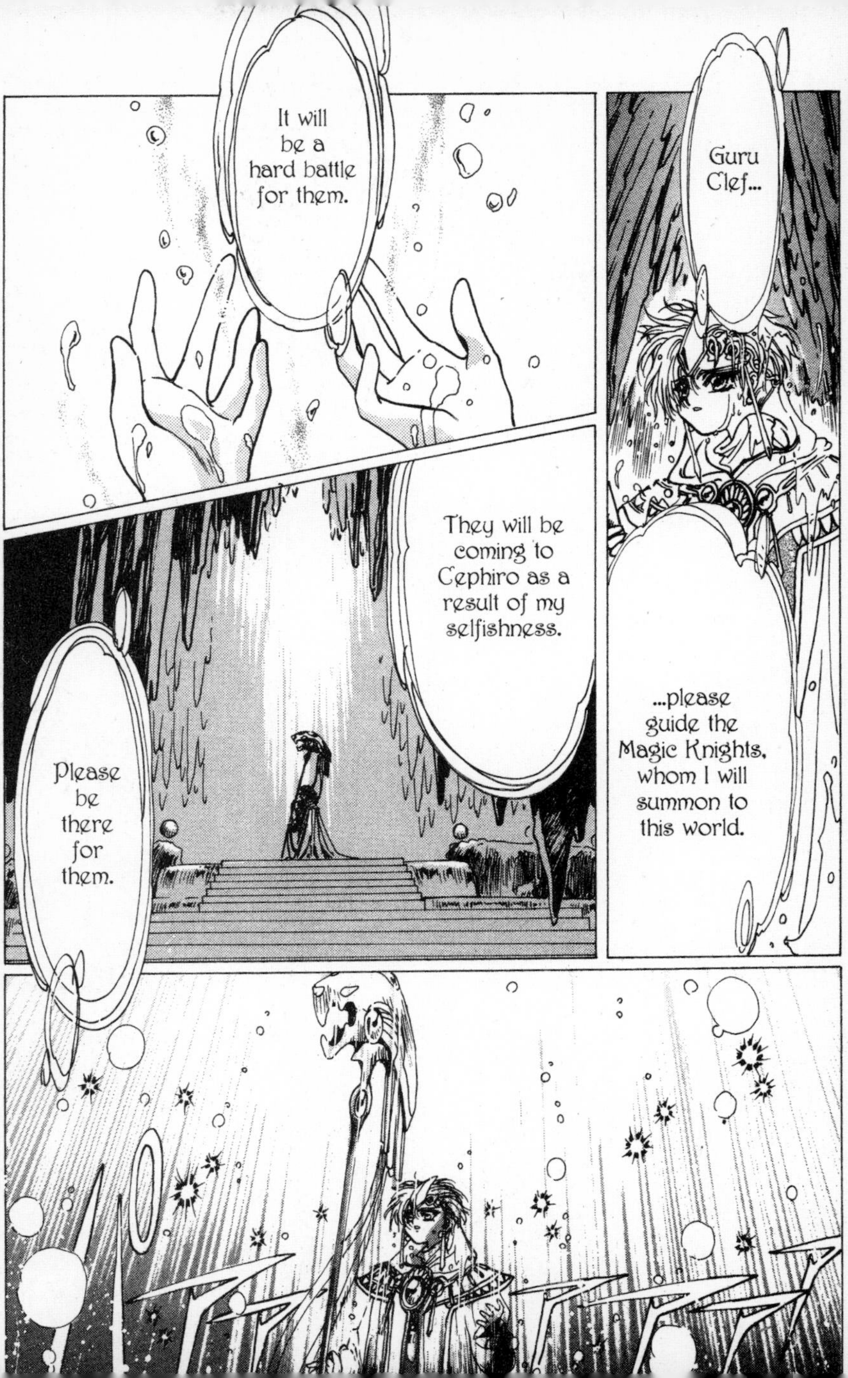

Guru Clef...
...please guide the Magic Knights, whom I will summon to this world.
It will be a hard battle for them.
They will be coming to Cephiro as a result of my selfishness.
Please be there for them.

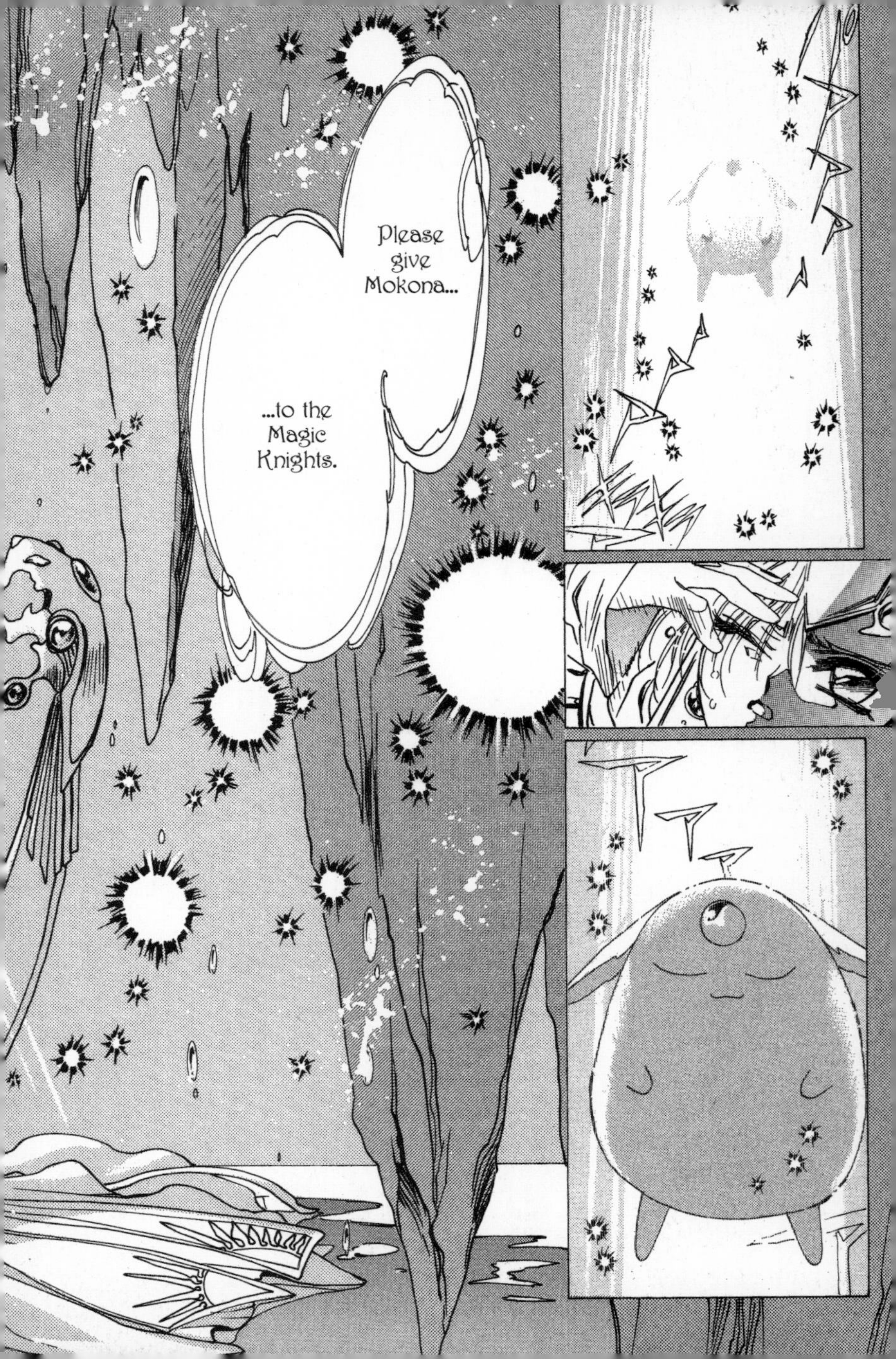
Please give Mokona...
...to the Magic Knights.

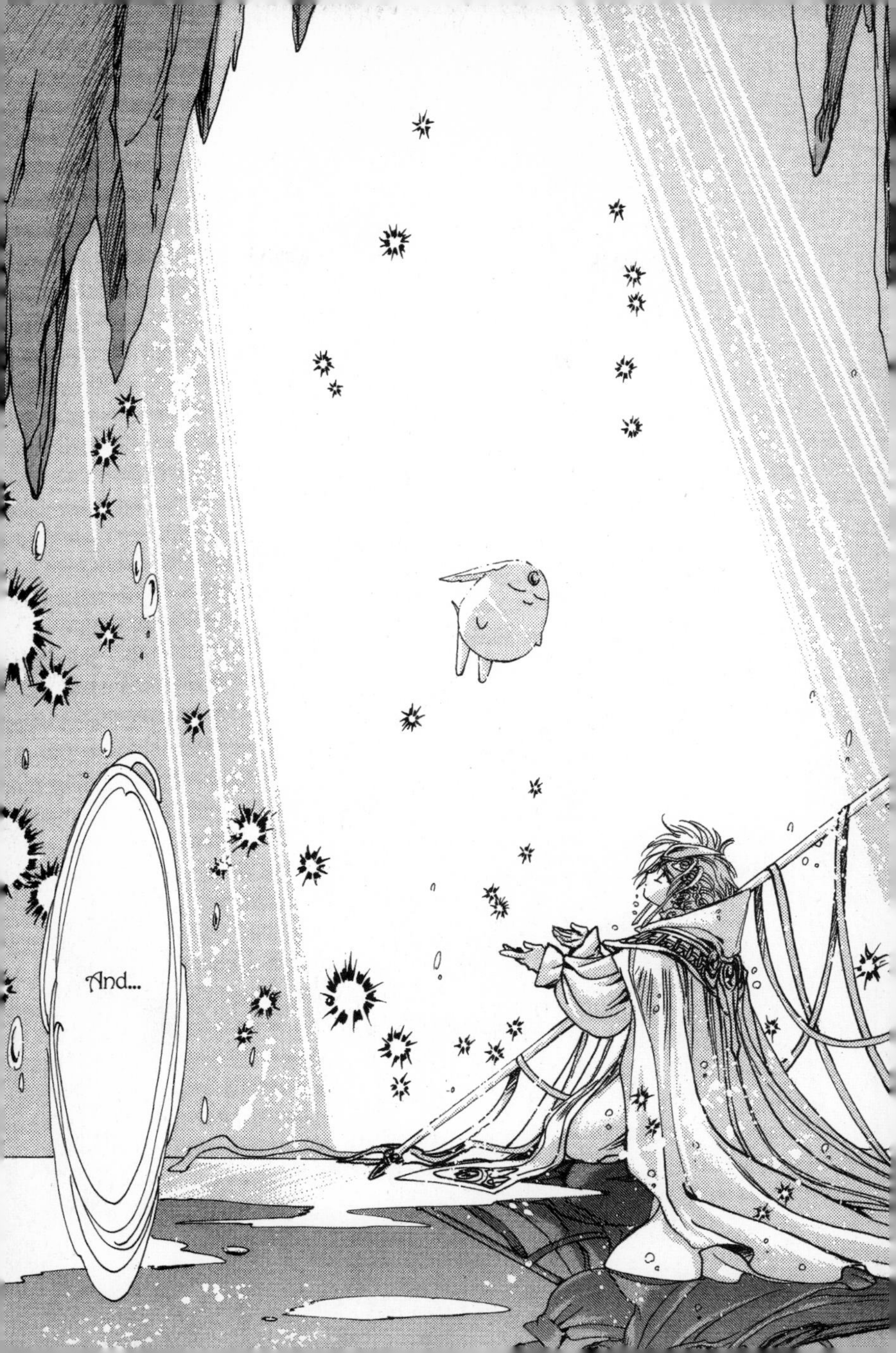
And...

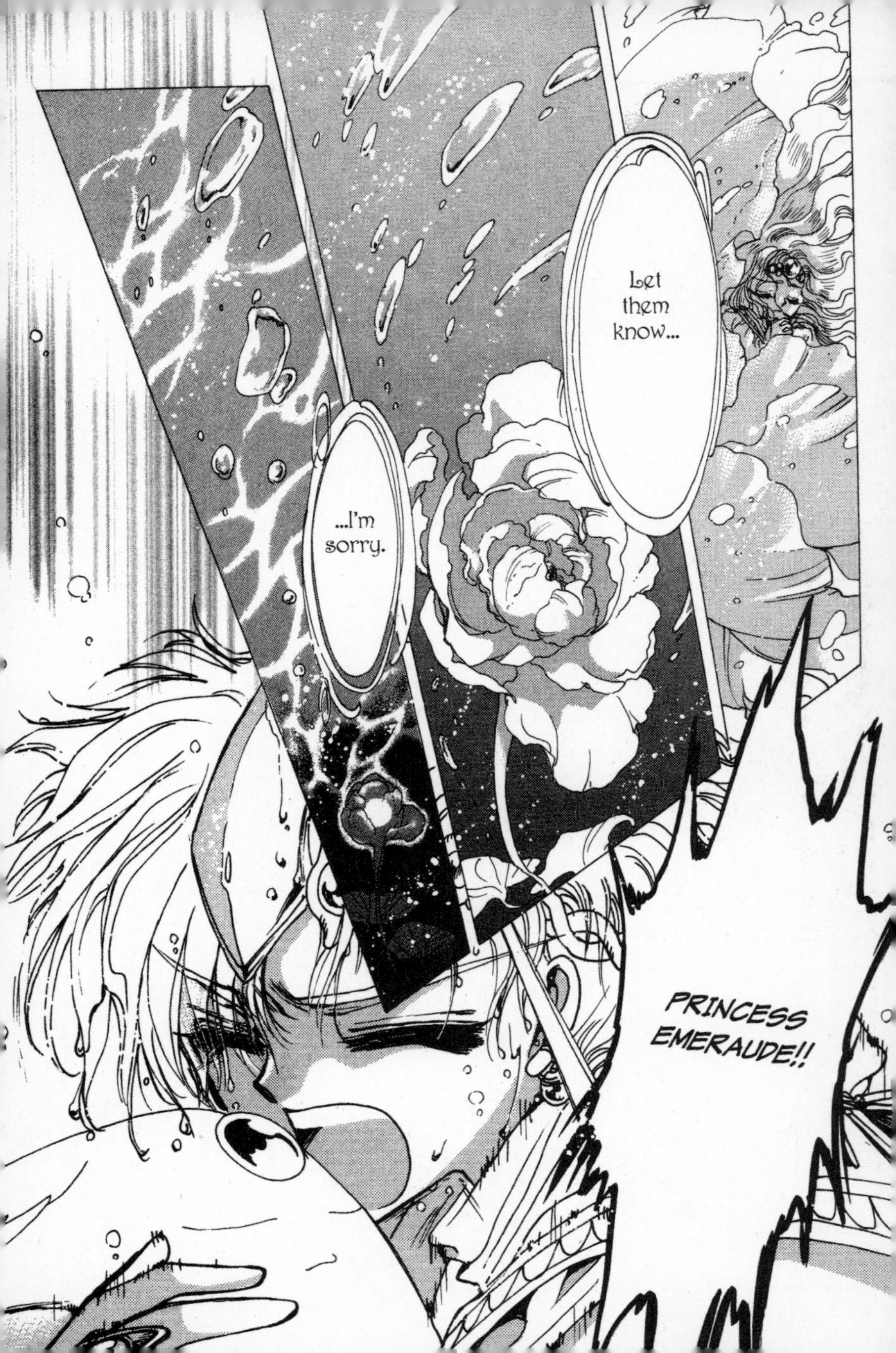
Let them know...
...I'm sorry.
PRINCESS EMERAUDE!!

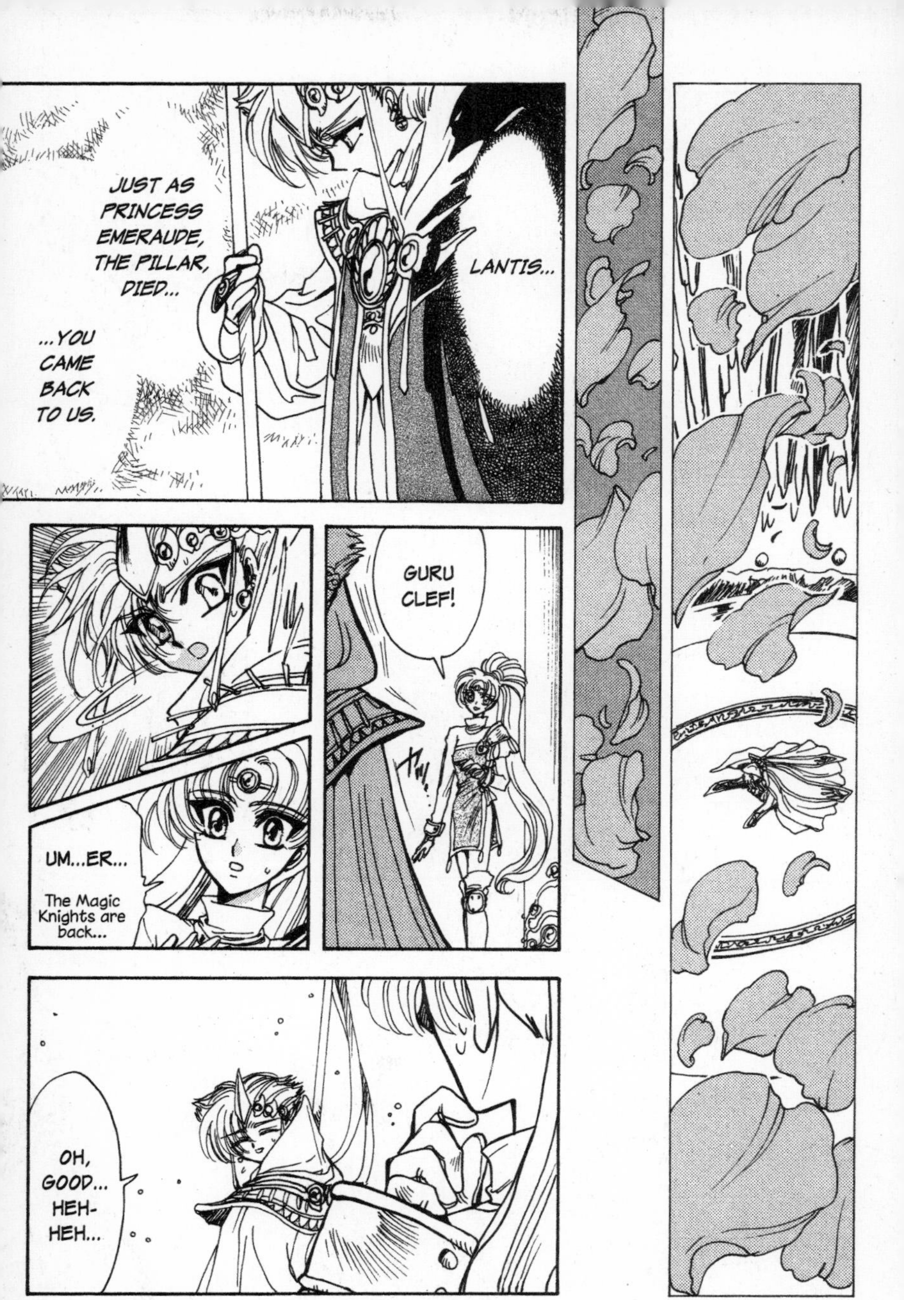
JUST AS PRINCESS EMERAUDE, THE PILLAR, DIED...
...YOU CAME BACK TO US.
LANTIS...
GURU CLEF!
UM...ER...
The Magic Knights are back...
OH, GOOD... HEH-HEH...

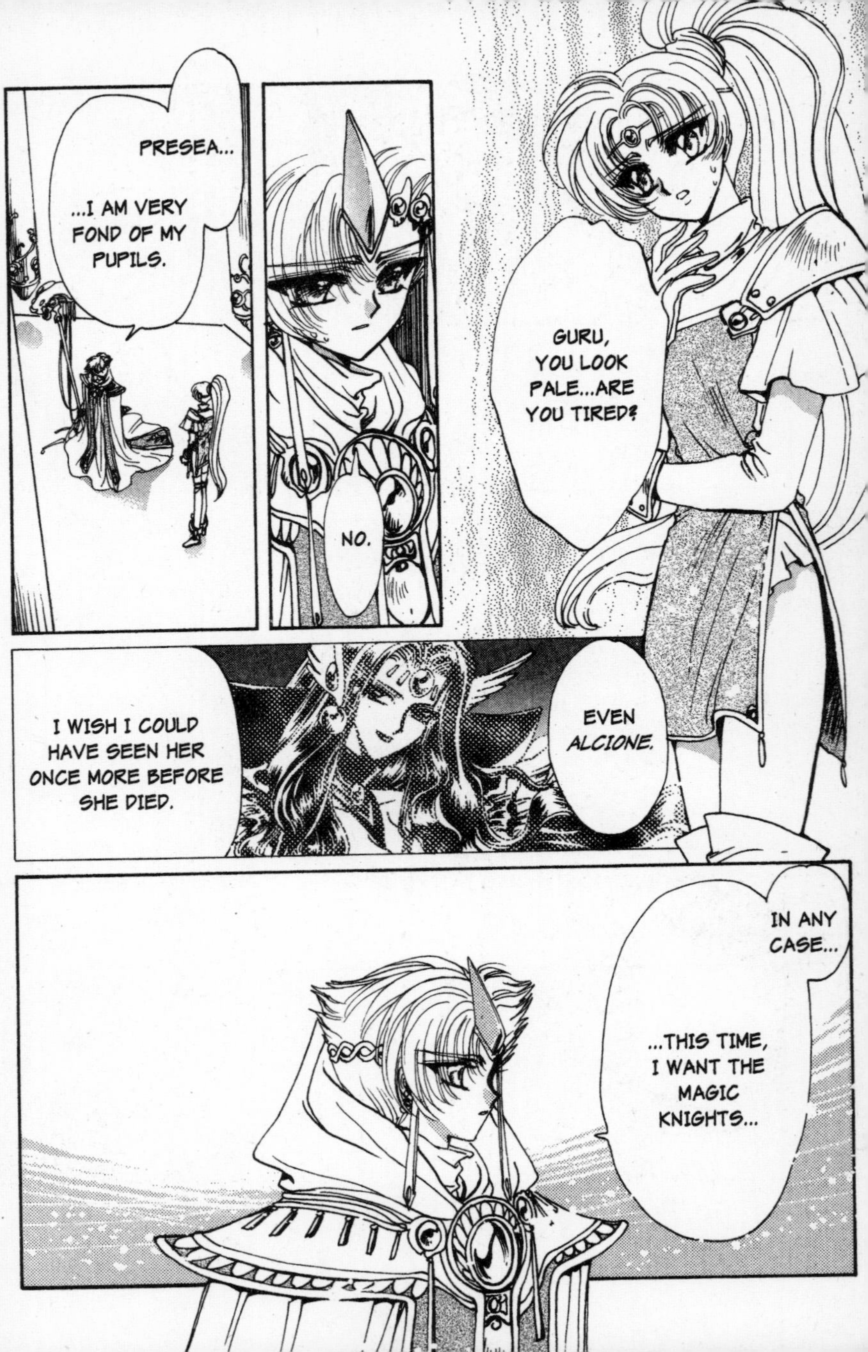
GURU, YOU LOOK PALE...ARE YOU TIRED?
NO.
PRESEA...
...I AM VERY FOND OF MY PUPILS.
EVEN ALCIONE.
I WISH I COULD HAVE SEEN HER ONCE MORE BEFORE SHE DIED.
IN ANY CASE...
...THIS TIME, I WANT THE MAGIC KNIGHTS...

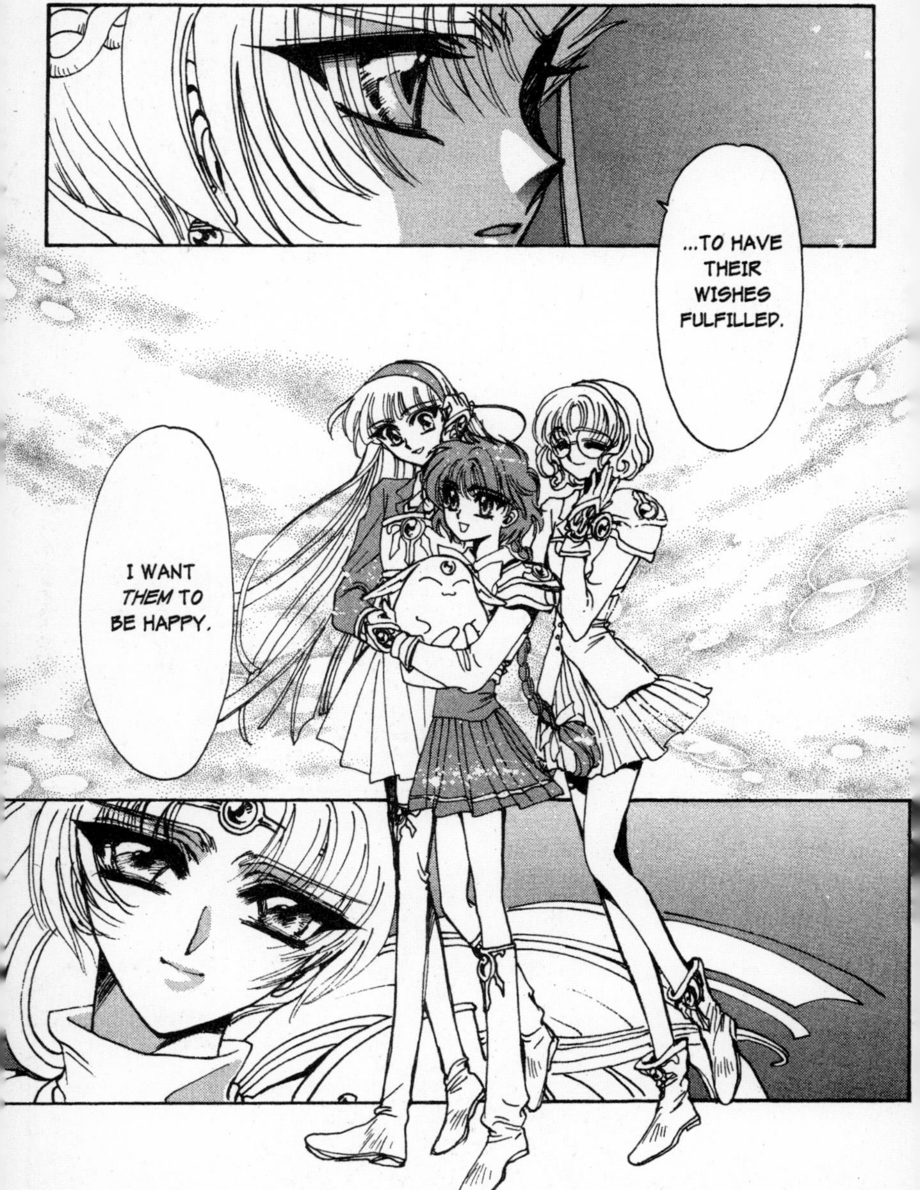
...TO HAVE THEIR WISHES FULFILLED.
I WANT *THEM* TO BE HAPPY.

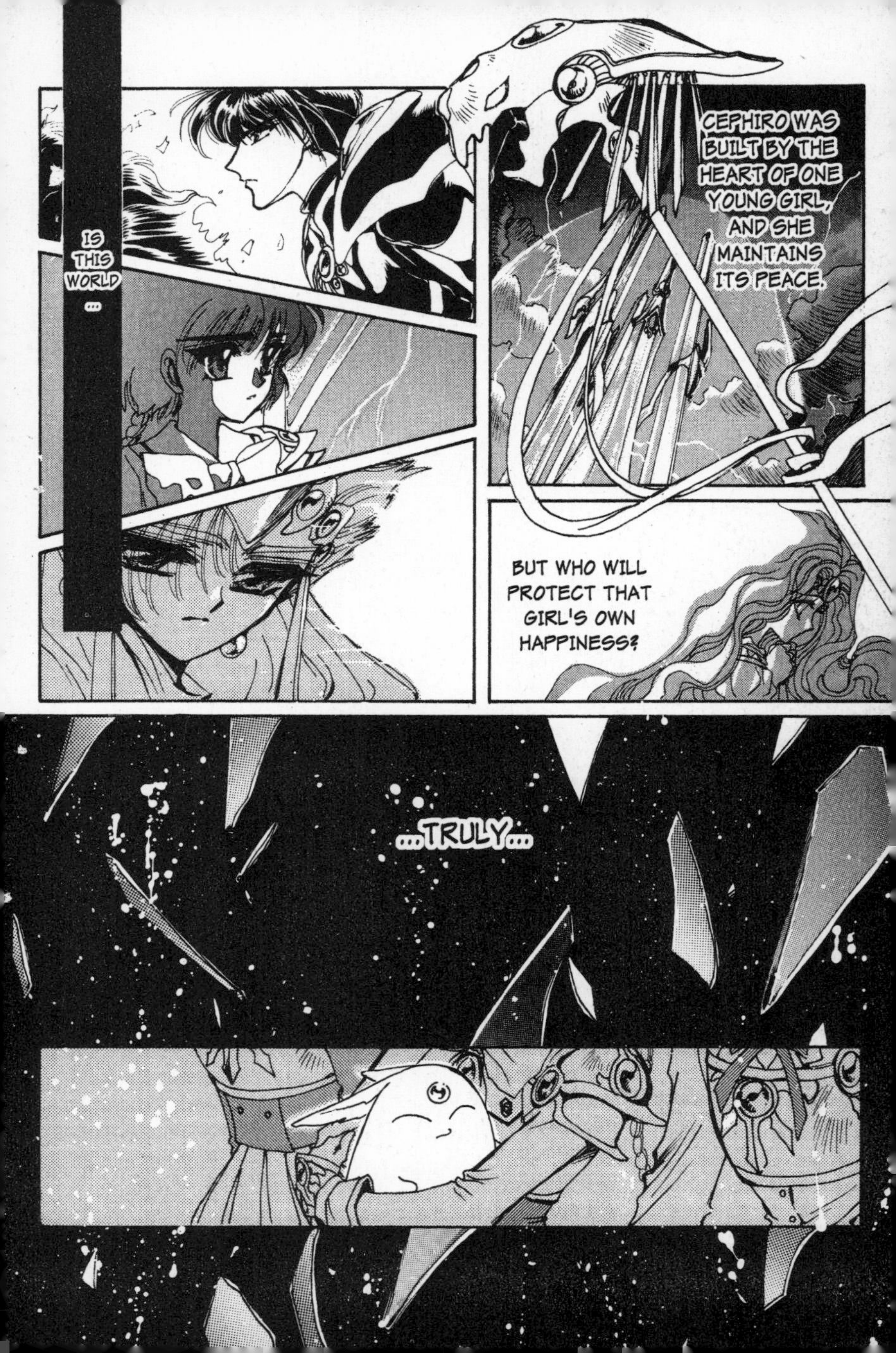
CEPHIRO WAS BUILT BY THE HEART OF ONE YOUNG GIRL, AND SHE MAINTAINS ITS PEACE.
BUT WHO WILL PROTECT THAT GIRL'S OWN HAPPINESS?
IS THIS WORLD ...
...TRULY...

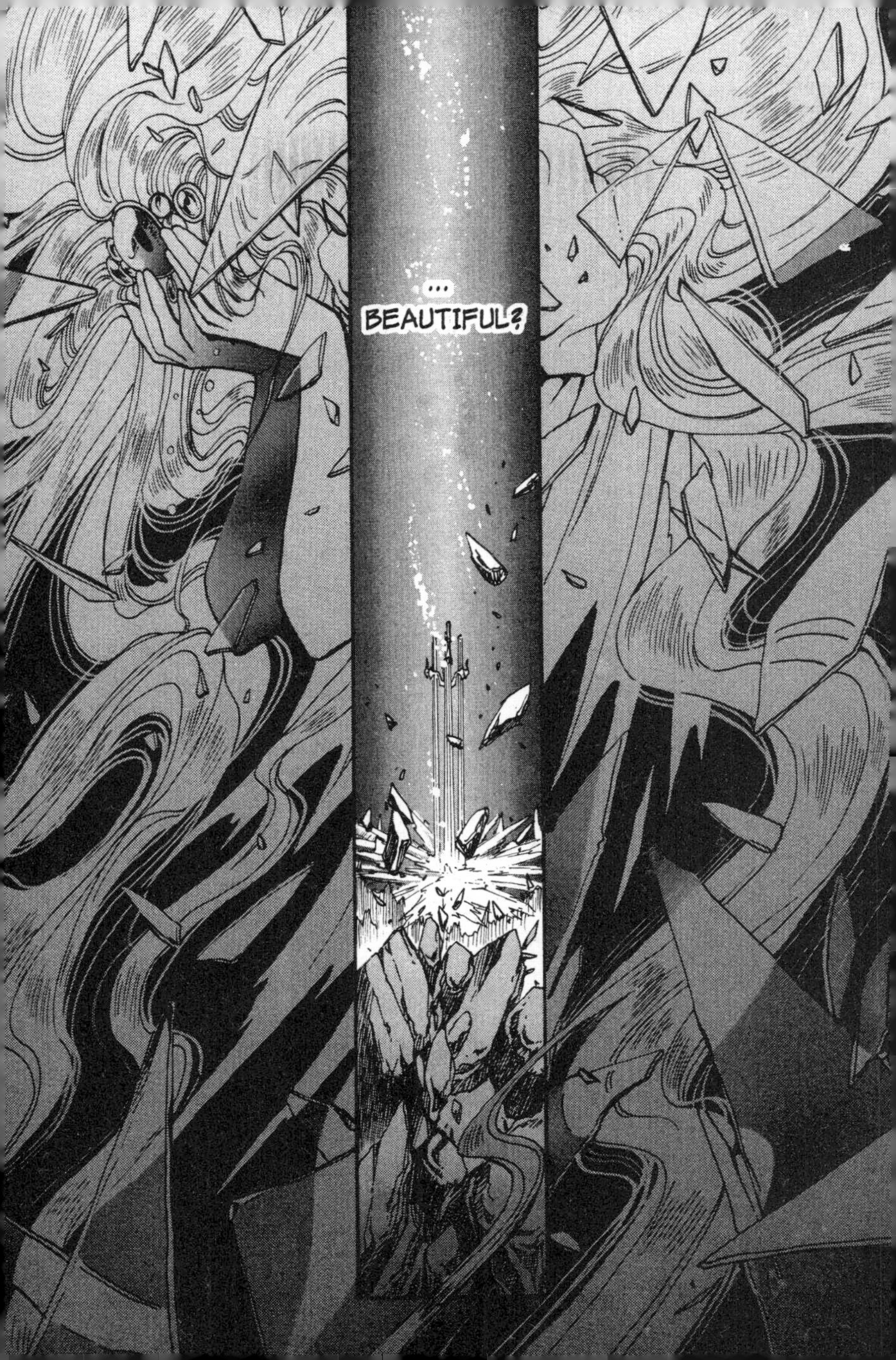
...
BEAUTIFUL?

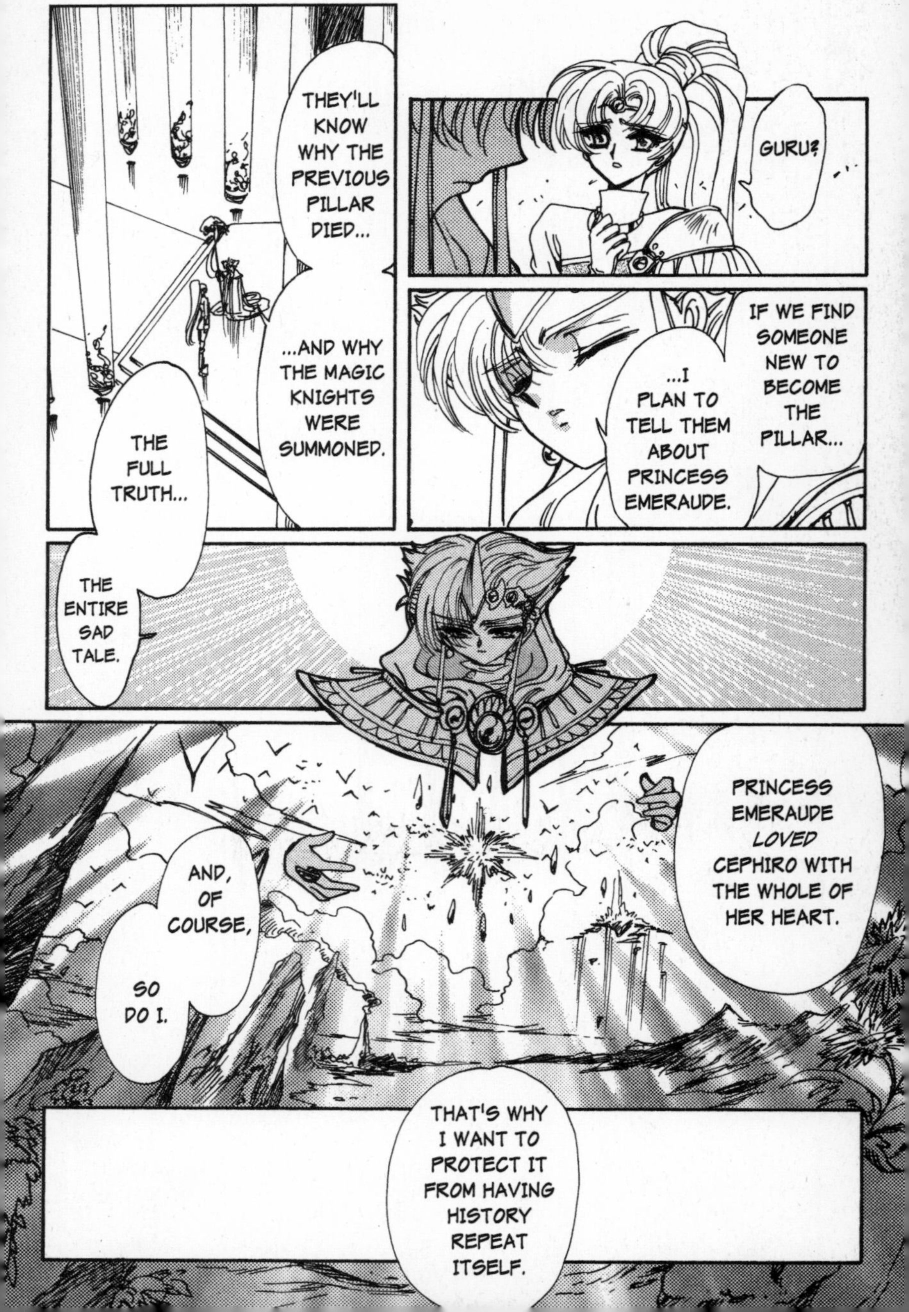
GURU?
IF WE FIND SOMEONE NEW TO BECOME THE PILLAR...
...I PLAN TO TELL THEM ABOUT PRINCESS EMERAUDE.
THEY'LL KNOW WHY THE PREVIOUS PILLAR DIED...
...AND WHY THE MAGIC KNIGHTS WERE SUMMONED.
THE FULL TRUTH...
THE ENTIRE SAD TALE.
PRINCESS EMERAUDE *LOVED* CEPHIRO WITH THE WHOLE OF HER HEART.
AND, OF COURSE,
SO DO I.
THAT'S WHY I WANT TO PROTECT IT FROM HAVING HISTORY REPEAT ITSELF.

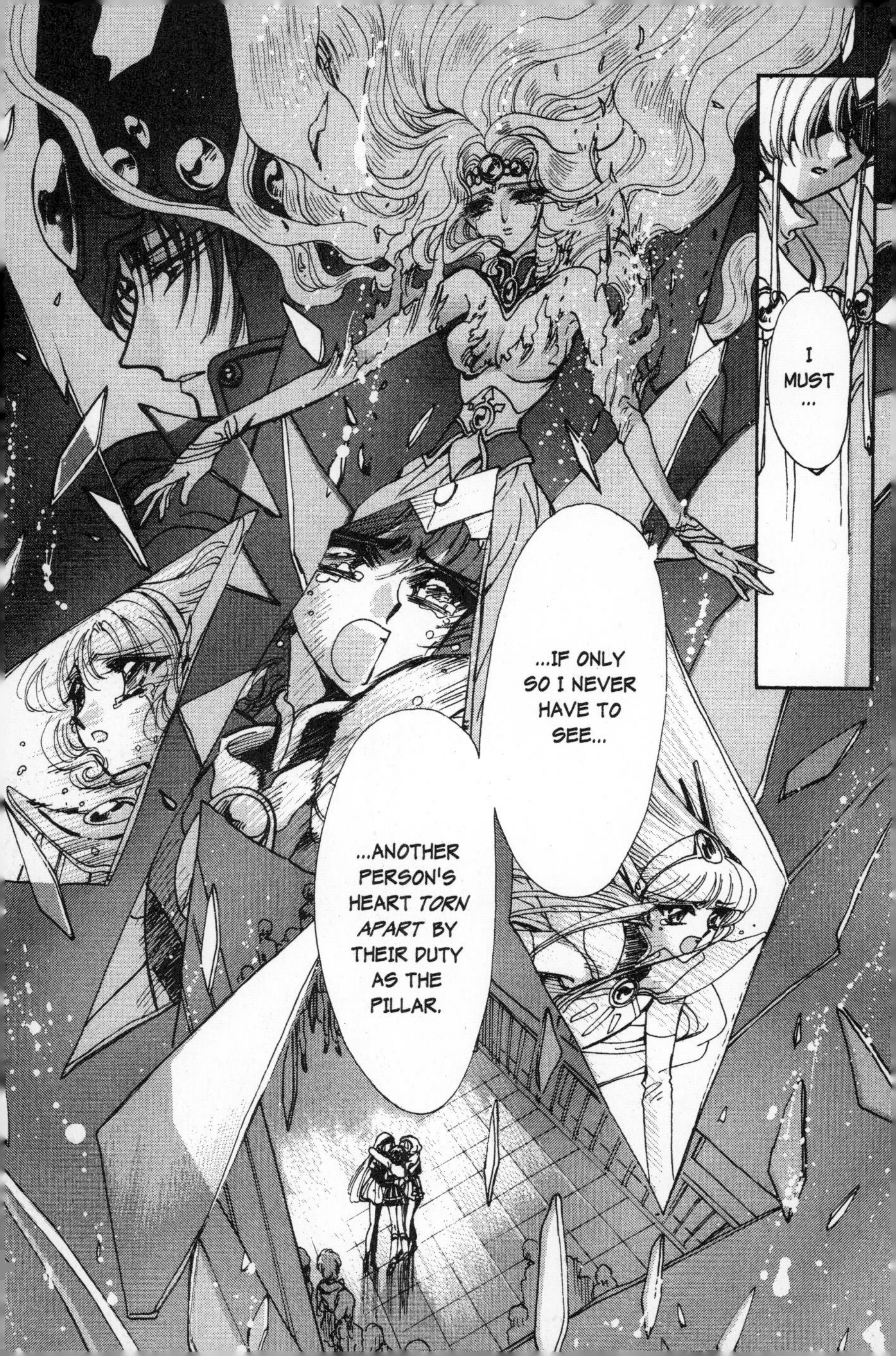
I MUST ...
...IF ONLY SO I NEVER HAVE TO SEE...
...ANOTHER PERSON'S HEART *TORN APART* BY THEIR DUTY AS THE PILLAR.

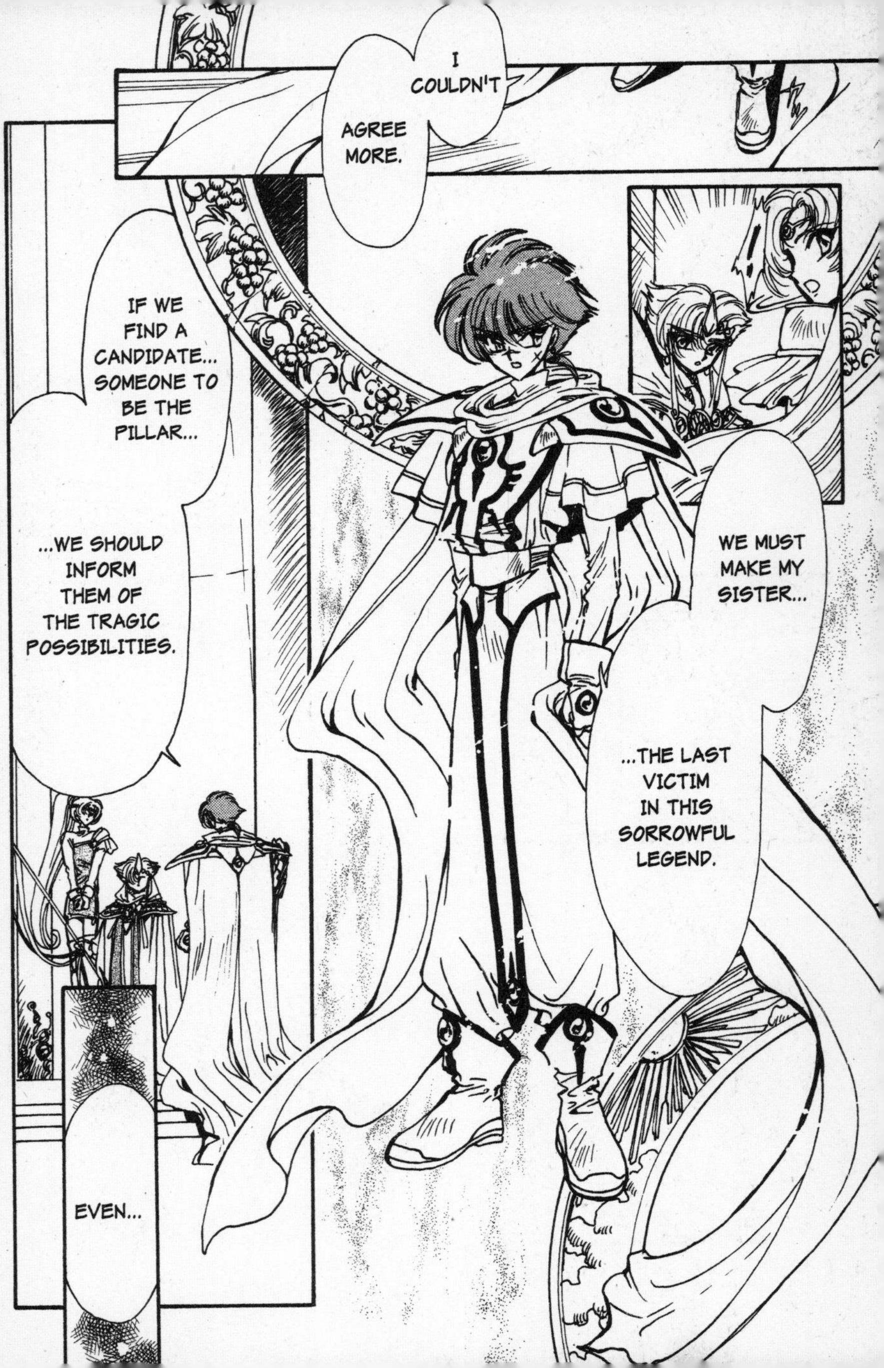
I COULDN'T AGREE MORE.
WE MUST MAKE MY SISTER...
...THE LAST VICTIM IN THIS SORROWFUL LEGEND.
IF WE FIND A CANDIDATE... SOMEONE TO BE THE PILLAR...
...WE SHOULD INFORM THEM OF THE TRAGIC POSSIBILITIES.
EVEN...

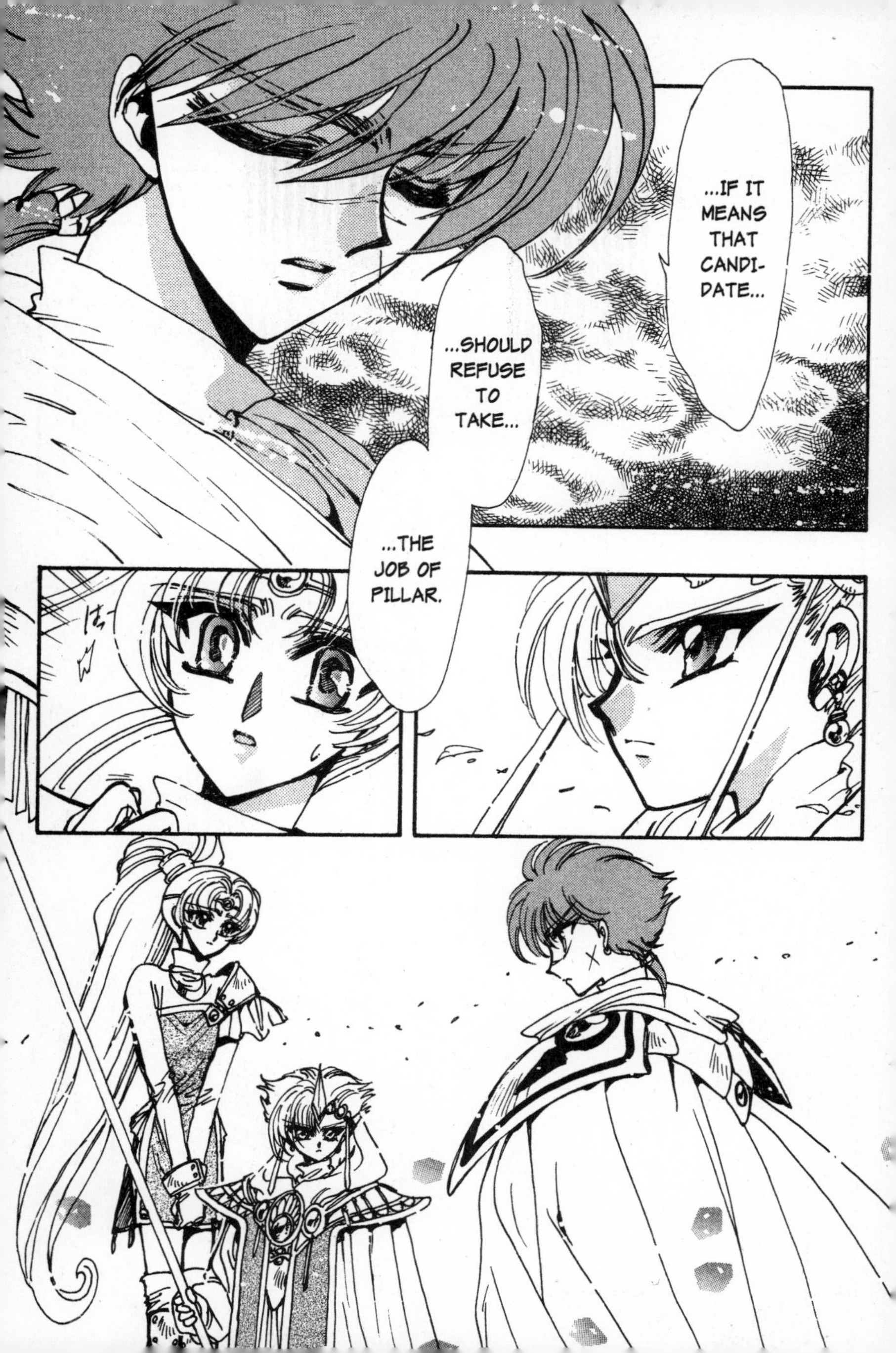
...IF IT MEANS THAT CANDI-DATE...
...SHOULD REFUSE TO TAKE...
...THE JOB OF PILLAR.

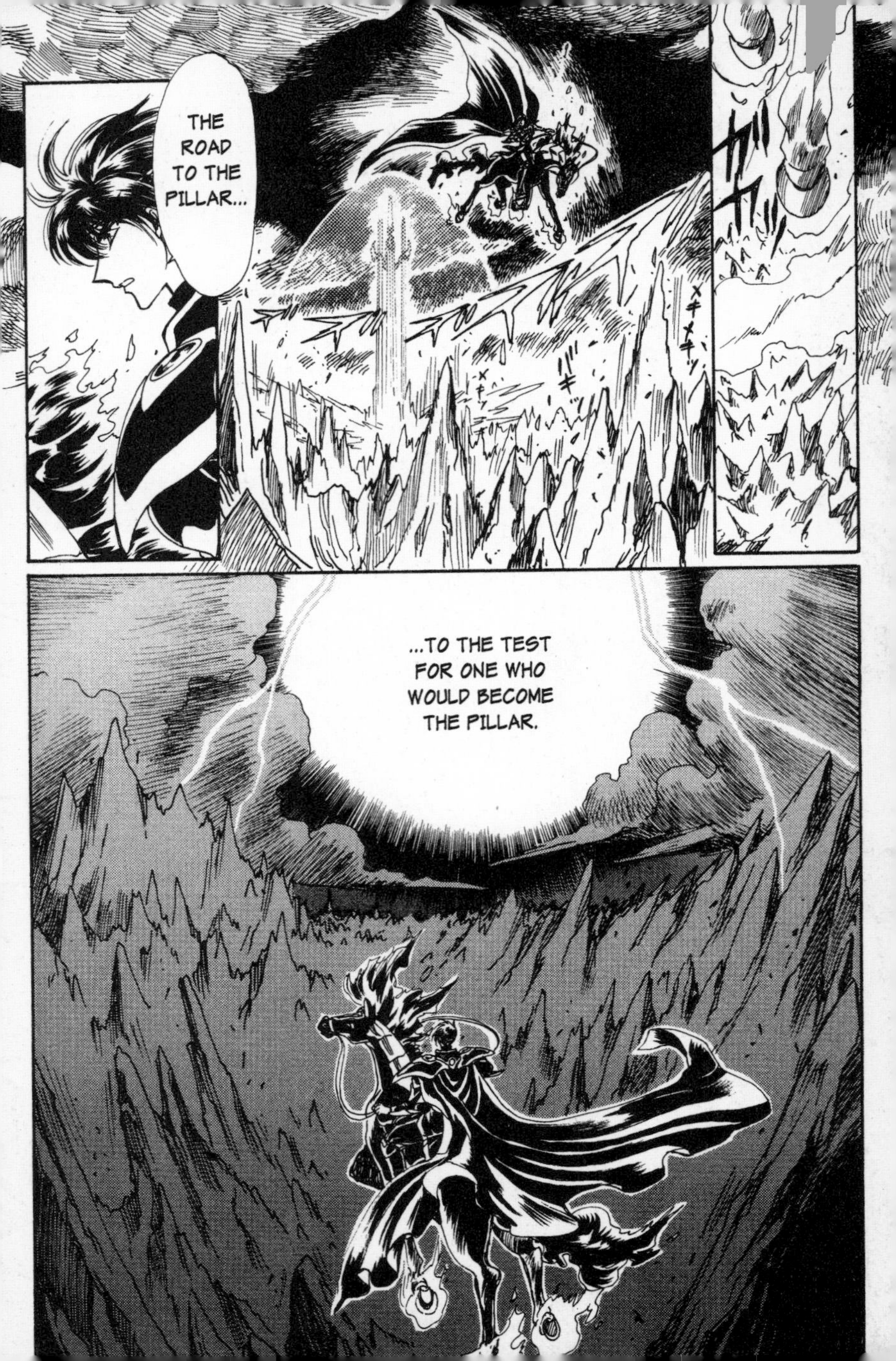
THE ROAD TO THE PILLAR...
...TO THE TEST FOR ONE WHO WOULD BECOME THE PILLAR.

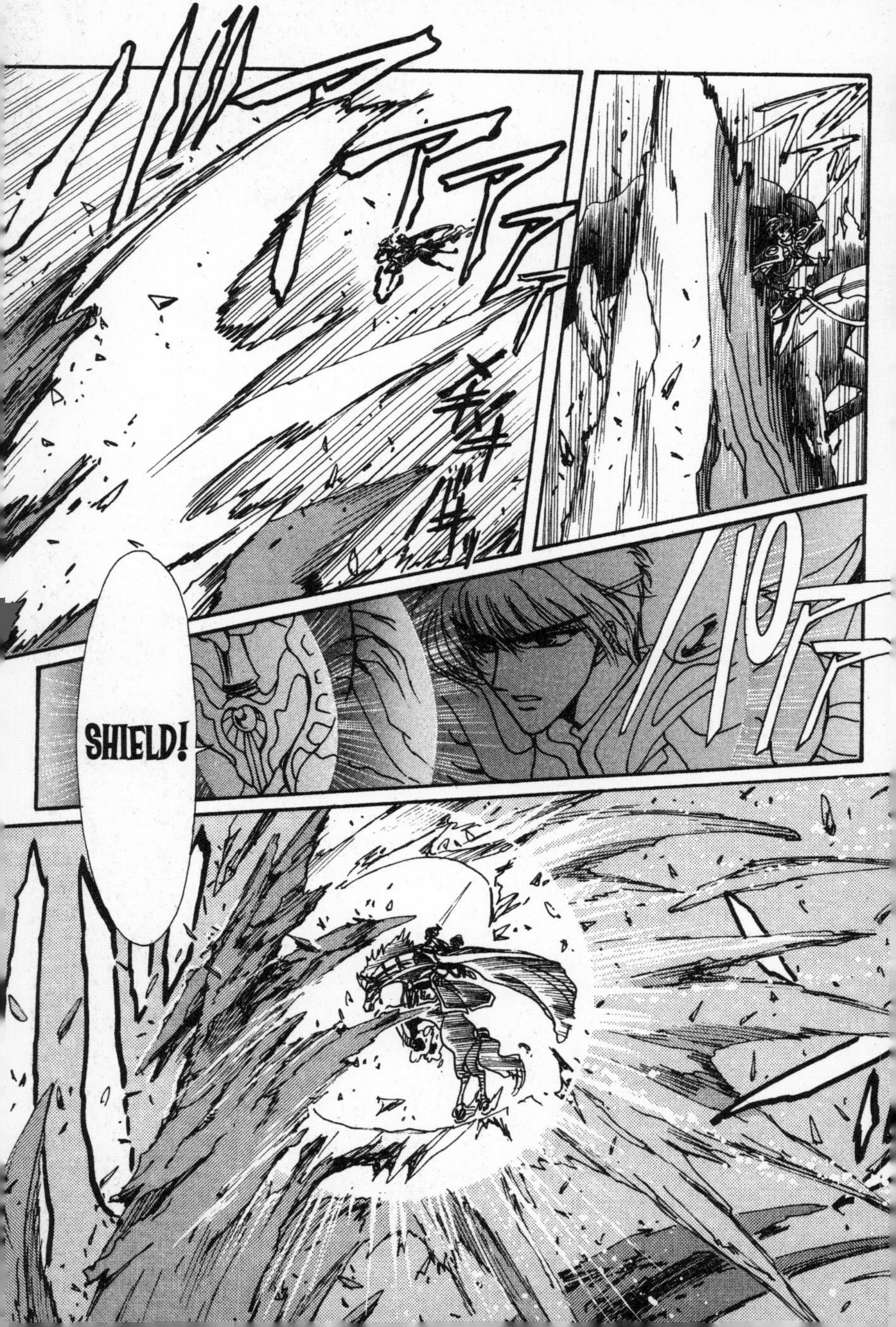
SHIELD!

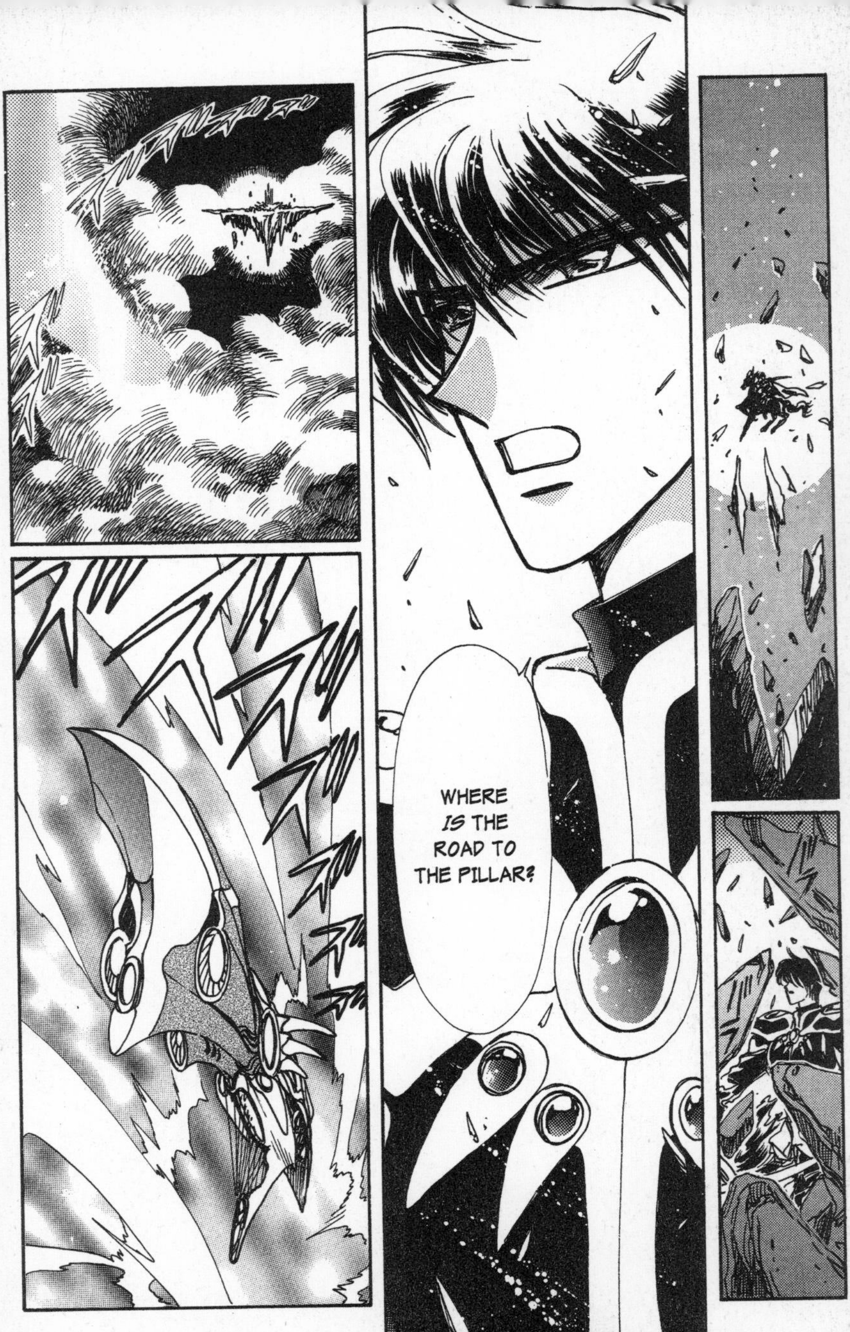
WHERE *IS* THE ROAD TO THE PILLAR?

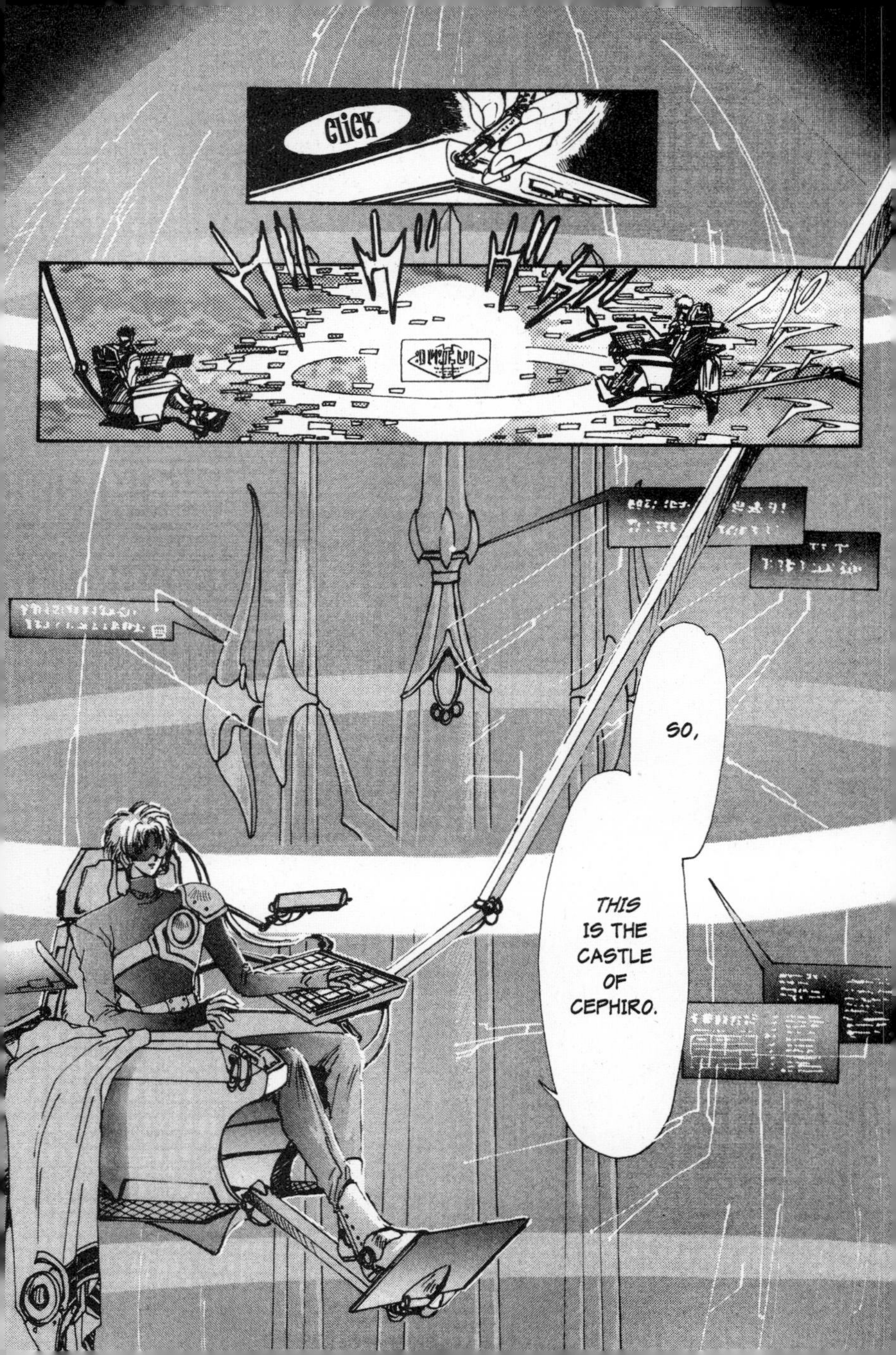
CLICK
SO,
THIS IS THE CASTLE OF CEPHIRO.

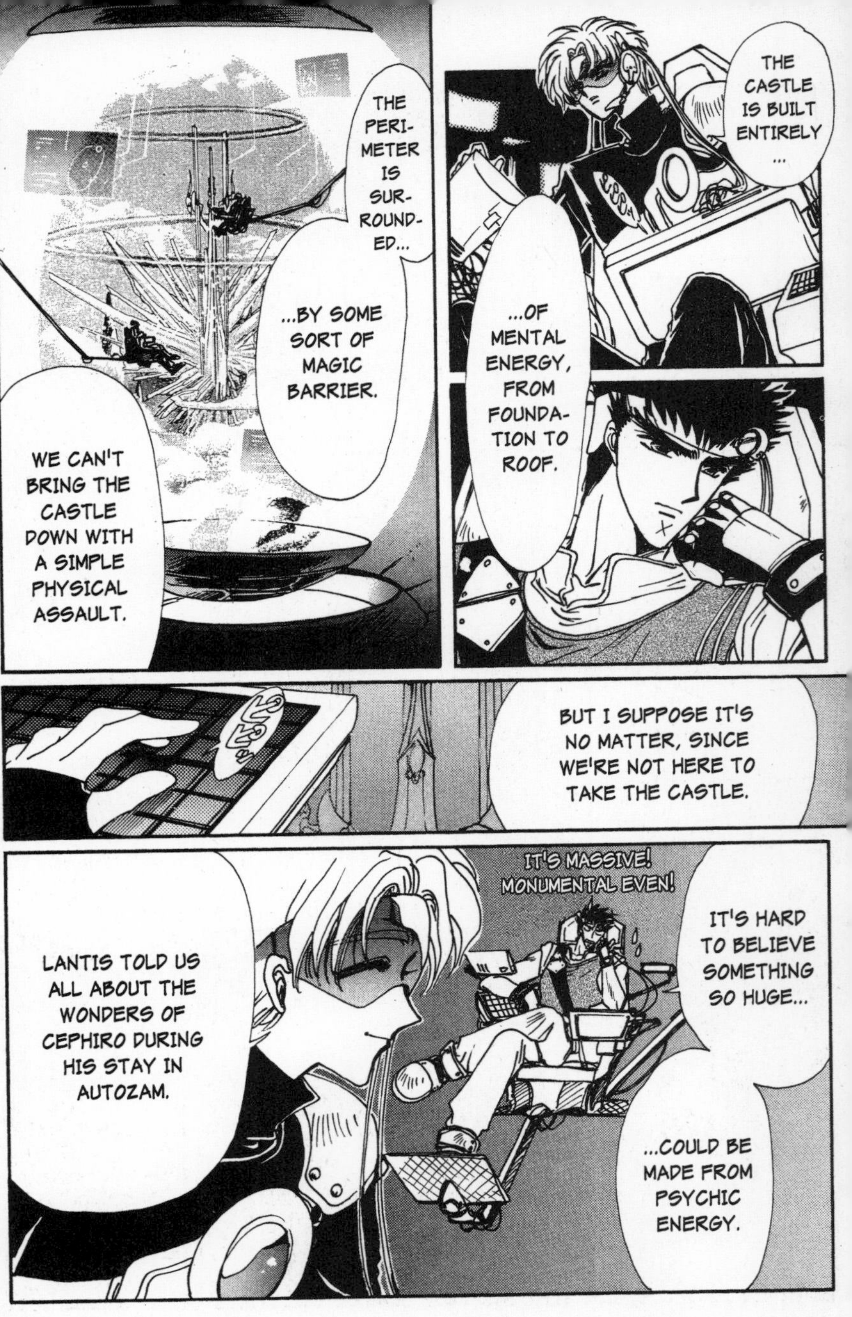
THE CASTLE IS BUILT ENTIRELY ...
...OF MENTAL ENERGY, FROM FOUNDATION TO ROOF.
THE PERIMETER IS SURROUNDED...
...BY SOME SORT OF MAGIC BARRIER.
WE CAN'T BRING THE CASTLE DOWN WITH A SIMPLE PHYSICAL ASSAULT.
BUT I SUPPOSE IT'S NO MATTER, SINCE WE'RE NOT HERE TO TAKE THE CASTLE.
IT'S MASSIVE! MONUMENTAL EVEN!
IT'S HARD TO BELIEVE SOMETHING SO HUGE...
...COULD BE MADE FROM PSYCHIC ENERGY.
LANTIS TOLD US ALL ABOUT THE WONDERS OF CEPHIRO DURING HIS STAY IN AUTOZAM.

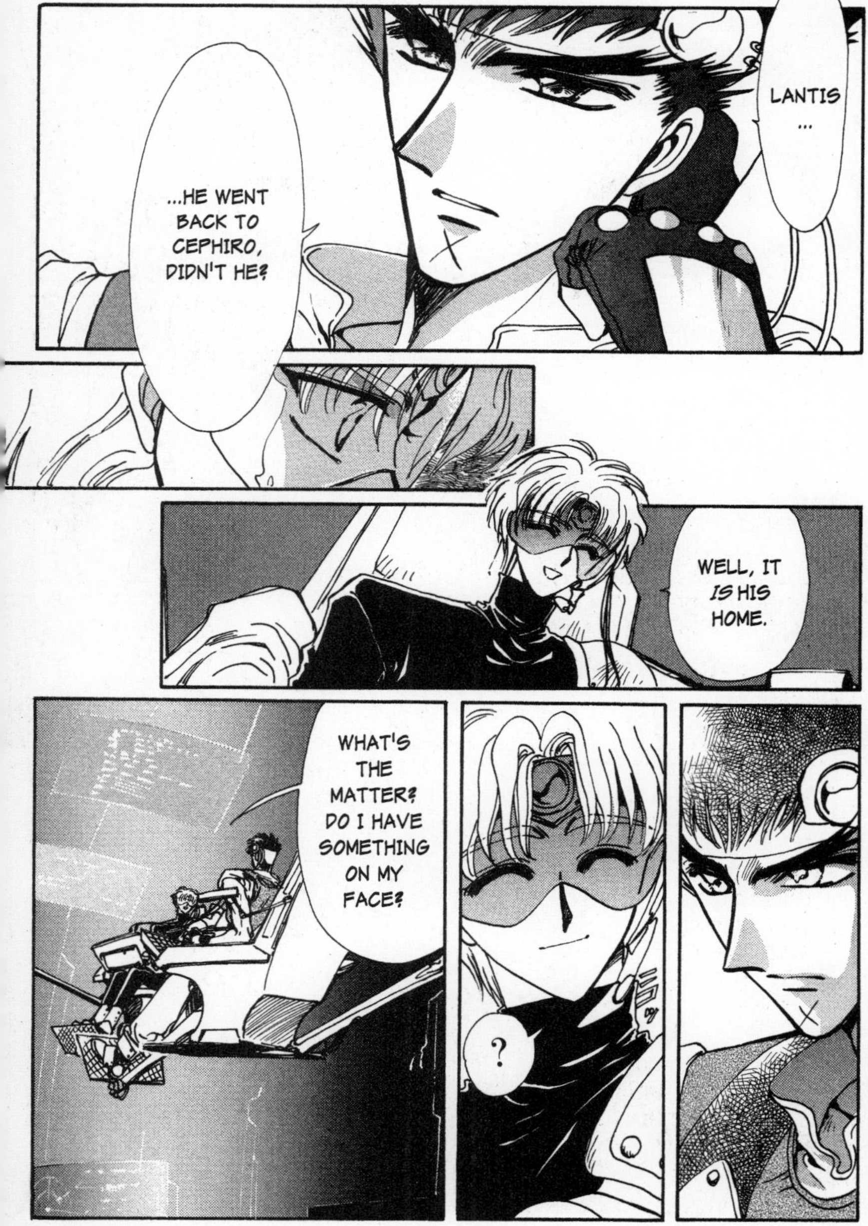
LANTIS ...
...HE WENT BACK TO CEPHIRO, DIDN'T HE?
WELL, IT *IS* HIS HOME.
?
WHAT'S THE MATTER? DO I HAVE SOMETHING ON MY FACE?

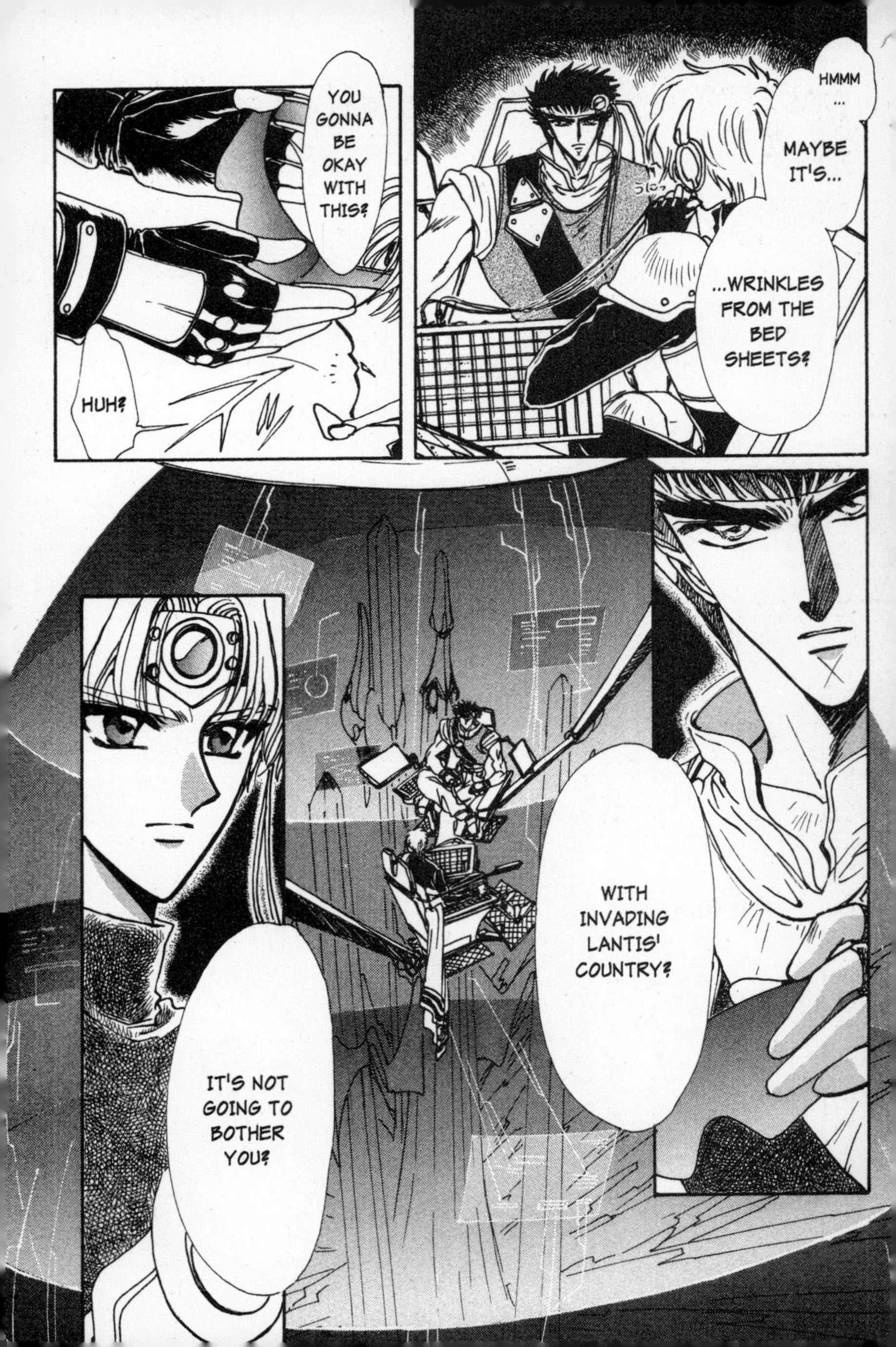
HMMM ...
MAYBE IT'S...
...WRINKLES FROM THE BED SHEETS?
YOU GONNA BE OKAY WITH THIS?
HUH?
WITH INVADING LANTIS' COUNTRY?
IT'S NOT GOING TO BOTHER YOU?

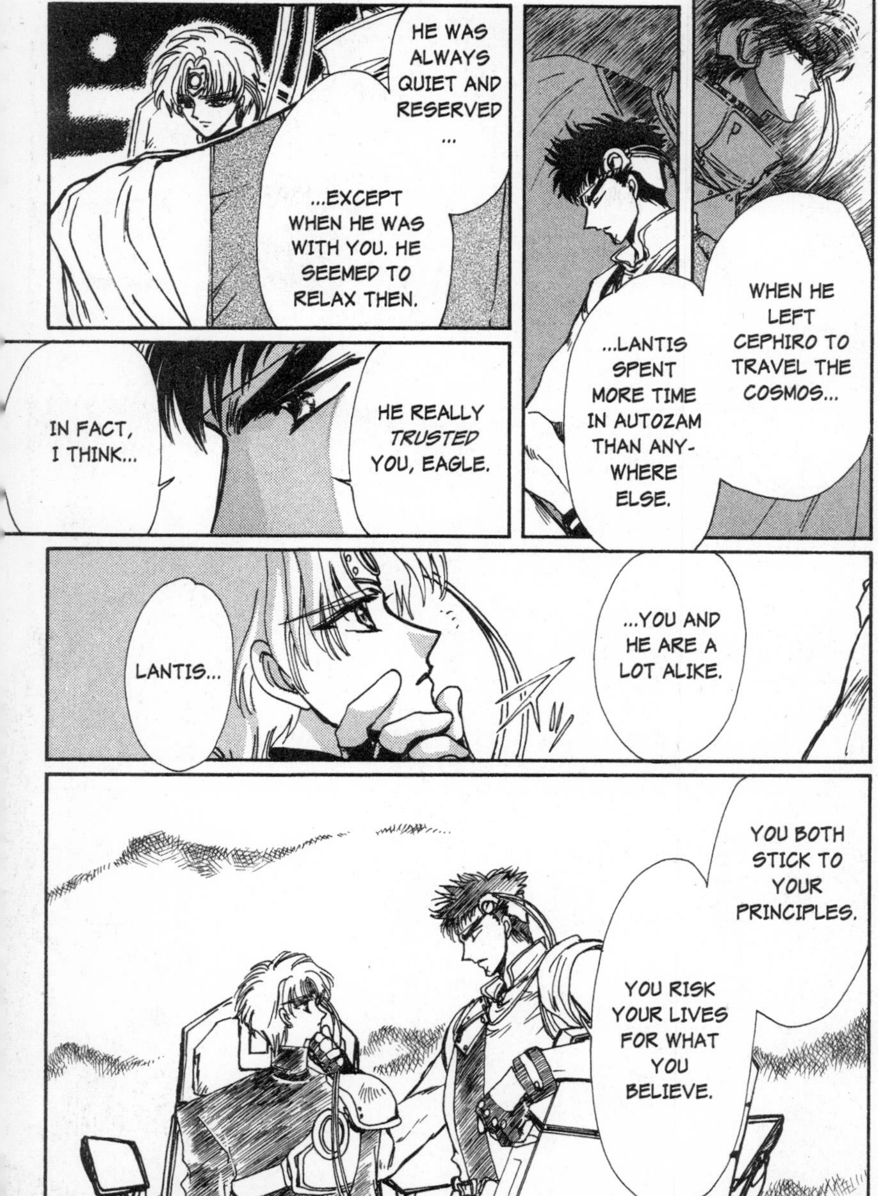
WHEN HE LEFT CEPHIRO TO TRAVEL THE COSMOS...
...LANTIS SPENT MORE TIME IN AUTOZAM THAN ANY-WHERE ELSE.
HE WAS ALWAYS QUIET AND RESERVED ...
...EXCEPT WHEN HE WAS WITH YOU. HE SEEMED TO RELAX THEN.
HE REALLY *TRUSTED* YOU, EAGLE.
IN FACT, I THINK...
...YOU AND HE ARE A LOT ALIKE.
LANTIS...
YOU BOTH STICK TO YOUR PRINCIPLES.
YOU RISK YOUR LIVES FOR WHAT YOU BELIEVE.

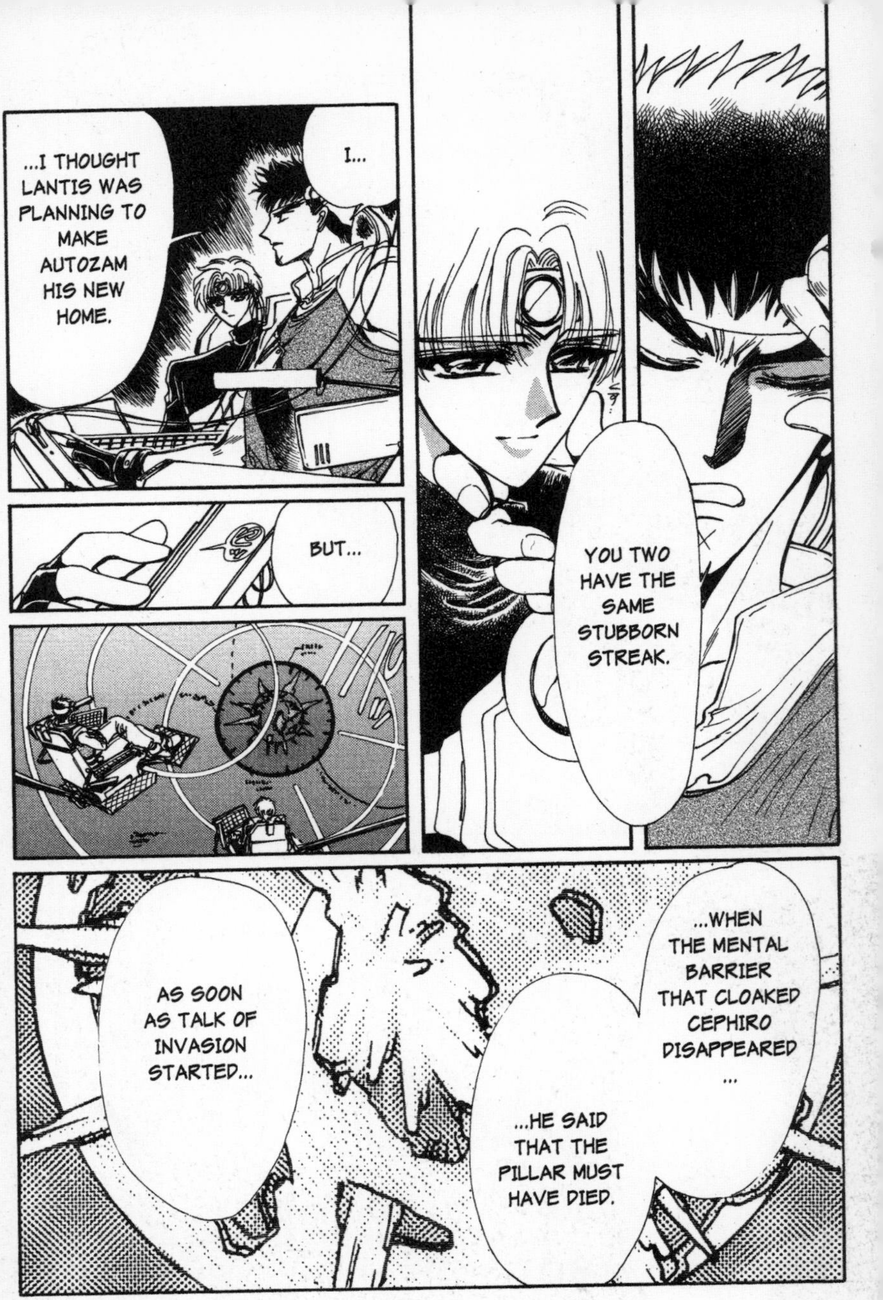
YOU TWO HAVE THE SAME STUBBORN STREAK.
I...
...I THOUGHT LANTIS WAS PLANNING TO MAKE AUTOZAM HIS NEW HOME.
BUT...
...WHEN THE MENTAL BARRIER THAT CLOAKED CEPHIRO DISAPPEARED ...
...HE SAID THAT THE PILLAR MUST HAVE DIED.
AS SOON AS TALK OF INVASION STARTED...

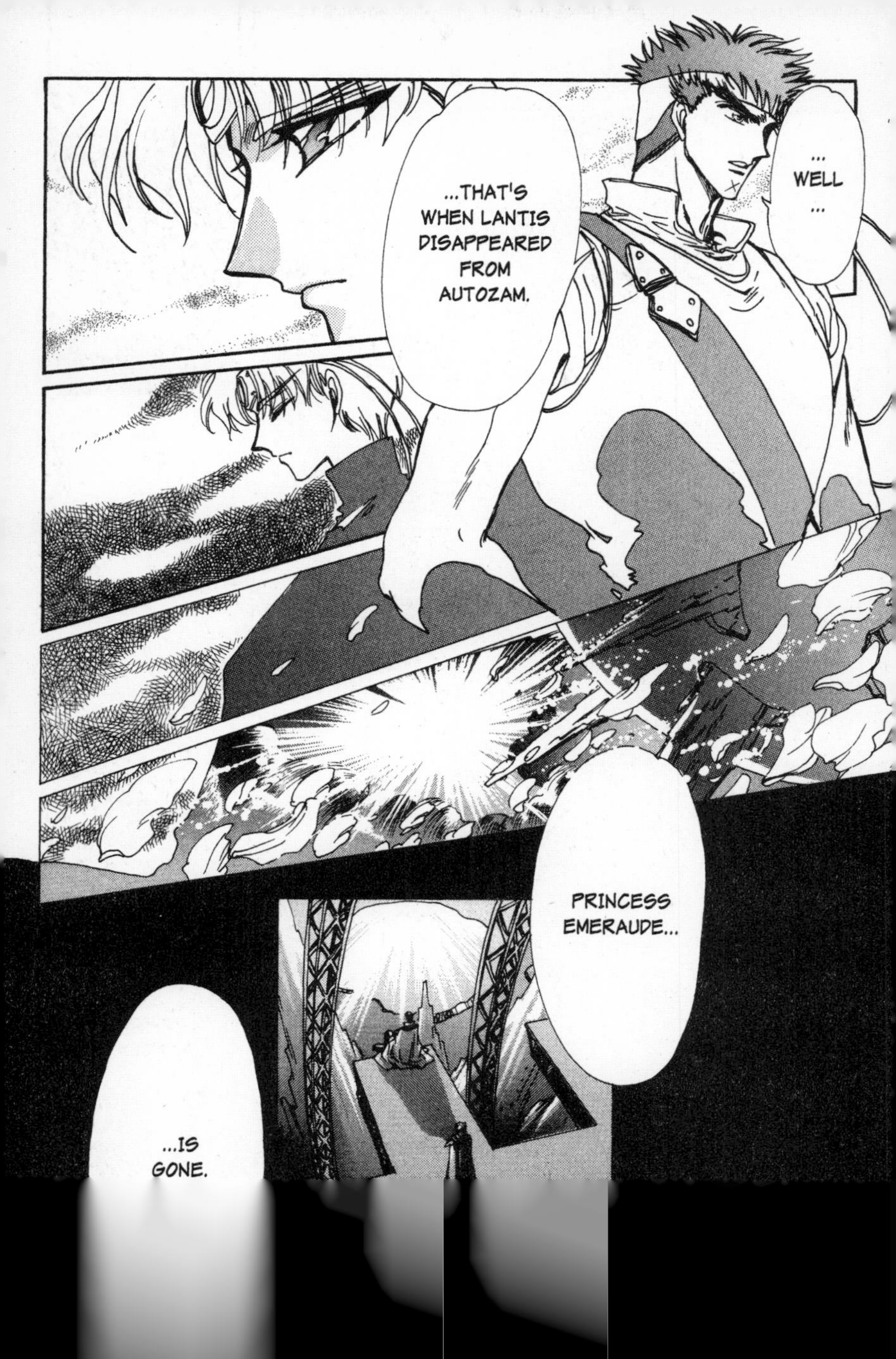
...WELL...
...THAT'S WHEN LANTIS DISAPPEARED FROM AUTOZAM.
PRINCESS EMERAUDE...
...IS GONE.

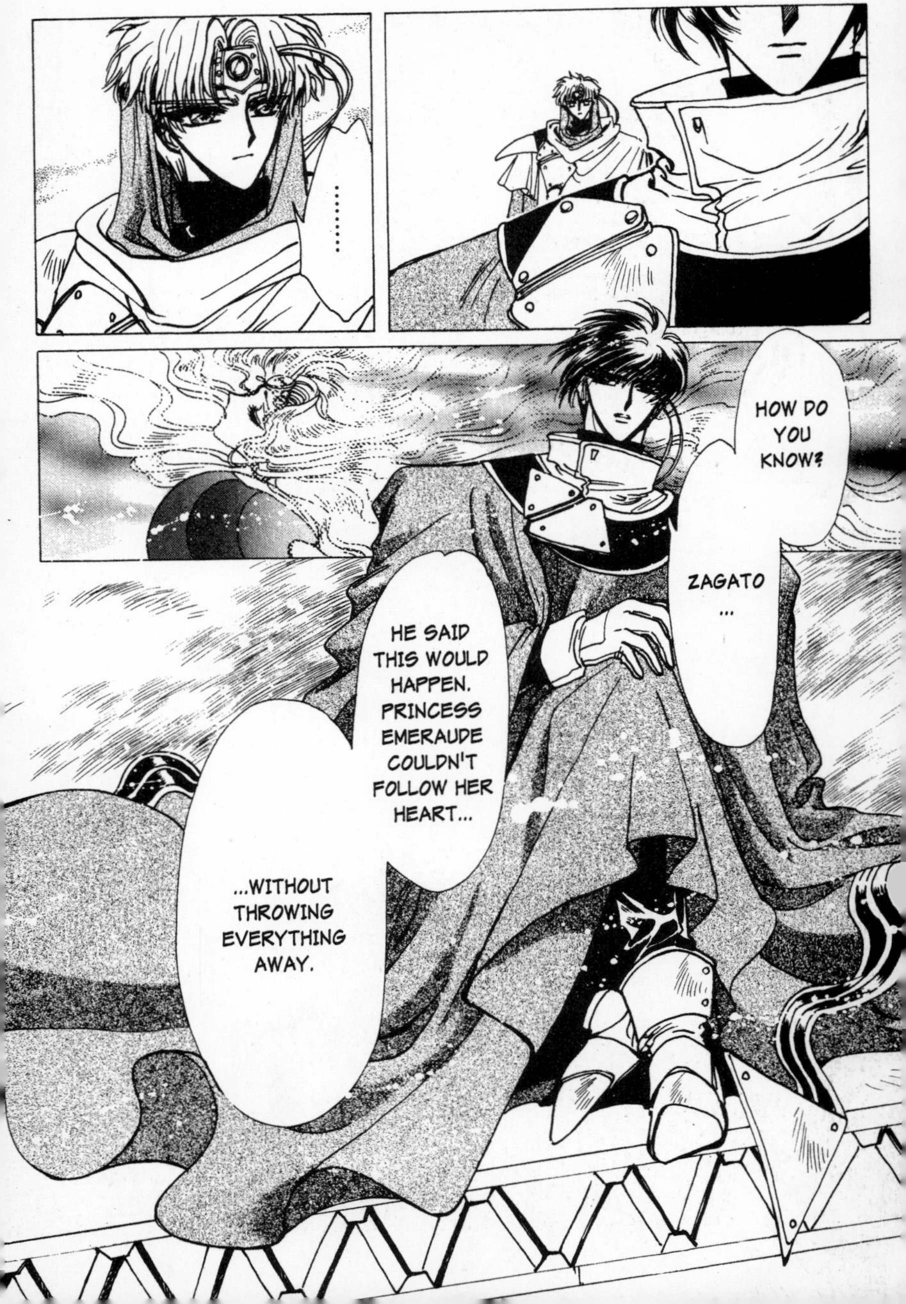
......
HOW DO YOU KNOW?
ZAGATO ...
HE SAID THIS WOULD HAPPEN. PRINCESS EMERAUDE COULDN'T FOLLOW HER HEART...
...WITHOUT THROWING EVERYTHING AWAY.

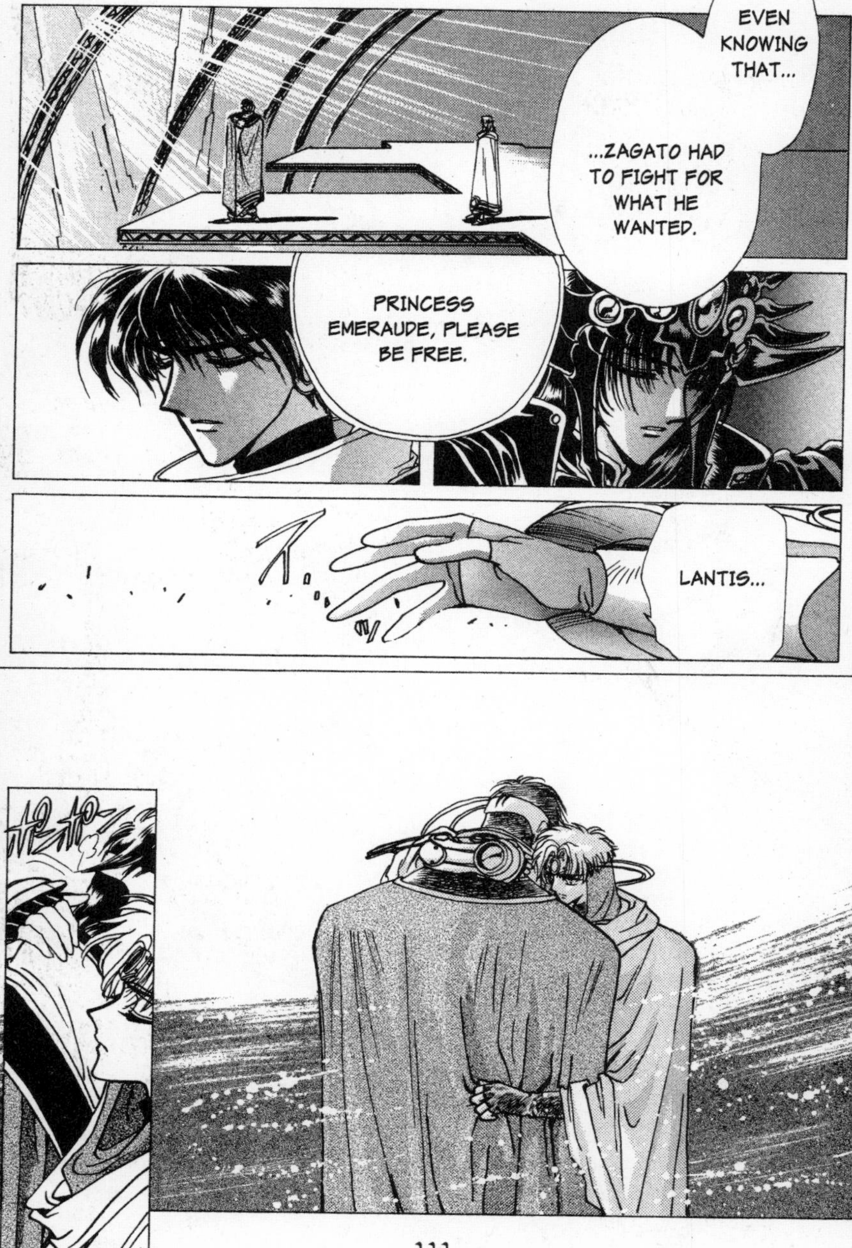
EVEN KNOWING THAT...
...ZAGATO HAD TO FIGHT FOR WHAT HE WANTED.
PRINCESS EMERAUDE, PLEASE BE FREE.
LANTIS...

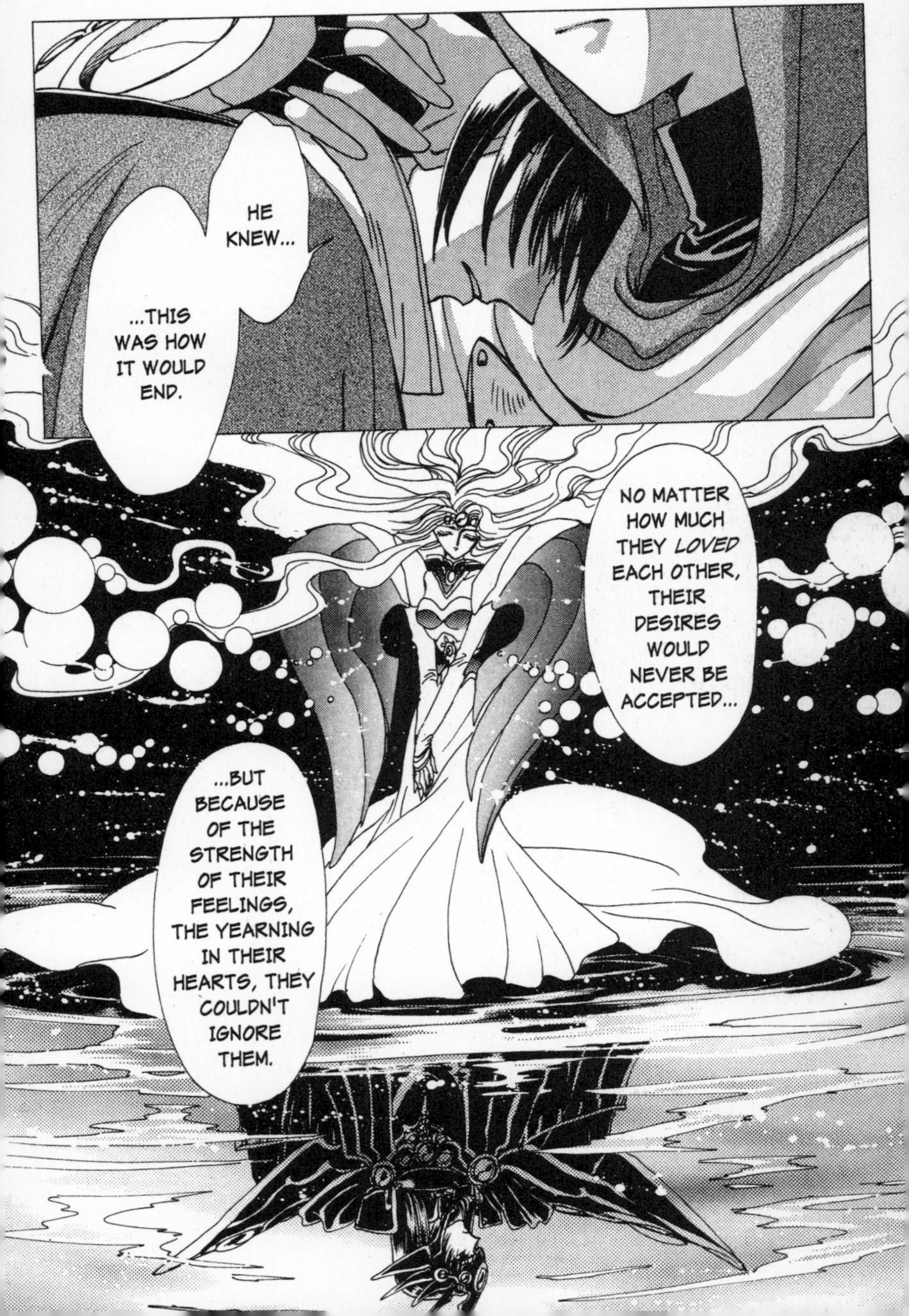
HE KNEW...
...THIS WAS HOW IT WOULD END.
NO MATTER HOW MUCH THEY *LOVED* EACH OTHER, THEIR DESIRES WOULD NEVER BE ACCEPTED...
...BUT BECAUSE OF THE STRENGTH OF THEIR FEELINGS, THE YEARNING IN THEIR HEARTS, THEY COULDN'T IGNORE THEM.

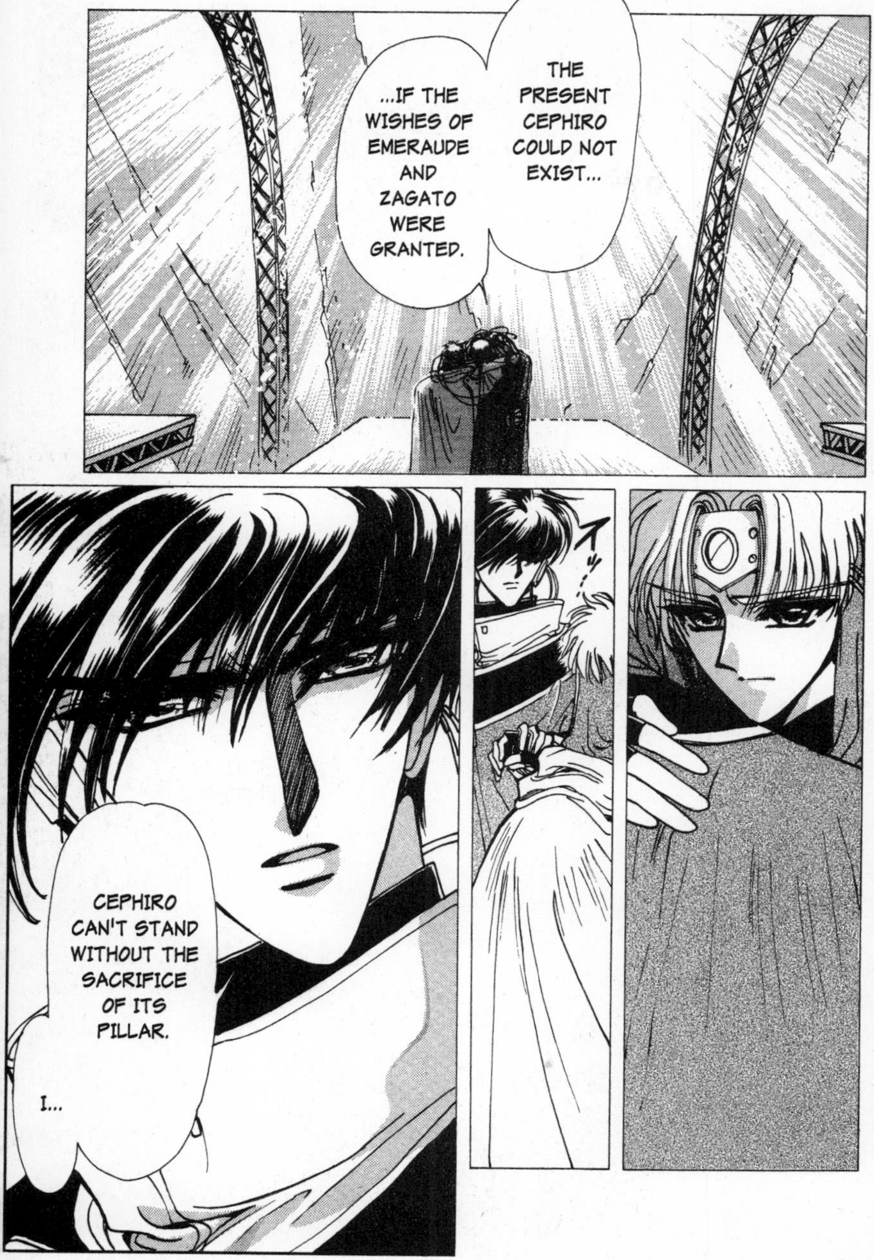
THE PRESENT CEPHIRO COULD NOT EXIST...
...IF THE WISHES OF EMERAUDE AND ZAGATO WERE GRANTED.
CEPHIRO CAN'T STAND WITHOUT THE SACRIFICE OF ITS PILLAR.
I...

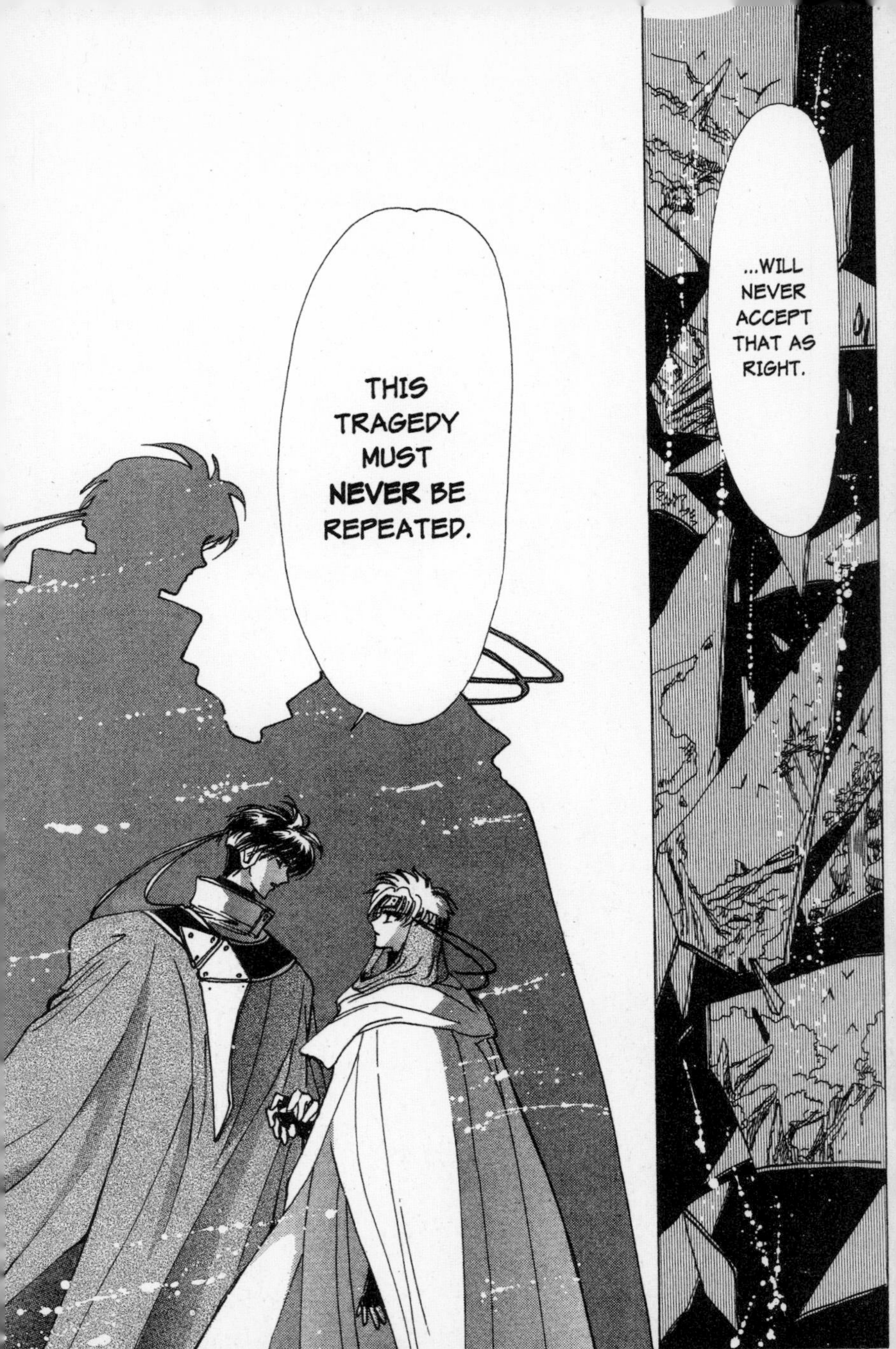
...WILL NEVER ACCEPT THAT AS RIGHT.
THIS TRAGEDY MUST **NEVER** BE REPEATED.

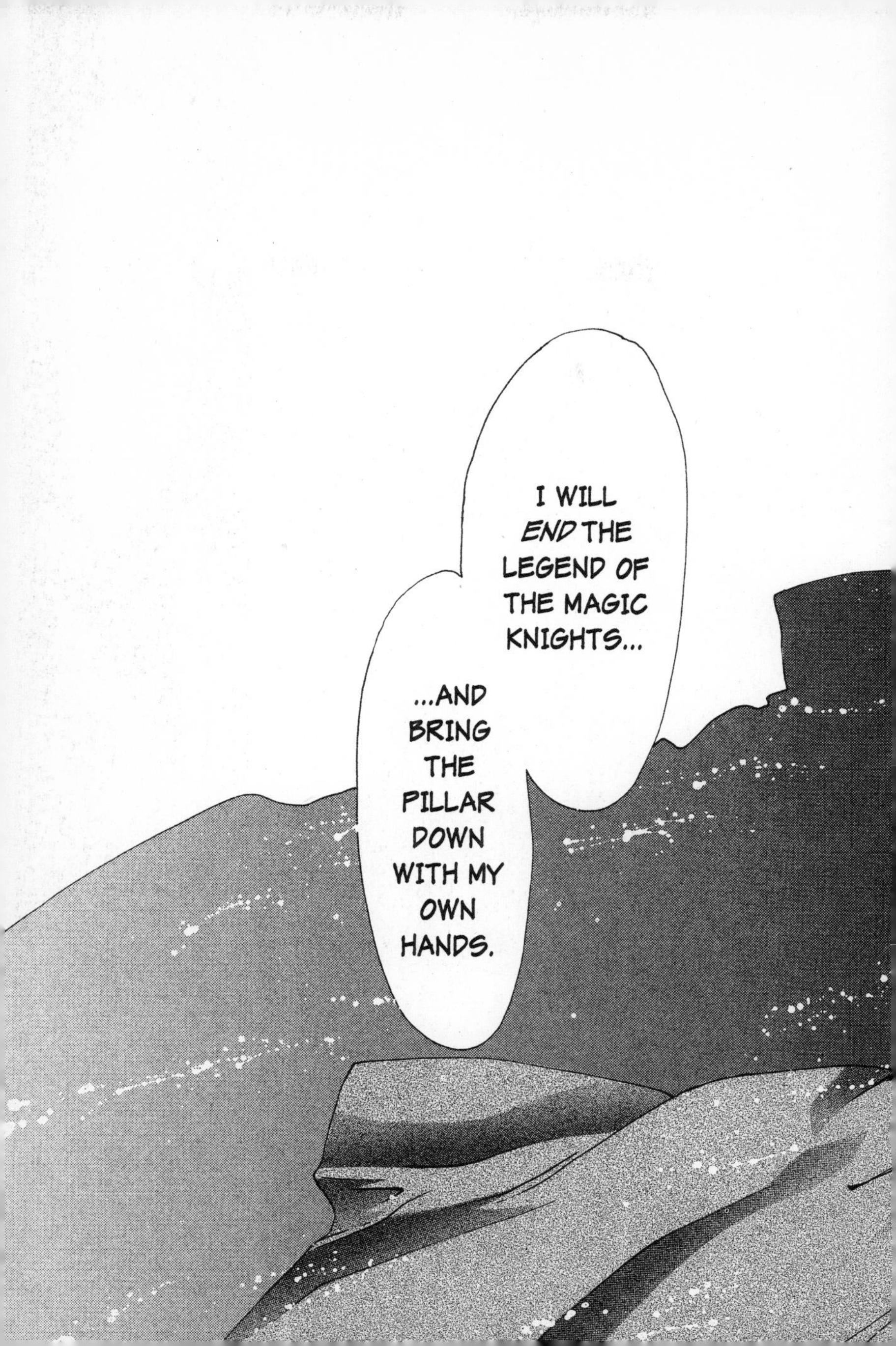
I WILL *END* THE LEGEND OF THE MAGIC KNIGHTS...
...AND BRING THE PILLAR DOWN WITH MY OWN HANDS.

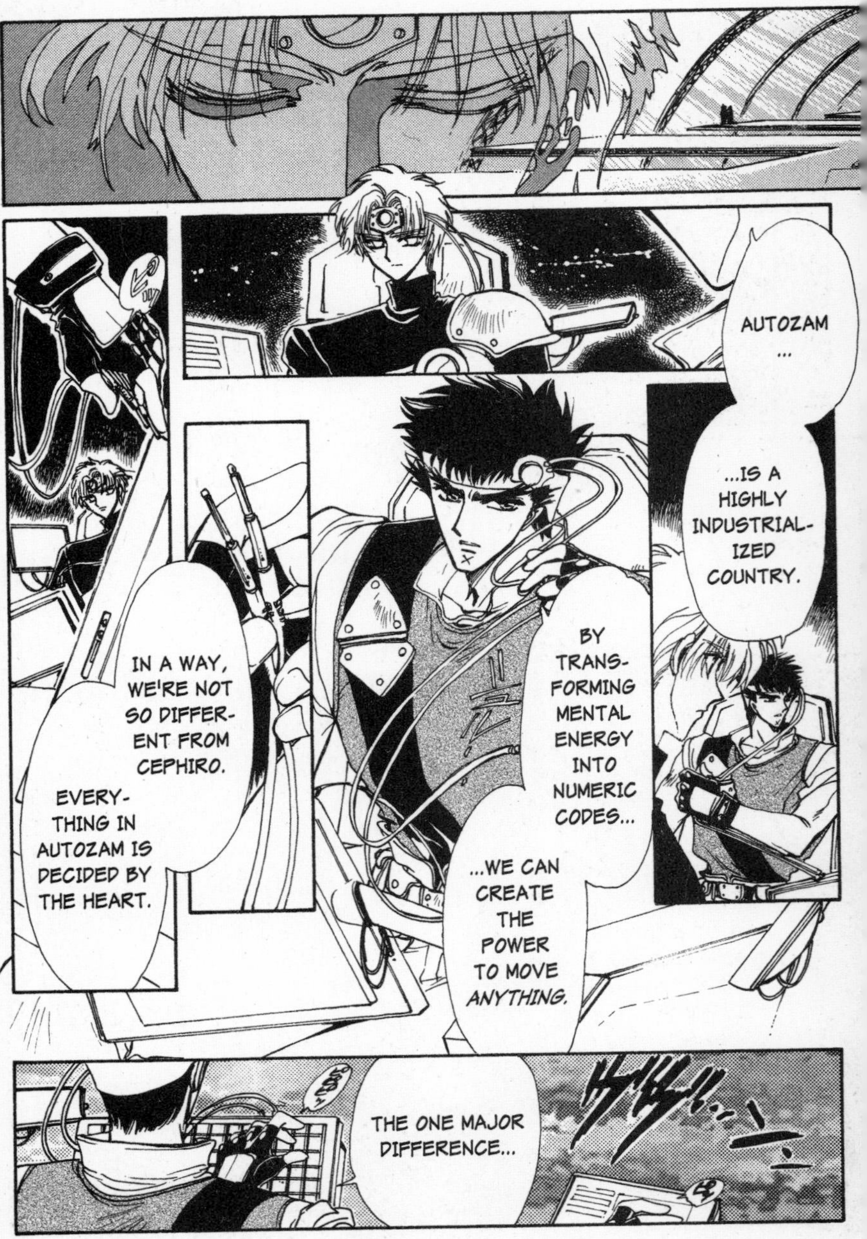
AUTOZAM ...
...IS A HIGHLY INDUSTRIAL-IZED COUNTRY.
BY TRANS-FORMING MENTAL ENERGY INTO NUMERIC CODES...
...WE CAN CREATE THE POWER TO MOVE *ANYTHING.*
IN A WAY, WE'RE NOT SO DIFFER-ENT FROM CEPHIRO.
EVERY-THING IN AUTOZAM IS DECIDED BY THE HEART.
THE ONE MAJOR DIFFERENCE...

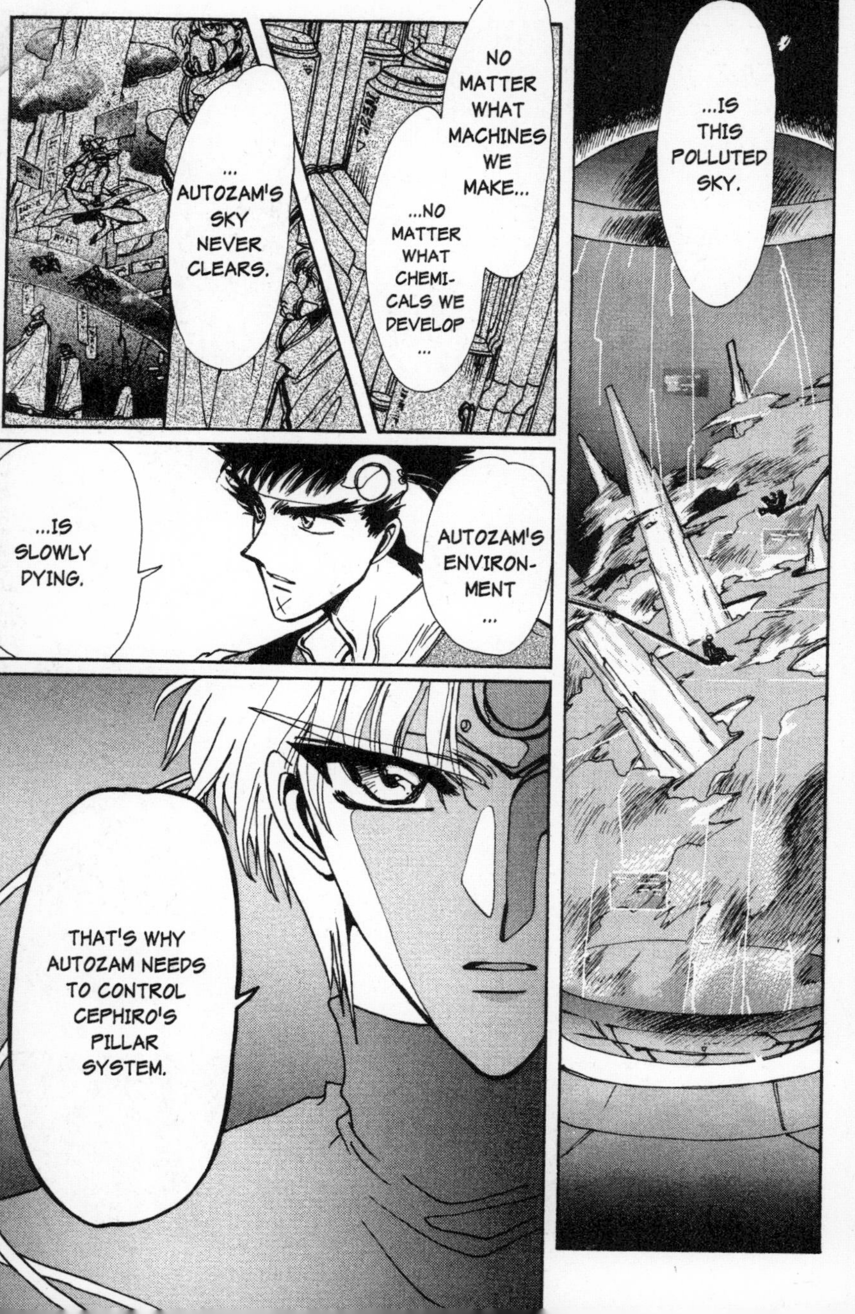
...IS THIS POLLUTED SKY.
NO MATTER WHAT MACHINES WE MAKE...
...NO MATTER WHAT CHEMI- CALS WE DEVELOP ...
... AUTOZAM'S SKY NEVER CLEARS.
AUTOZAM'S ENVIRON- MENT ...
...IS SLOWLY DYING.
THAT'S WHY AUTOZAM NEEDS TO CONTROL CEPHIRO'S PILLAR SYSTEM.

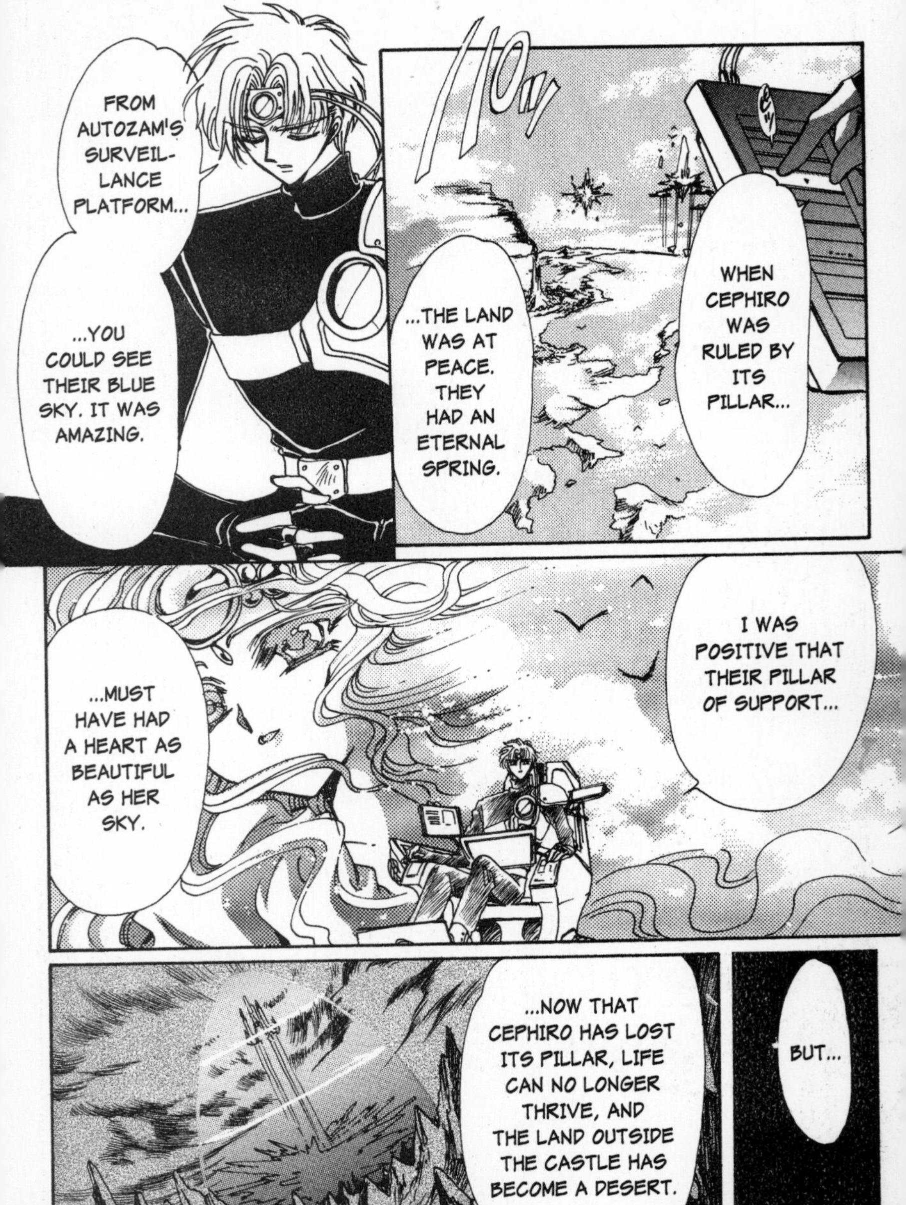
WHEN CEPHIRO WAS RULED BY ITS PILLAR...
...THE LAND WAS AT PEACE. THEY HAD AN ETERNAL SPRING.
FROM AUTOZAM'S SURVEIL-LANCE PLATFORM...
...YOU COULD SEE THEIR BLUE SKY. IT WAS AMAZING.
I WAS POSITIVE THAT THEIR PILLAR OF SUPPORT...
...MUST HAVE HAD A HEART AS BEAUTIFUL AS HER SKY.
BUT...
...NOW THAT CEPHIRO HAS LOST ITS PILLAR, LIFE CAN NO LONGER THRIVE, AND THE LAND OUTSIDE THE CASTLE HAS BECOME A DESERT.

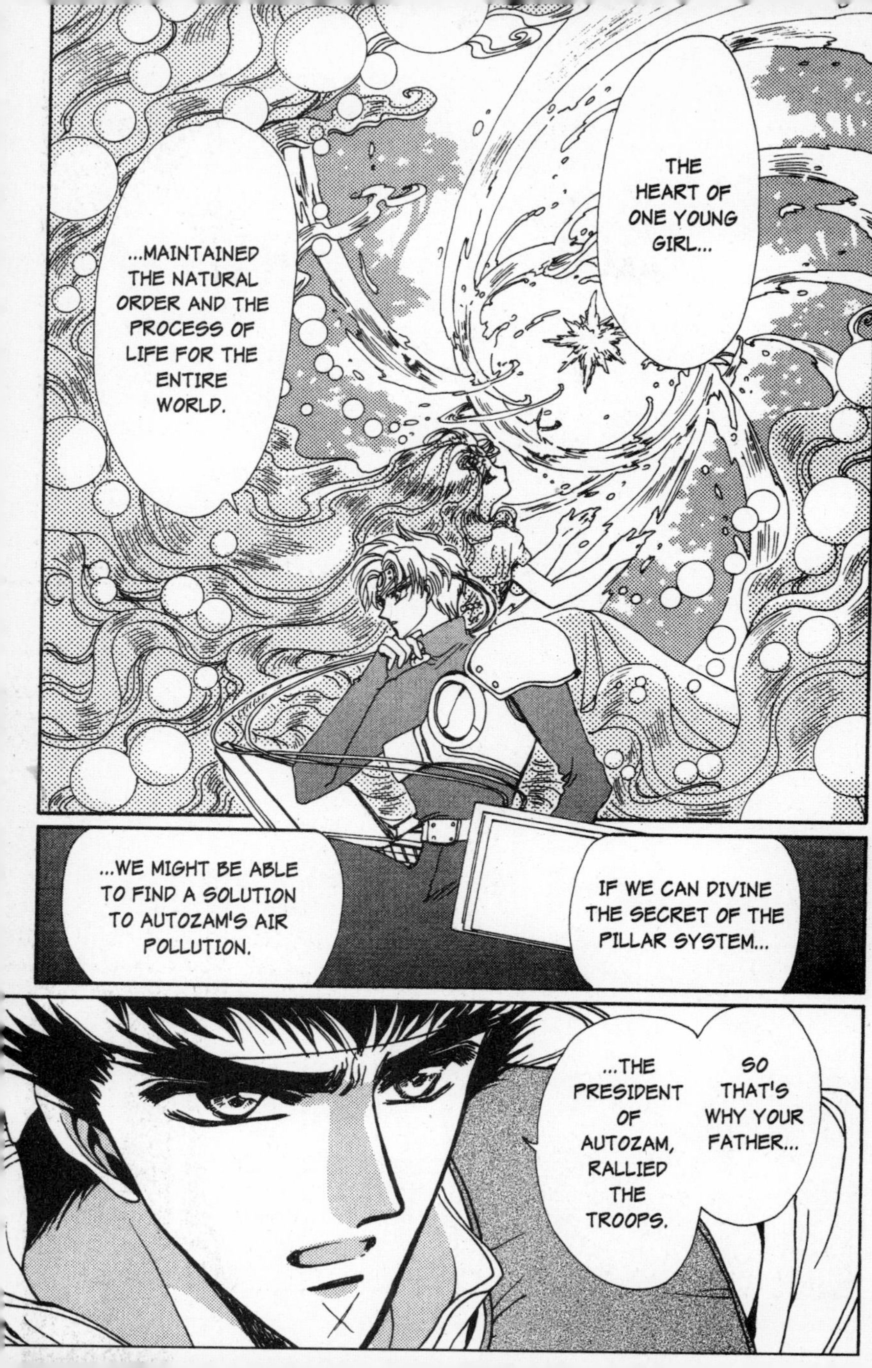
THE HEART OF ONE YOUNG GIRL...
...MAINTAINED THE NATURAL ORDER AND THE PROCESS OF LIFE FOR THE ENTIRE WORLD.
IF WE CAN DIVINE THE SECRET OF THE PILLAR SYSTEM...
...WE MIGHT BE ABLE TO FIND A SOLUTION TO AUTOZAM'S AIR POLLUTION.
SO THAT'S WHY YOUR FATHER...
...THE PRESIDENT OF AUTOZAM, RALLIED THE TROOPS.

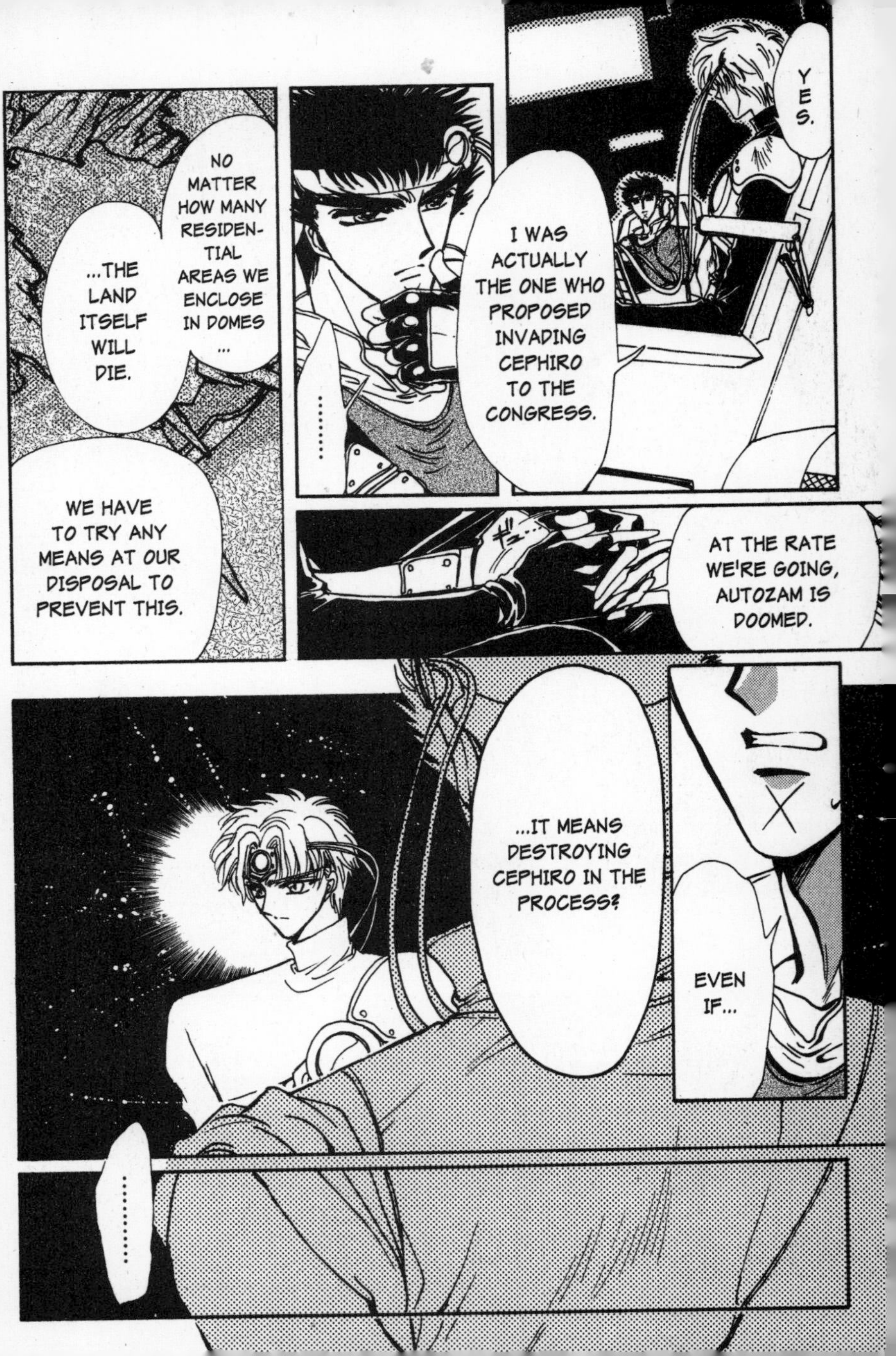
YES.
I WAS ACTUALLY THE ONE WHO PROPOSED INVADING CEPHIRO TO THE CONGRESS.
......
AT THE RATE WE'RE GOING, AUTOZAM IS DOOMED.
NO MATTER HOW MANY RESIDEN-TIAL AREAS WE ENCLOSE IN DOMES ...
...THE LAND ITSELF WILL DIE.
WE HAVE TO TRY ANY MEANS AT OUR DISPOSAL TO PREVENT THIS.
EVEN IF...
...IT MEANS DESTROYING CEPHIRO IN THE PROCESS?
......

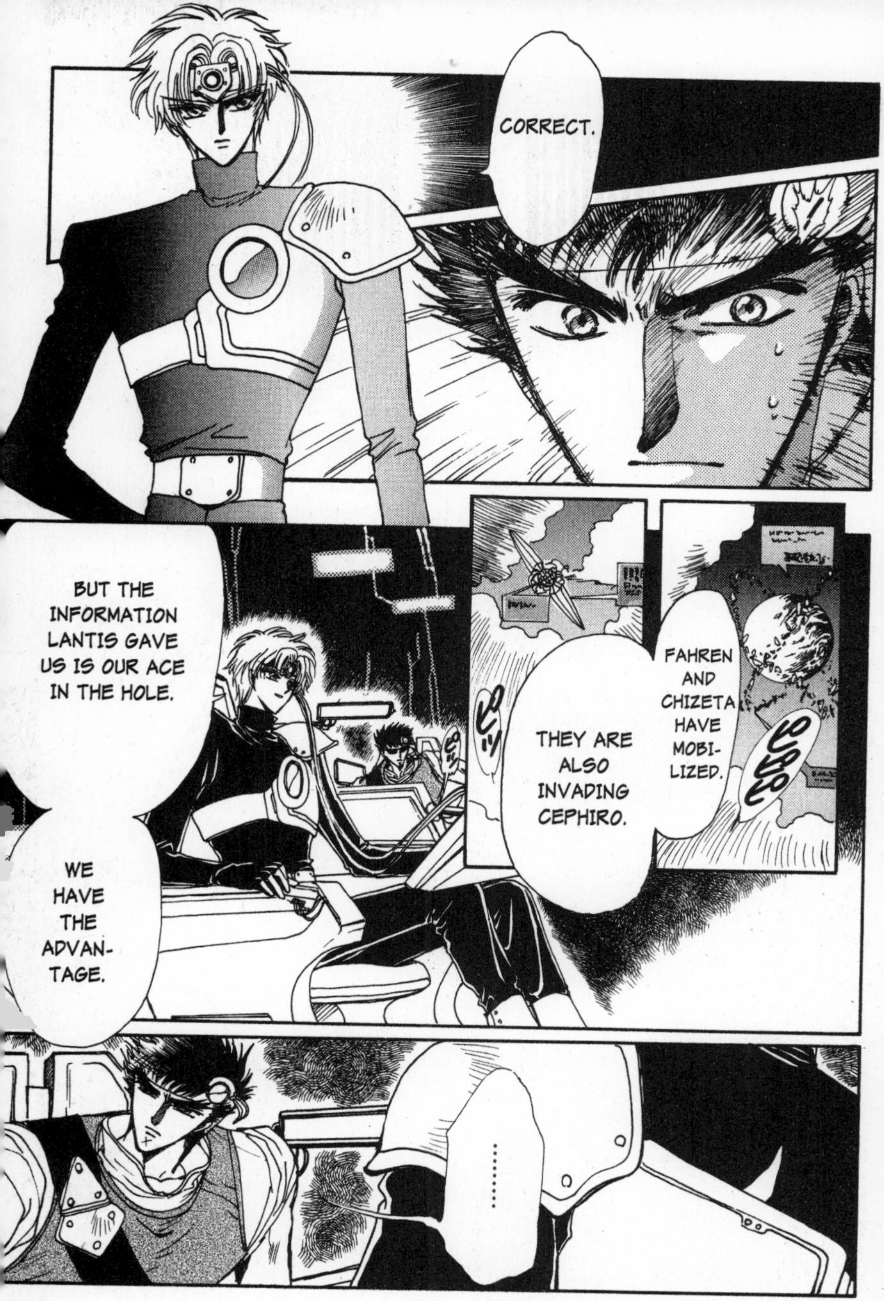
CORRECT.
FAHREN AND CHIZETA HAVE MOBILIZED.
THEY ARE ALSO INVADING CEPHIRO.
ピッ
BUT THE INFORMATION LANTIS GAVE US IS OUR ACE IN THE HOLE.
WE HAVE THE ADVANTAGE.
......

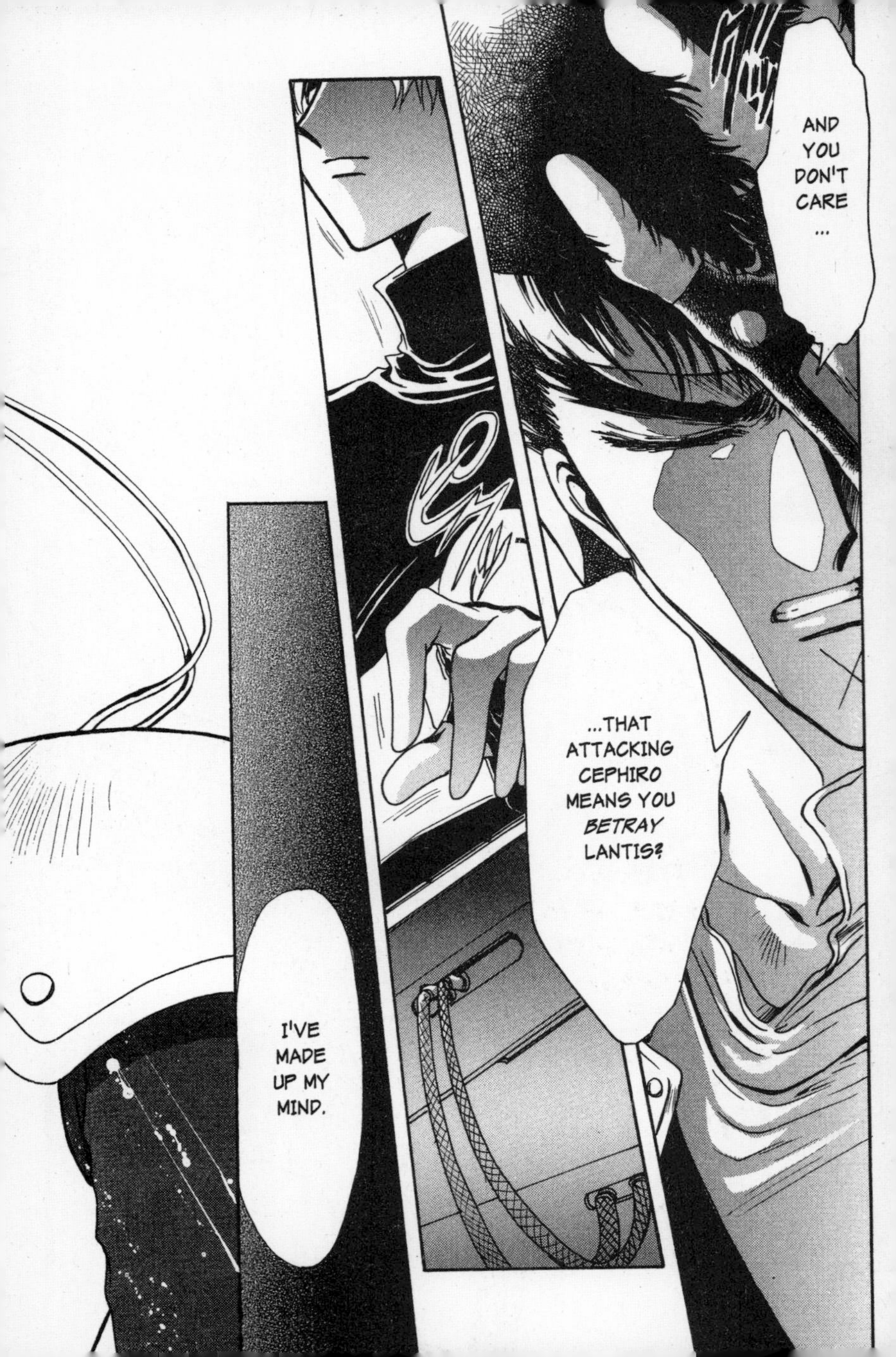
AND YOU DON'T CARE ...
...THAT ATTACKING CEPHIRO MEANS YOU *BETRAY* LANTIS?
I'VE MADE UP MY MIND.

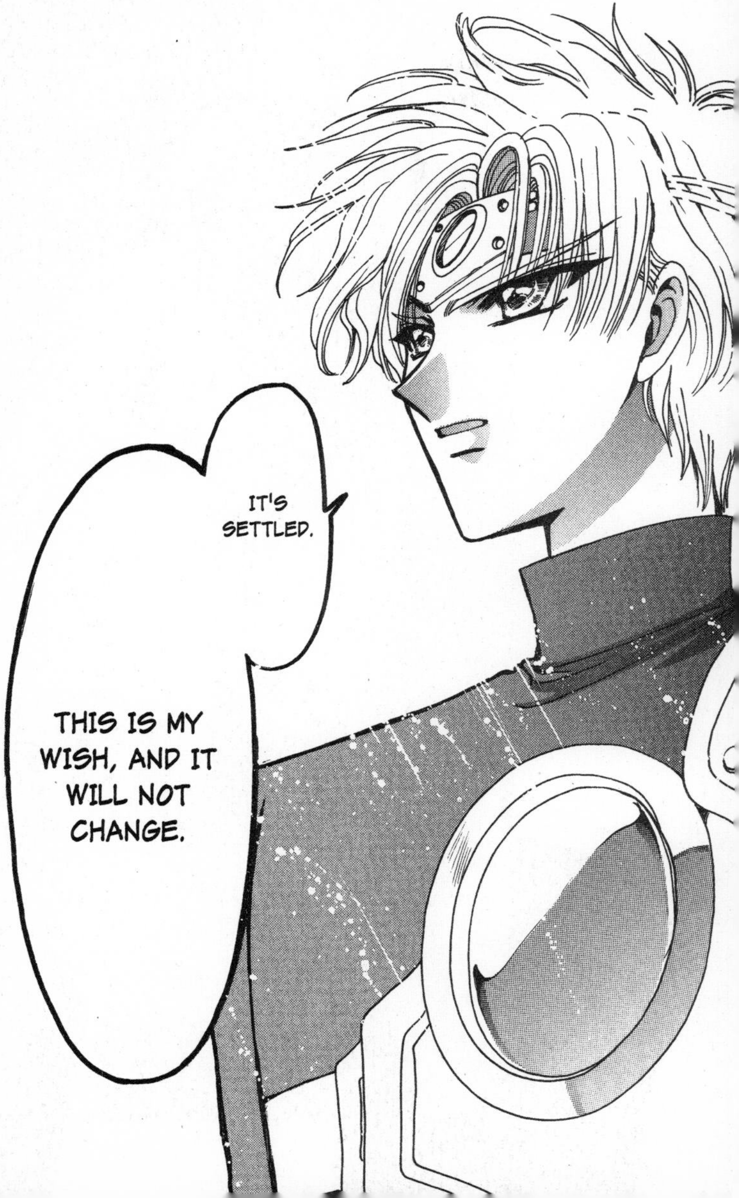
IT'S SETTLED.
THIS IS MY WISH, AND IT WILL NOT CHANGE.

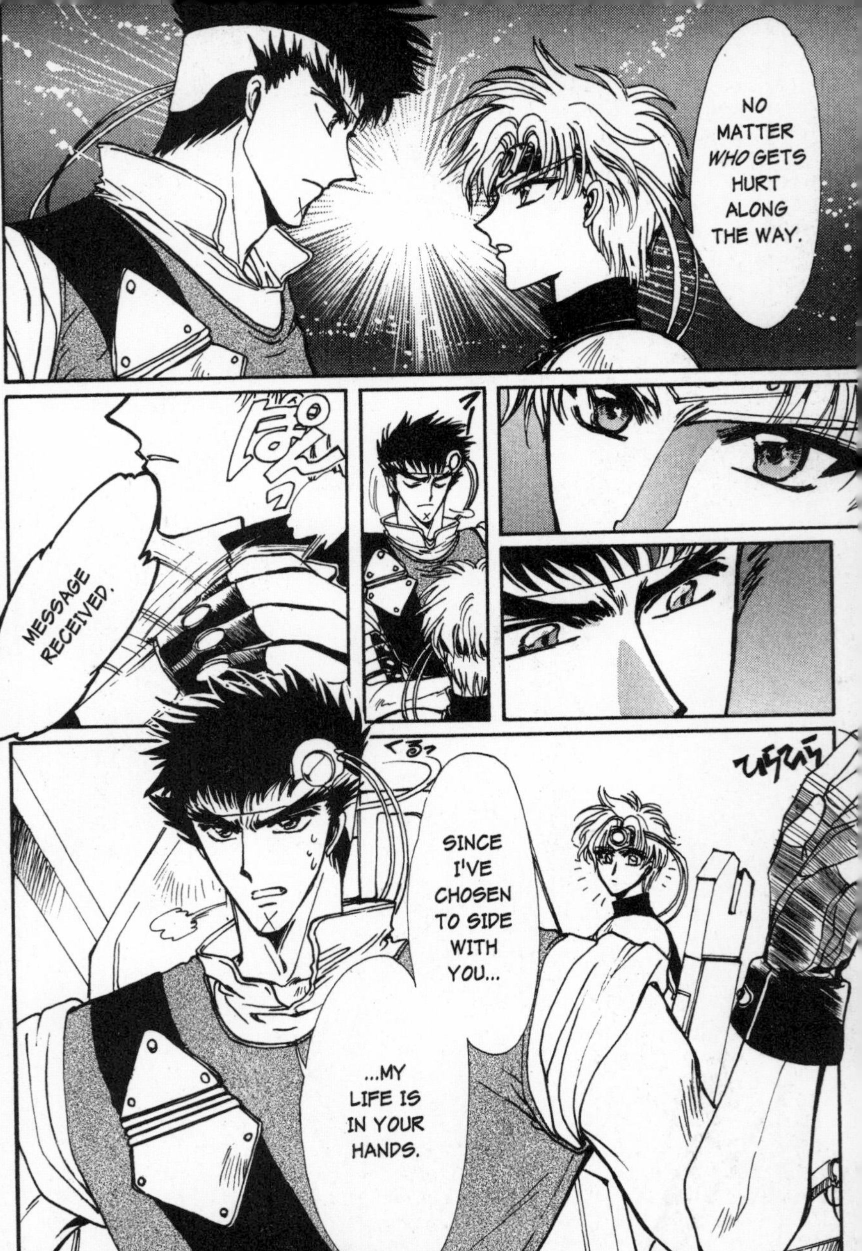
NO MATTER *WHO* GETS HURT ALONG THE WAY.
MESSAGE RECEIVED.
ひらひら
くるっ
SINCE I'VE CHOSEN TO SIDE WITH YOU...
...MY LIFE IS IN YOUR HANDS.

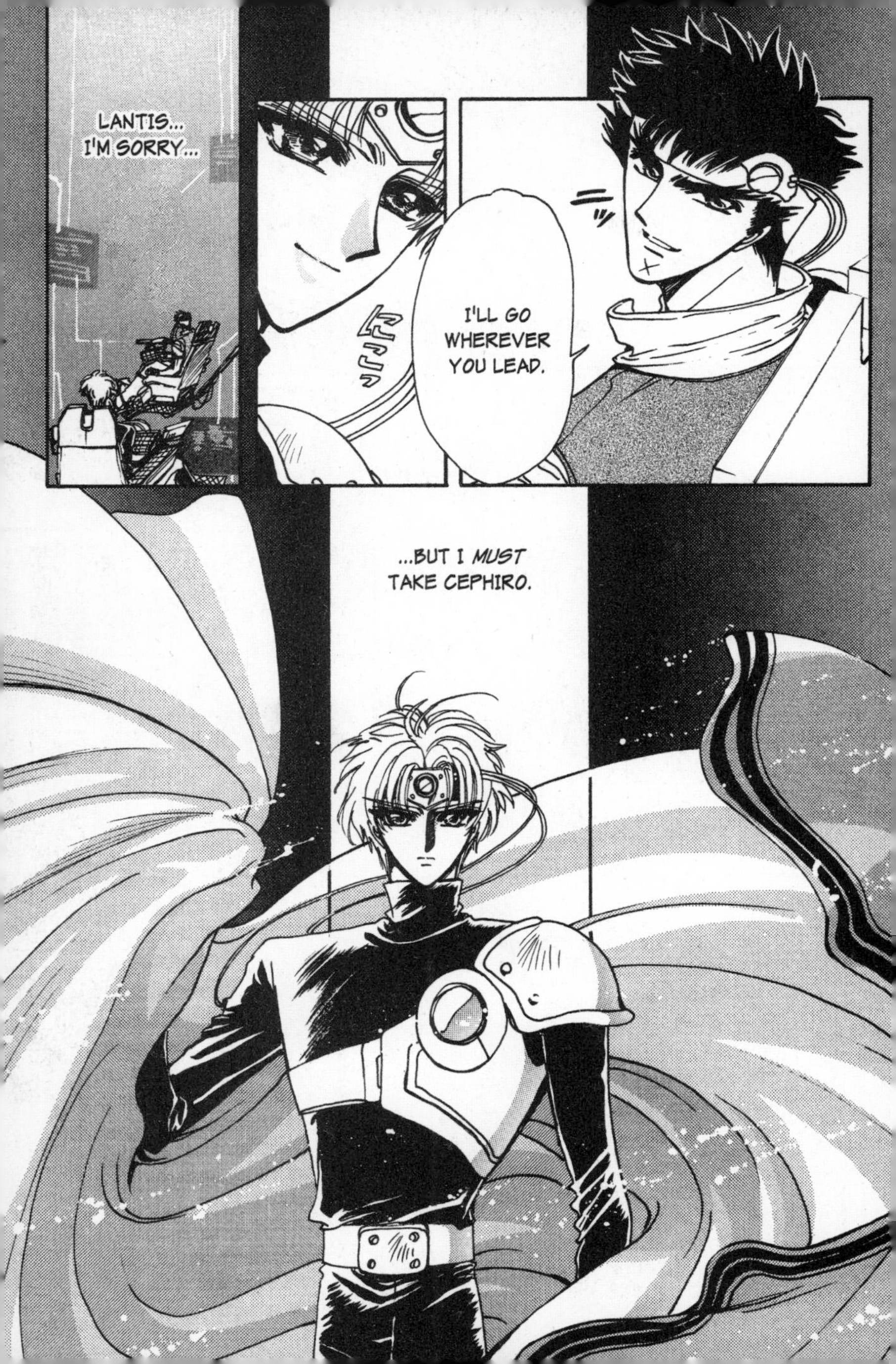
I'LL GO WHEREVER YOU LEAD.
LANTIS... I'M SORRY...
...BUT I *MUST* TAKE CEPHIRO.

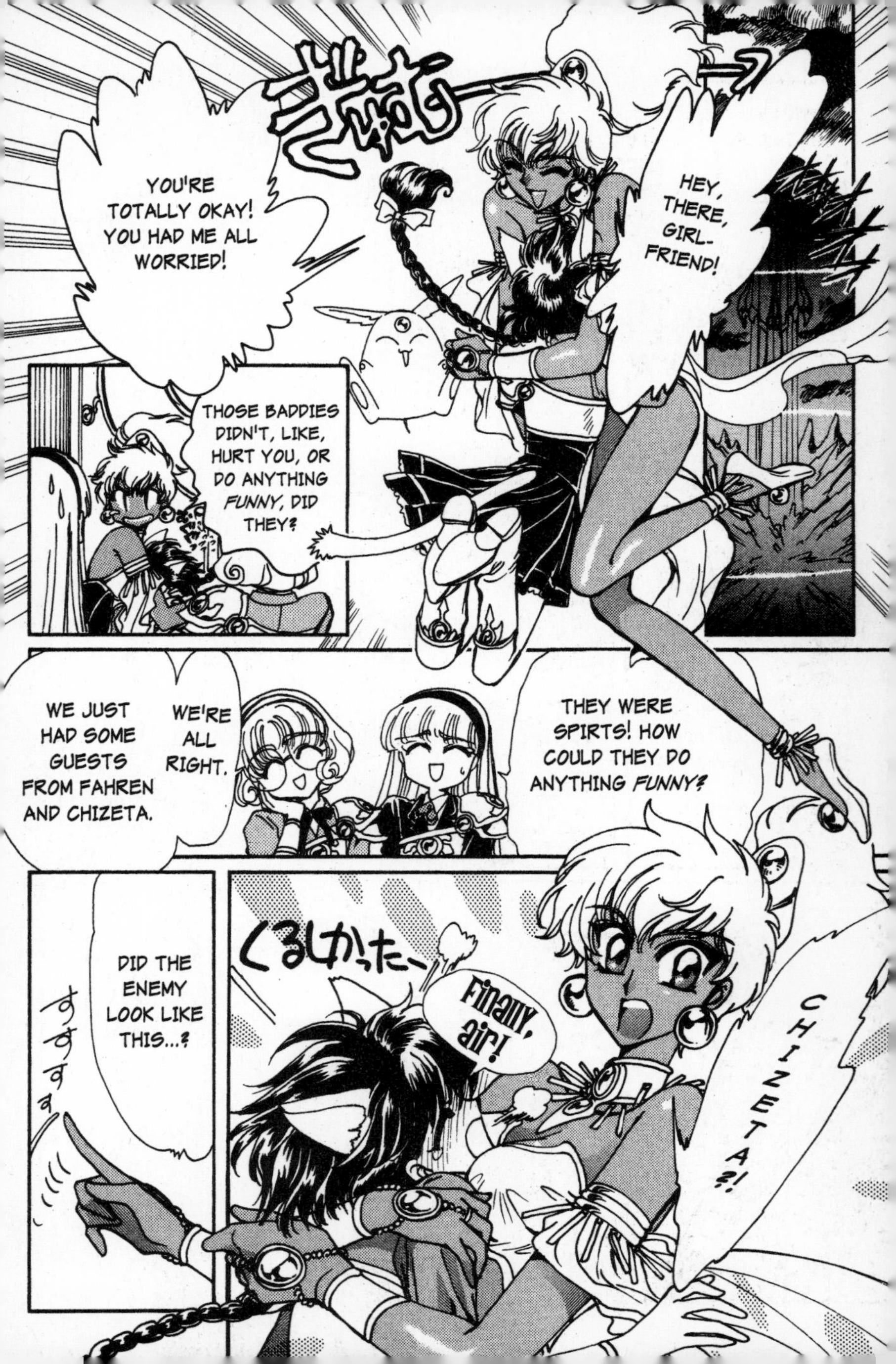
HEY, THERE, GIRL-FRIEND!
YOU'RE TOTALLY OKAY! YOU HAD ME ALL WORRIED!
THOSE BADDIES DIDN'T, LIKE, HURT YOU, OR DO ANYTHING *FUNNY*, DID THEY?
THEY WERE SPIRTS! HOW COULD THEY DO ANYTHING *FUNNY*?
WE'RE ALL RIGHT.
WE JUST HAD SOME GUESTS FROM FAHREN AND CHIZETA.
CHIZETA?!
Finally, air!
くるしかった～
DID THE ENEMY LOOK LIKE THIS...?
すすす

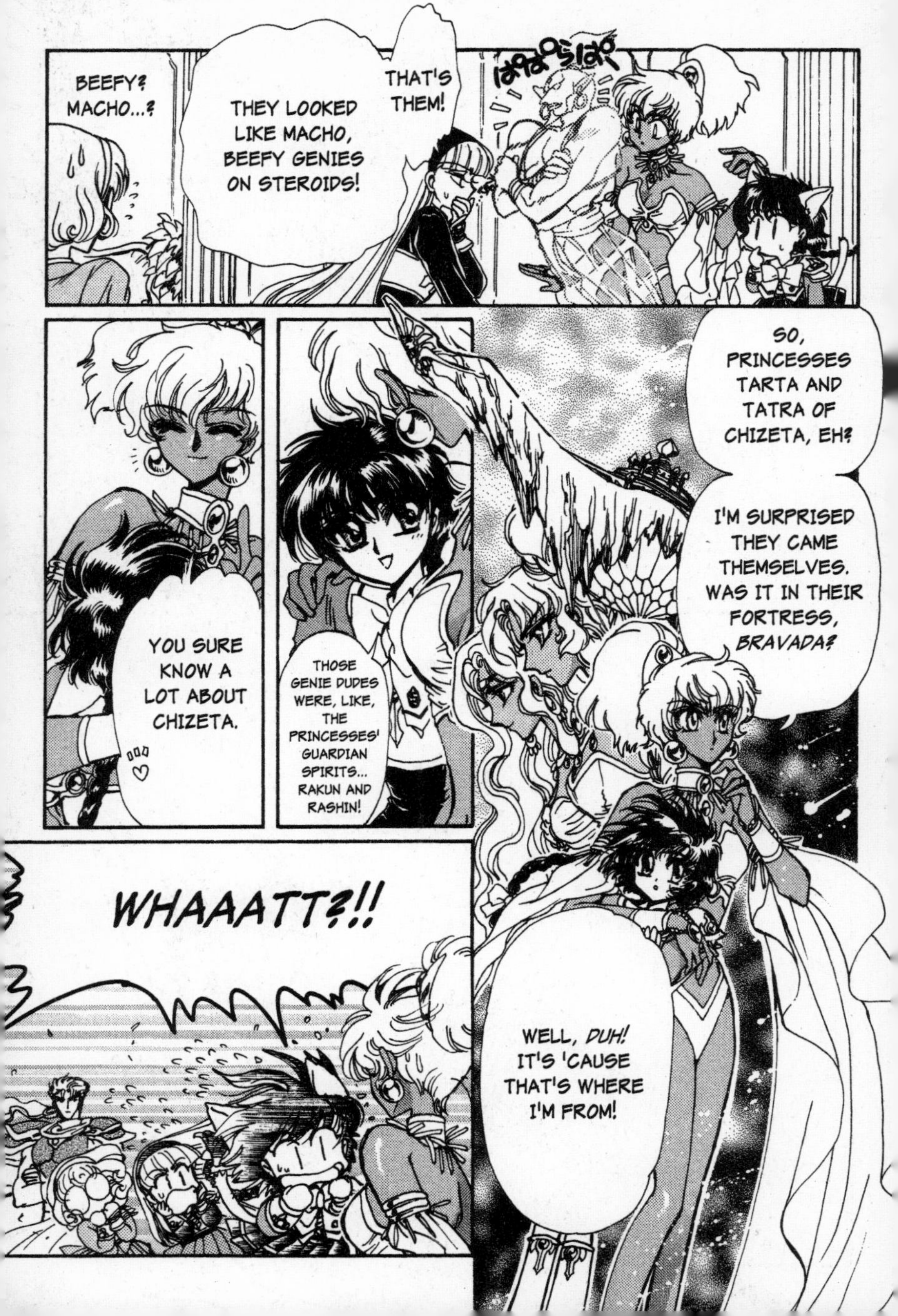
THAT'S THEM!
THEY LOOKED LIKE MACHO, BEEFY GENIES ON STEROIDS!
BEEFY? MACHO...?
SO, PRINCESSES TARTA AND TATRA OF CHIZETA, EH?
I'M SURPRISED THEY CAME THEMSELVES. WAS IT IN THEIR FORTRESS, *BRAVADA*?
WELL, *DUH!* IT'S 'CAUSE THAT'S WHERE I'M FROM!
THOSE GENIE DUDES WERE, LIKE, THE PRINCESSES' GUARDIAN SPIRITS... RAKUN AND RASHIN!
YOU SURE KNOW A LOT ABOUT CHIZETA.
WHAAATT?!!

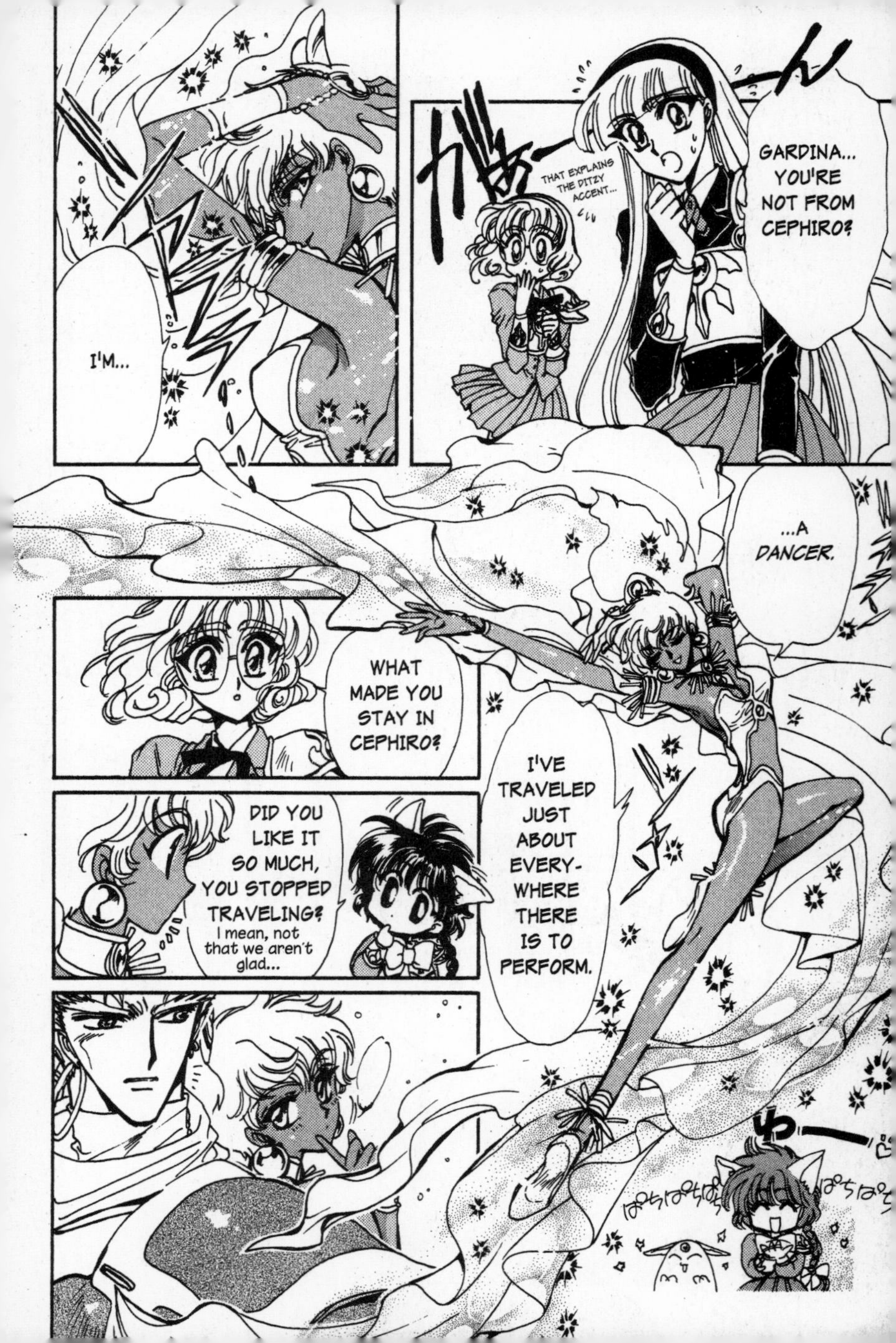
GARDINA... YOU'RE NOT FROM CEPHIRO?
THAT EXPLAINS THE DITZY ACCENT...
I'M...
...A DANCER.
I'VE TRAVELED JUST ABOUT EVERY-WHERE THERE IS TO PERFORM.
WHAT MADE YOU STAY IN CEPHIRO?
DID YOU LIKE IT SO MUCH, YOU STOPPED TRAVELING?
I mean, not that we aren't glad...
ぱちぱちぱち

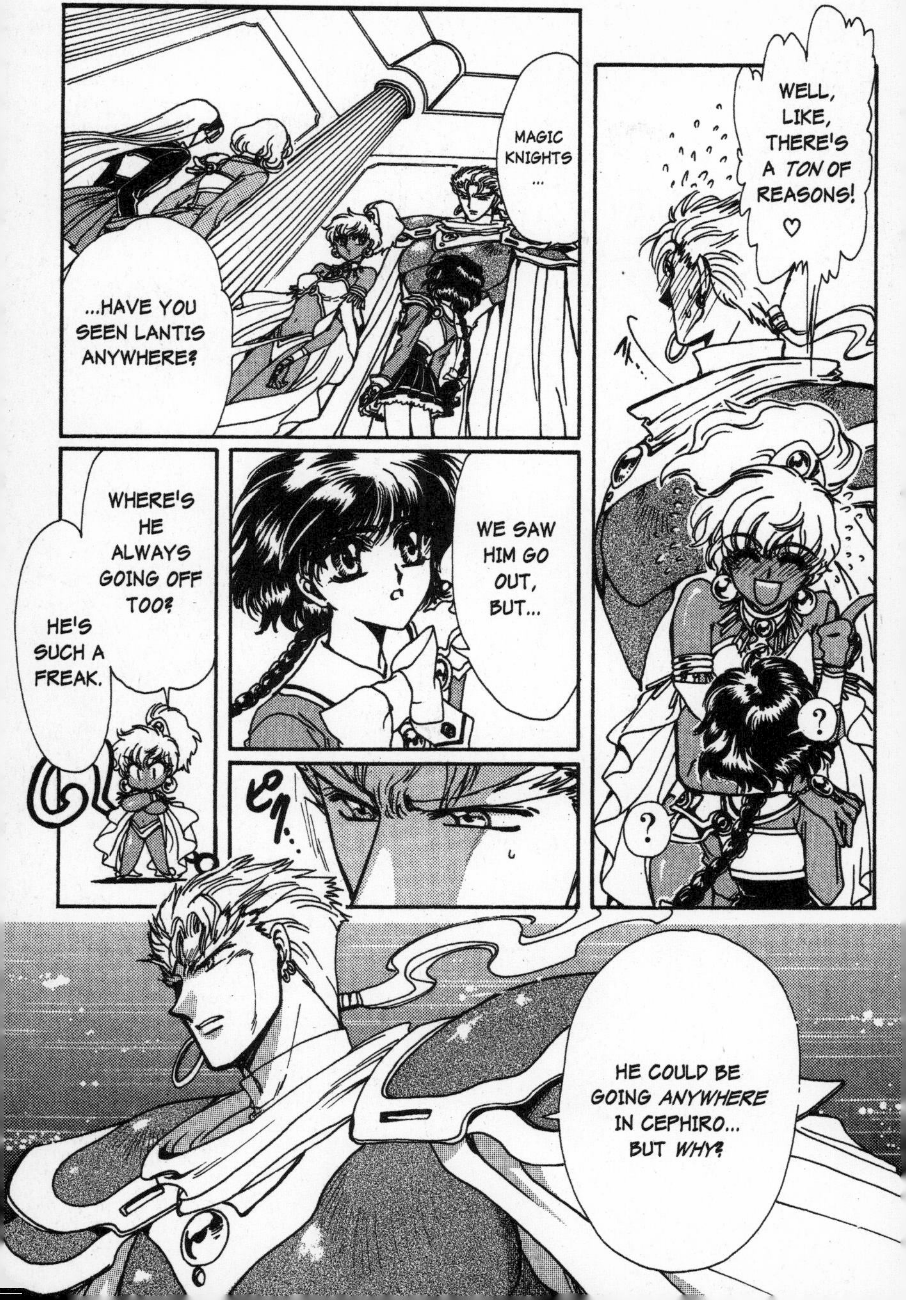

MAGIC KNIGHTS ...
...HAVE YOU SEEN LANTIS ANYWHERE?
WE SAW HIM GO OUT, BUT...
WHERE'S HE ALWAYS GOING OFF TOO?
HE'S SUCH A FREAK.
WELL, LIKE, THERE'S A *TON* OF REASONS! ♡
?
?
HE COULD BE GOING *ANYWHERE* IN CEPHIRO... BUT *WHY*?

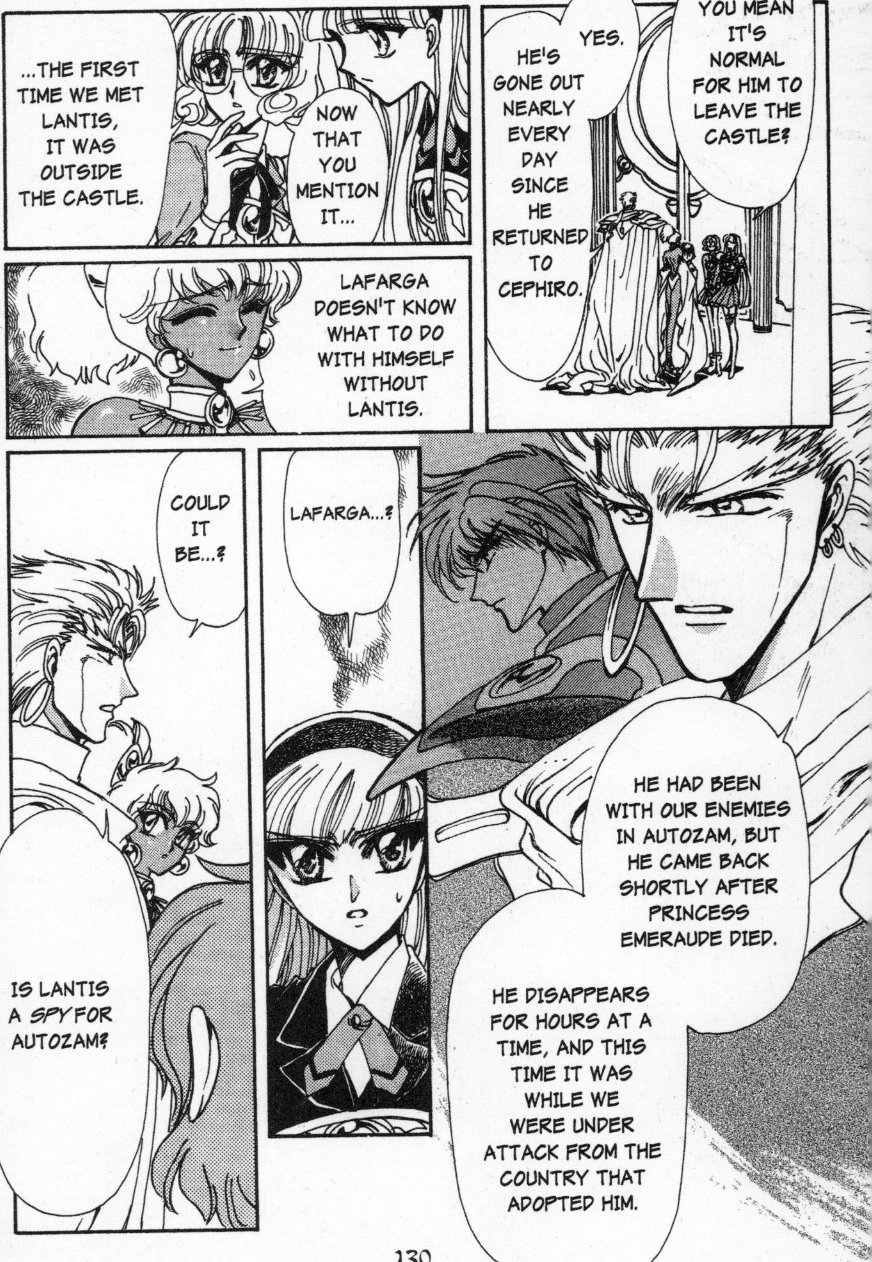
YOU MEAN IT'S NORMAL FOR HIM TO LEAVE THE CASTLE?
YES.
HE'S GONE OUT NEARLY EVERY DAY SINCE HE RETURNED TO CEPHIRO.
NOW THAT YOU MENTION IT...
...THE FIRST TIME WE MET LANTIS, IT WAS OUTSIDE THE CASTLE.
LAFARGA DOESN'T KNOW WHAT TO DO WITH HIMSELF WITHOUT LANTIS.
HE HAD BEEN WITH OUR ENEMIES IN AUTOZAM, BUT HE CAME BACK SHORTLY AFTER PRINCESS EMERAUDE DIED.
HE DISAPPEARS FOR HOURS AT A TIME, AND THIS TIME IT WAS WHILE WE WERE UNDER ATTACK FROM THE COUNTRY THAT ADOPTED HIM.
LAFARGA...?
COULD IT BE...?
IS LANTIS A *SPY* FOR AUTOZAM?

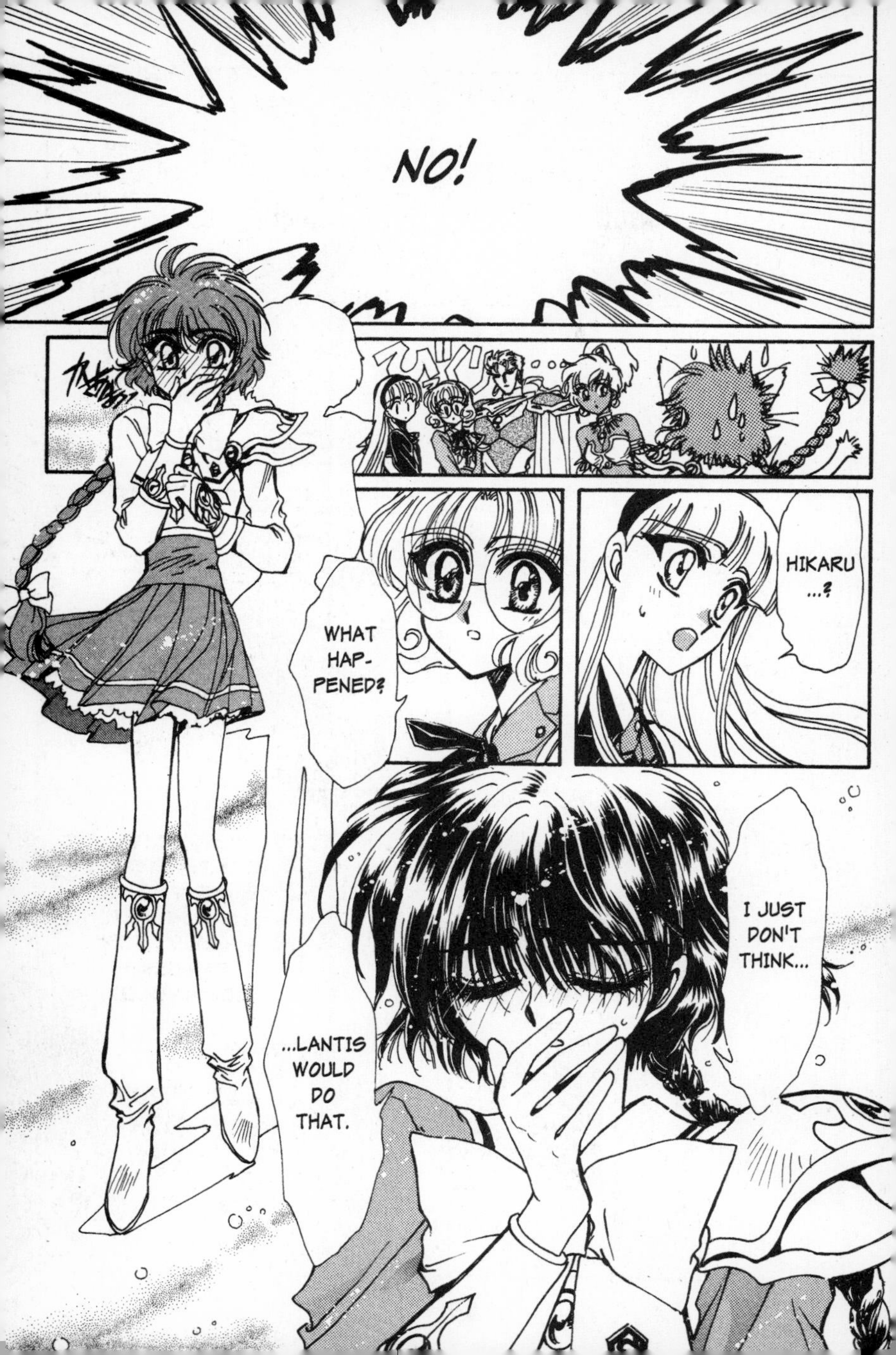
NO!
HIKARU ...?
WHAT HAPPENED?
I JUST DON'T THINK...
...LANTIS WOULD DO THAT.

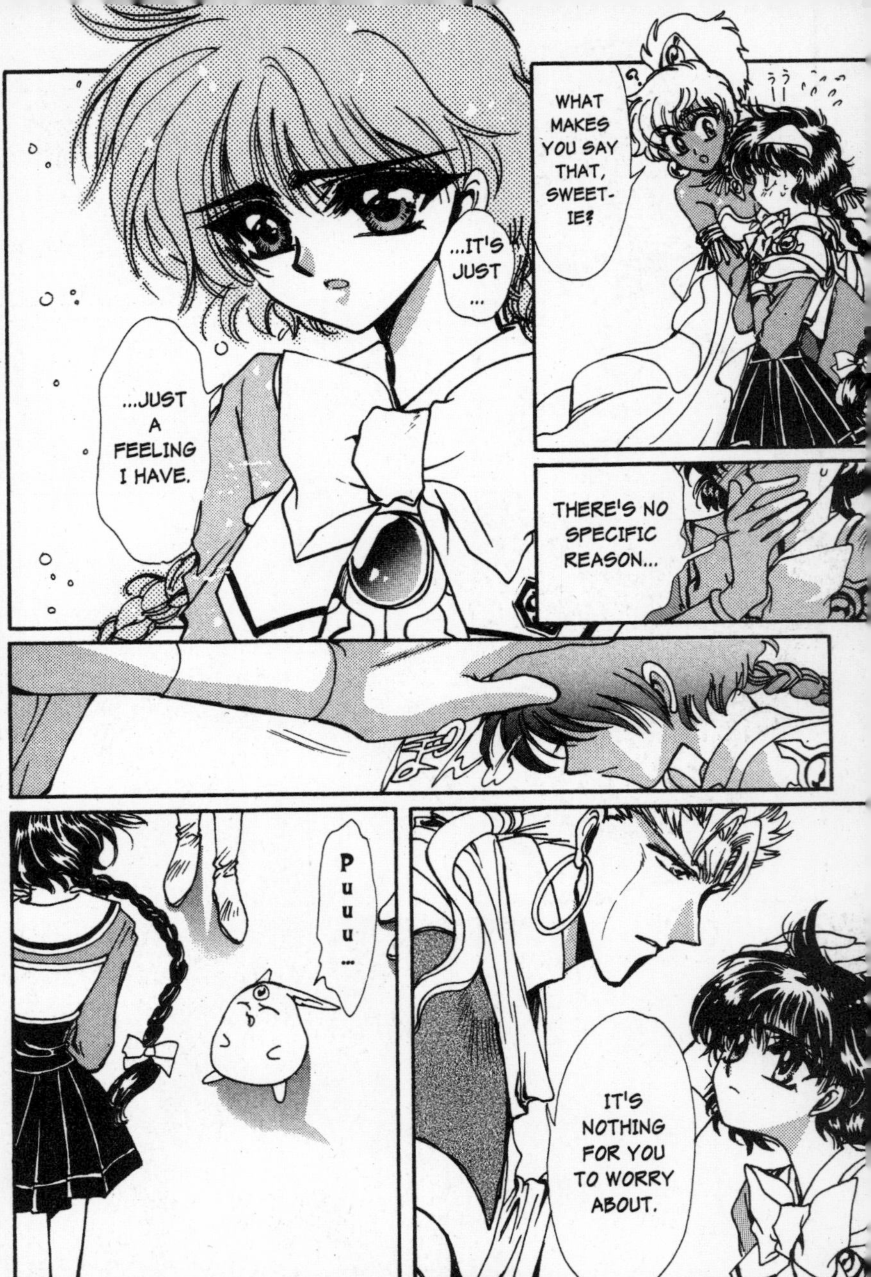
WHAT MAKES YOU SAY THAT, SWEET-IE?
THERE'S NO SPECIFIC REASON...
...IT'S JUST ...
...JUST A FEELING I HAVE.
IT'S NOTHING FOR YOU TO WORRY ABOUT.
Puuu...

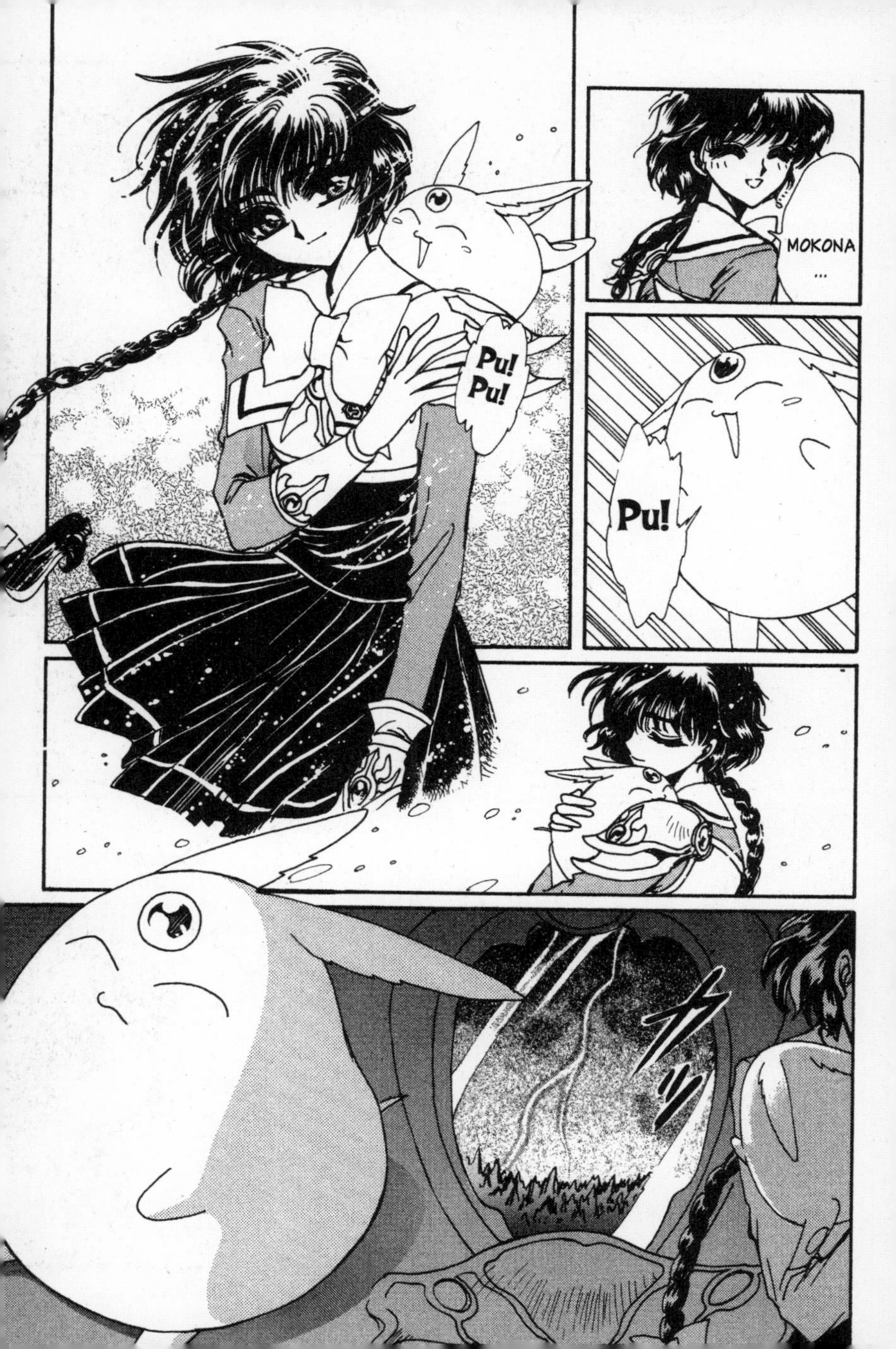
MOKONA ...
Pu!
Pu! Pu!

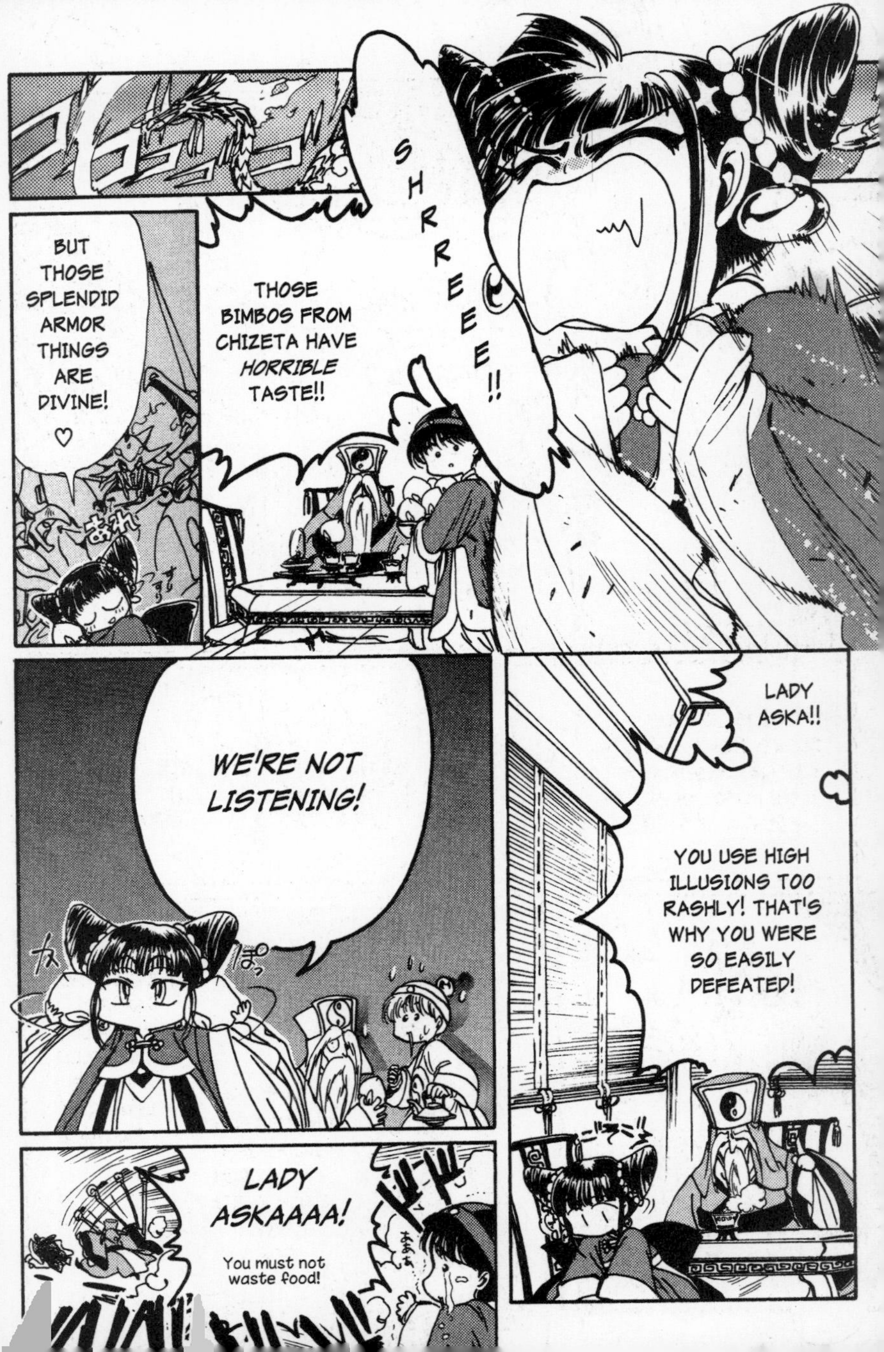
SHRREEEE!!
THOSE BIMBOS FROM CHIZETA HAVE *HORRIBLE* TASTE!!
BUT THOSE SPLENDID ARMOR THINGS ARE DIVINE! ♡
LADY ASKA!!
YOU USE HIGH ILLUSIONS TOO RASHLY! THAT'S WHY YOU WERE SO EASILY DEFEATED!
WE'RE NOT LISTENING!
LADY ASKAAAA!
You must not waste food!

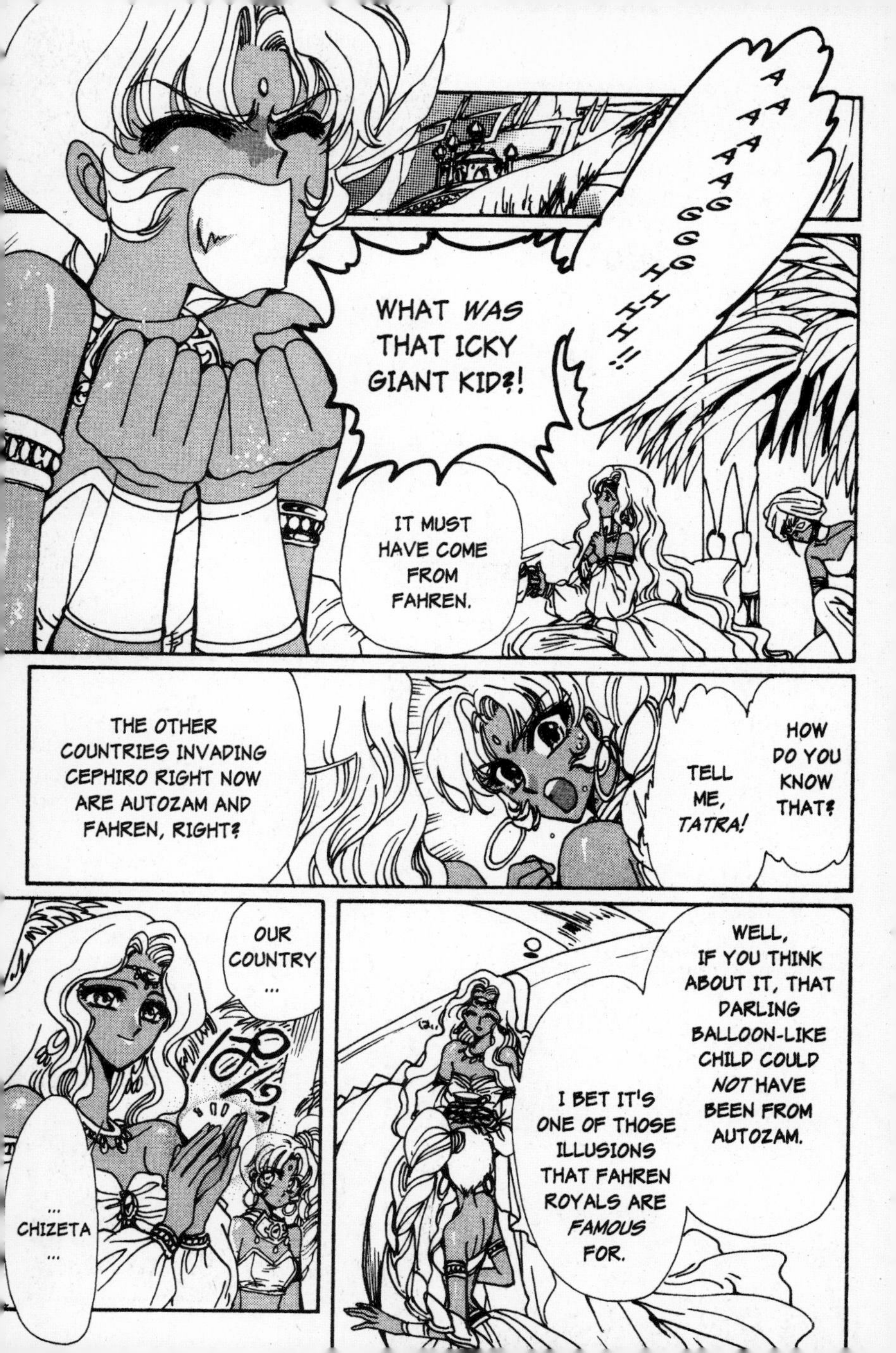
AAAAAAGGGGHHHH!!
WHAT *WAS* THAT ICKY GIANT KID?!
IT MUST HAVE COME FROM FAHREN.
HOW DO YOU KNOW THAT?
TELL ME, *TATRA!*
THE OTHER COUNTRIES INVADING CEPHIRO RIGHT NOW ARE AUTOZAM AND FAHREN, RIGHT?
WELL, IF YOU THINK ABOUT IT, THAT DARLING BALLOON-LIKE CHILD COULD *NOT* HAVE BEEN FROM AUTOZAM.
I BET IT'S ONE OF THOSE ILLUSIONS THAT FAHREN ROYALS ARE *FAMOUS* FOR.
OUR COUNTRY ...
... CHIZETA ...

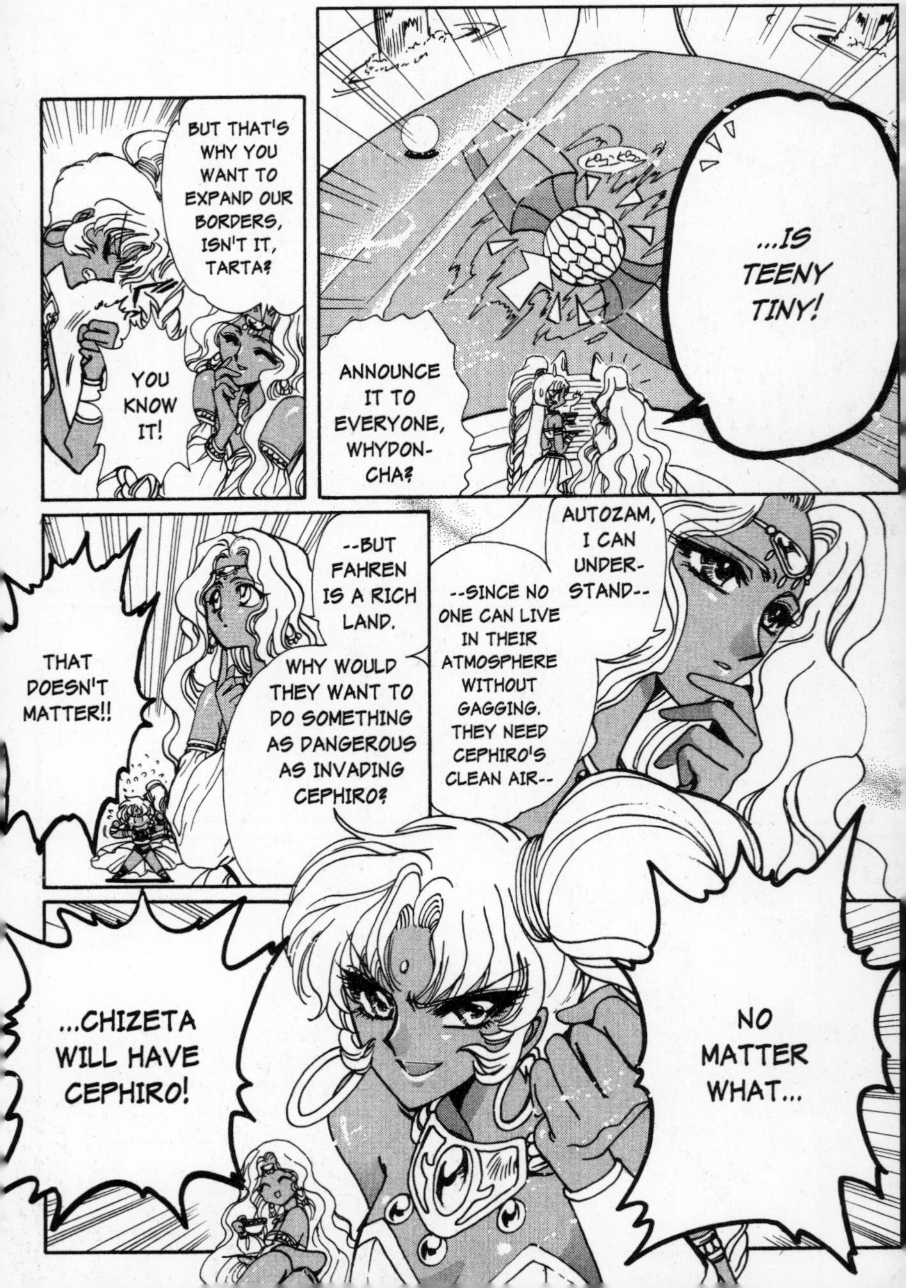
...IS TEENY TINY!
ANNOUNCE IT TO EVERYONE, WHYDONCHA?
BUT THAT'S WHY YOU WANT TO EXPAND OUR BORDERS, ISN'T IT, TARTA?
YOU KNOW IT!
AUTOZAM, I CAN UNDER-STAND--
--SINCE NO ONE CAN LIVE IN THEIR ATMOSPHERE WITHOUT GAGGING. THEY NEED CEPHIRO'S CLEAN AIR--
--BUT FAHREN IS A RICH LAND.
WHY WOULD THEY WANT TO DO SOMETHING AS DANGEROUS AS INVADING CEPHIRO?
THAT DOESN'T MATTER!!
NO MATTER WHAT...
...CHIZETA WILL HAVE CEPHIRO!

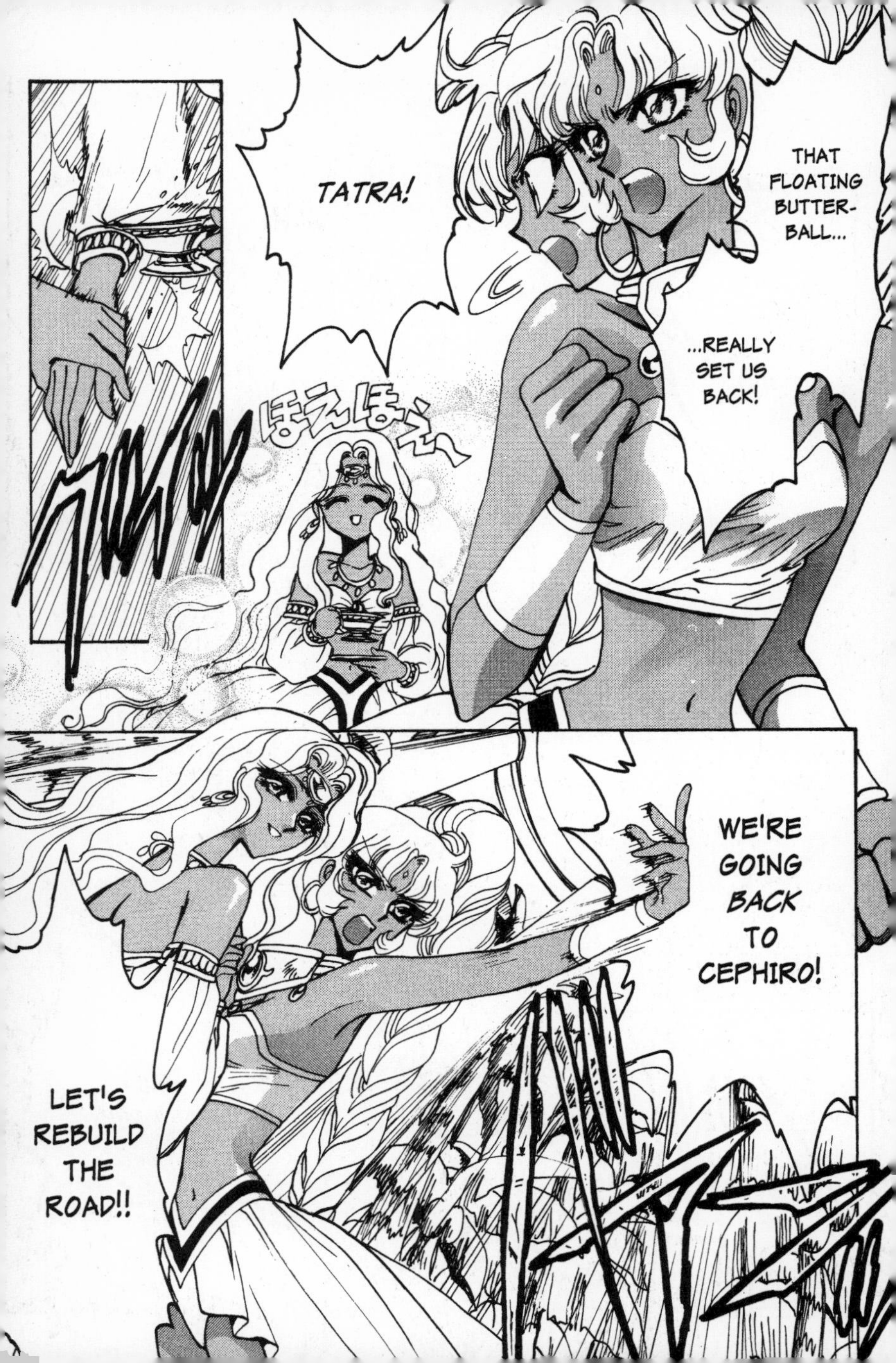
TATRA!
THAT FLOATING BUTTER-BALL...
...REALLY SET US BACK!
ほえほえ~
WE'RE GOING *BACK* TO CEPHIRO!
LET'S REBUILD THE ROAD!!

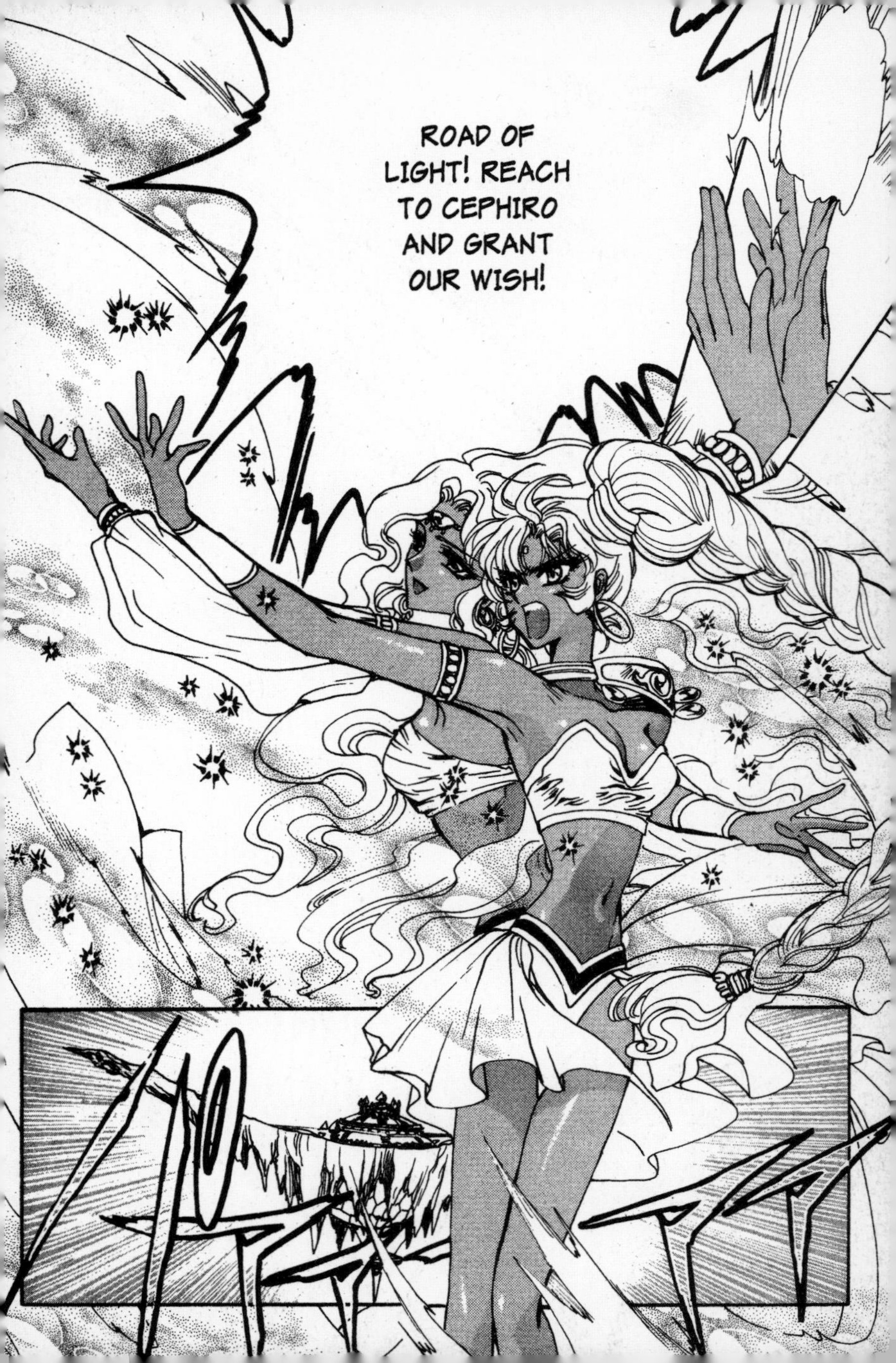
ROAD OF LIGHT! REACH TO CEPHIRO AND GRANT OUR WISH!

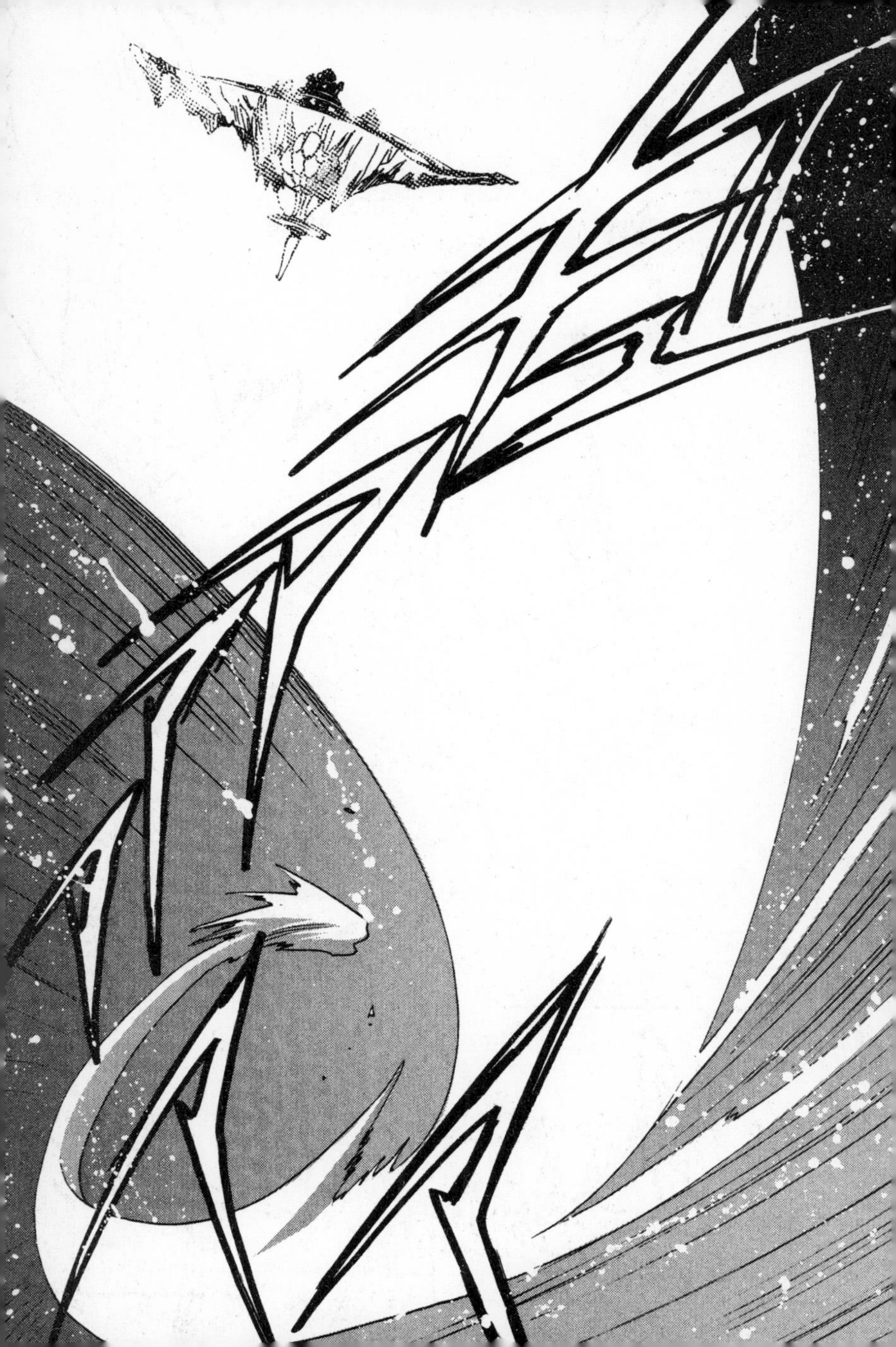

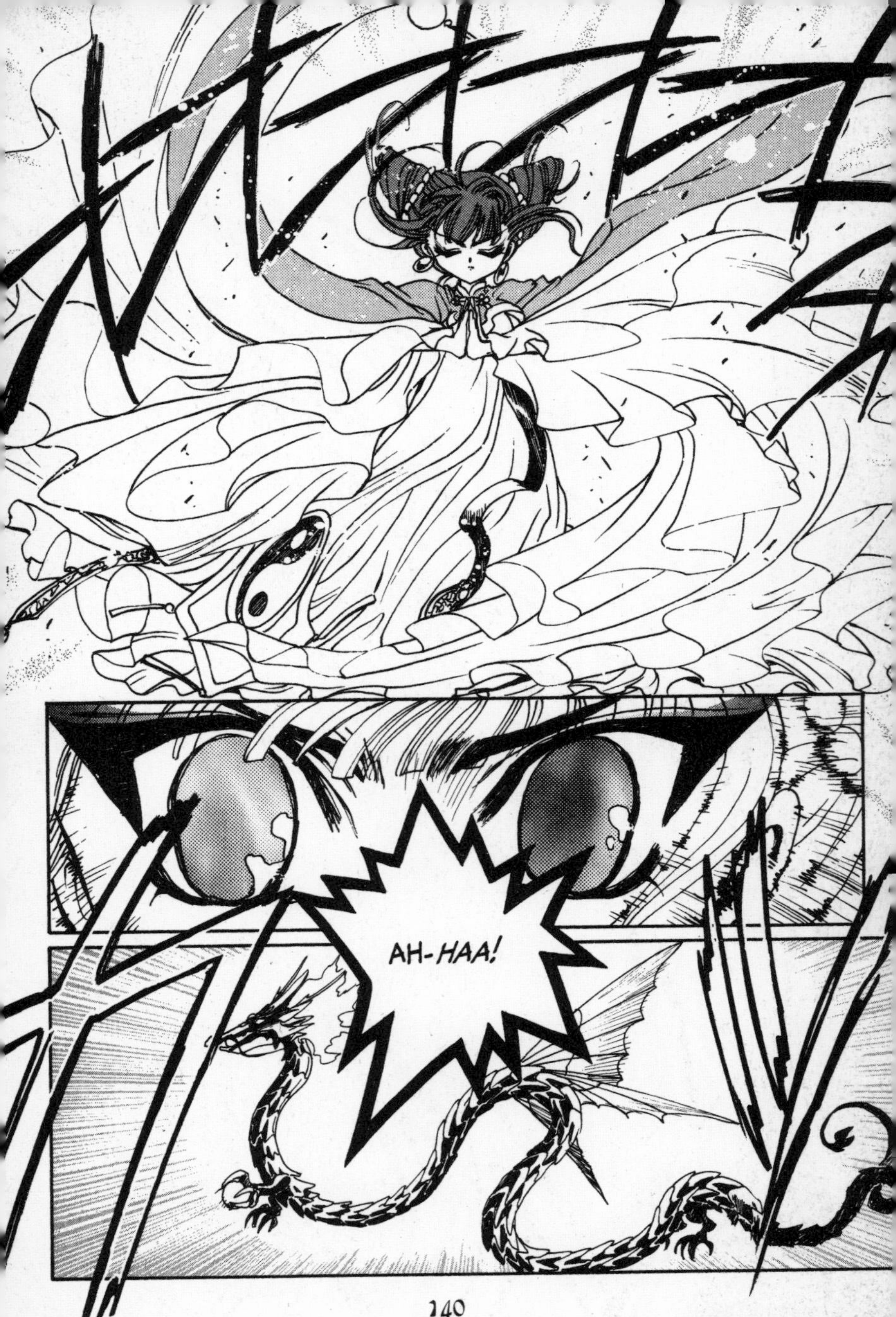
AH-HAA!

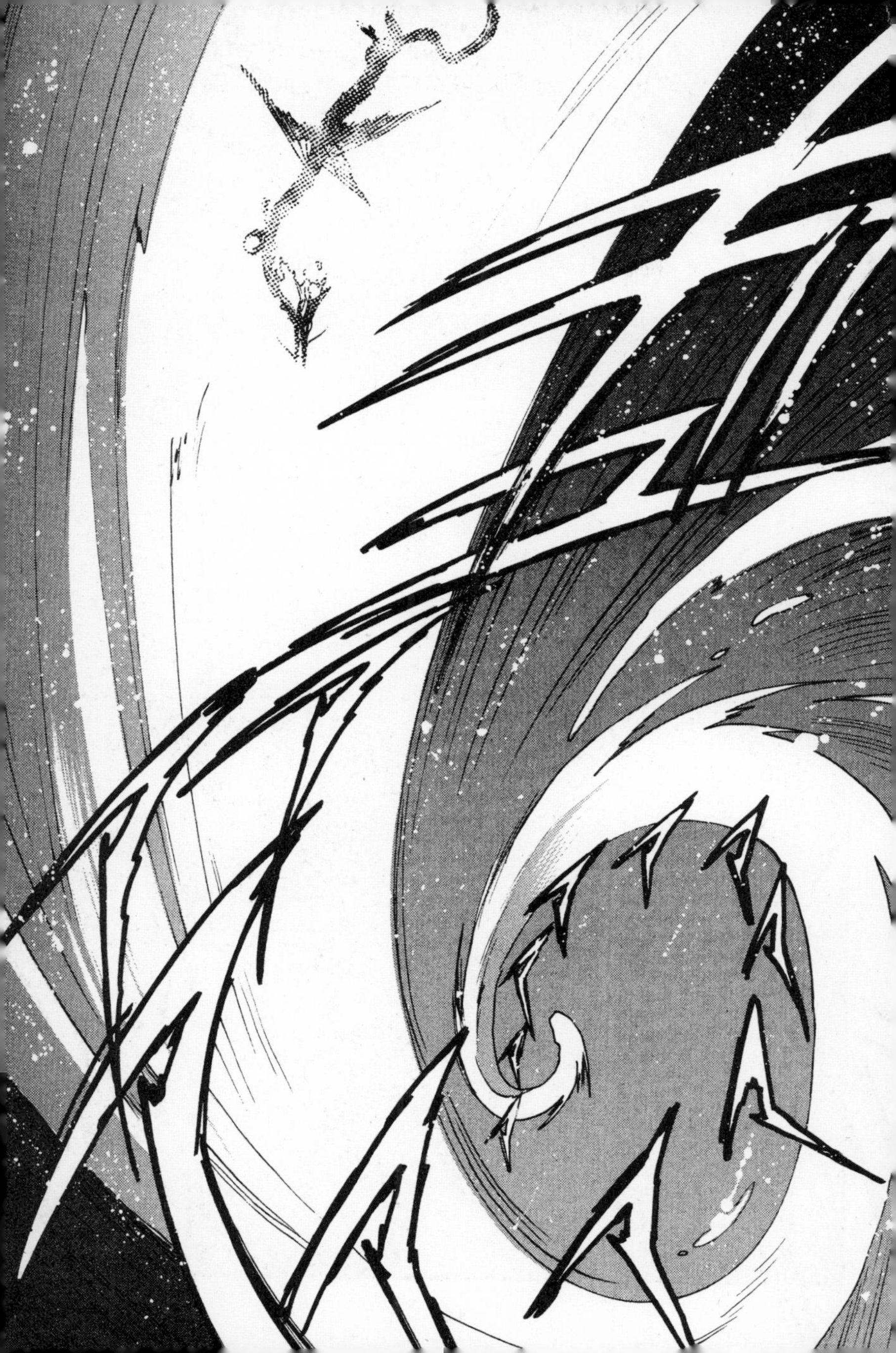

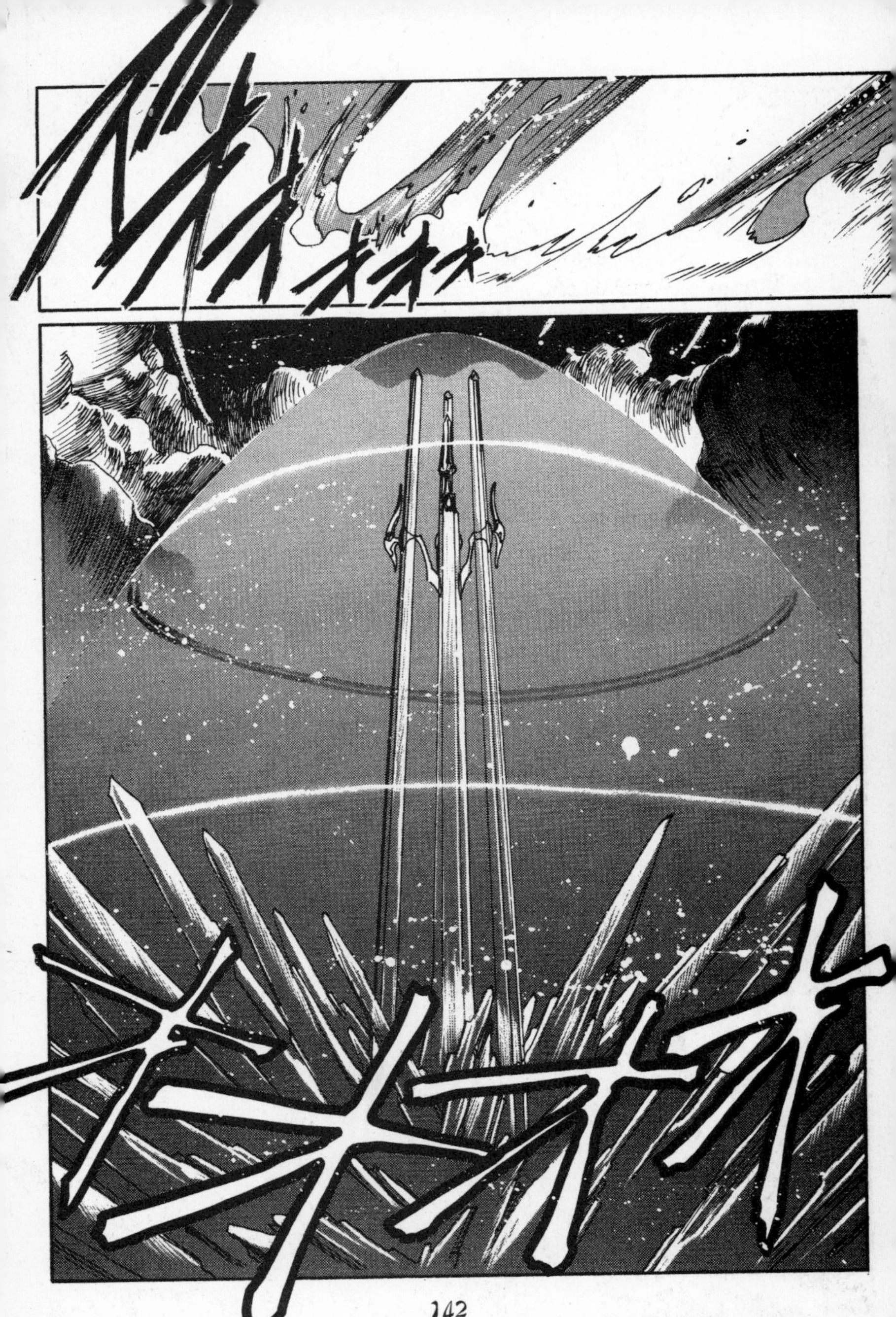

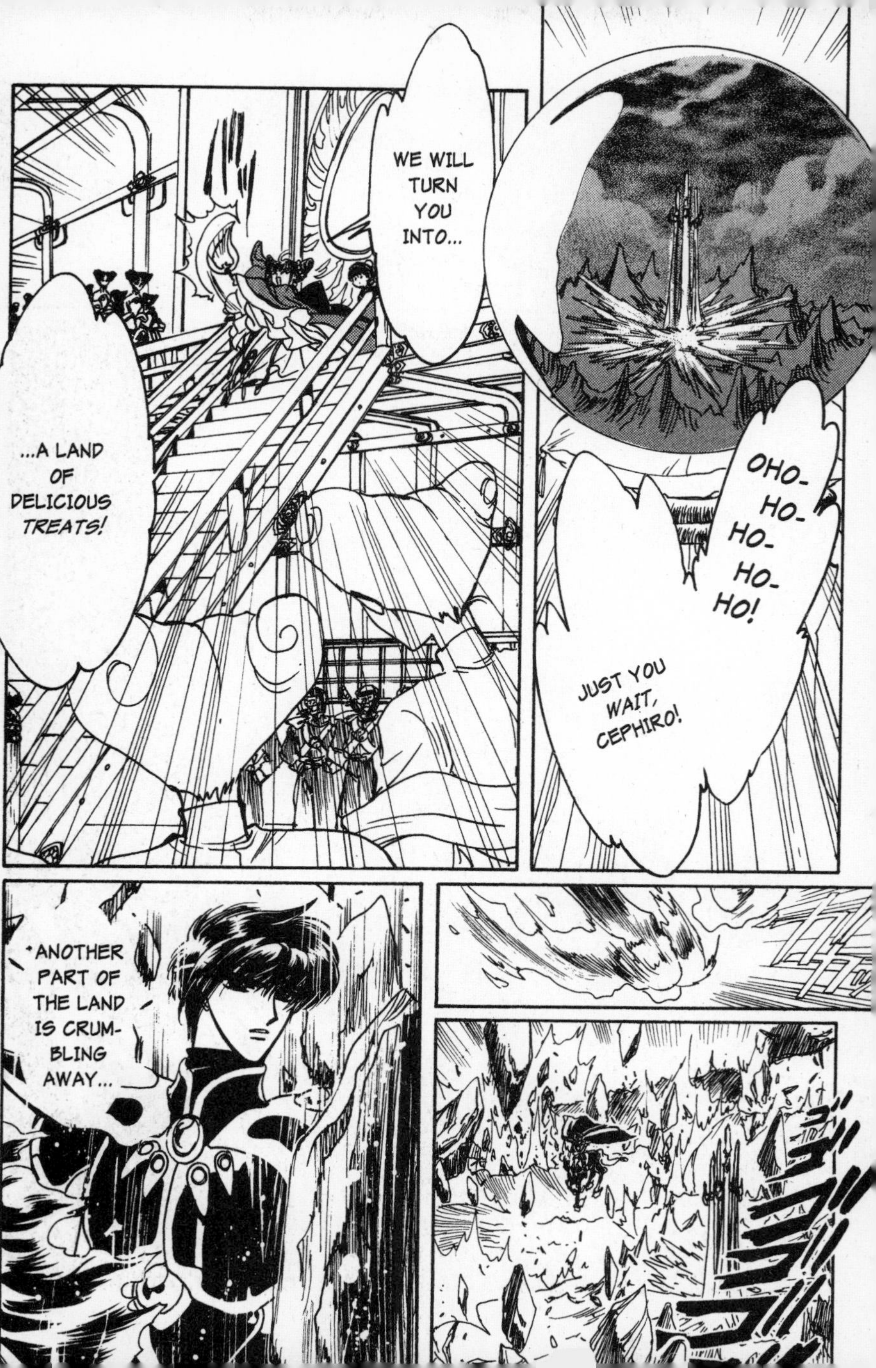
WE WILL TURN YOU INTO...
...A LAND OF DELICIOUS TREATS!
OHO-HO-HO-HO-HO!
JUST YOU WAIT, CEPHIRO!
ANOTHER PART OF THE LAND IS CRUM-BLING AWAY...

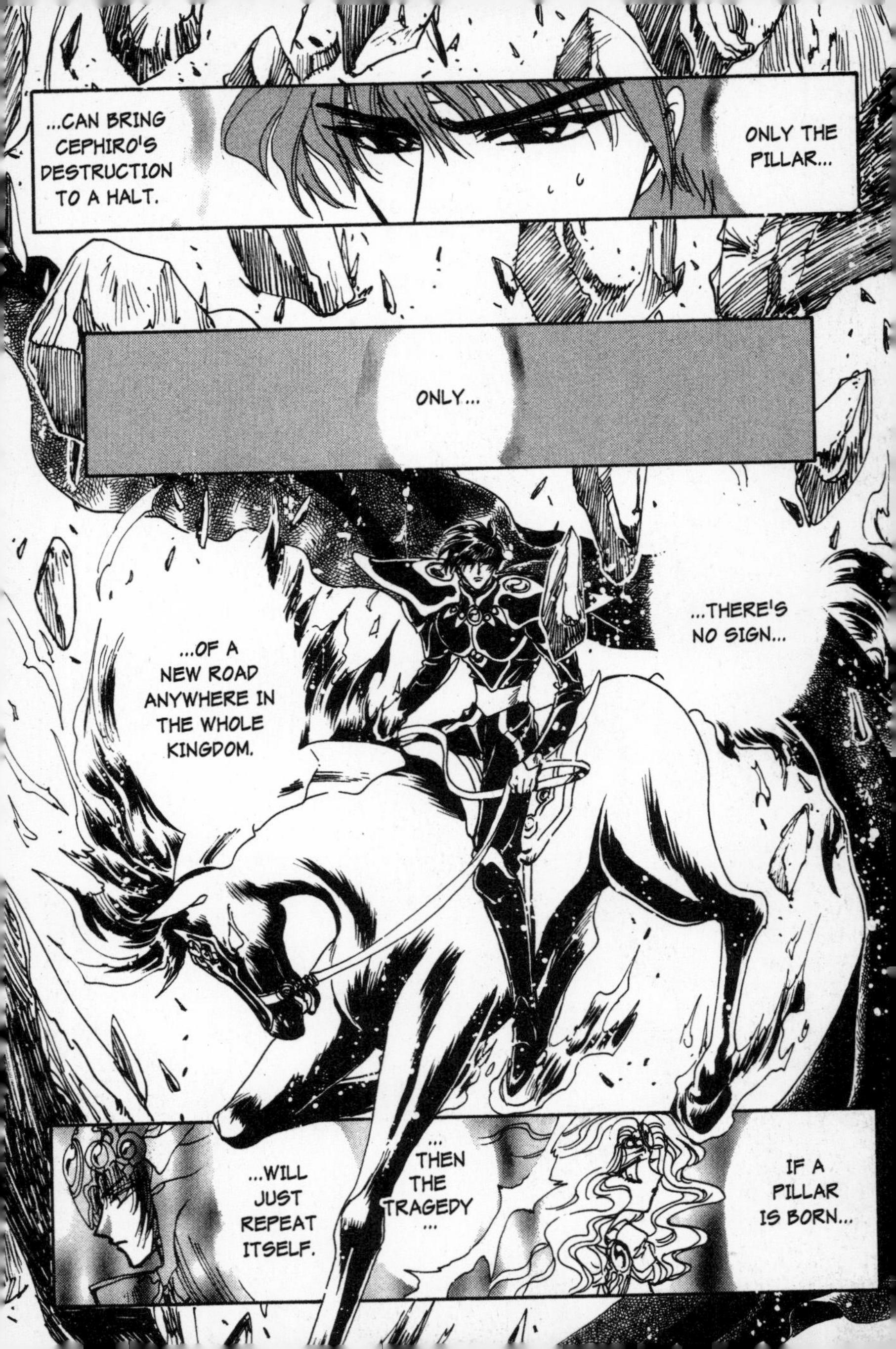
ONLY THE PILLAR...
...CAN BRING CEPHIRO'S DESTRUCTION TO A HALT.
ONLY...
...THERE'S NO SIGN...
...OF A NEW ROAD ANYWHERE IN THE WHOLE KINGDOM.
IF A PILLAR IS BORN...
...THEN THE TRAGEDY...
...WILL JUST REPEAT ITSELF.

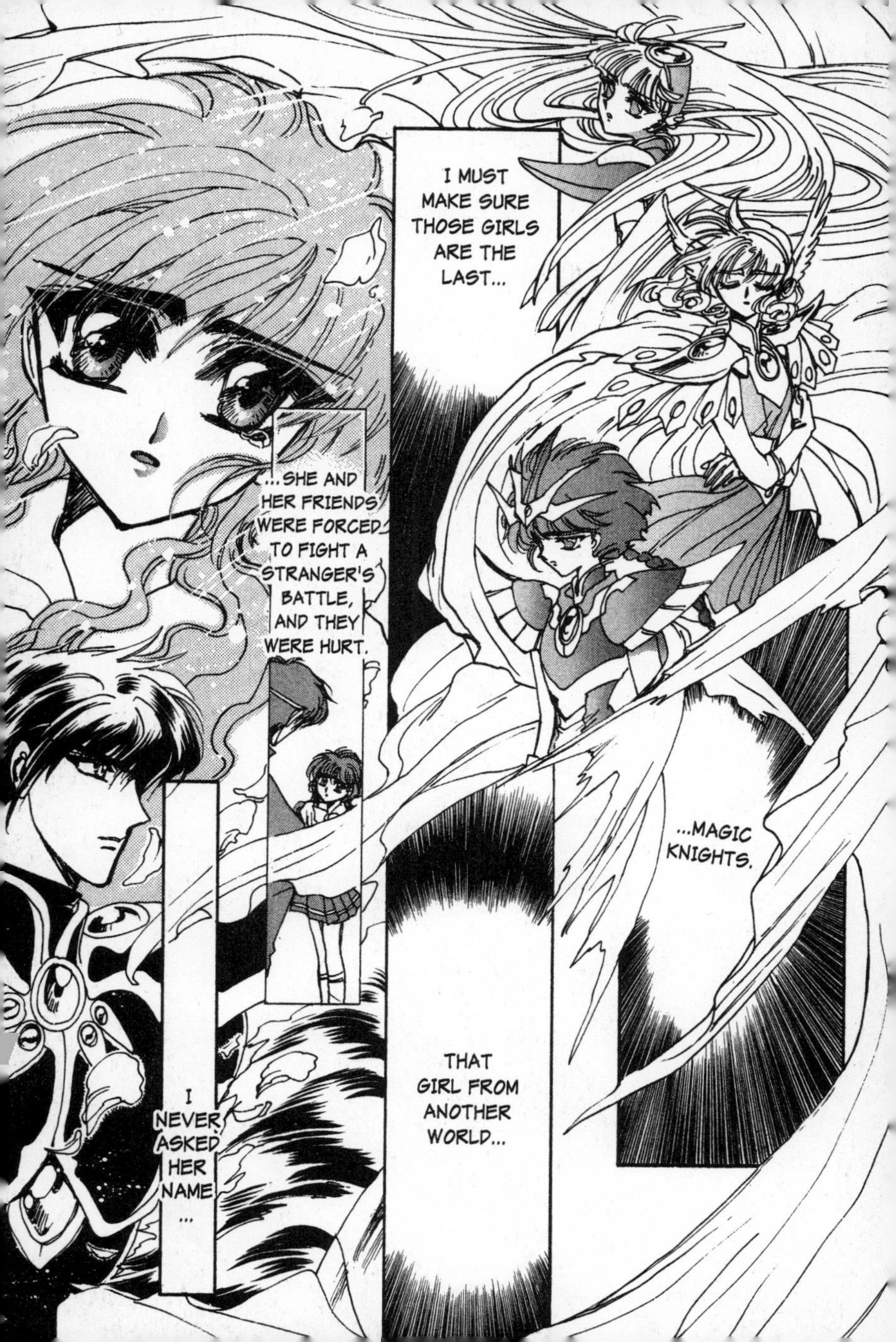
I MUST MAKE SURE THOSE GIRLS ARE THE LAST...
...MAGIC KNIGHTS.
THAT GIRL FROM ANOTHER WORLD...
...SHE AND HER FRIENDS WERE FORCED TO FIGHT A STRANGER'S BATTLE, AND THEY WERE HURT.
I NEVER ASKED HER NAME...

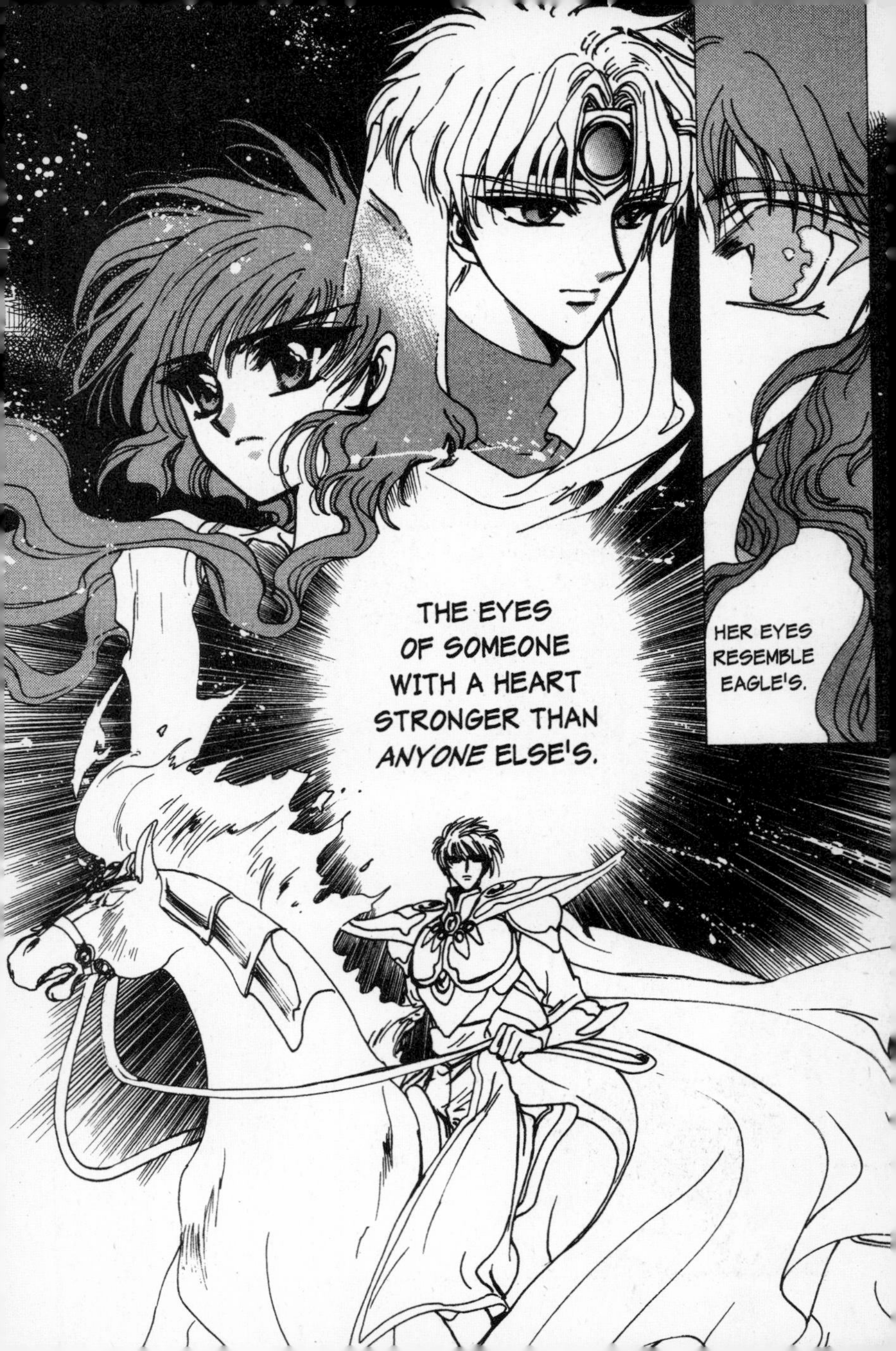
HER EYES RESEMBLE EAGLE'S.
THE EYES OF SOMEONE WITH A HEART STRONGER THAN *ANYONE* ELSE'S.

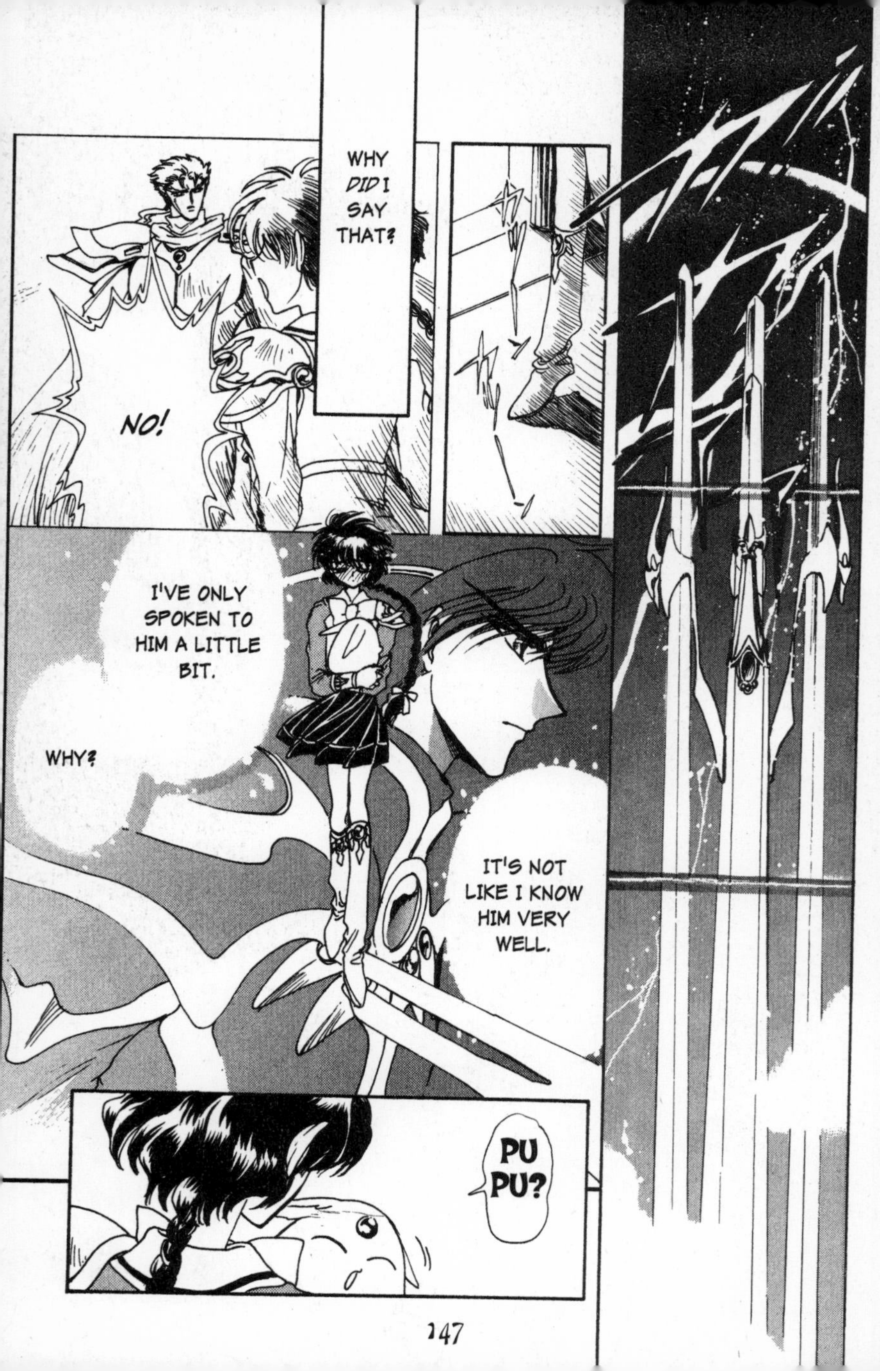
WHY *DID* I SAY THAT?
NO!
I'VE ONLY SPOKEN TO HIM A LITTLE BIT.
WHY?
IT'S NOT LIKE I KNOW HIM VERY WELL.
PU PU?

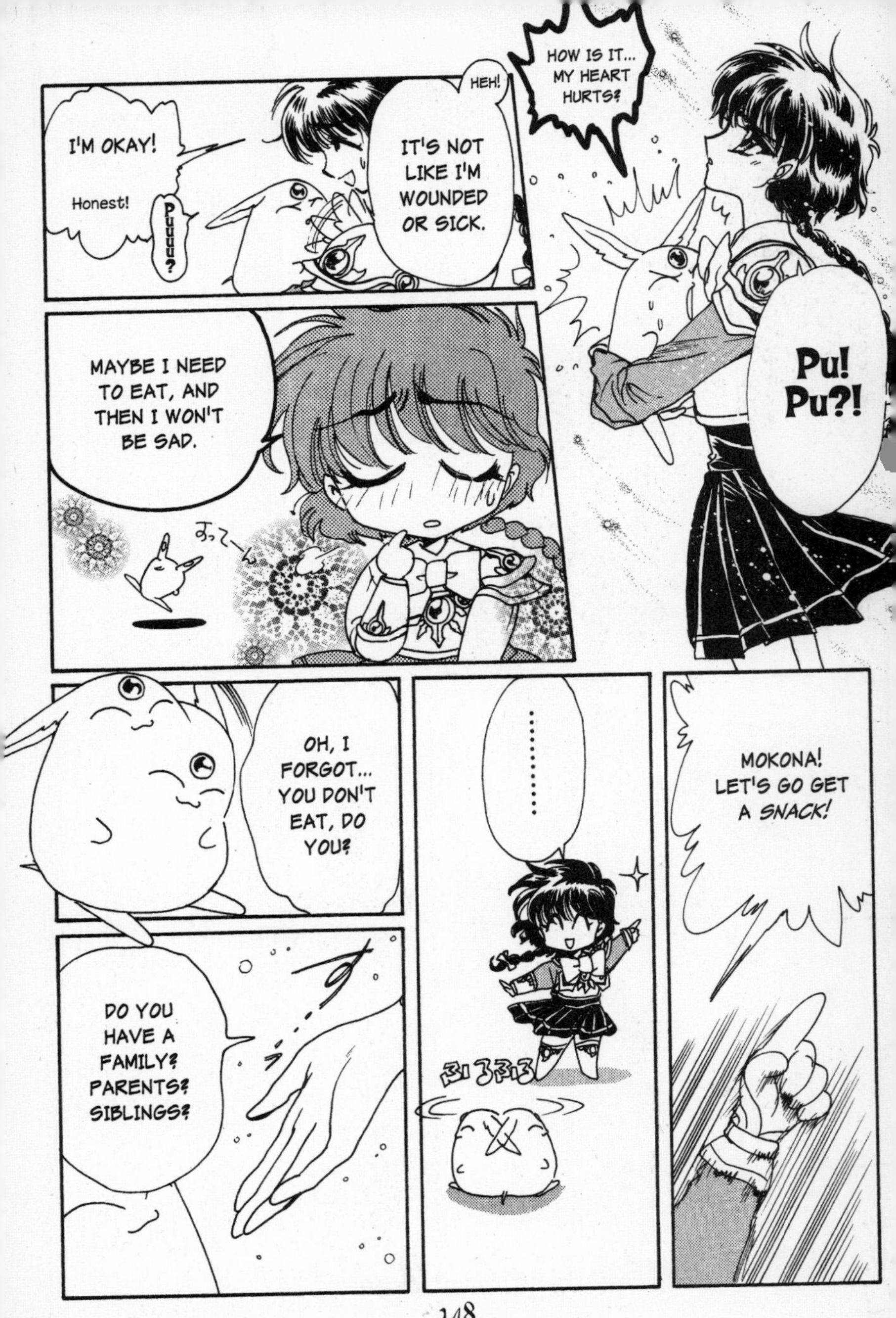
HOW IS IT... MY HEART HURTS?
Pu! Pu?!
HEH!
IT'S NOT LIKE I'M WOUNDED OR SICK.
I'M OKAY!
Puuuu?
Honest!
MAYBE I NEED TO EAT, AND THEN I WON'T BE SAD.
すって～ん
MOKONA! LET'S GO GET A SNACK!
......
OH, I FORGOT... YOU DON'T EAT, DO YOU?
DO YOU HAVE A FAMILY? PARENTS? SIBLINGS?

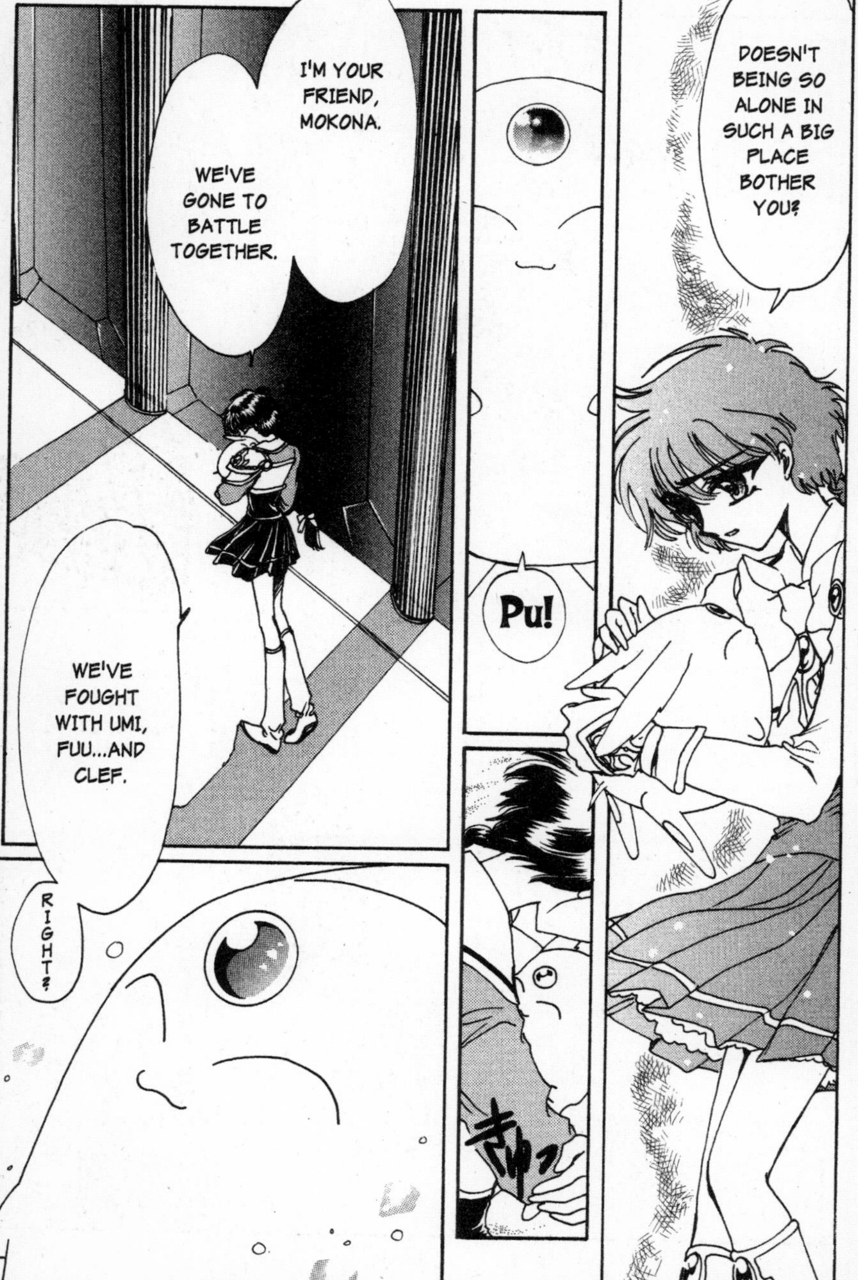

DOESN'T BEING SO ALONE IN SUCH A BIG PLACE BOTHER YOU?
Pu!
I'M YOUR FRIEND, MOKONA.
WE'VE GONE TO BATTLE TOGETHER.
WE'VE FOUGHT WITH UMI, FUU...AND CLEF.
きゅっ
RIGHT?

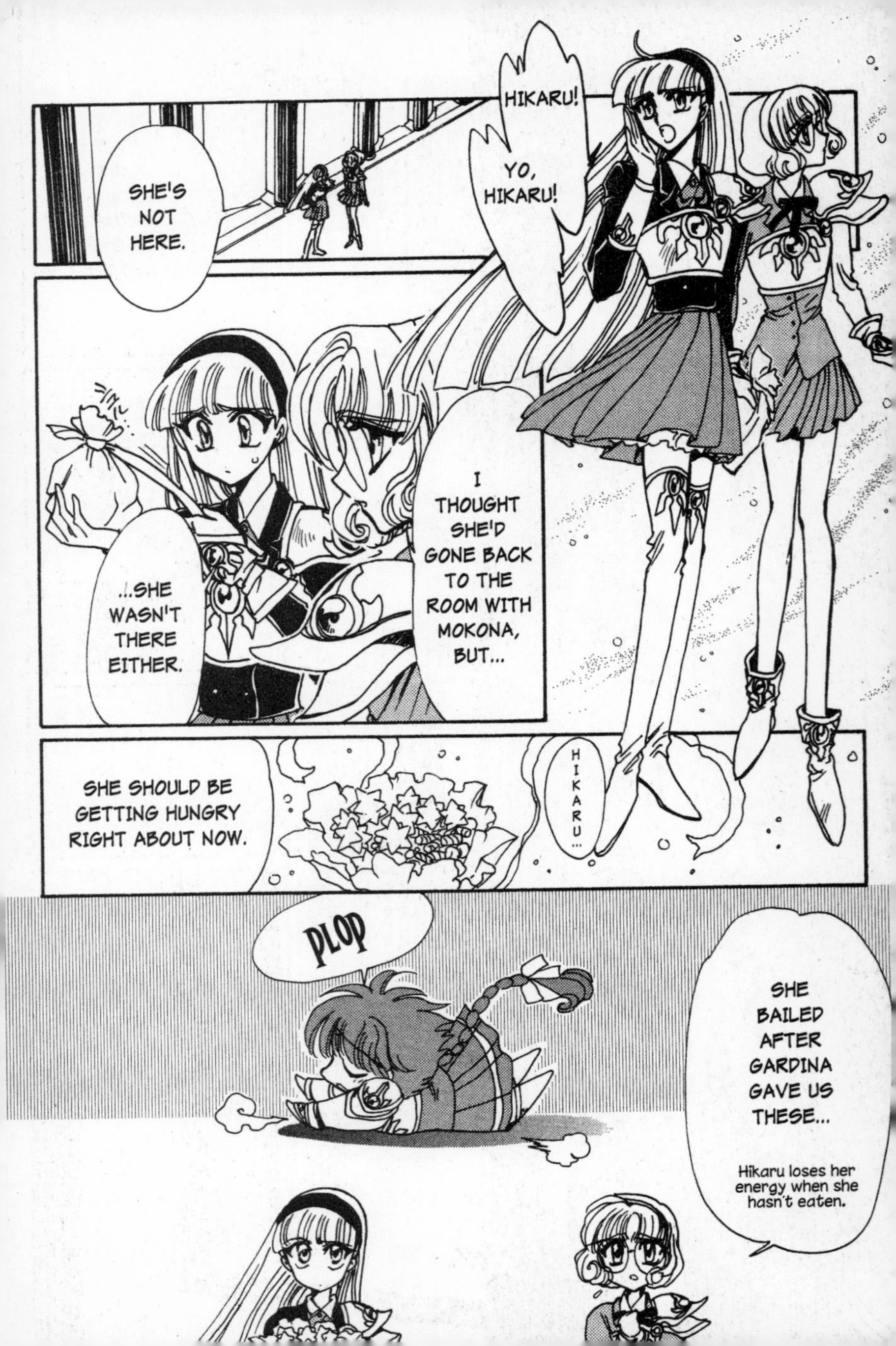
HIKARU!
YO, HIKARU!
SHE'S NOT HERE.
I THOUGHT SHE'D GONE BACK TO THE ROOM WITH MOKONA, BUT...
...SHE WASN'T THERE EITHER.
HIKARU...
SHE SHOULD BE GETTING HUNGRY RIGHT ABOUT NOW.
SHE BAILED AFTER GARDINA GAVE US THESE...
Hikaru loses her energy when she hasn't eaten.
PLOP

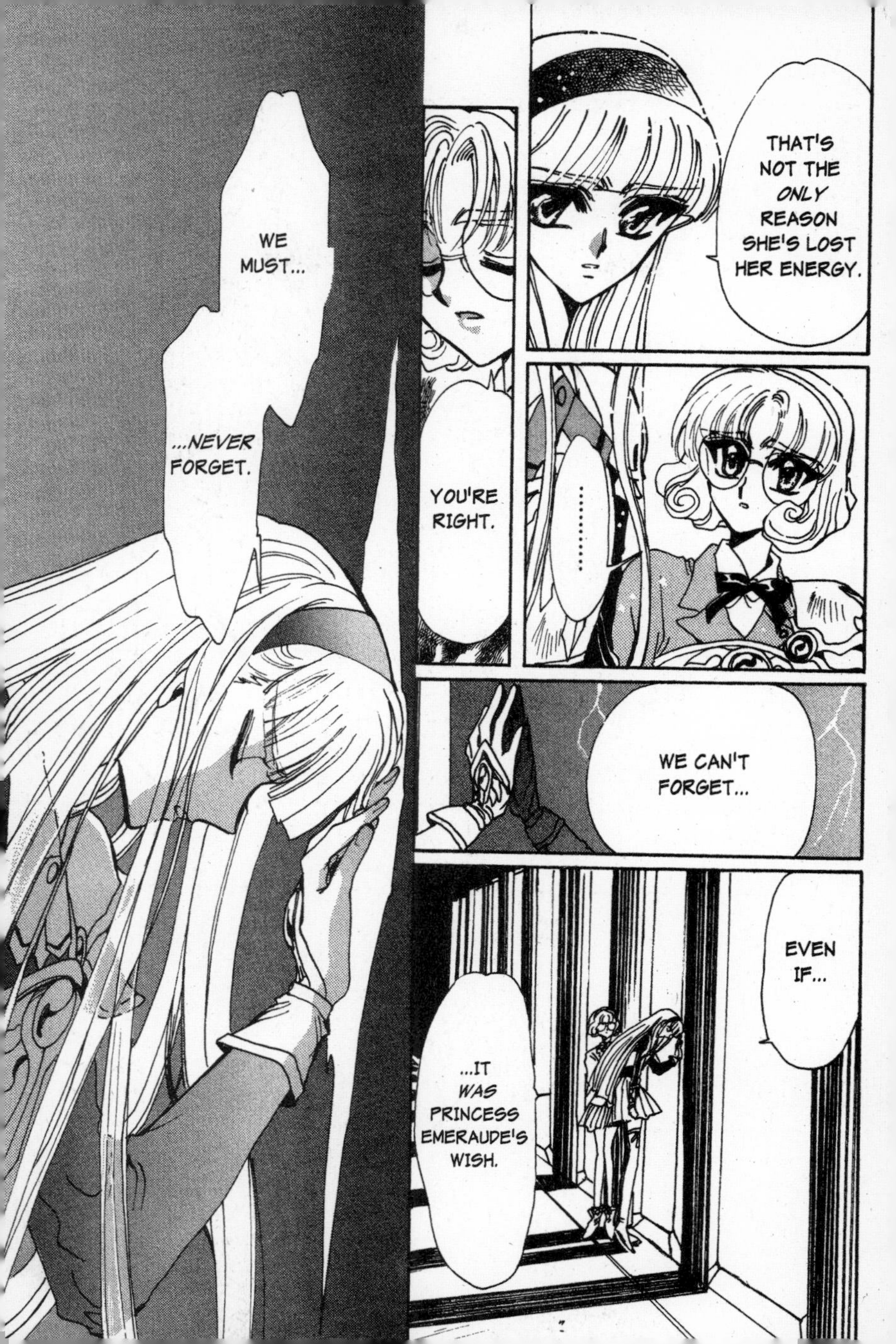
THAT'S NOT THE *ONLY* REASON SHE'S LOST HER ENERGY.
......
YOU'RE RIGHT.
WE CAN'T FORGET...
EVEN IF...
...IT *WAS* PRINCESS EMERAUDE'S WISH.
WE MUST...
...*NEVER* FORGET.

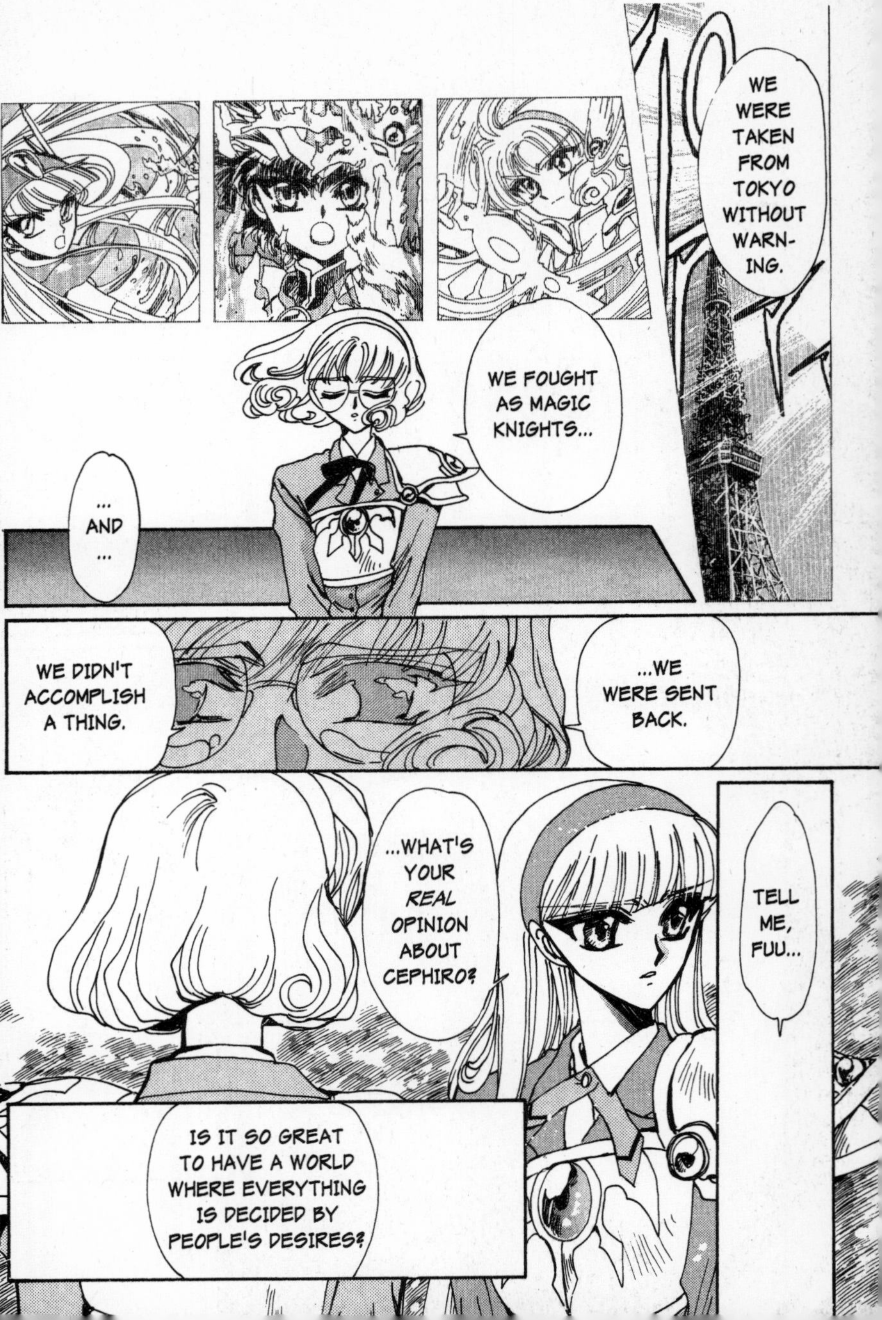
WE WERE TAKEN FROM TOKYO WITHOUT WARN-ING.
WE FOUGHT AS MAGIC KNIGHTS...
... AND ...
...WE WERE SENT BACK.
WE DIDN'T ACCOMPLISH A THING.
TELL ME, FUU...
...WHAT'S YOUR *REAL* OPINION ABOUT CEPHIRO?
IS IT SO GREAT TO HAVE A WORLD WHERE EVERYTHING IS DECIDED BY PEOPLE'S DESIRES?

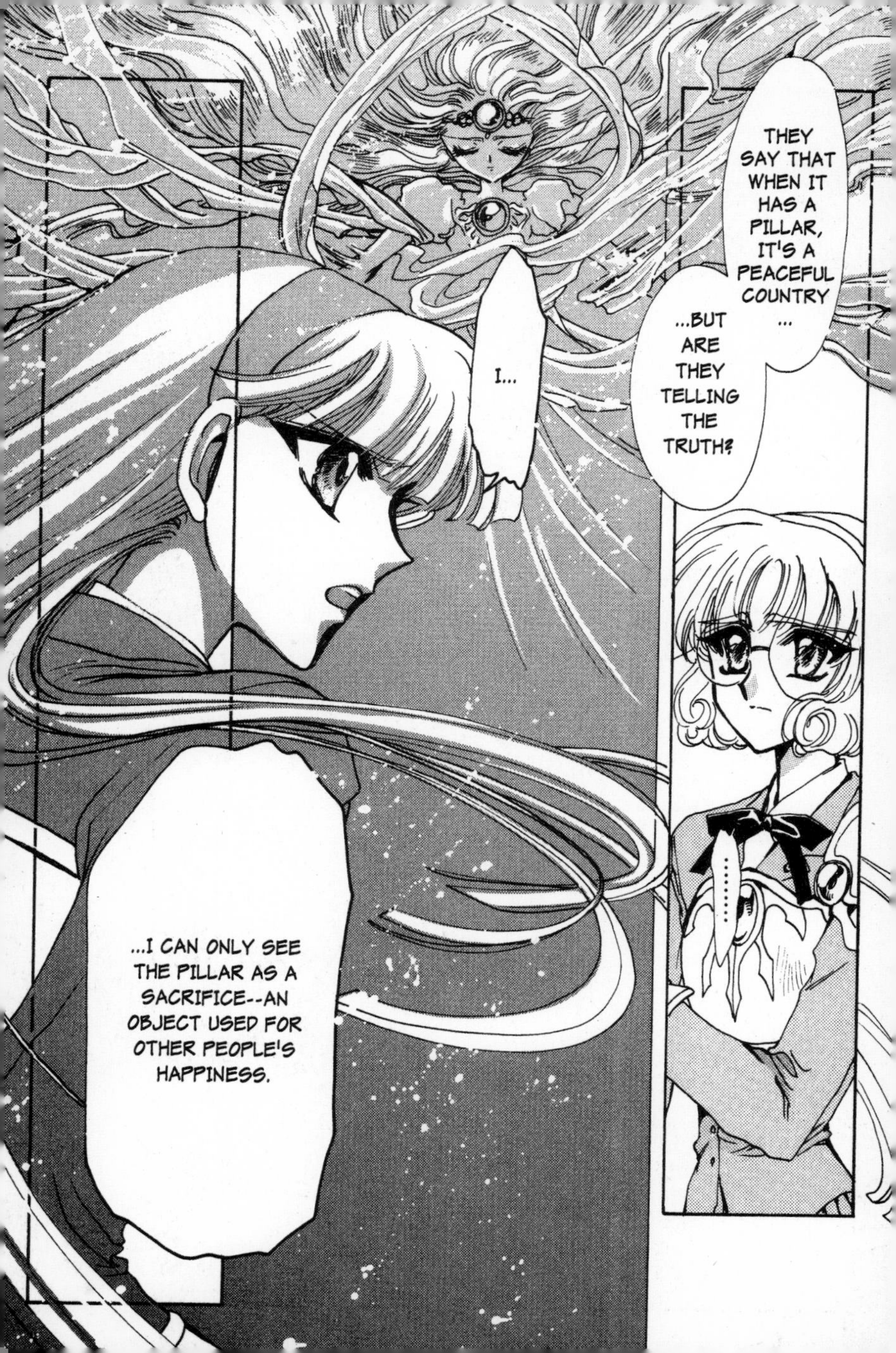
THEY SAY THAT WHEN IT HAS A PILLAR, IT'S A PEACEFUL COUNTRY ...
...BUT ARE THEY TELLING THE TRUTH?
......
I...
...I CAN ONLY SEE THE PILLAR AS A SACRIFICE--AN OBJECT USED FOR OTHER PEOPLE'S HAPPINESS.

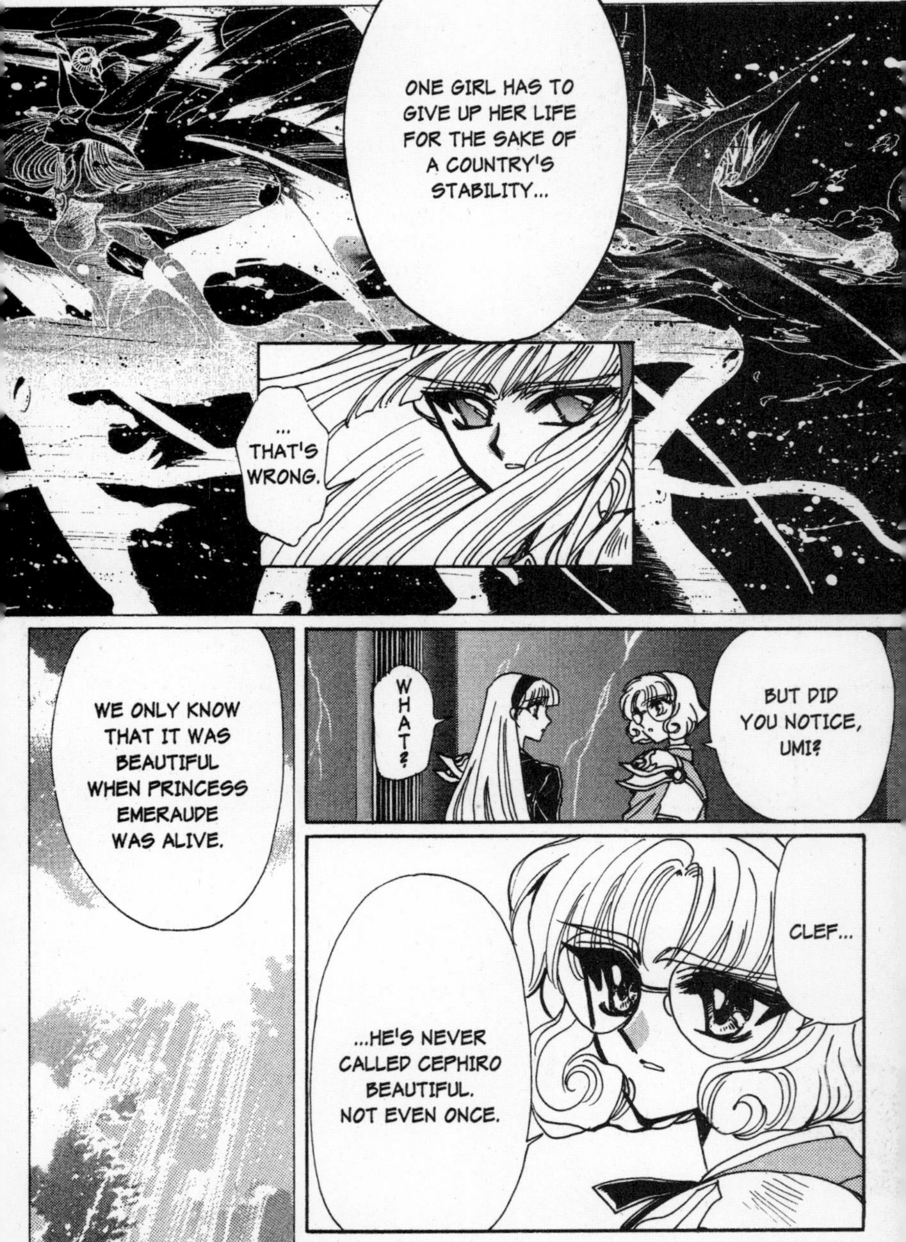
ONE GIRL HAS TO GIVE UP HER LIFE FOR THE SAKE OF A COUNTRY'S STABILITY...
... THAT'S WRONG.
BUT DID YOU NOTICE, UMI?
WHAT?
CLEF...
...HE'S NEVER CALLED CEPHIRO BEAUTIFUL. NOT EVEN ONCE.
WE ONLY KNOW THAT IT WAS BEAUTIFUL WHEN PRINCESS EMERAUDE WAS ALIVE.

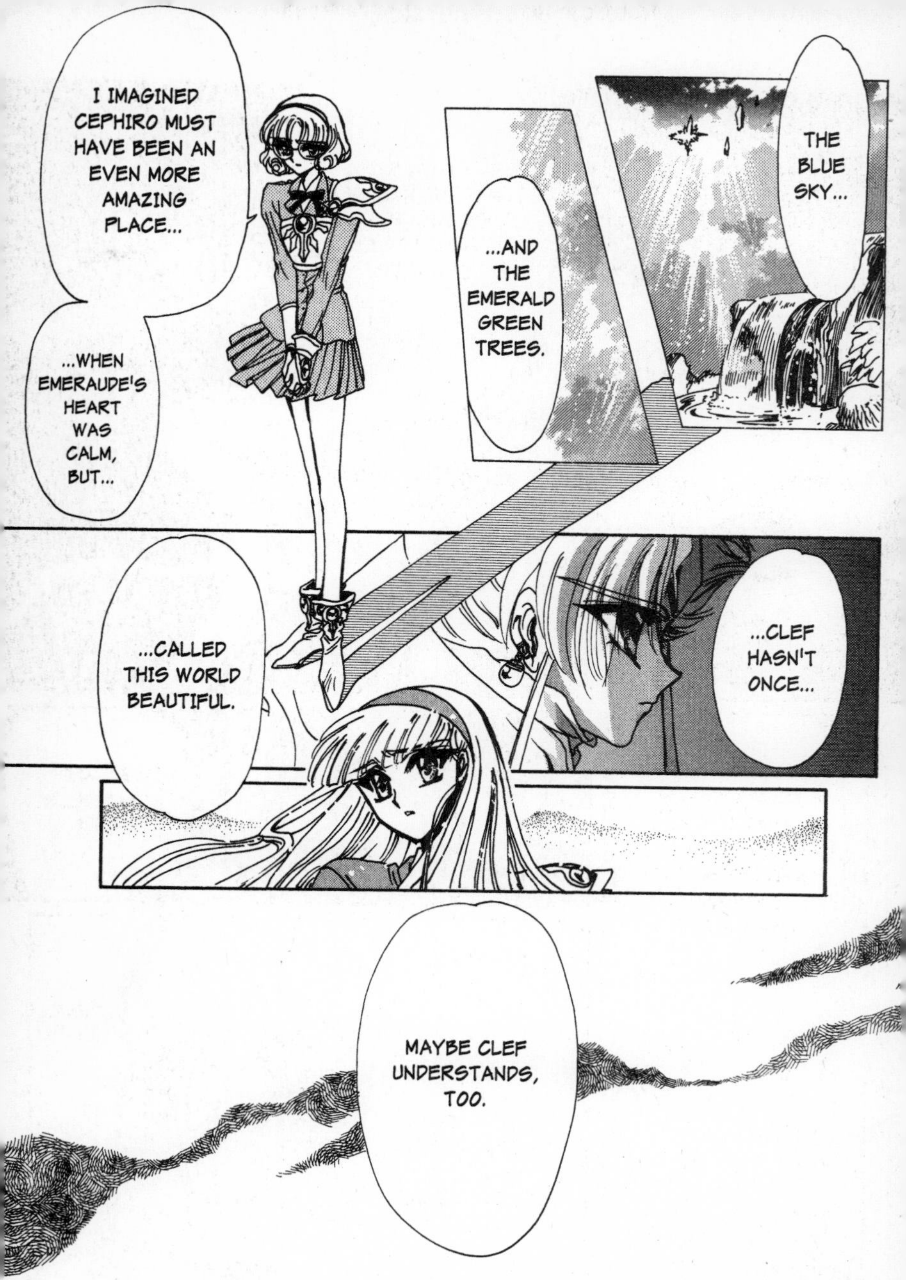
THE BLUE SKY...
...AND THE EMERALD GREEN TREES.
I IMAGINED CEPHIRO MUST HAVE BEEN AN EVEN MORE AMAZING PLACE...
...WHEN EMERAUDE'S HEART WAS CALM, BUT...
...CLEF HASN'T ONCE...
...CALLED THIS WORLD BEAUTIFUL.
MAYBE CLEF UNDERSTANDS, TOO.

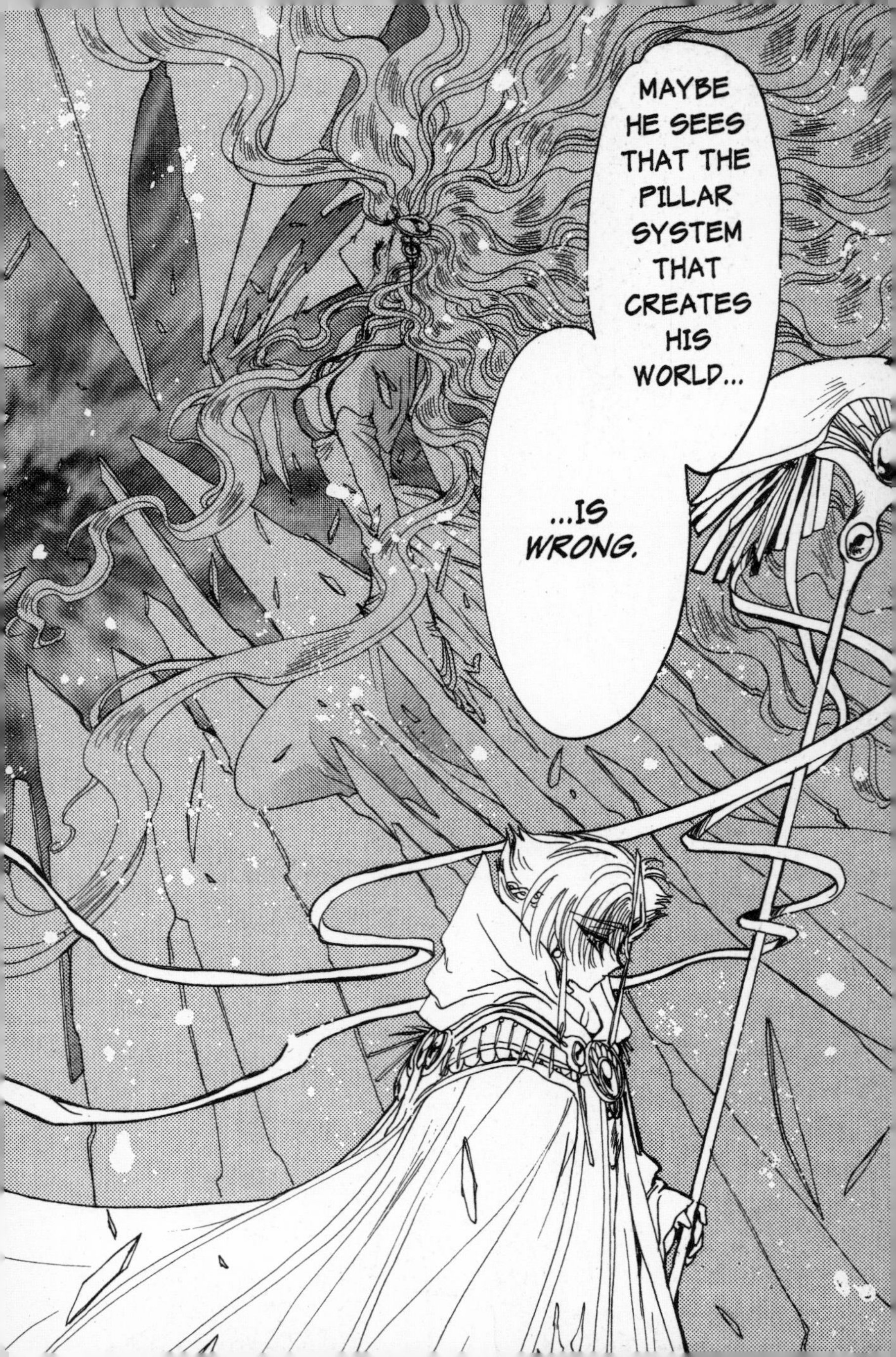
MAYBE HE SEES THAT THE PILLAR SYSTEM THAT CREATES HIS WORLD...
...IS WRONG.

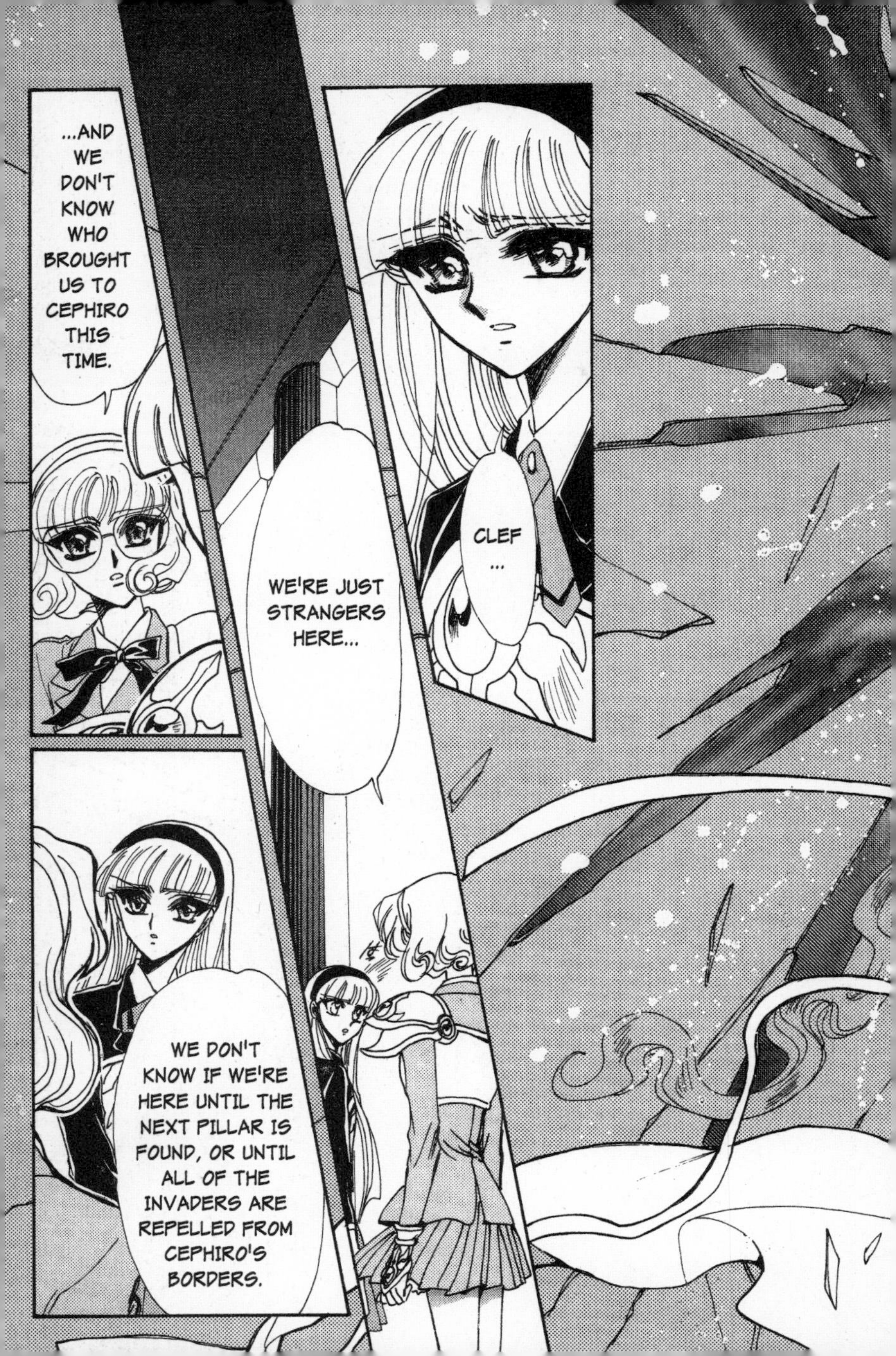
CLEF ...
WE'RE JUST STRANGERS HERE...
...AND WE DON'T KNOW WHO BROUGHT US TO CEPHIRO THIS TIME.
WE DON'T KNOW IF WE'RE HERE UNTIL THE NEXT PILLAR IS FOUND, OR UNTIL ALL OF THE INVADERS ARE REPELLED FROM CEPHIRO'S BORDERS.

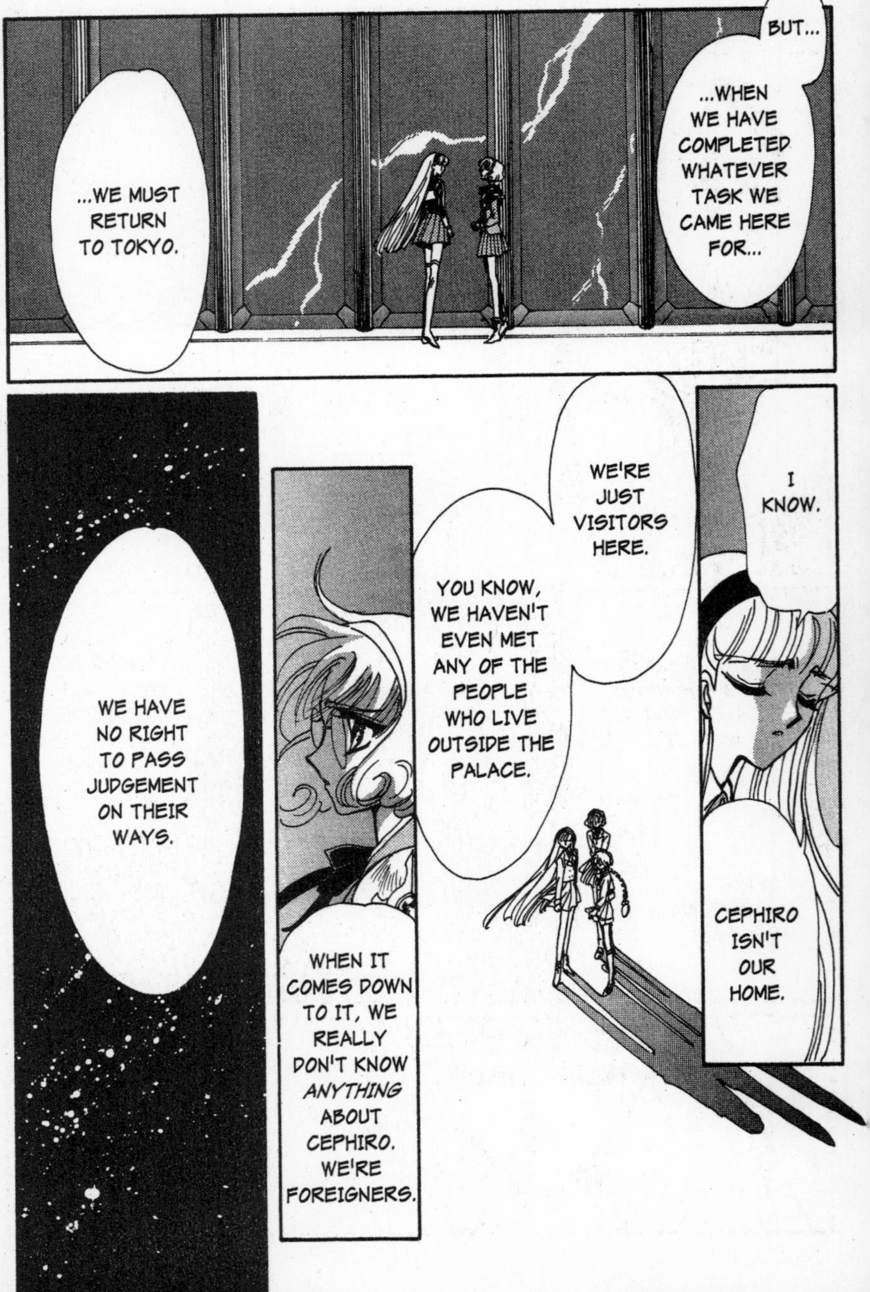
BUT...
...WHEN WE HAVE COMPLETED WHATEVER TASK WE CAME HERE FOR...
...WE MUST RETURN TO TOKYO.
I KNOW.
CEPHIRO ISN'T OUR HOME.
WE'RE JUST VISITORS HERE.
YOU KNOW, WE HAVEN'T EVEN MET ANY OF THE PEOPLE WHO LIVE OUTSIDE THE PALACE.
WHEN IT COMES DOWN TO IT, WE REALLY DON'T KNOW *ANYTHING* ABOUT CEPHIRO. WE'RE FOREIGNERS.
WE HAVE NO RIGHT TO PASS JUDGEMENT ON THEIR WAYS.

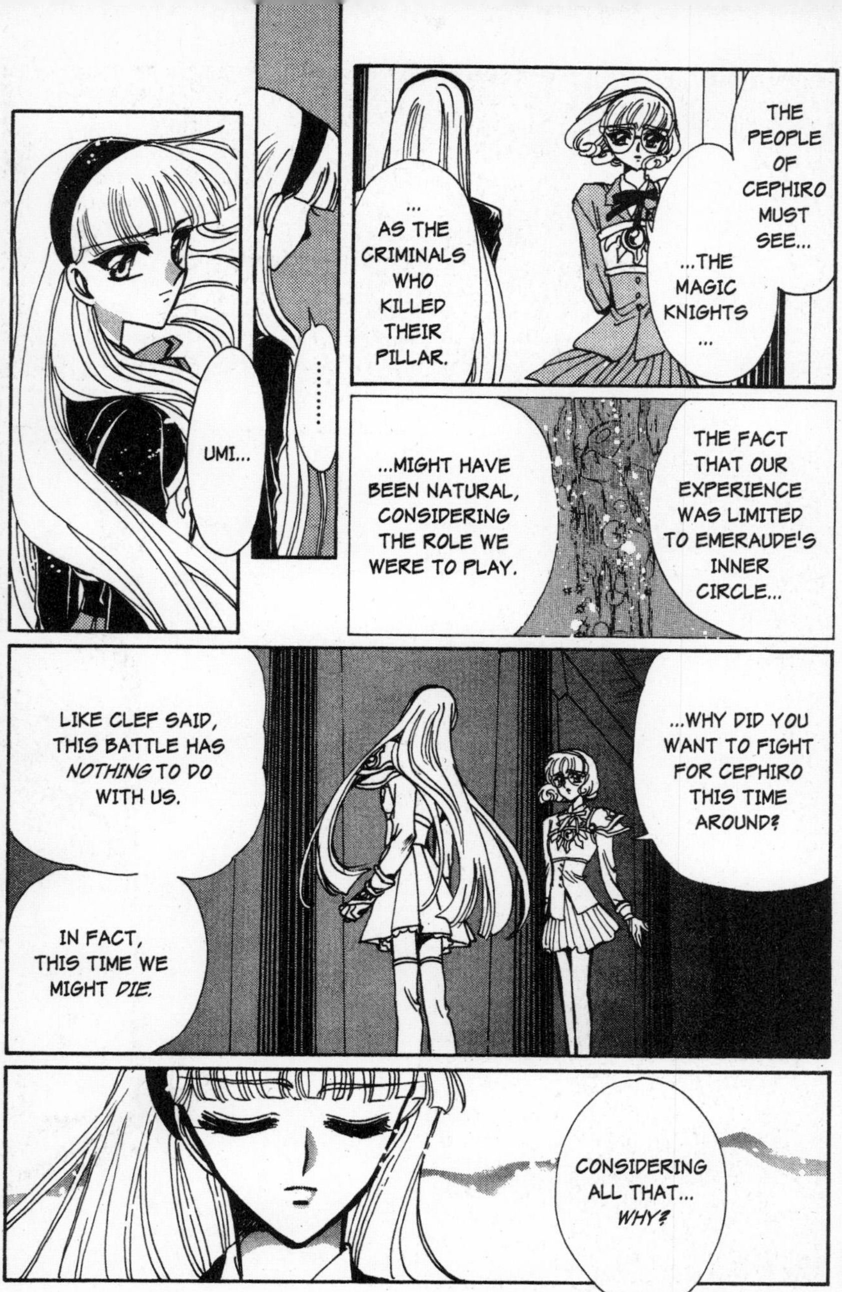
THE PEOPLE OF CEPHIRO MUST SEE...
...THE MAGIC KNIGHTS ...
... AS THE CRIMINALS WHO KILLED THEIR PILLAR.
THE FACT THAT OUR EXPERIENCE WAS LIMITED TO EMERAUDE'S INNER CIRCLE...
...MIGHT HAVE BEEN NATURAL, CONSIDERING THE ROLE WE WERE TO PLAY.
......
UMI...
...WHY DID YOU WANT TO FIGHT FOR CEPHIRO THIS TIME AROUND?
LIKE CLEF SAID, THIS BATTLE HAS *NOTHING* TO DO WITH US.
IN FACT, THIS TIME WE MIGHT *DIE*.
CONSIDERING ALL THAT... *WHY?*

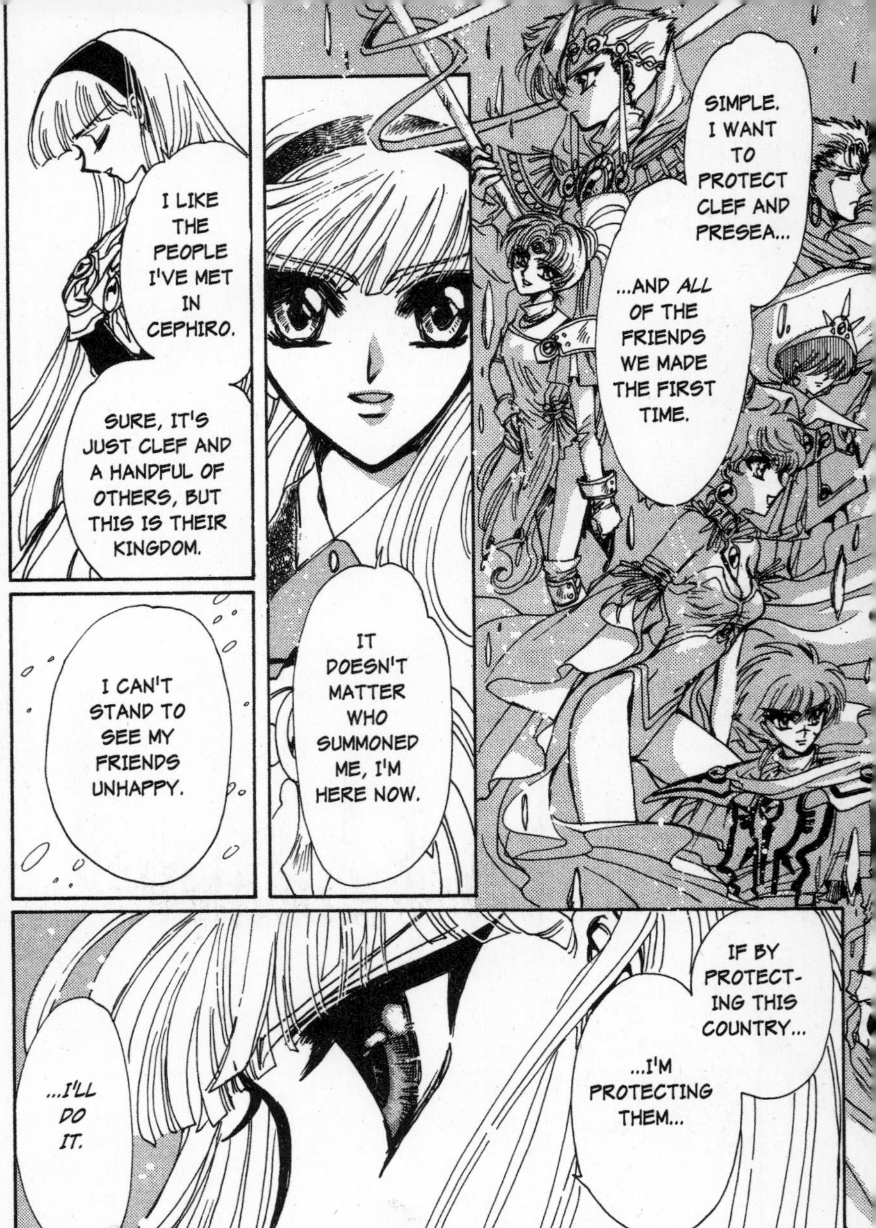
SIMPLE. I WANT TO PROTECT CLEF AND PRESEA...
...AND *ALL* OF THE FRIENDS WE MADE THE FIRST TIME.
IT DOESN'T MATTER WHO SUMMONED ME, I'M HERE NOW.
I LIKE THE PEOPLE I'VE MET IN CEPHIRO.
SURE, IT'S JUST CLEF AND A HANDFUL OF OTHERS, BUT THIS IS THEIR KINGDOM.
I CAN'T STAND TO SEE MY FRIENDS UNHAPPY.
IF BY PROTECTING THIS COUNTRY...
...I'M PROTECTING THEM...
...I'LL DO IT.

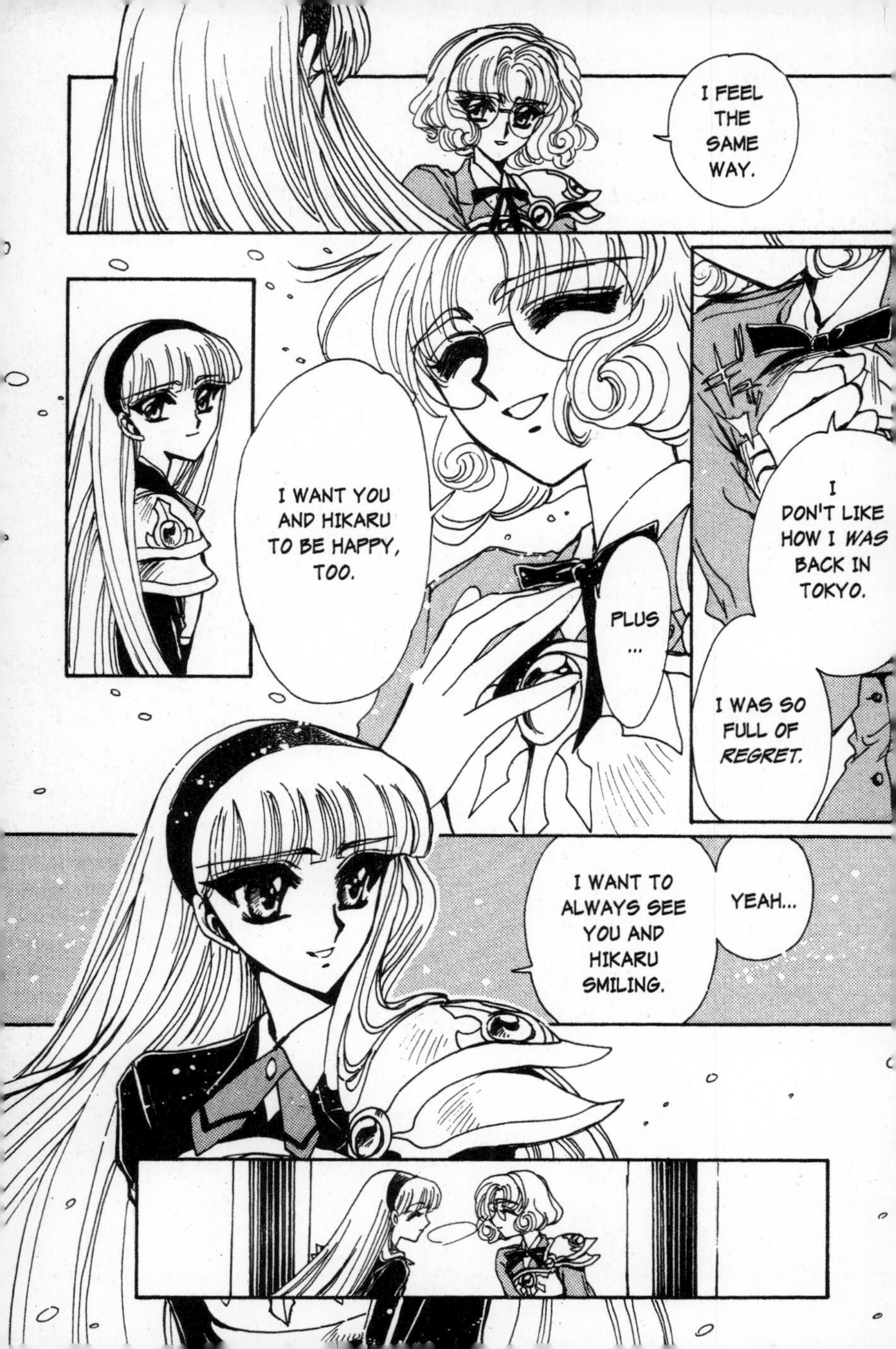
I FEEL THE SAME WAY.
I DON'T LIKE HOW I *WAS* BACK IN TOKYO.
I WAS SO FULL OF *REGRET*.
PLUS ...
I WANT YOU AND HIKARU TO BE HAPPY, TOO.
YEAH...
I WANT TO ALWAYS SEE YOU AND HIKARU SMILING.

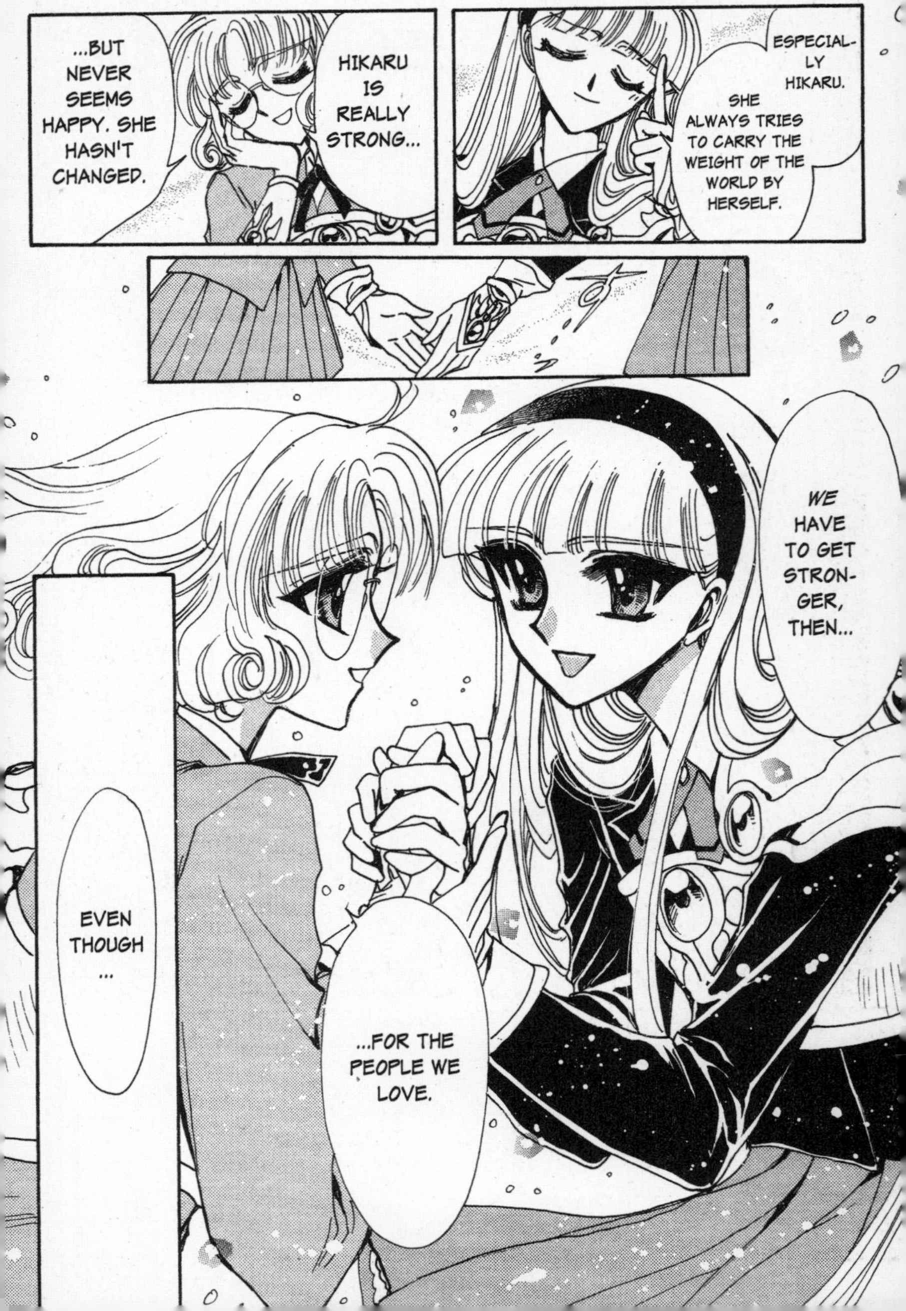
ESPECIAL-LY HIKARU.
SHE ALWAYS TRIES TO CARRY THE WEIGHT OF THE WORLD BY HERSELF.
HIKARU IS REALLY STRONG...
...BUT NEVER SEEMS HAPPY. SHE HASN'T CHANGED.
WE HAVE TO GET STRON-GER, THEN...
...FOR THE PEOPLE WE LOVE.
EVEN THOUGH ...

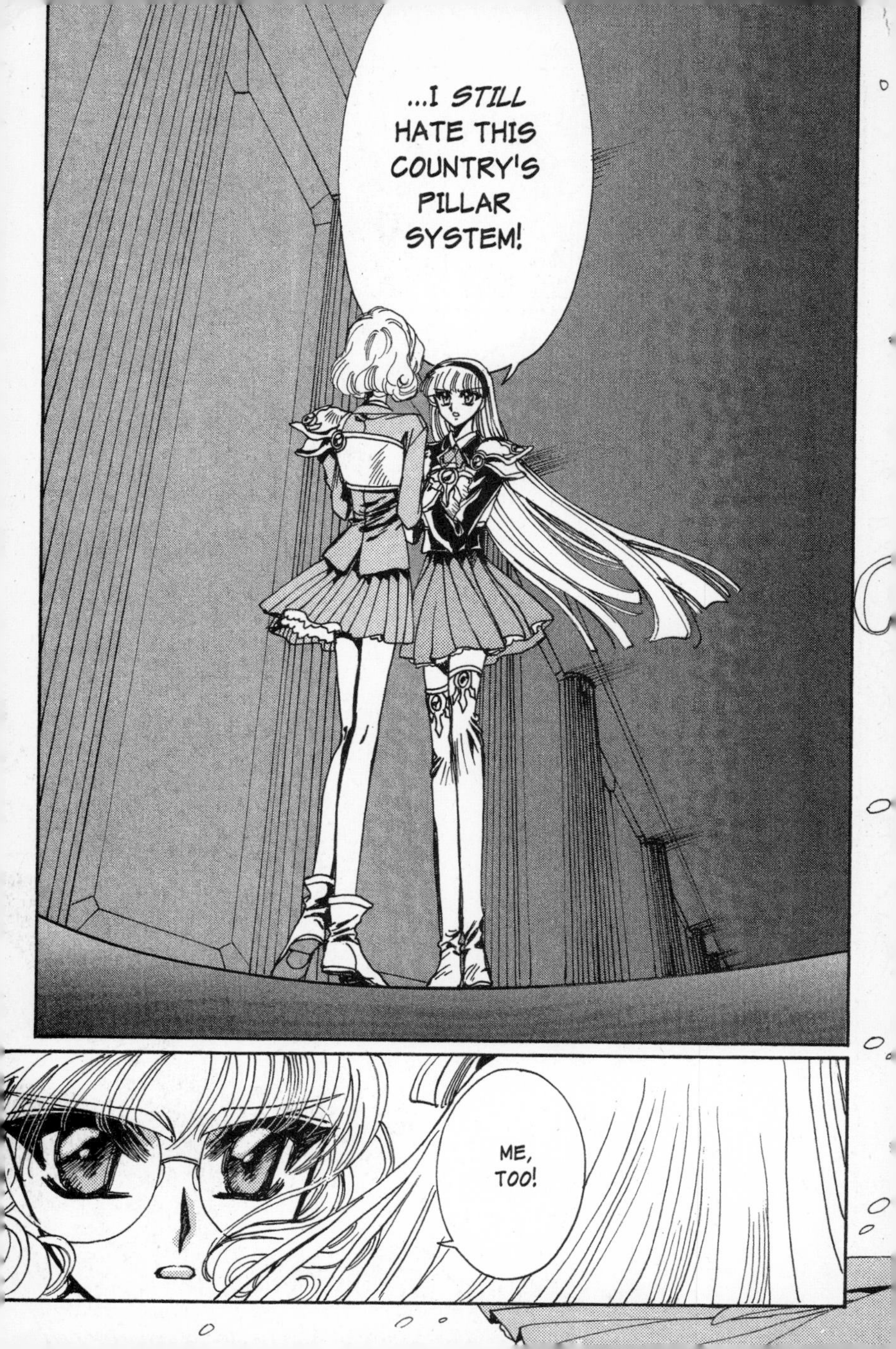
...I *STILL* HATE THIS COUNTRY'S PILLAR SYSTEM!
ME, TOO!

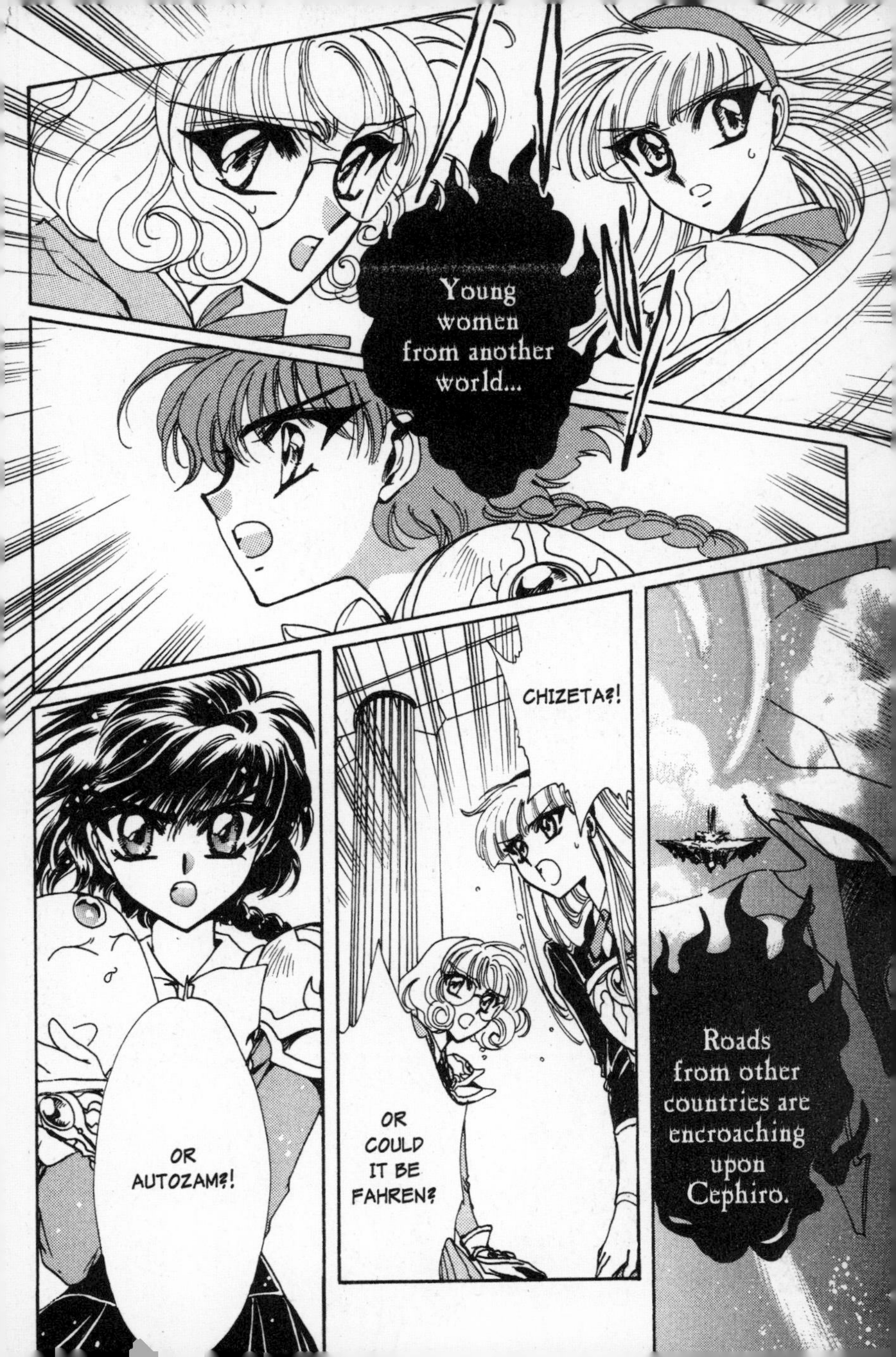

Young women from another world...
Roads from other countries are encroaching upon Cephiro.
CHIZETA?!
OR COULD IT BE FAHREN?
OR AUTOZAM?!

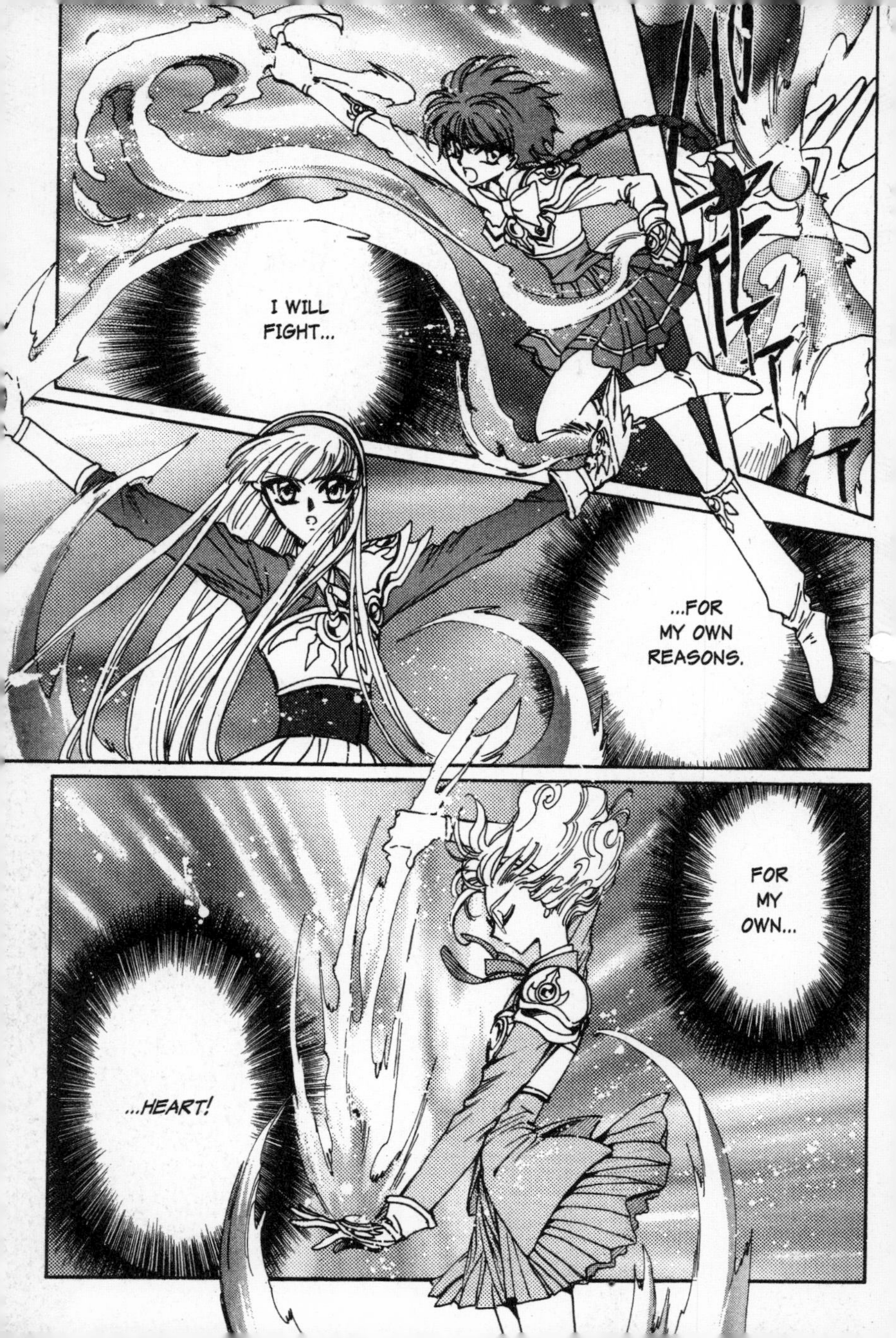
I WILL FIGHT...
...FOR MY OWN REASONS.
FOR MY OWN...
...HEART!

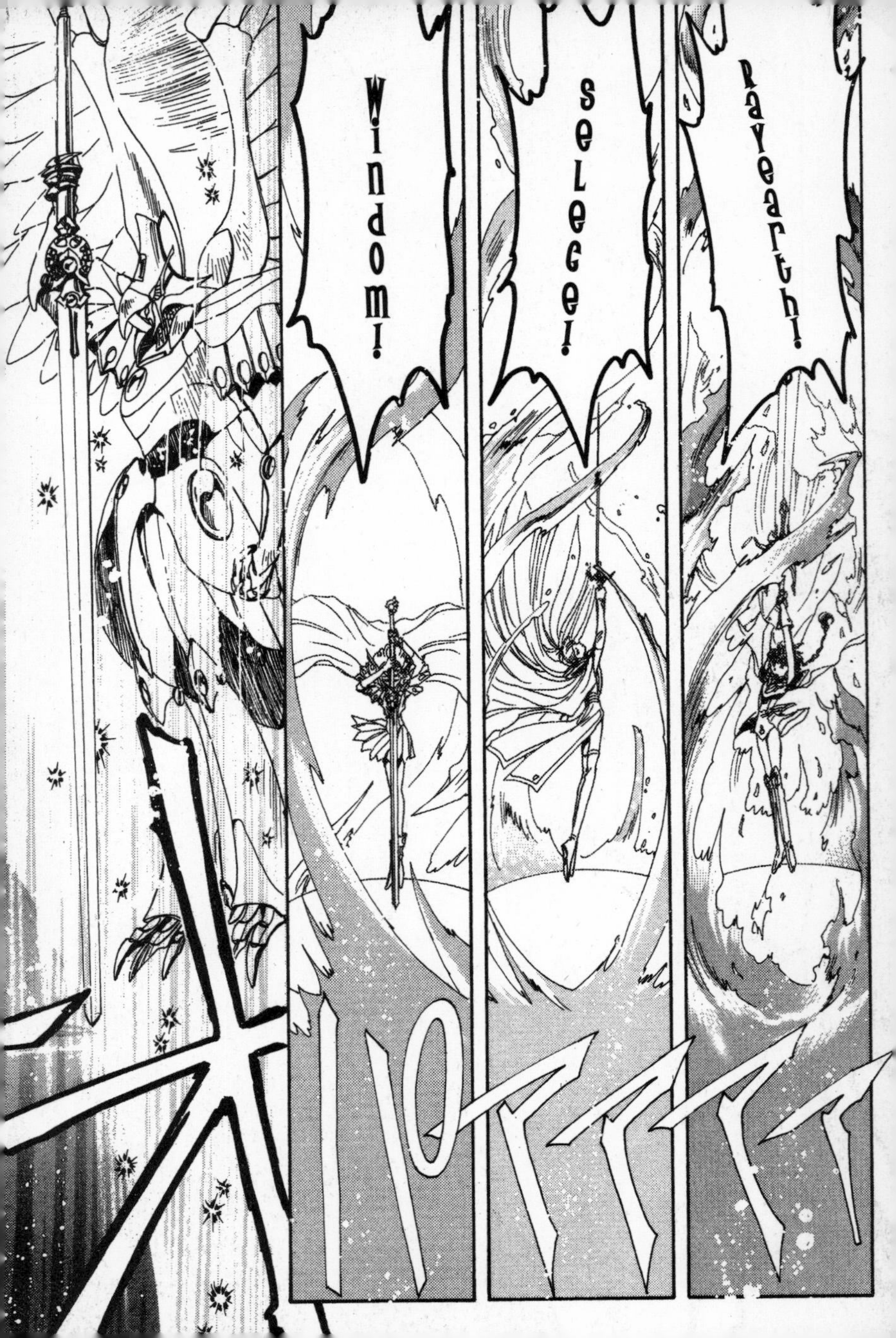
Rayearth!
Selece!
Windom!

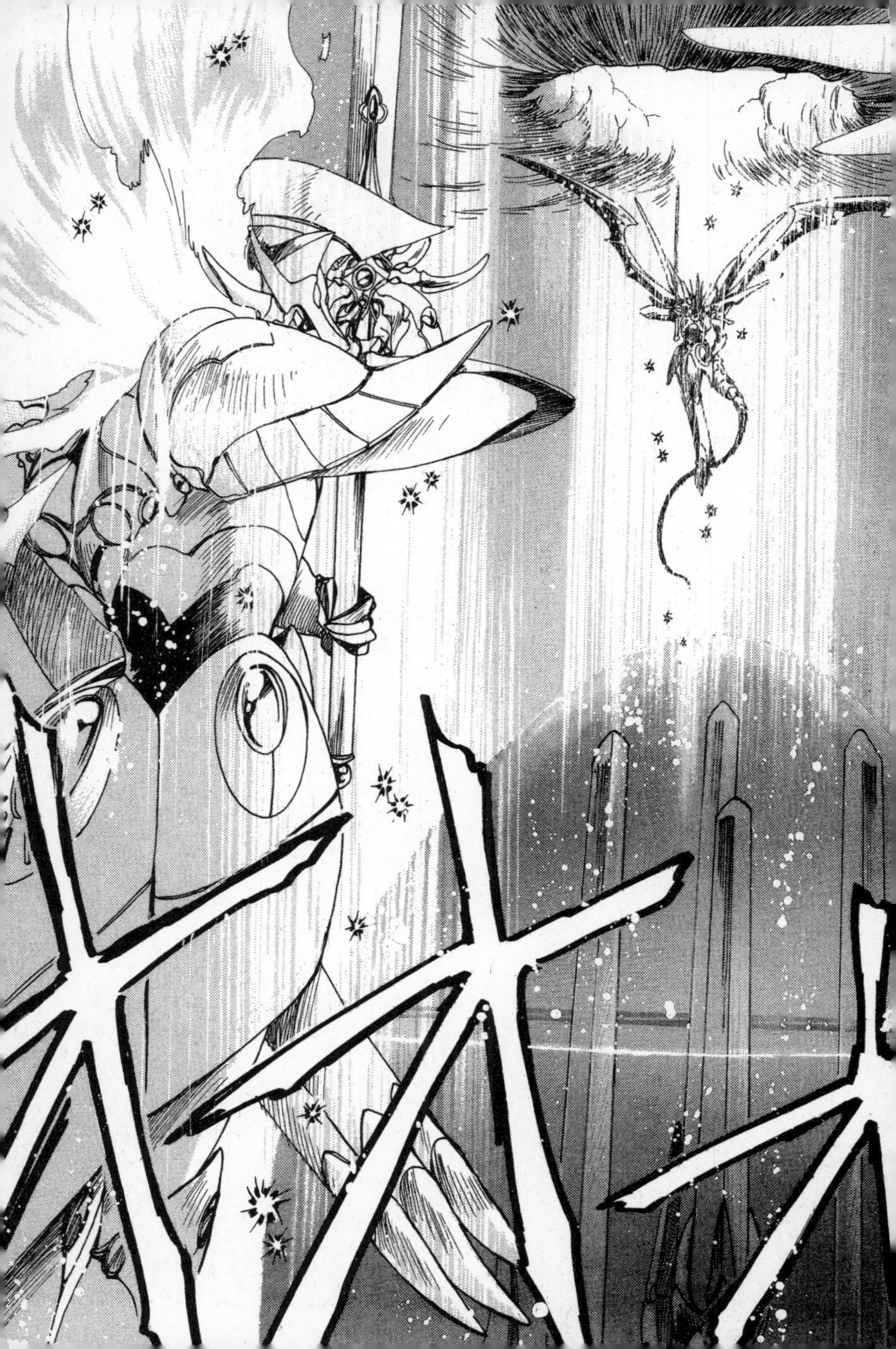

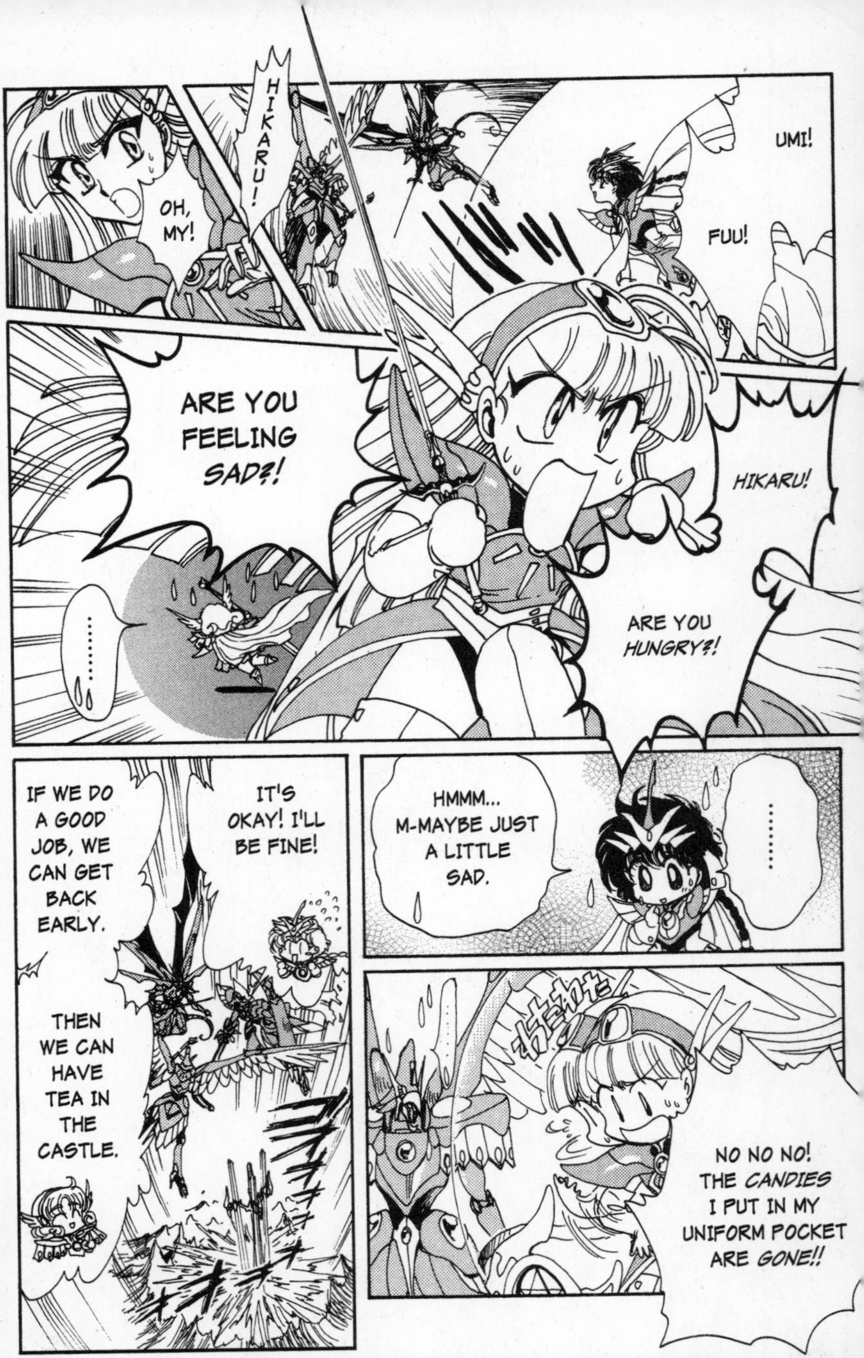
UMI!
FUU!
HIKARU!
OH, MY!
HIKARU!
ARE YOU FEELING SAD?!
ARE YOU HUNGRY?!
......
......
HMMM... M-MAYBE JUST A LITTLE SAD.
NO NO NO! THE CANDIES I PUT IN MY UNIFORM POCKET ARE GONE!!
IT'S OKAY! I'LL BE FINE!
IF WE DO A GOOD JOB, WE CAN GET BACK EARLY.
THEN WE CAN HAVE TEA IN THE CASTLE.

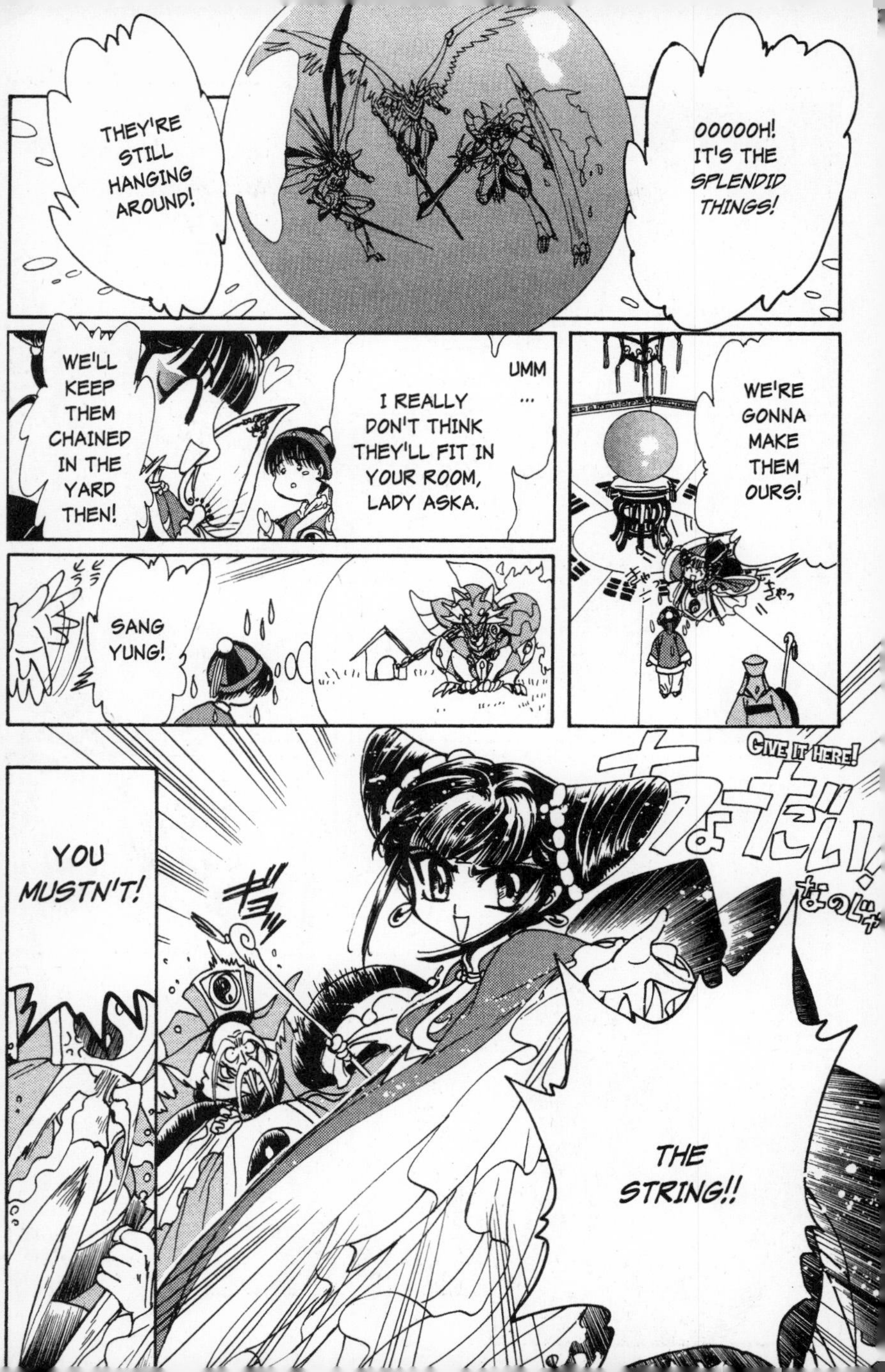
OOOOOH! IT'S THE SPLENDID THINGS!
THEY'RE STILL HANGING AROUND!
WE'RE GONNA MAKE THEM OURS!
きゃっ
UMM ...
I REALLY DON'T THINK THEY'LL FIT IN YOUR ROOM, LADY ASKA.
WE'LL KEEP THEM CHAINED IN THE YARD THEN!
ヒラヒラ
SANG YUNG!
GIVE IT HERE!
ちょだい!
なのじゃ
THE STRING!!
YOU MUSTN'T!

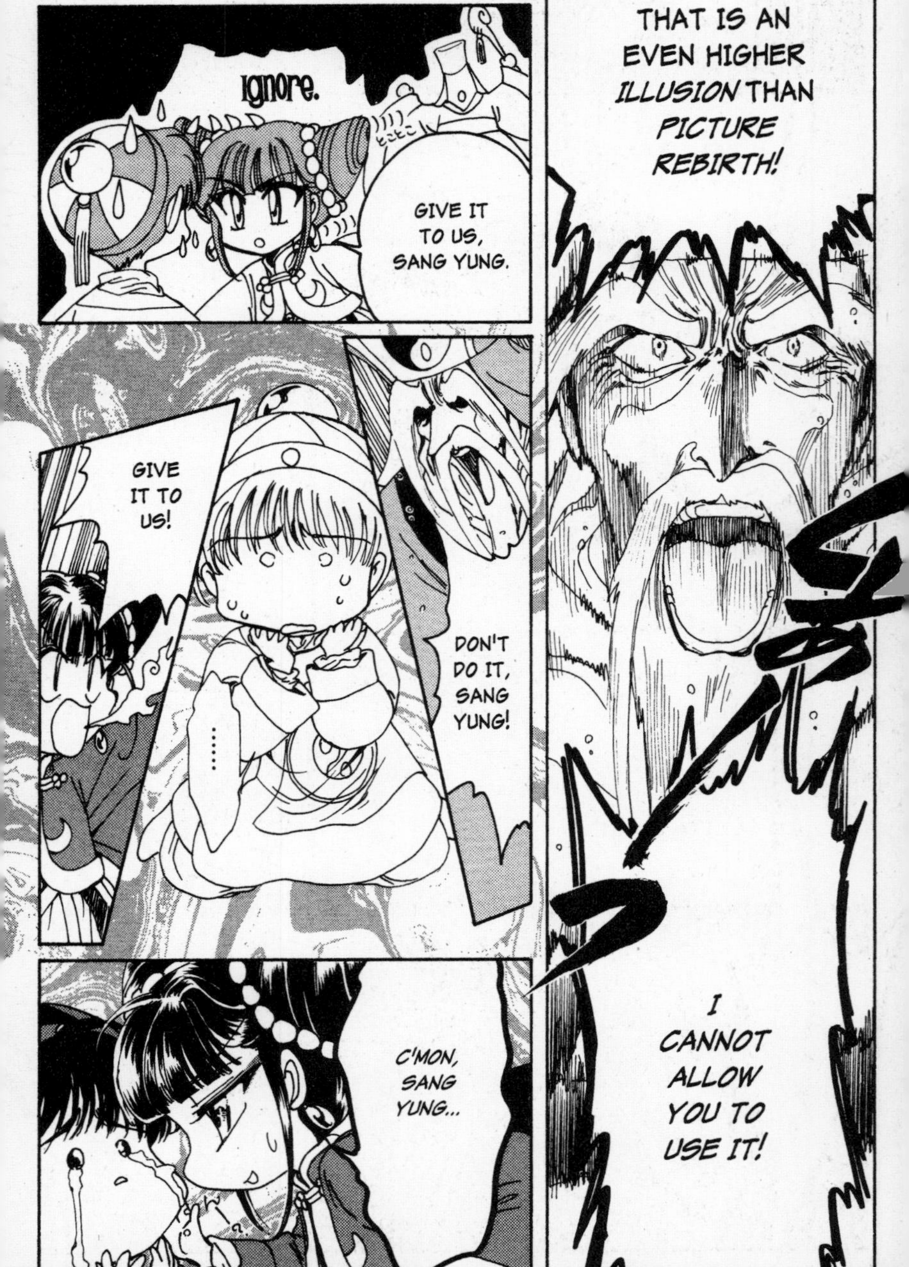

THAT IS AN EVEN HIGHER ILLUSION THAN PICTURE REBIRTH!
I CANNOT ALLOW YOU TO USE IT!
Ignore.
GIVE IT TO US, SANG YUNG.
DON'T DO IT, SANG YUNG!
......
GIVE IT TO US!
C'MON, SANG YUNG...

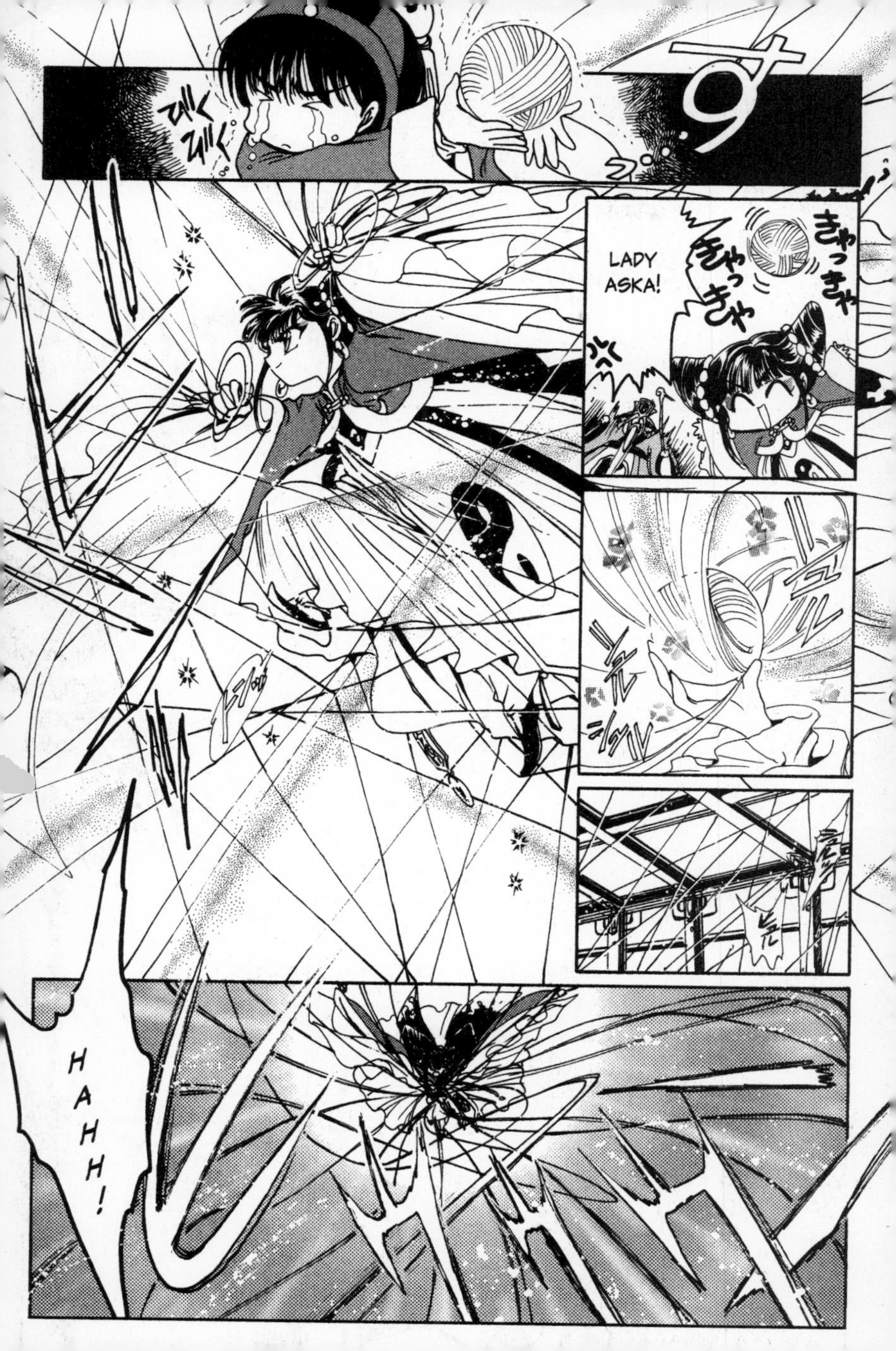
す
びくびく
きゃっきゃ
きゃっきゃ
LADY ASKA!
HAHHH!

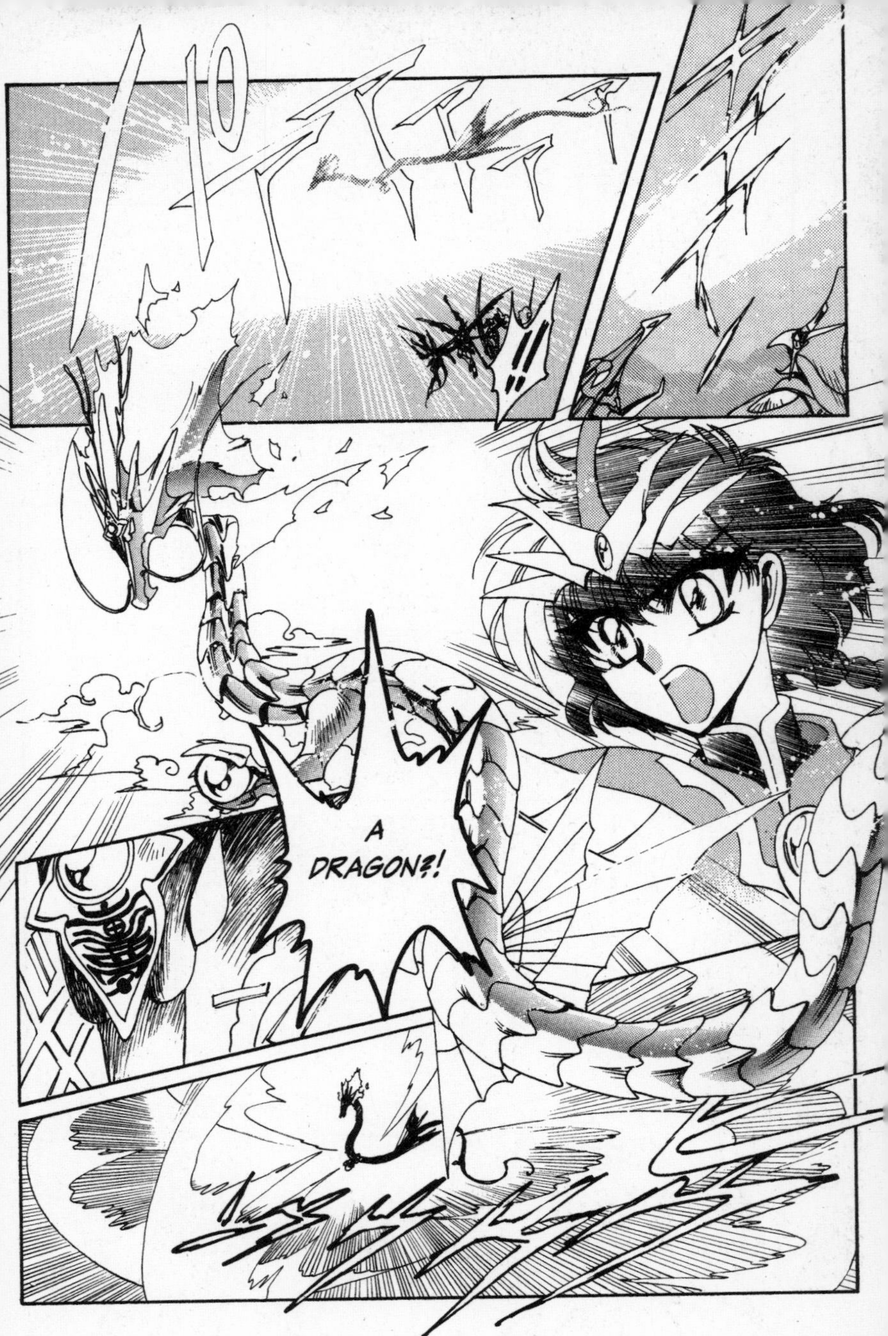
A DRAGON?!

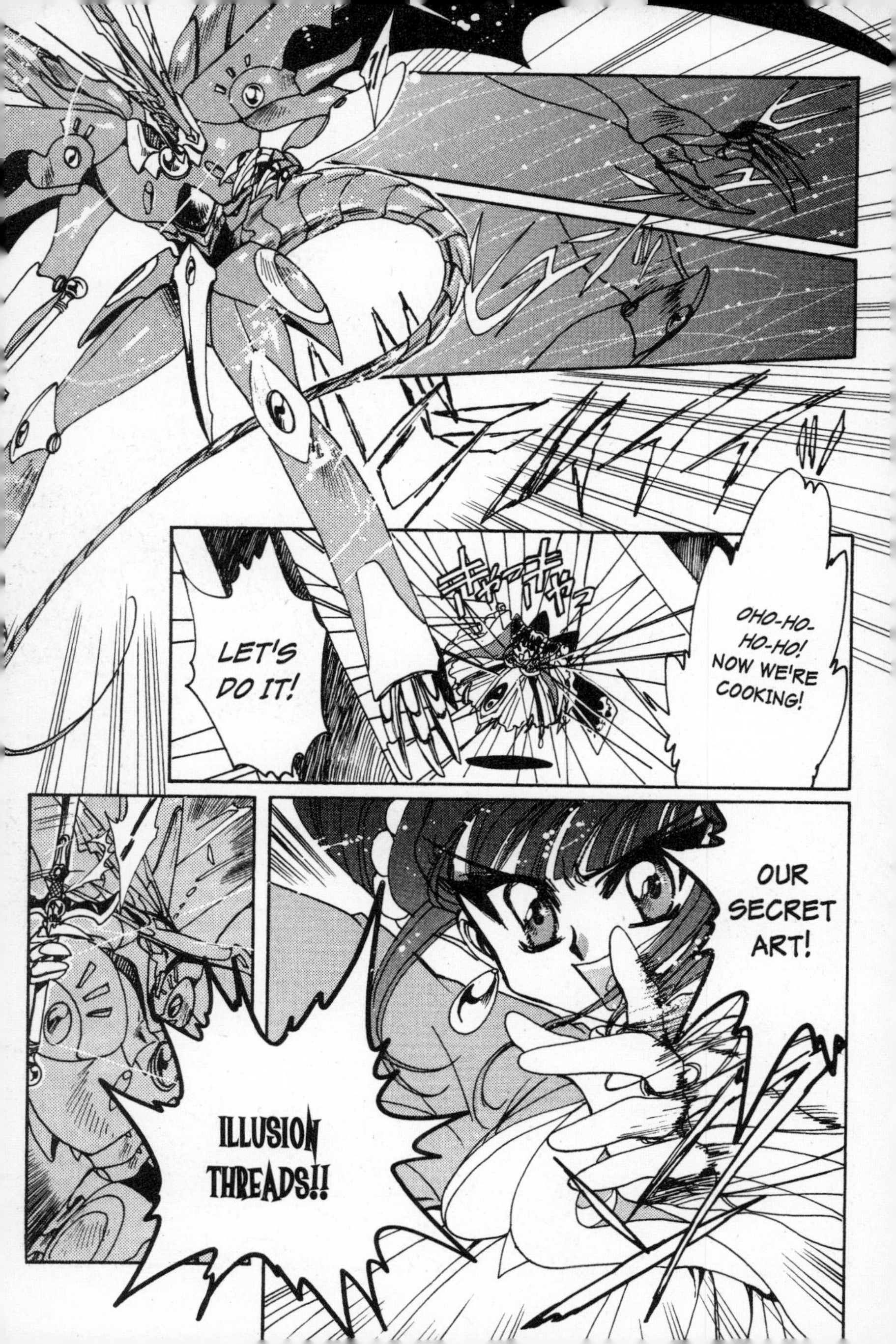
OHO-HO-HO-HO! NOW WE'RE COOKING!
LET'S DO IT!
OUR SECRET ART!
ILLUSION THREADS!!

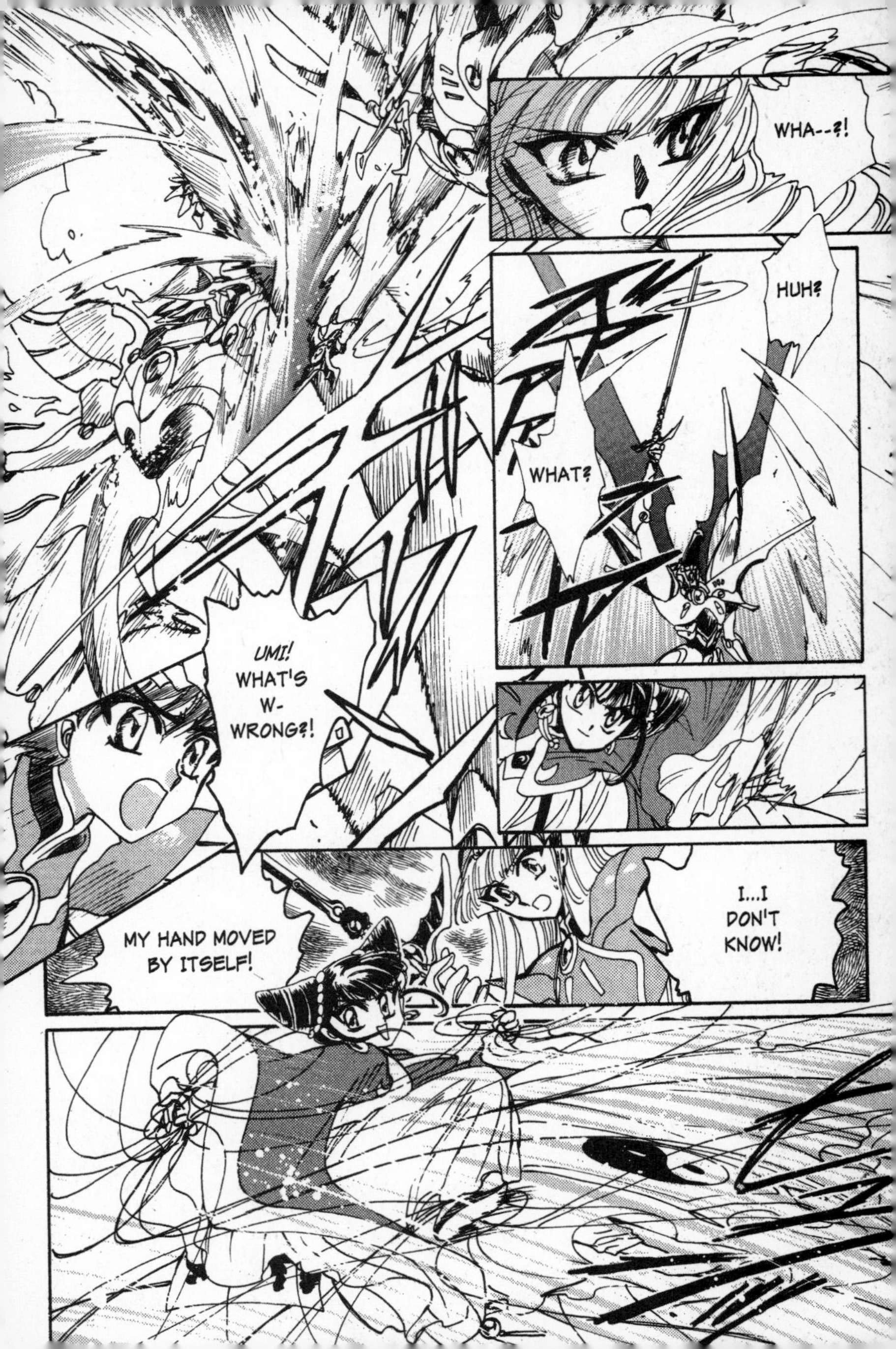
WHA--?!
HUH?
WHAT?
UMI! WHAT'S W-WRONG?!
I...I DON'T KNOW!
MY HAND MOVED BY ITSELF!

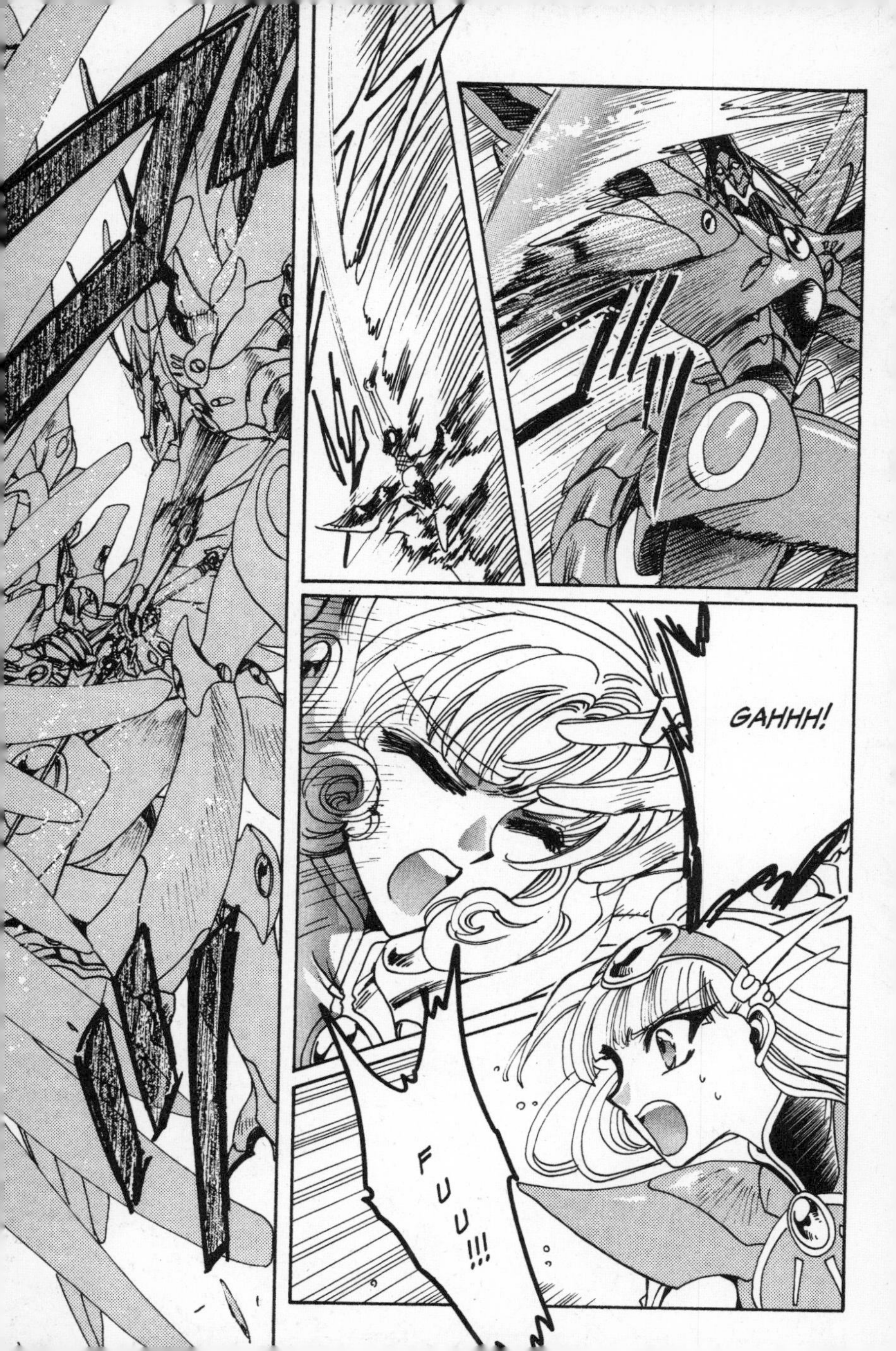
GAHHH!
FUUU!!!

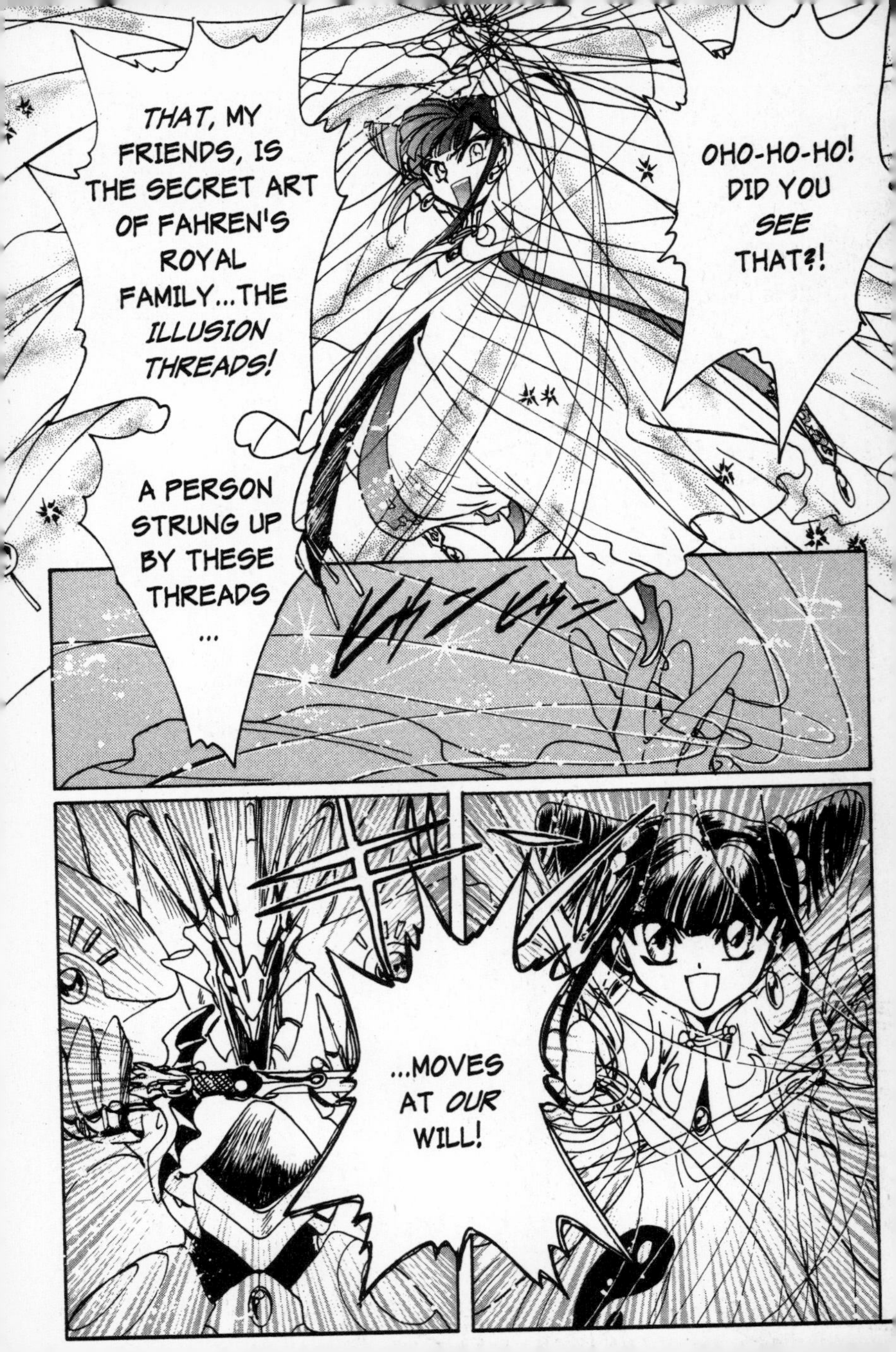
OHO-HO-HO! DID YOU *SEE* THAT?!
THAT, MY FRIENDS, IS THE SECRET ART OF FAHREN'S ROYAL FAMILY...THE *ILLUSION THREADS!*
A PERSON STRUNG UP BY THESE THREADS ...
...MOVES AT *OUR* WILL!

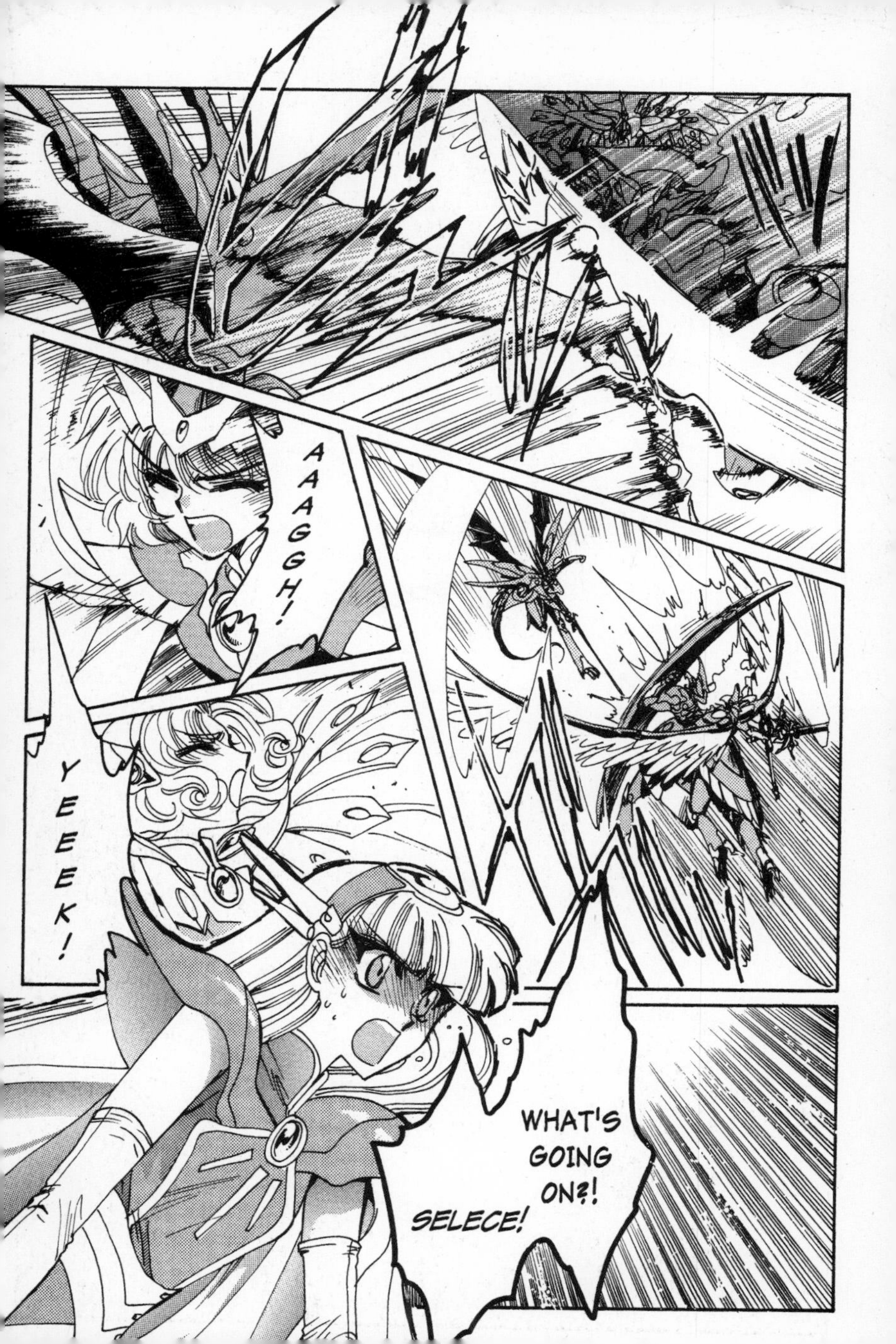
AAAAGGH!
YEEEEK!
WHAT'S GOING ON?!
SELECE!

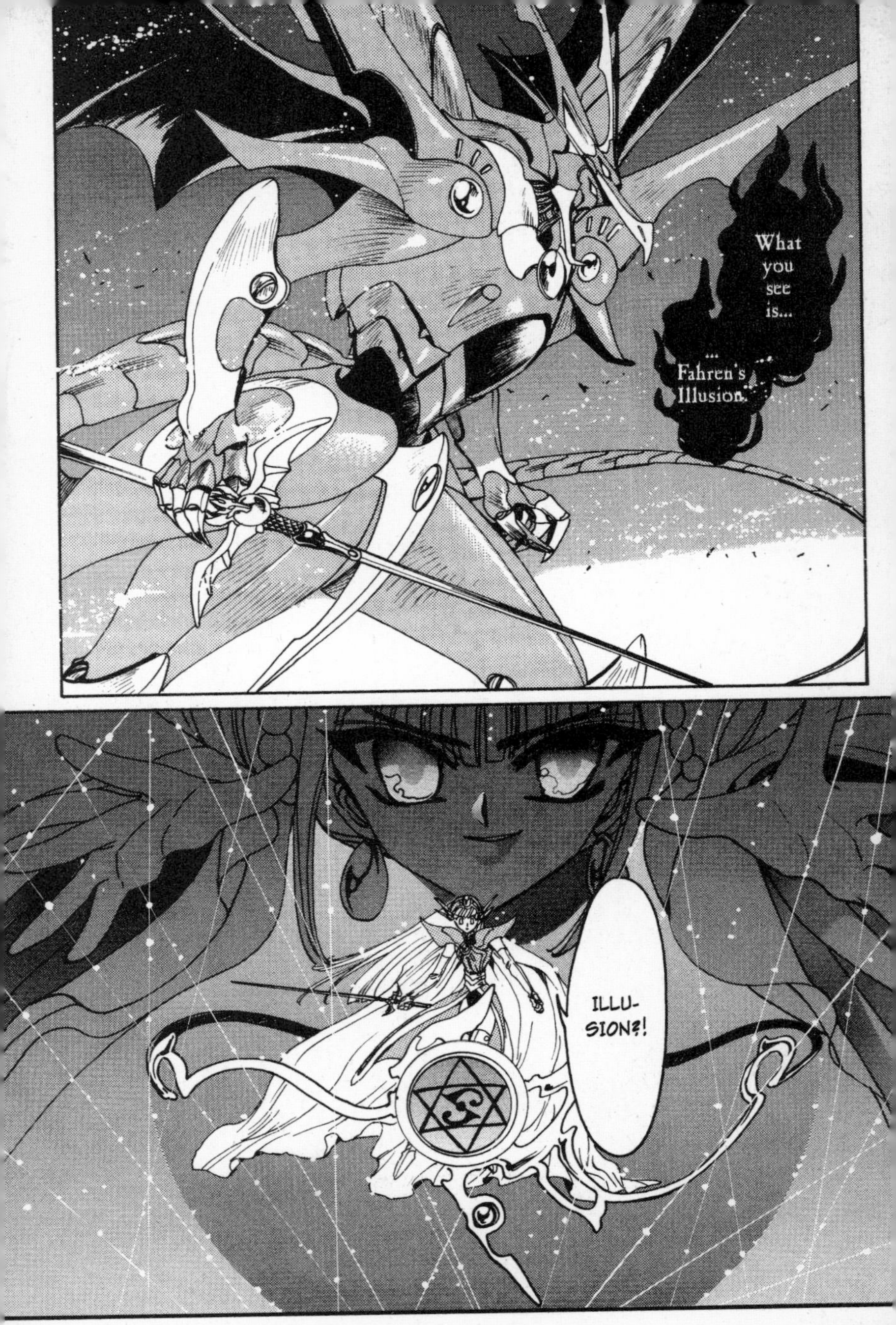
What you see is...
...Fahren's Illusion.
ILLUSION?!

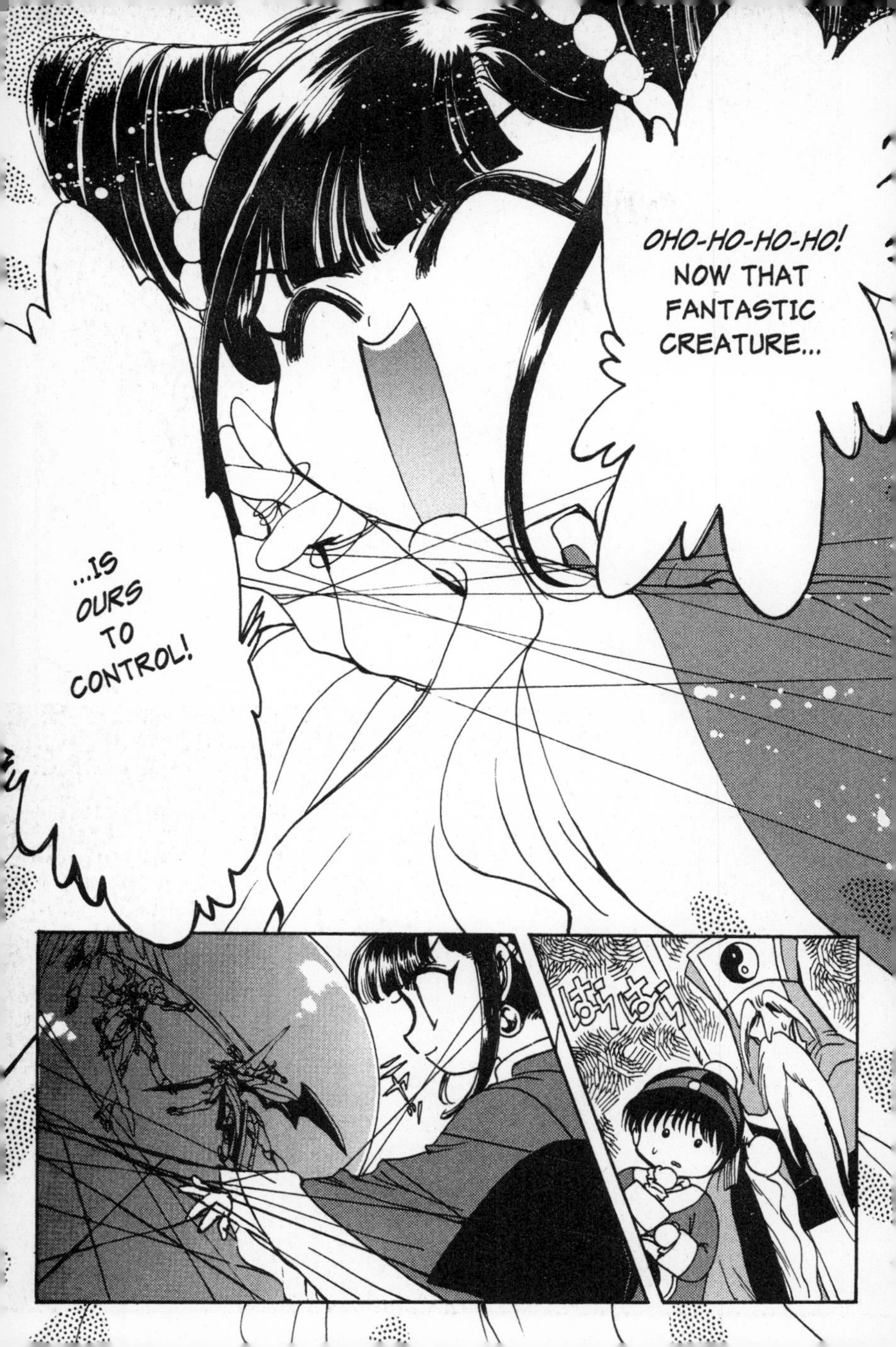
OHO-HO-HO-HO! NOW THAT FANTASTIC CREATURE...
...IS OURS TO CONTROL!
はらはら

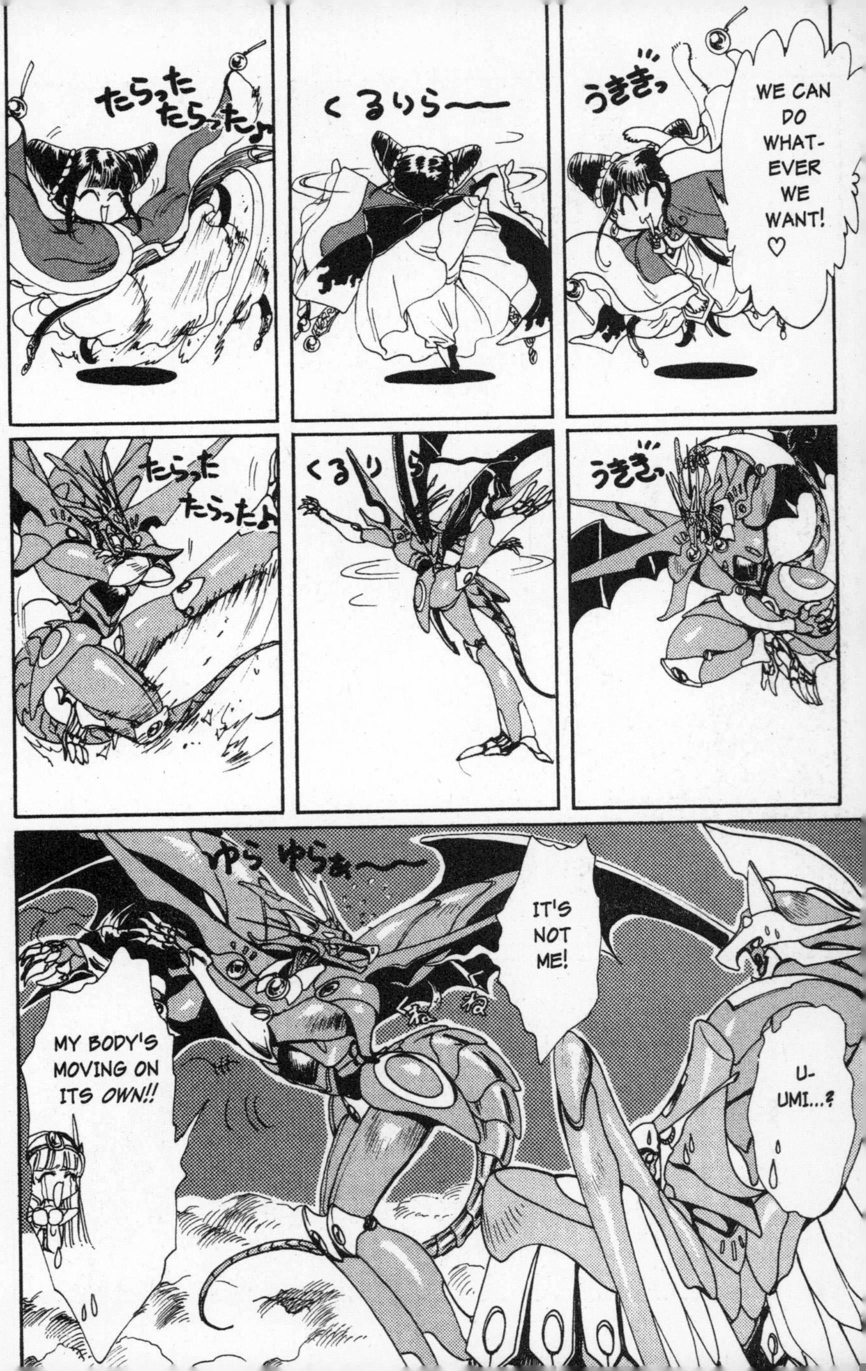
うききっ
WE CAN DO WHATEVER WE WANT! ♡
くるりら〜〜
たらったたらったた♪
うききっ
くるりら
たらった たらったた
ゆら ゆらぁ〜〜
IT'S NOT ME!
U-UMI...?
くね くね
MY BODY'S MOVING ON ITS OWN!!

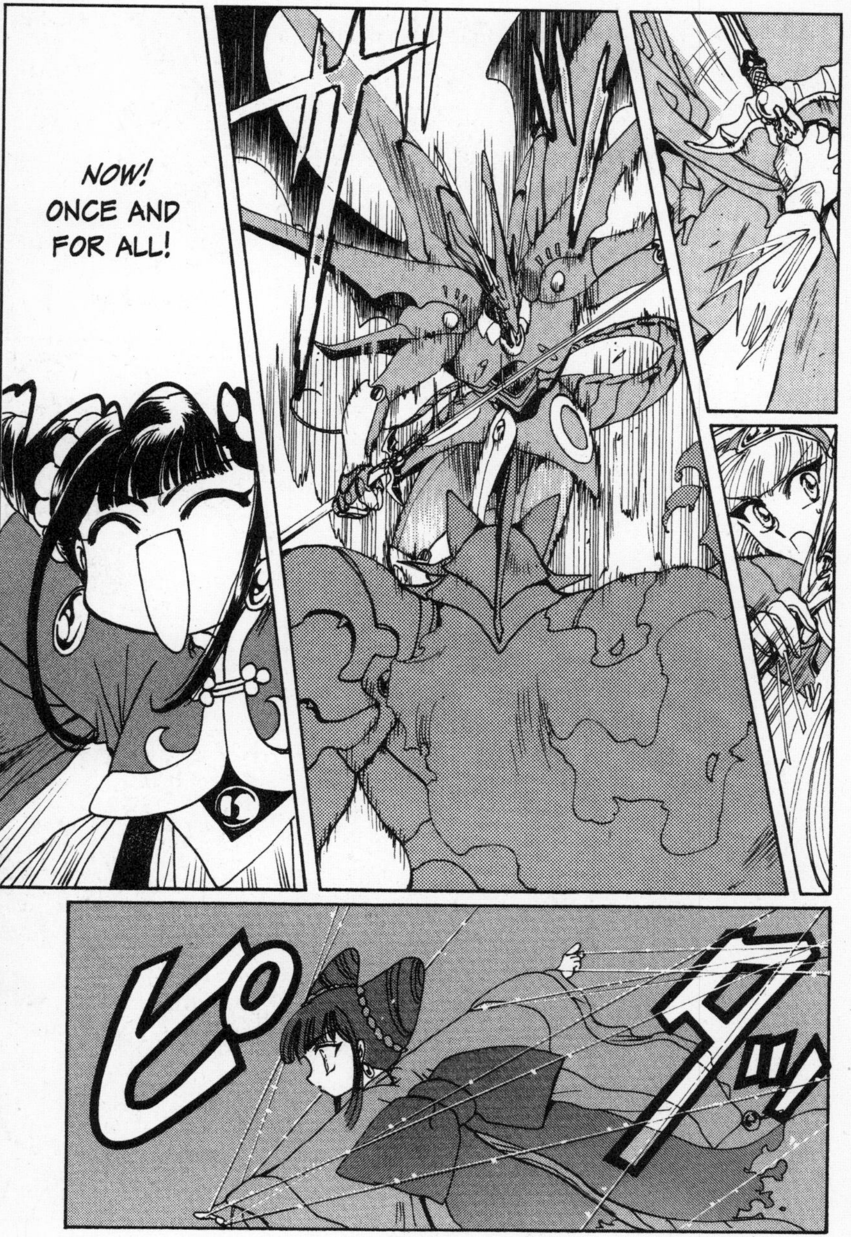
NOW! ONCE AND FOR ALL!

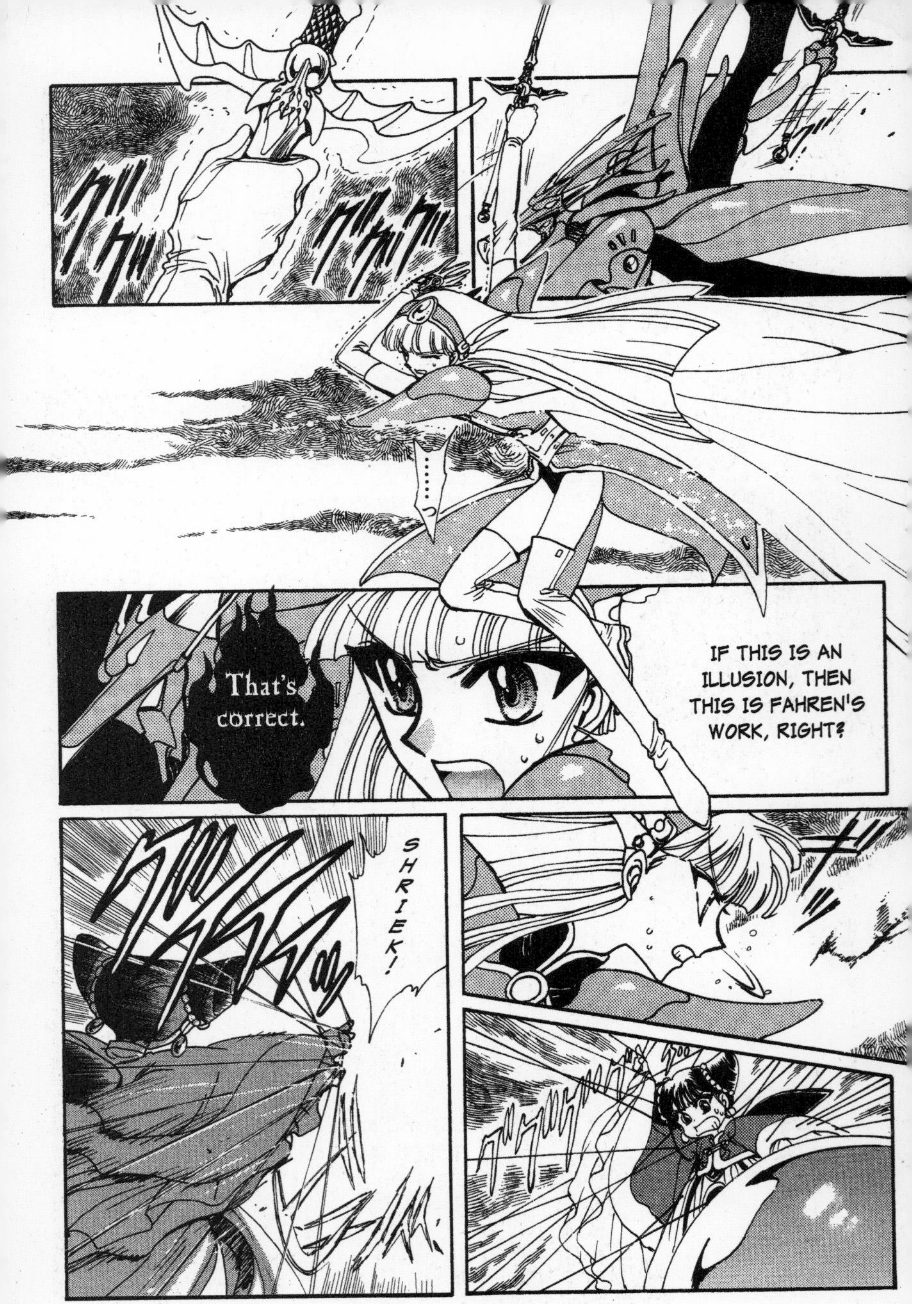
IF THIS IS AN ILLUSION, THEN THIS IS FAHREN'S WORK, RIGHT?
That's correct.
SHRIEK!

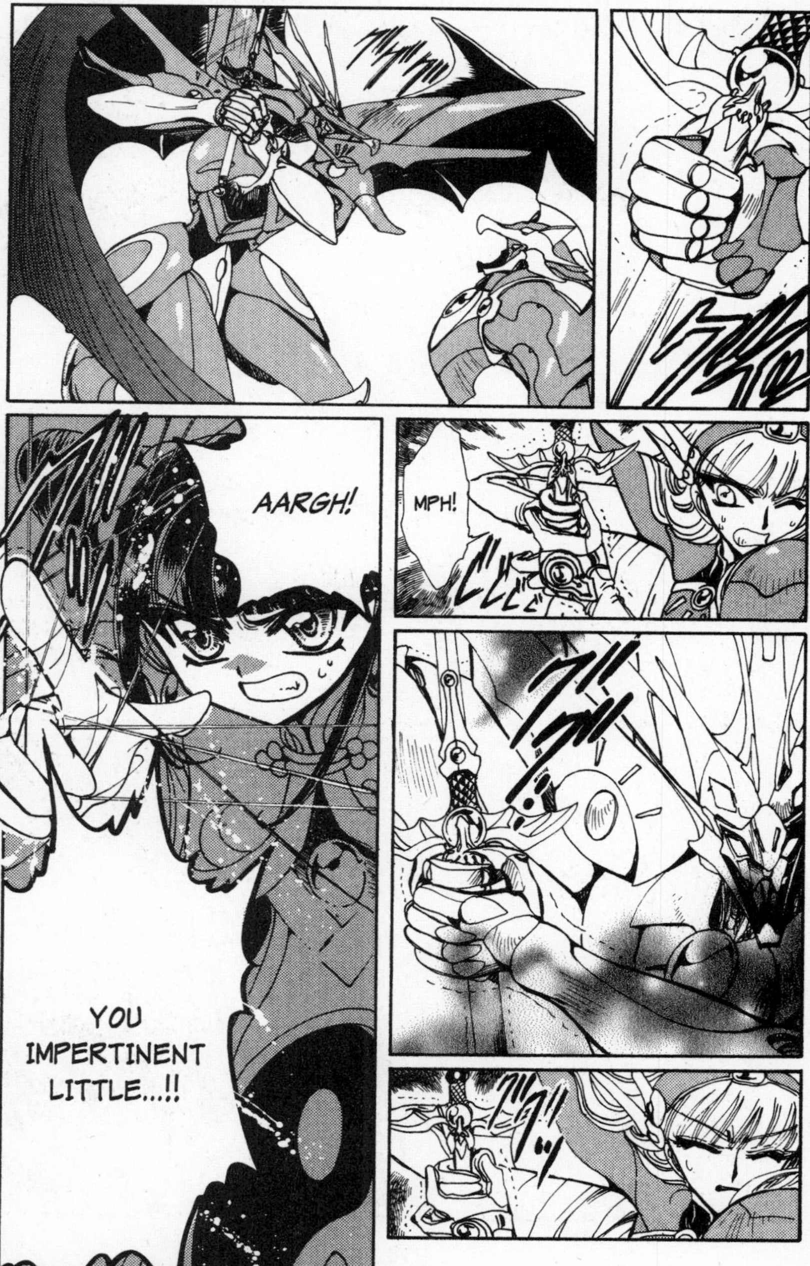
MPH!
AARGH!
YOU IMPERTINENT LITTLE...!!

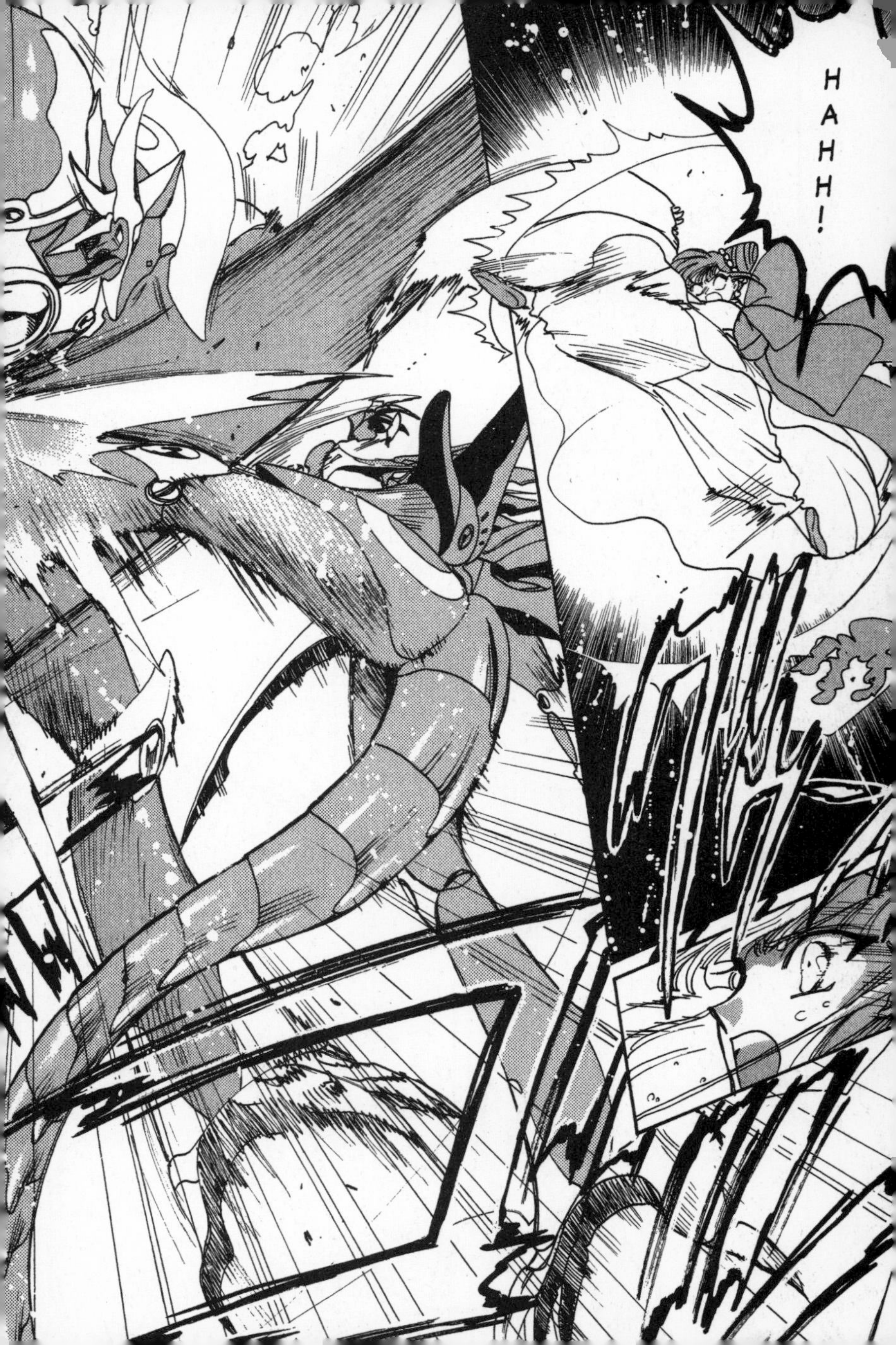
HAHHH!

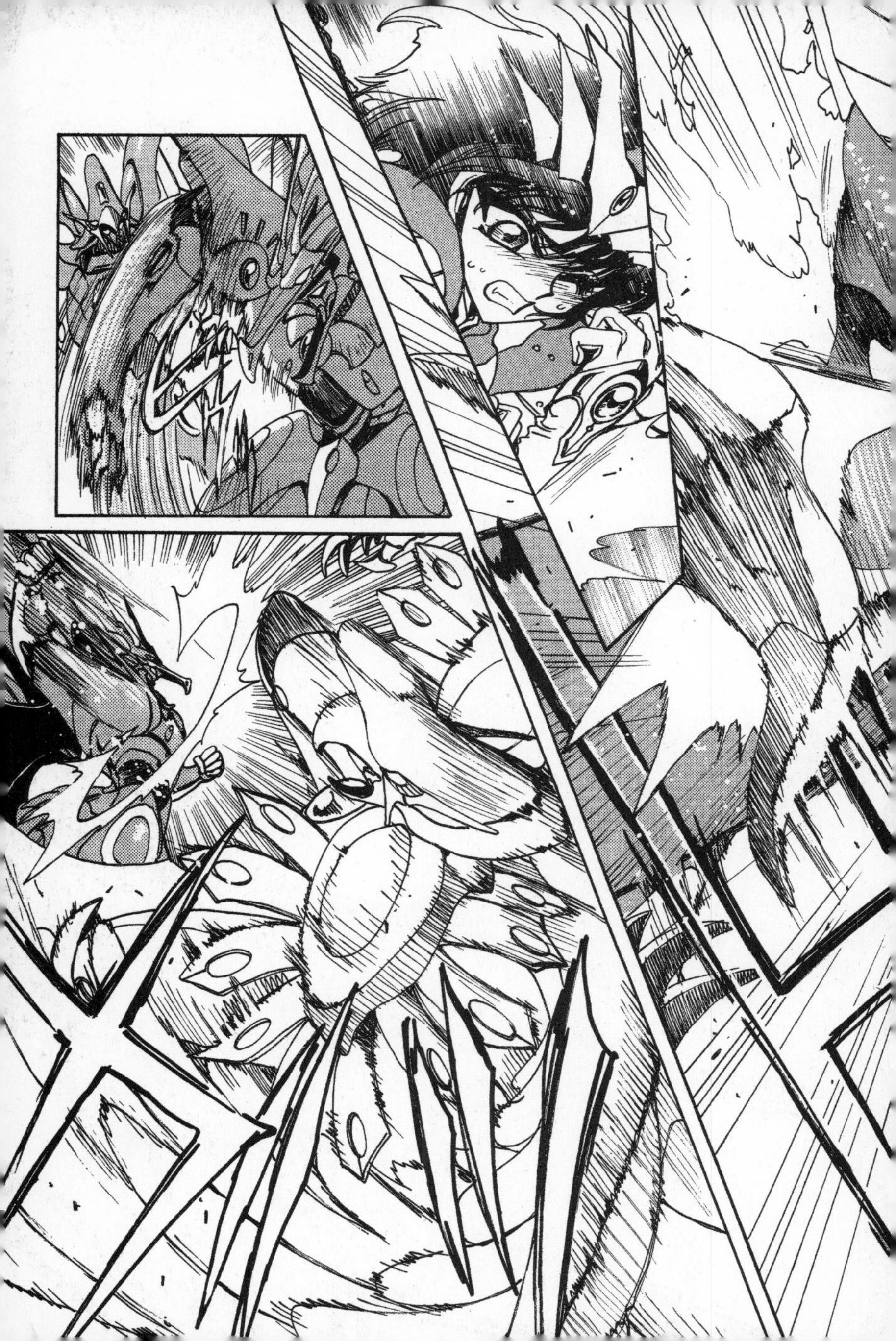

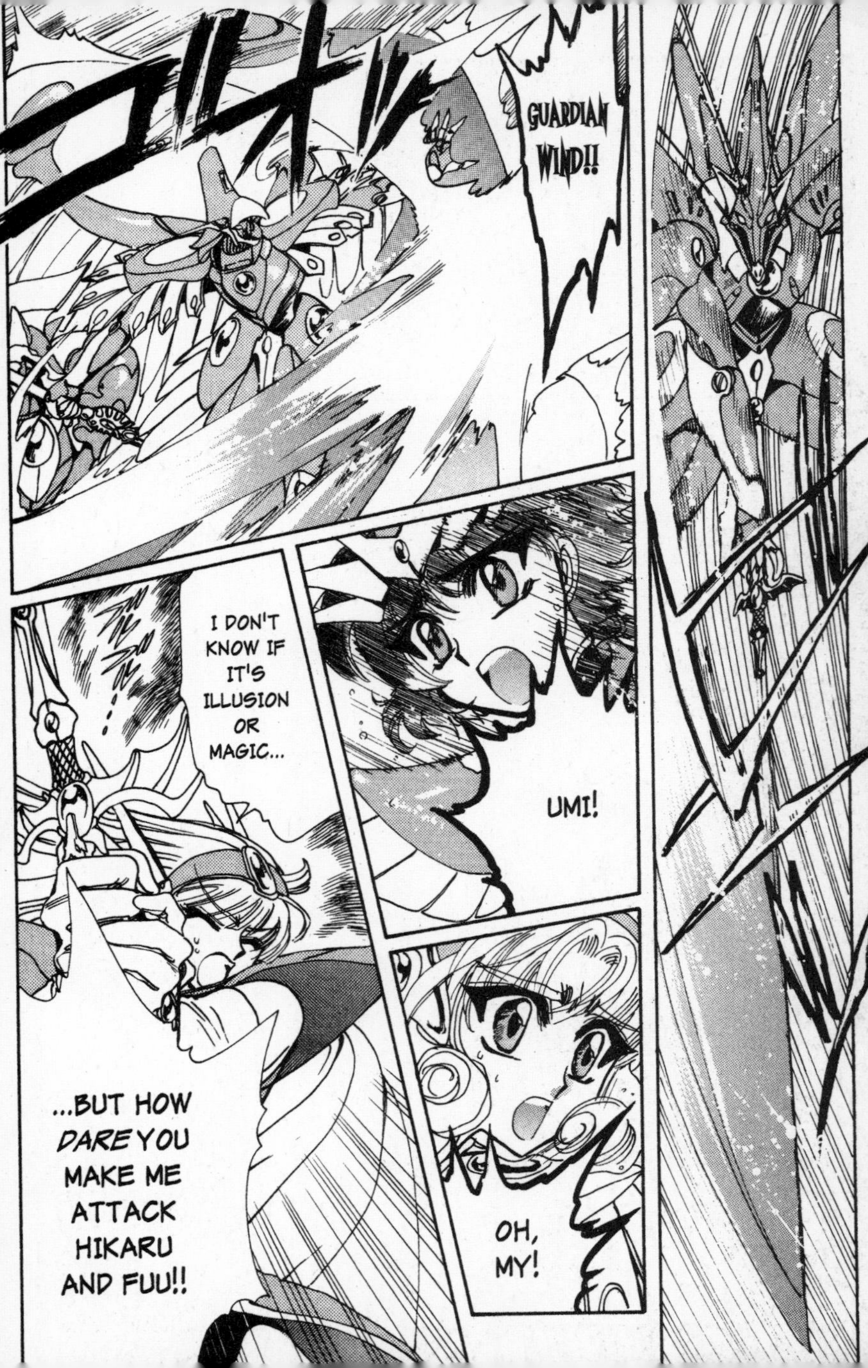
GUARDIAN WIND!!
UMI!
OH, MY!
I DON'T KNOW IF IT'S ILLUSION OR MAGIC...
...BUT HOW *DARE* YOU MAKE ME ATTACK HIKARU AND FUU!!

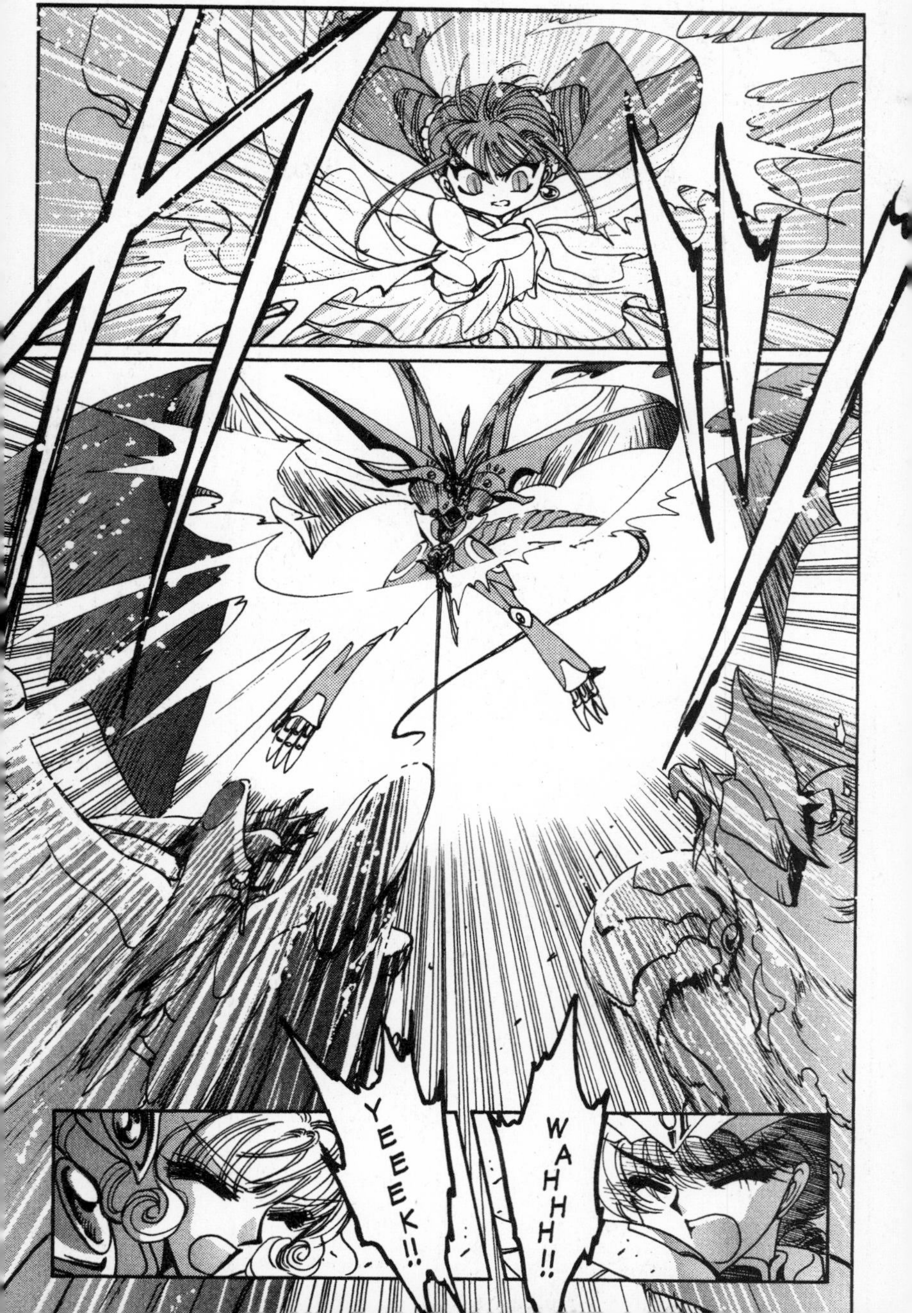
WAHHH!!
YEEEK!!

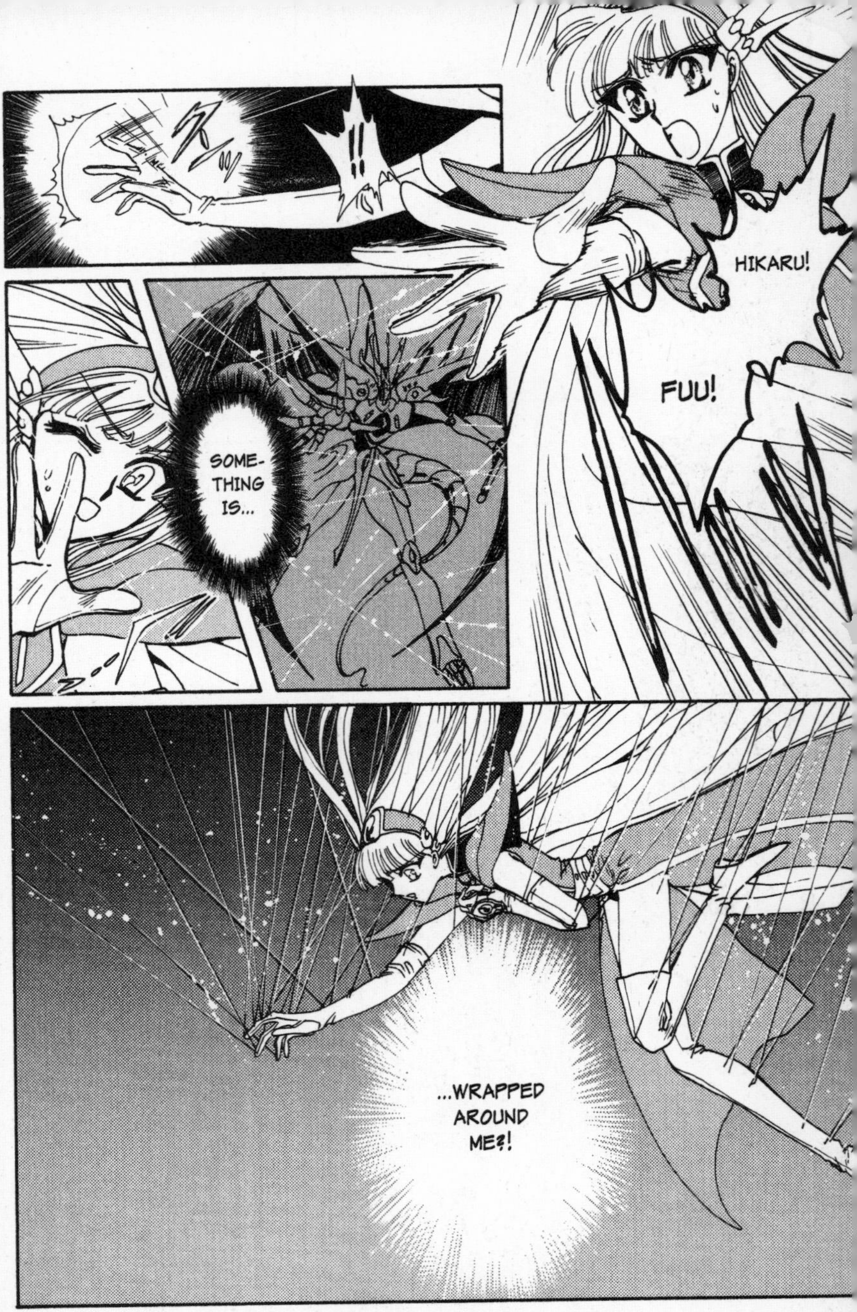
HIKARU!
FUU!
!!
SOME-
THING
IS...
...WRAPPED
AROUND
ME?!

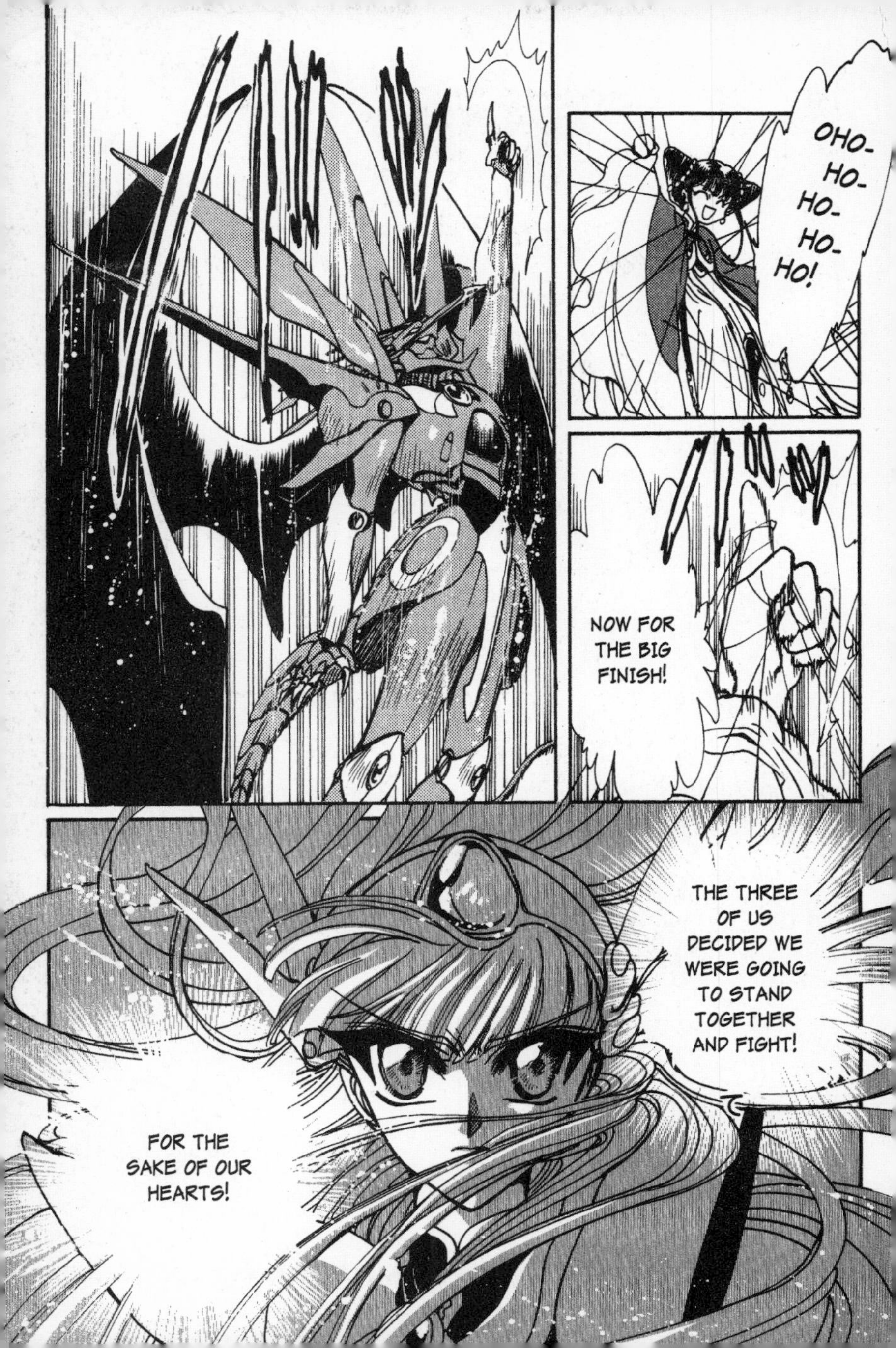
OHO-HO-HO-HO-HO!
NOW FOR THE BIG FINISH!
THE THREE OF US DECIDED WE WERE GOING TO STAND TOGETHER AND FIGHT!
FOR THE SAKE OF OUR HEARTS!

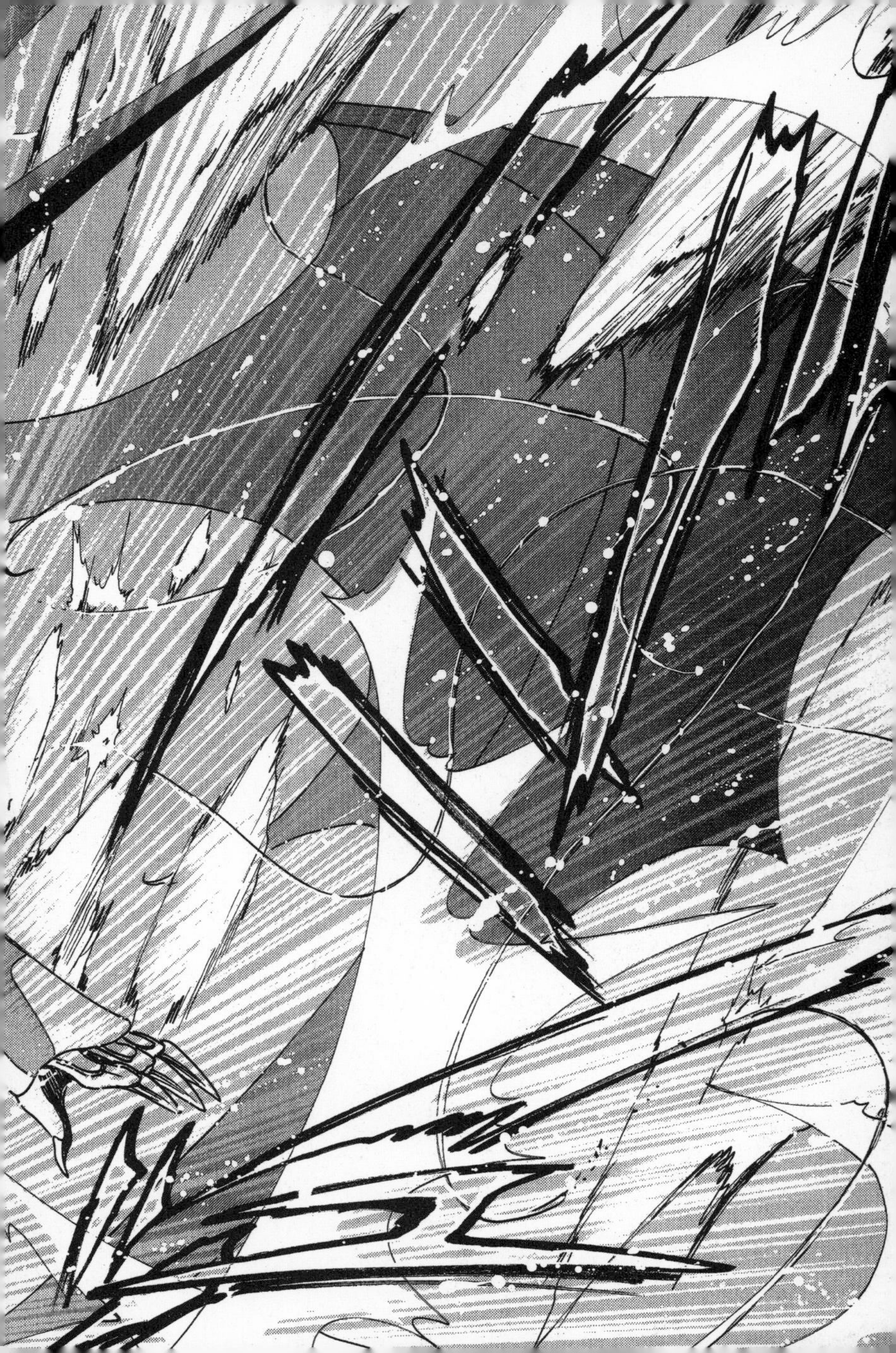

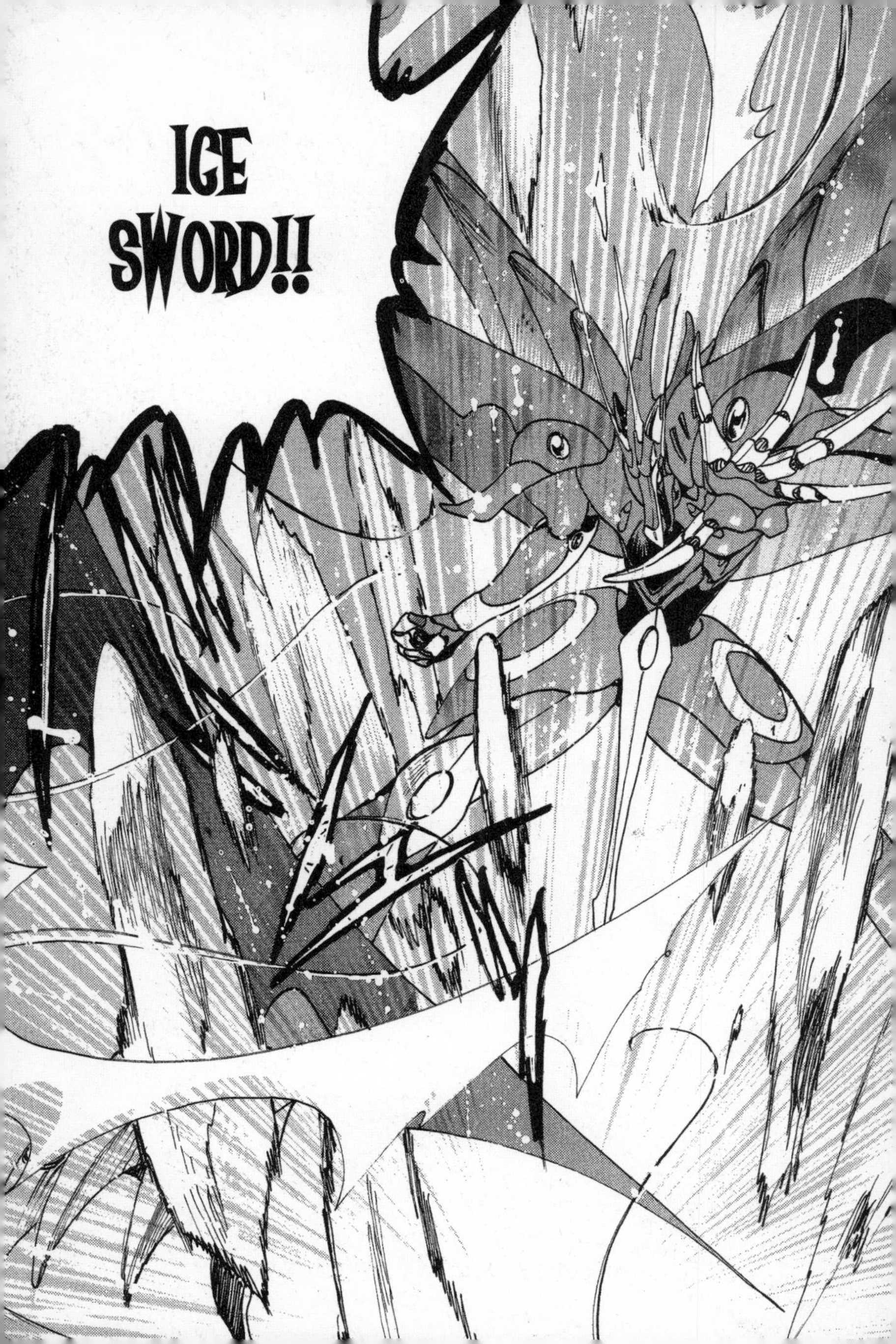
ICE SWORD!!

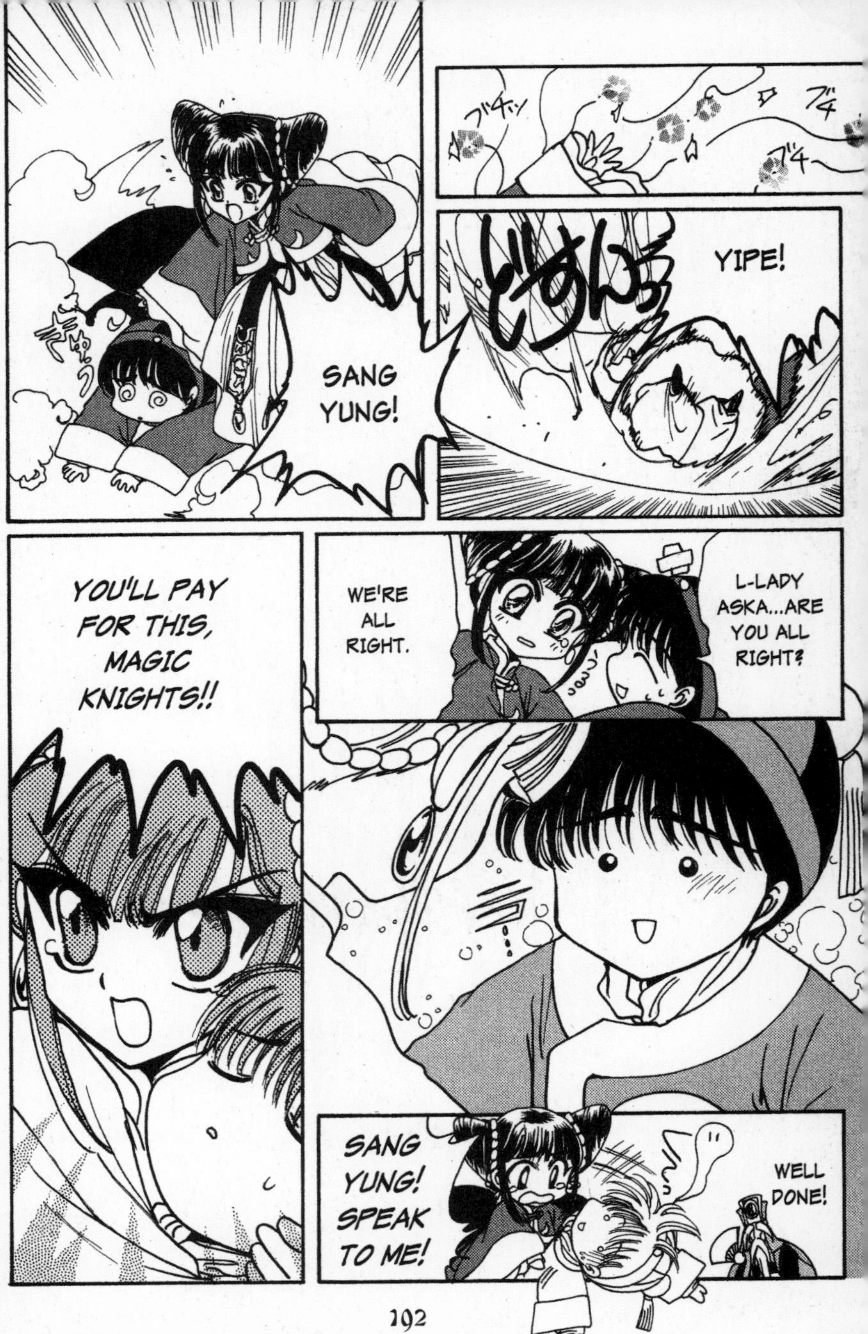
YIPE!
SANG YUNG!
L-LADY ASKA...ARE YOU ALL RIGHT?
WE'RE ALL RIGHT.
WELL DONE!
SANG YUNG! SPEAK TO ME!
YOU'LL PAY FOR THIS, MAGIC KNIGHTS!!

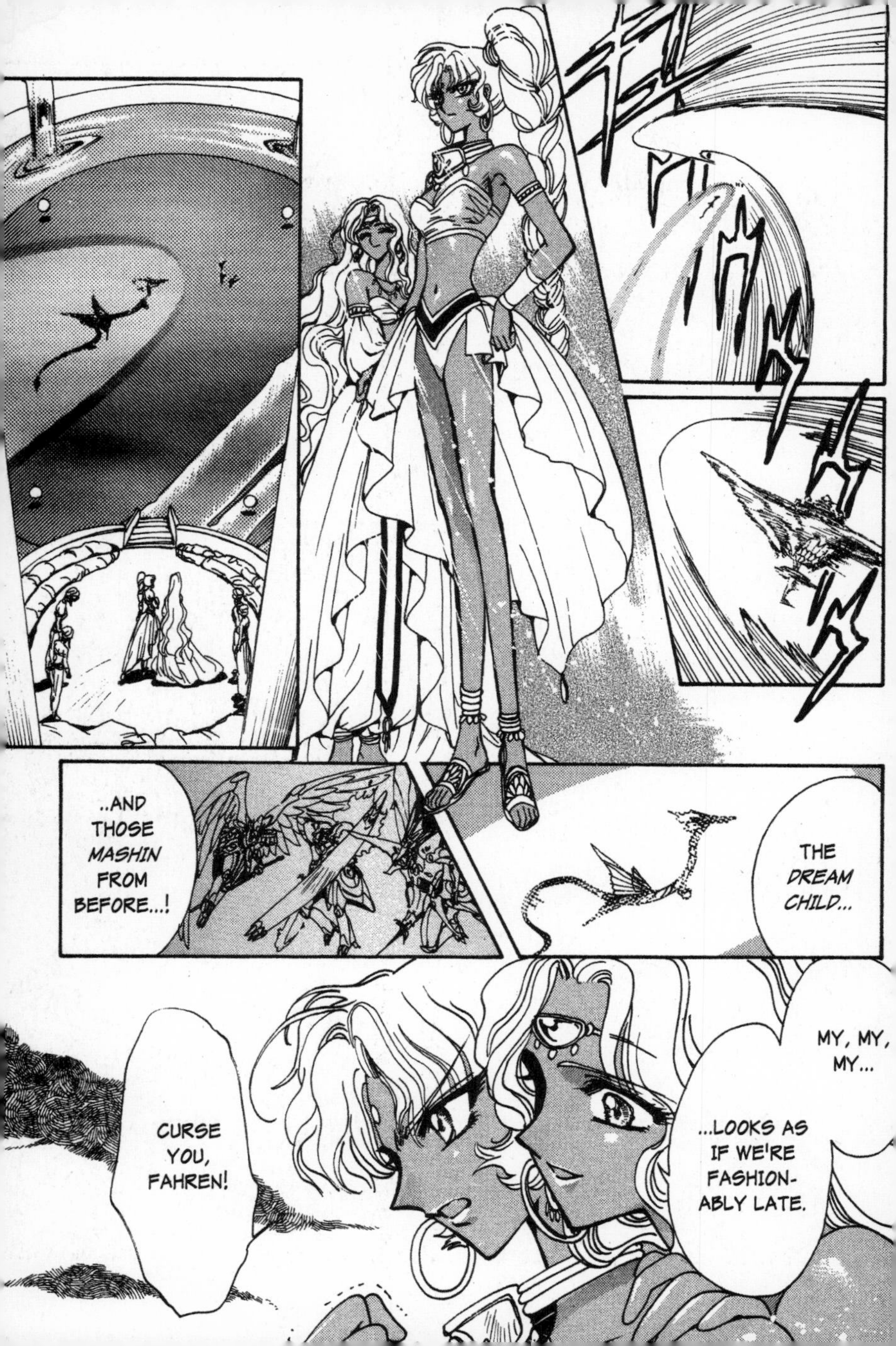
THE DREAM CHILD...
..AND THOSE MASHIN FROM BEFORE...!
MY, MY, MY...
...LOOKS AS IF WE'RE FASHION-ABLY LATE.
CURSE YOU, FAHREN!

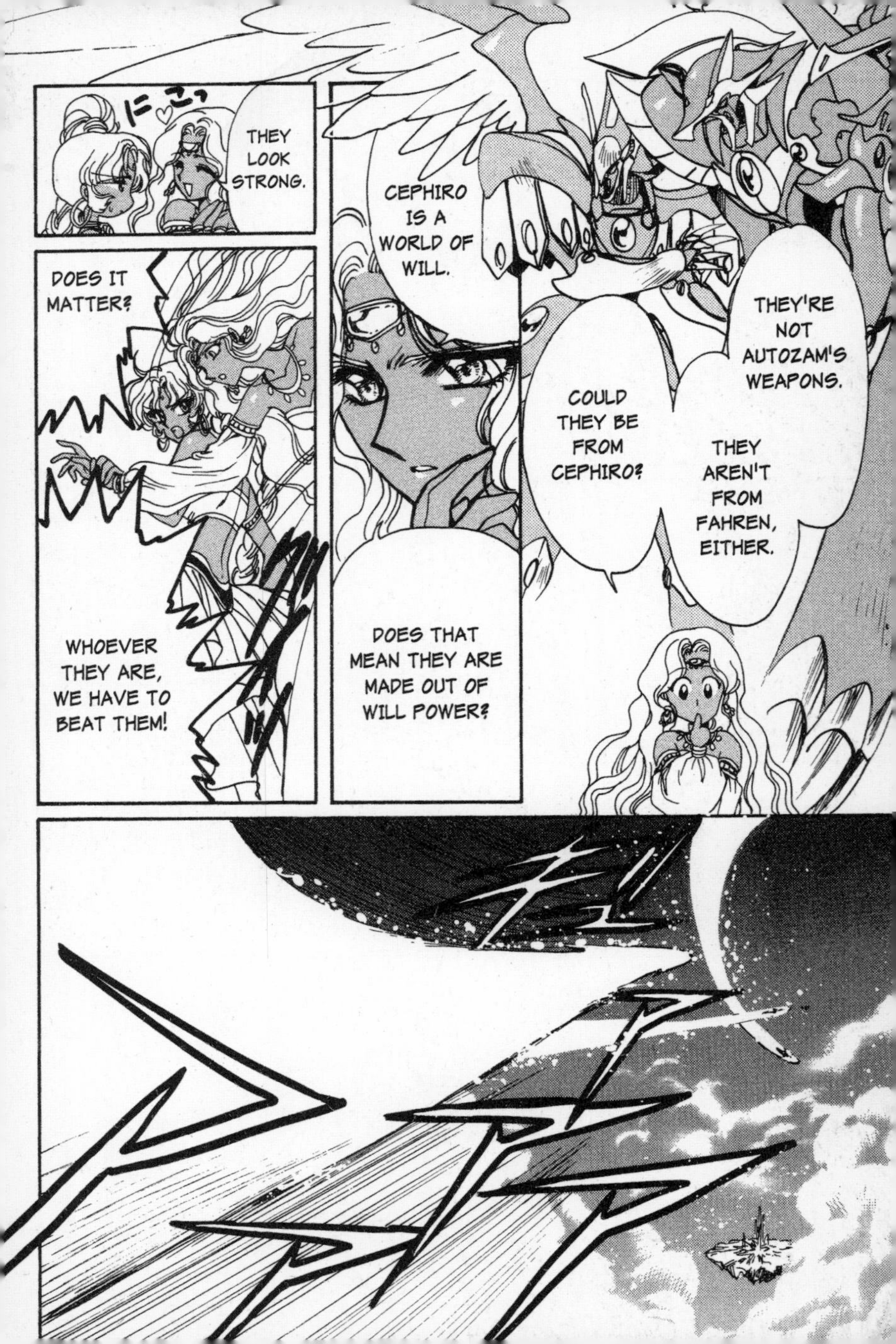
THEY'RE NOT AUTOZAM'S WEAPONS.
THEY AREN'T FROM FAHREN, EITHER.
COULD THEY BE FROM CEPHIRO?
CEPHIRO IS A WORLD OF WILL.
DOES THAT MEAN THEY ARE MADE OUT OF WILL POWER?
にこっ
THEY LOOK STRONG.
DOES IT MATTER?
WHOEVER THEY ARE, WE HAVE TO BEAT THEM!

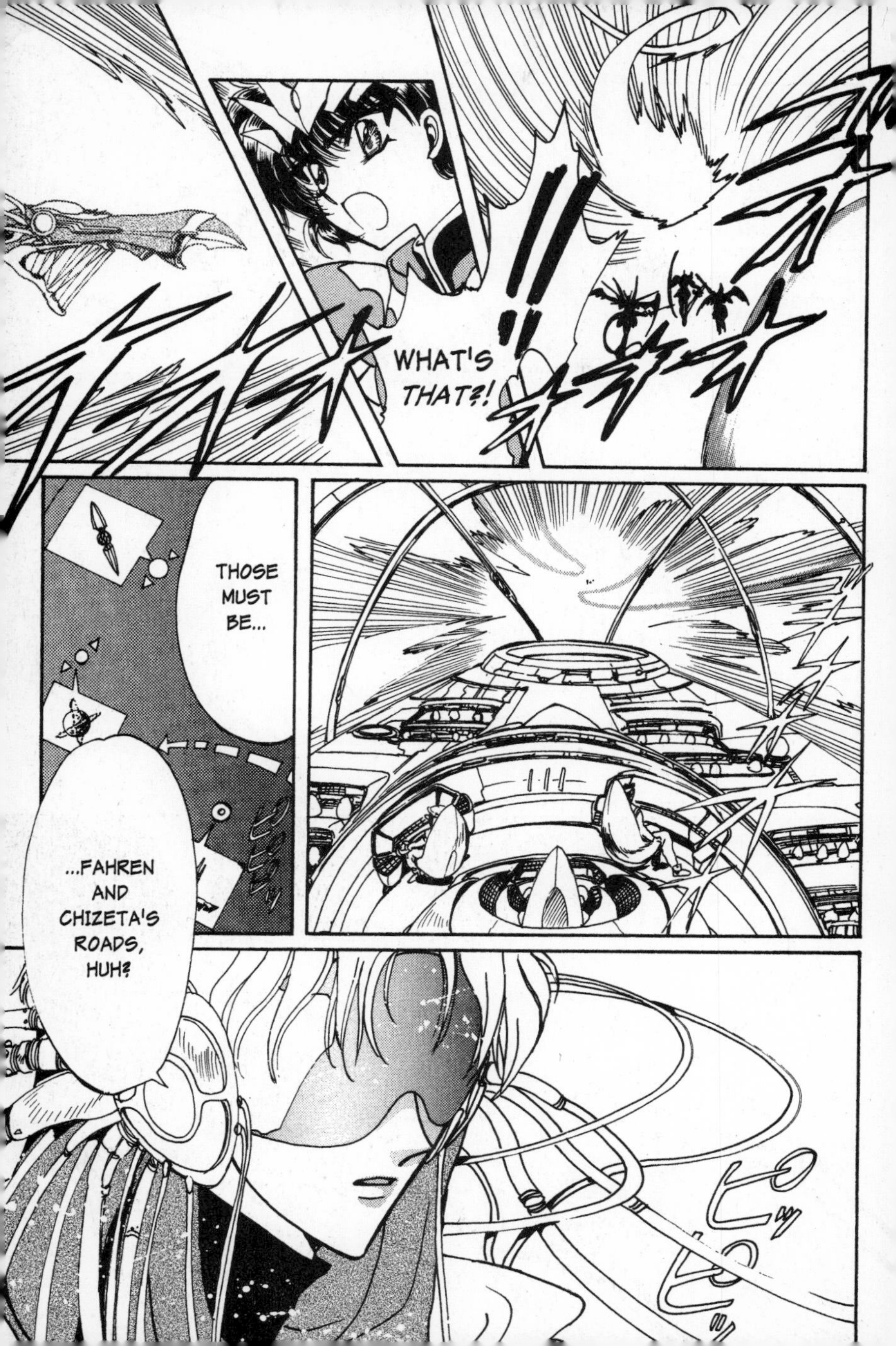
WHAT'S THAT?!
THOSE MUST BE...
...FAHREN AND CHIZETA'S ROADS, HUH?

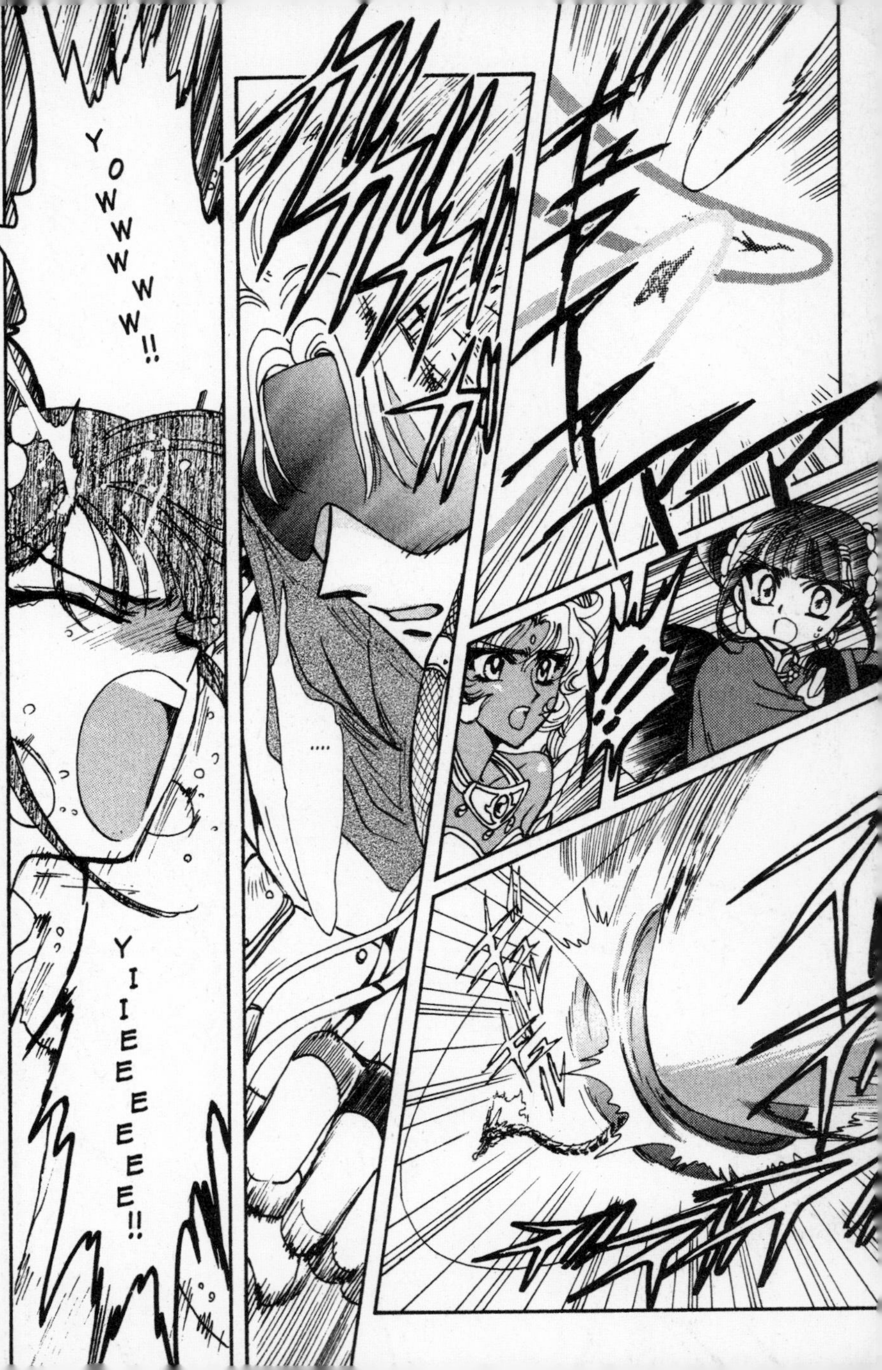
....
YOWWWWW!!
YIIEEEEEE!!

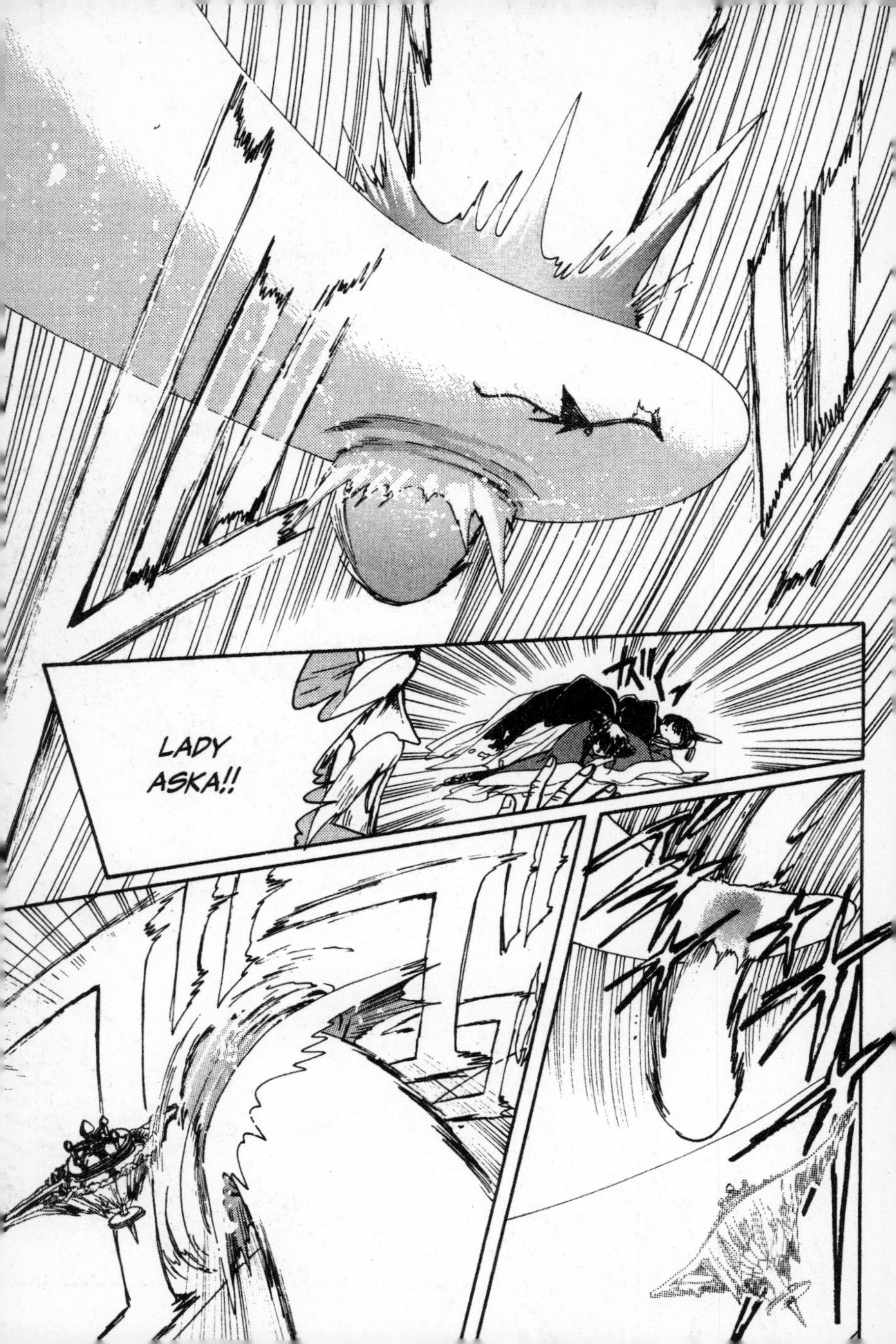
LADY
ASKA!!

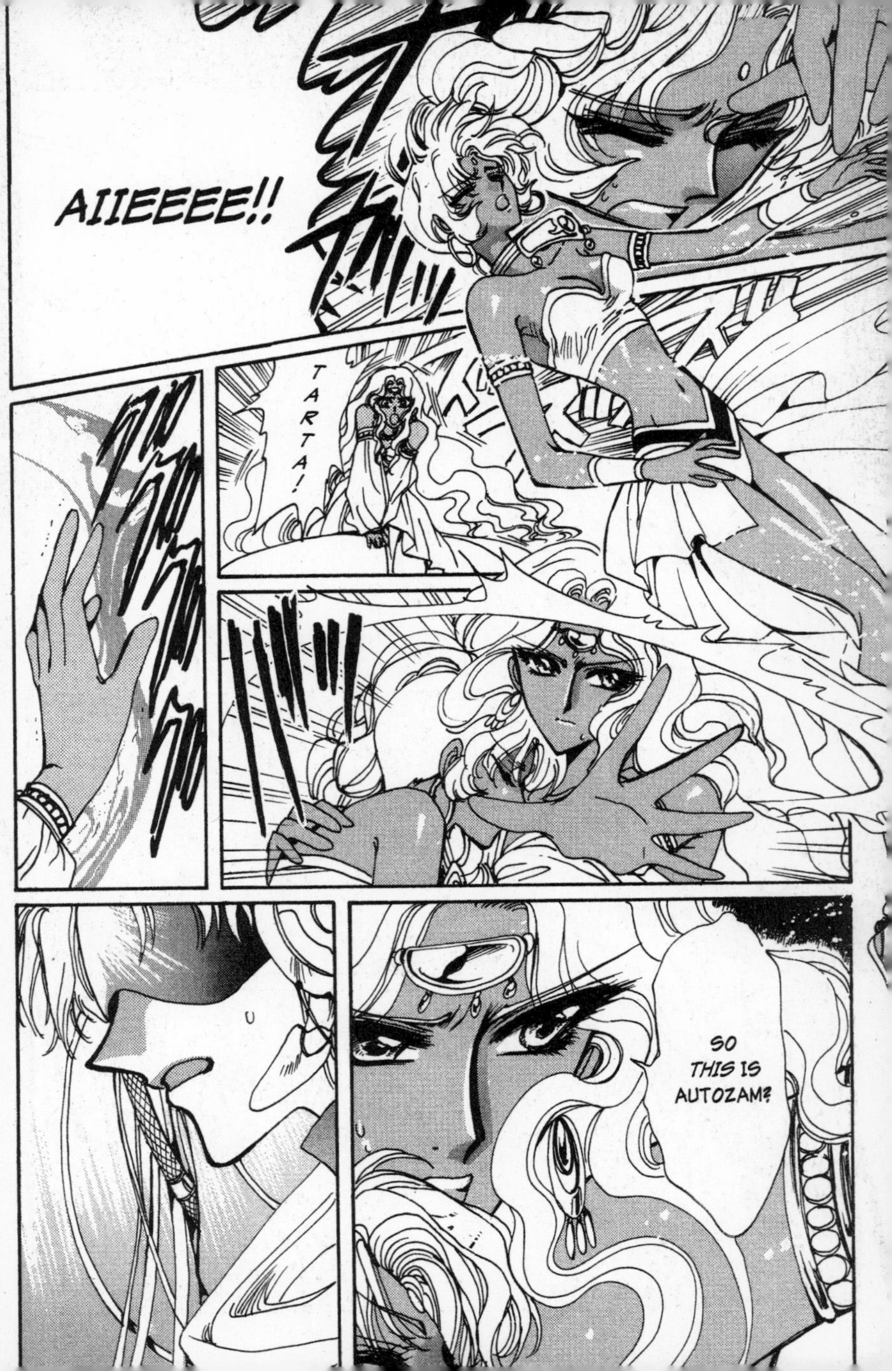
AIIEEEE!!
TARTA!
SO THIS IS AUTOZAM?

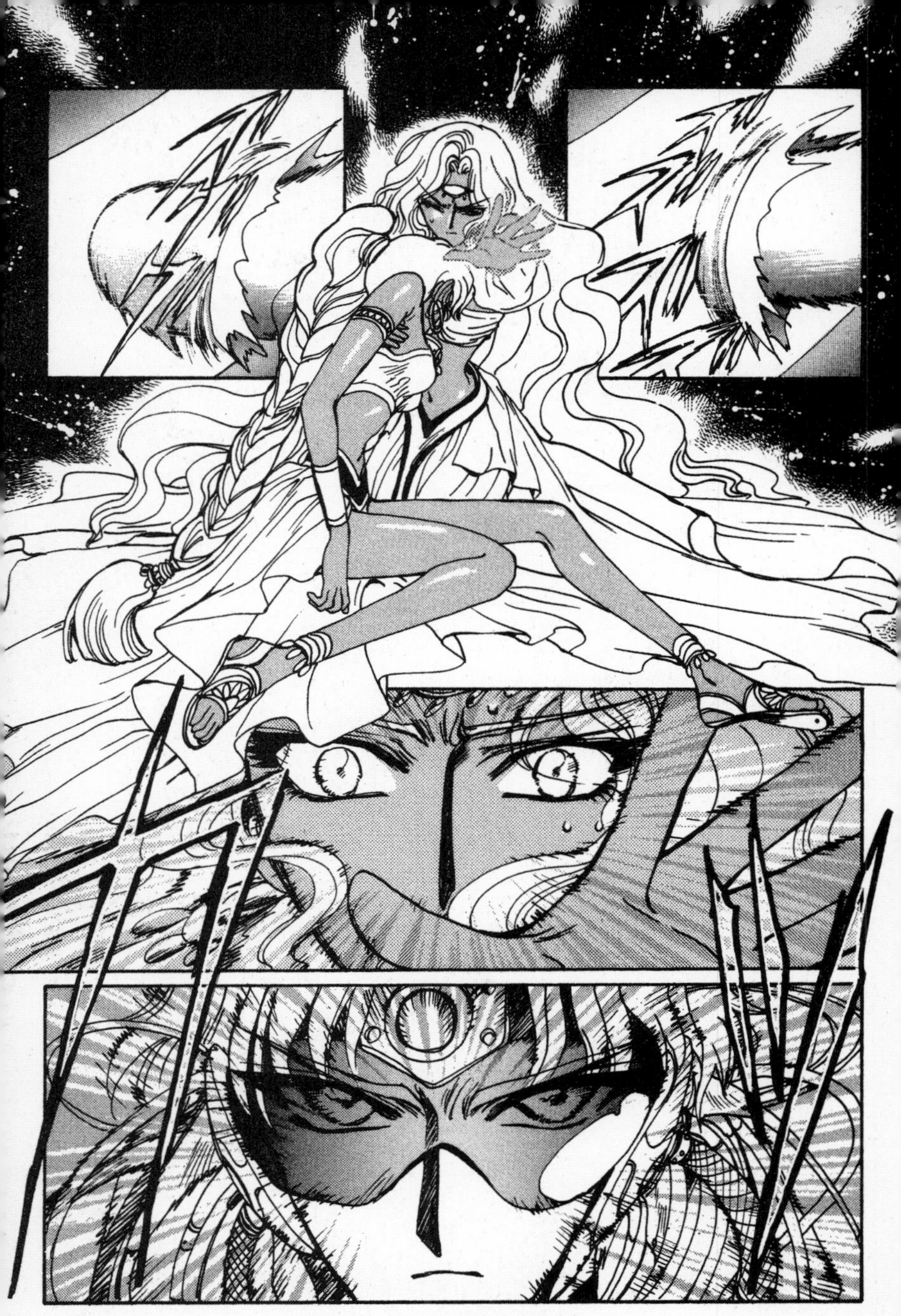

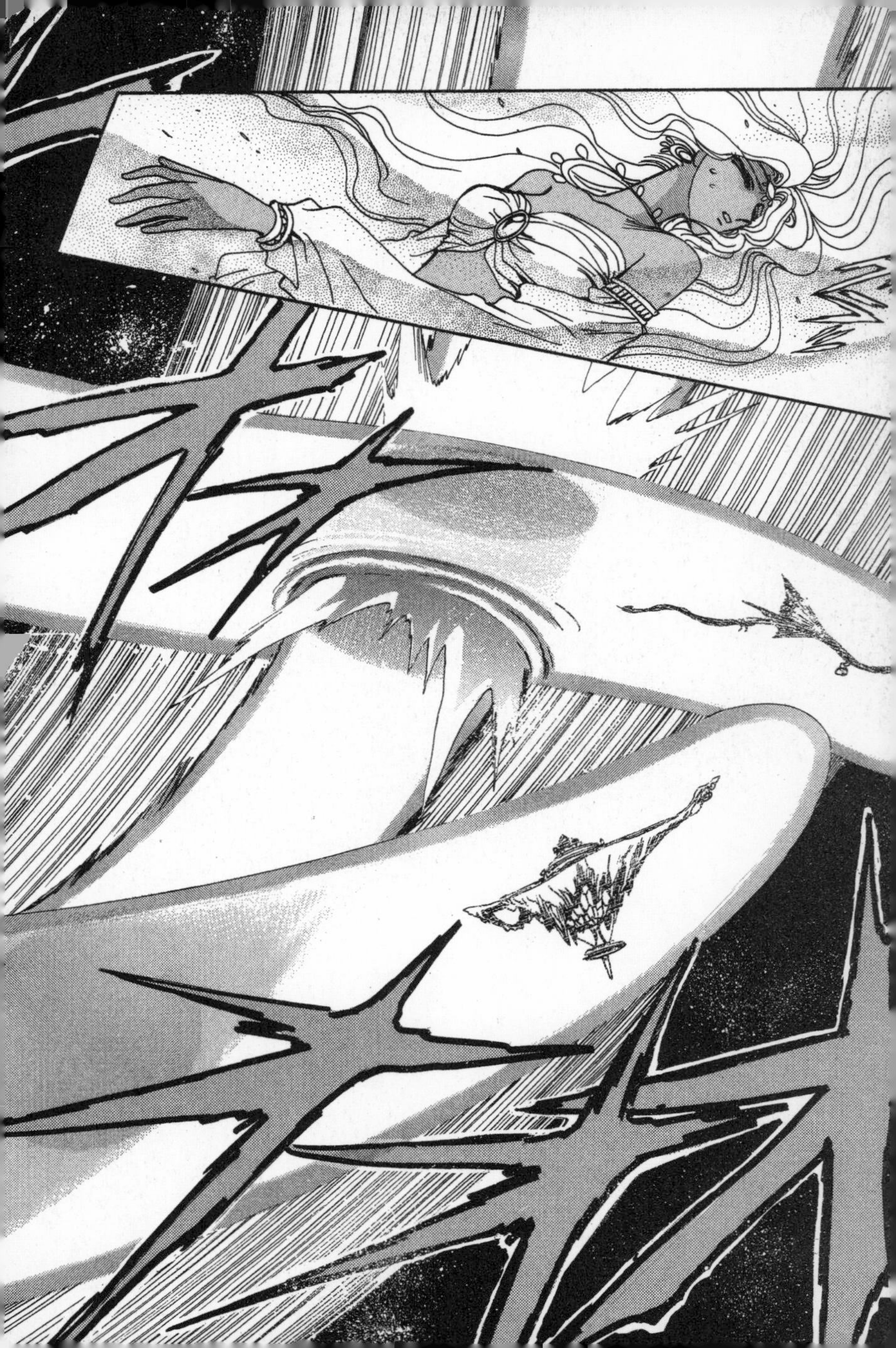

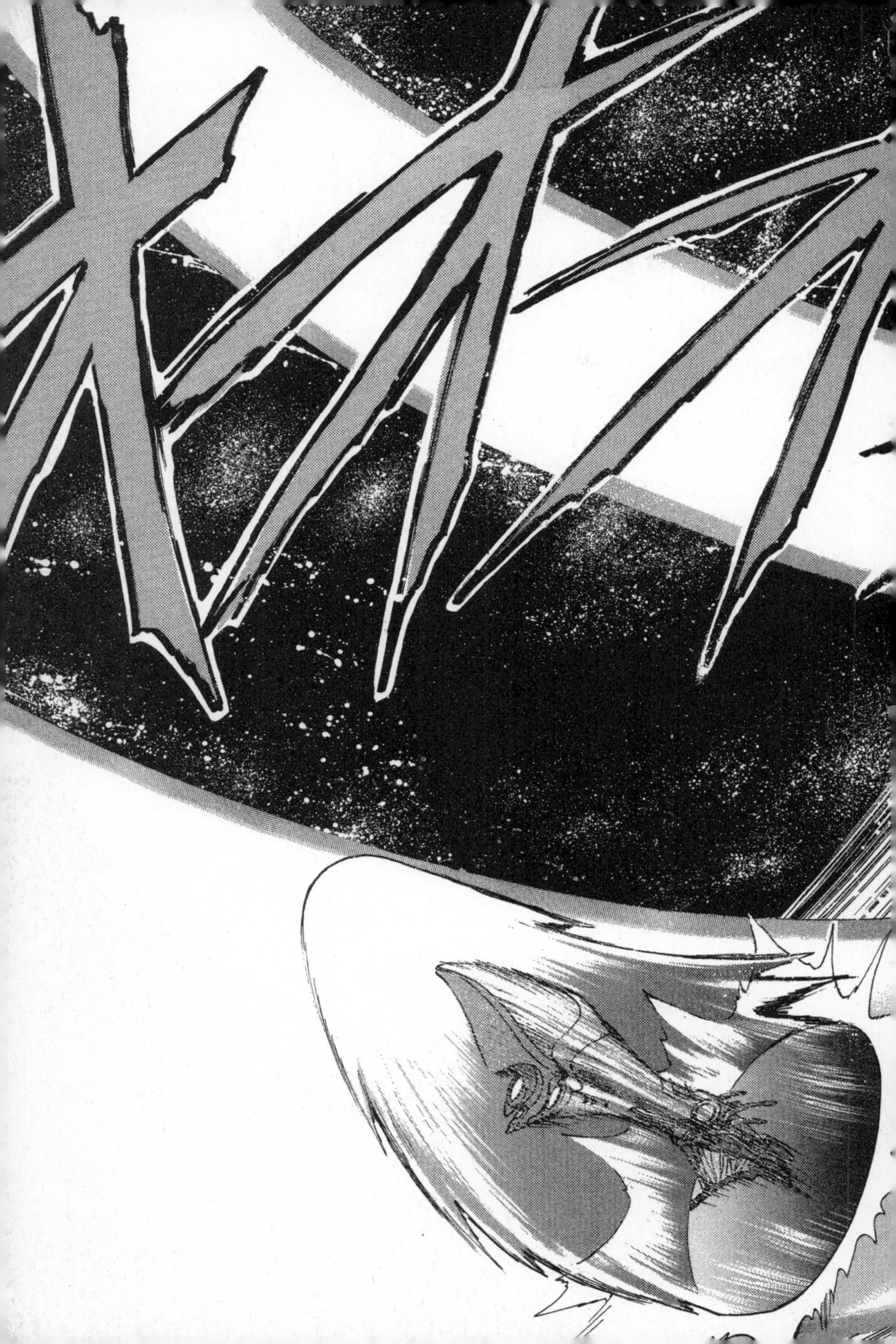

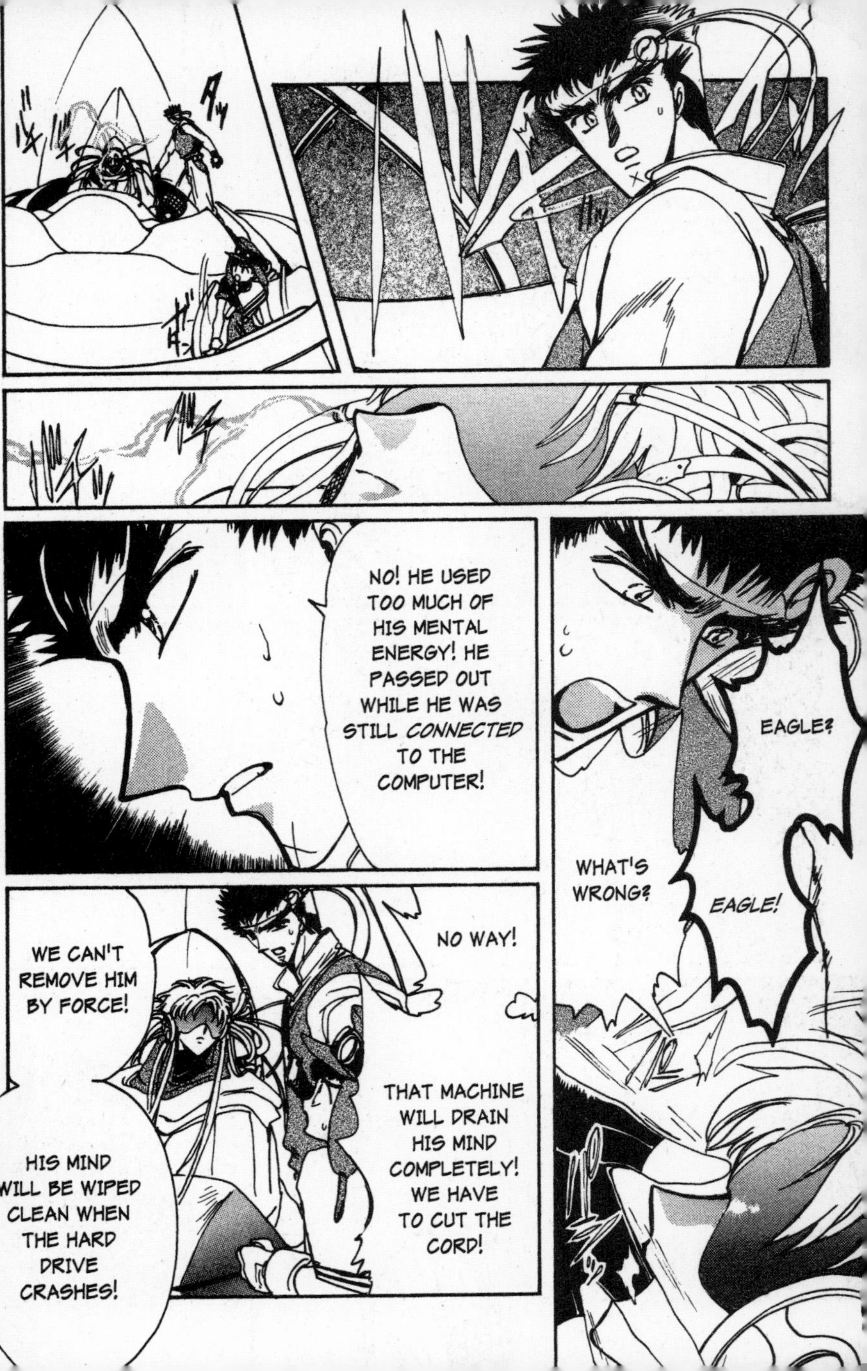
EAGLE?
WHAT'S WRONG?
EAGLE!
NO! HE USED TOO MUCH OF HIS MENTAL ENERGY! HE PASSED OUT WHILE HE WAS STILL *CONNECTED* TO THE COMPUTER!
NO WAY!
THAT MACHINE WILL DRAIN HIS MIND COMPLETELY! WE HAVE TO CUT THE CORD!
WE CAN'T REMOVE HIM BY FORCE!
HIS MIND WILL BE WIPED CLEAN WHEN THE HARD DRIVE CRASHES!

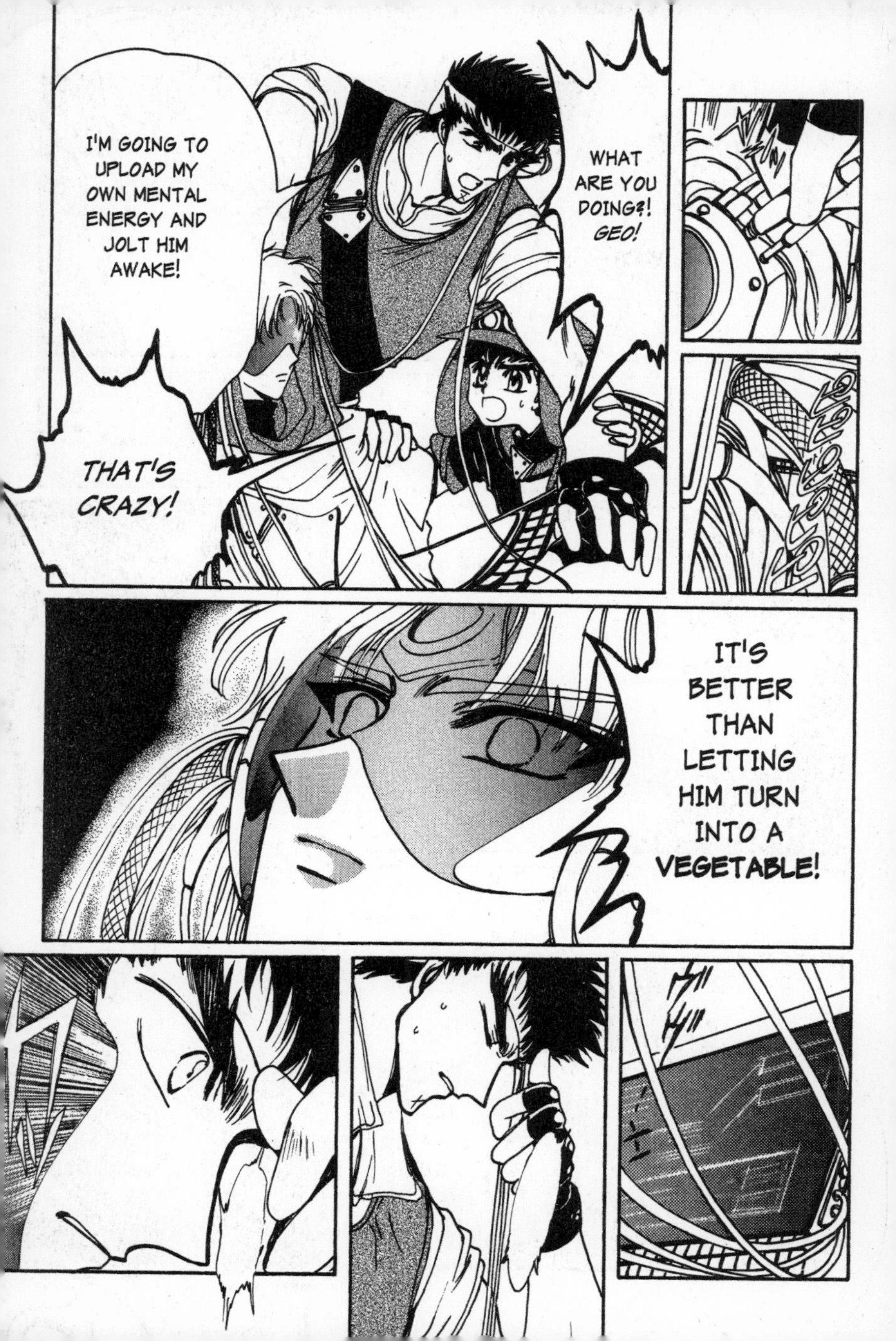
WHAT ARE YOU DOING?! GEO!
I'M GOING TO UPLOAD MY OWN MENTAL ENERGY AND JOLT HIM AWAKE!
THAT'S CRAZY!
IT'S BETTER THAN LETTING HIM TURN INTO A VEGETABLE!

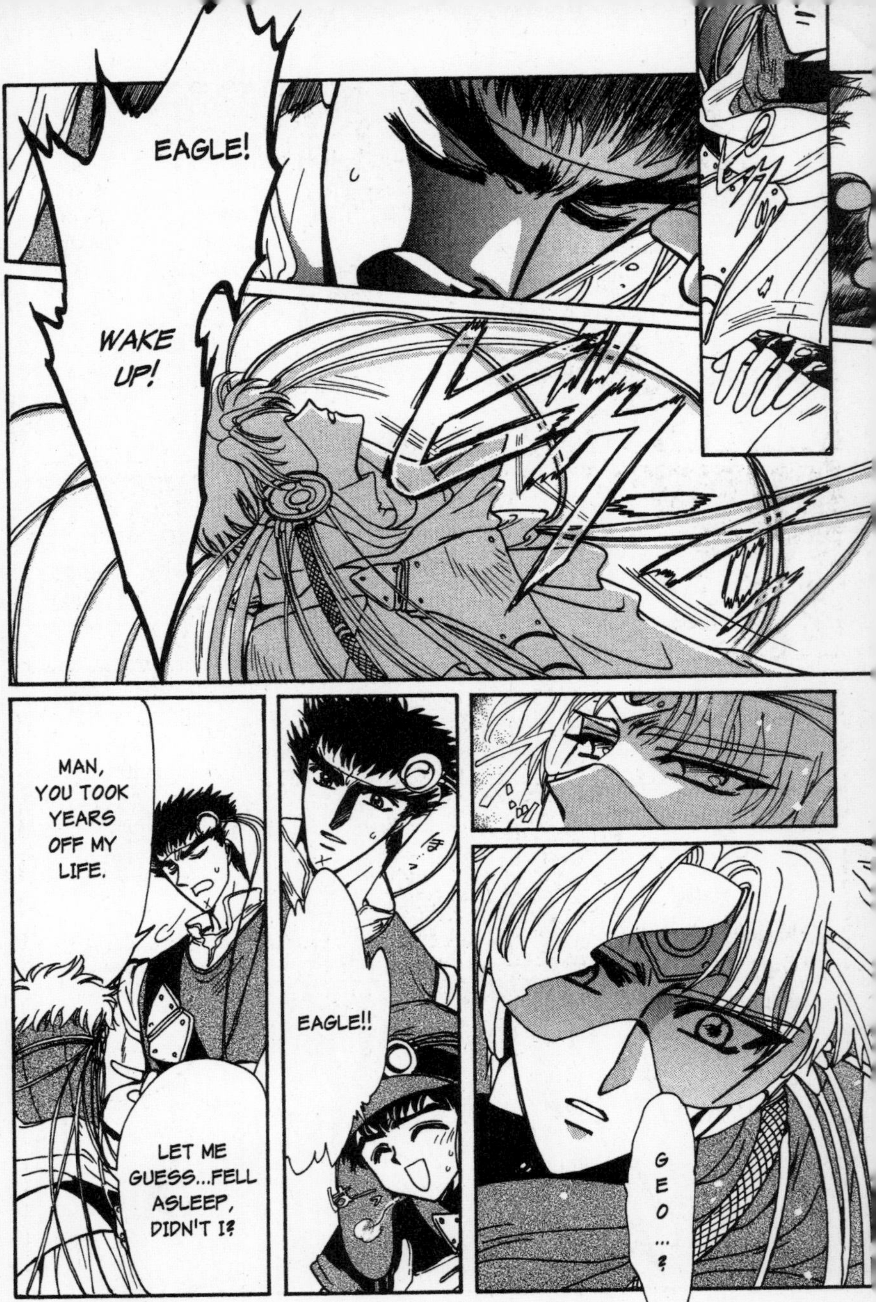
EAGLE!
WAKE UP!
GEO...?
EAGLE!!
MAN, YOU TOOK YEARS OFF MY LIFE.
LET ME GUESS...FELL ASLEEP, DIDN'T I?

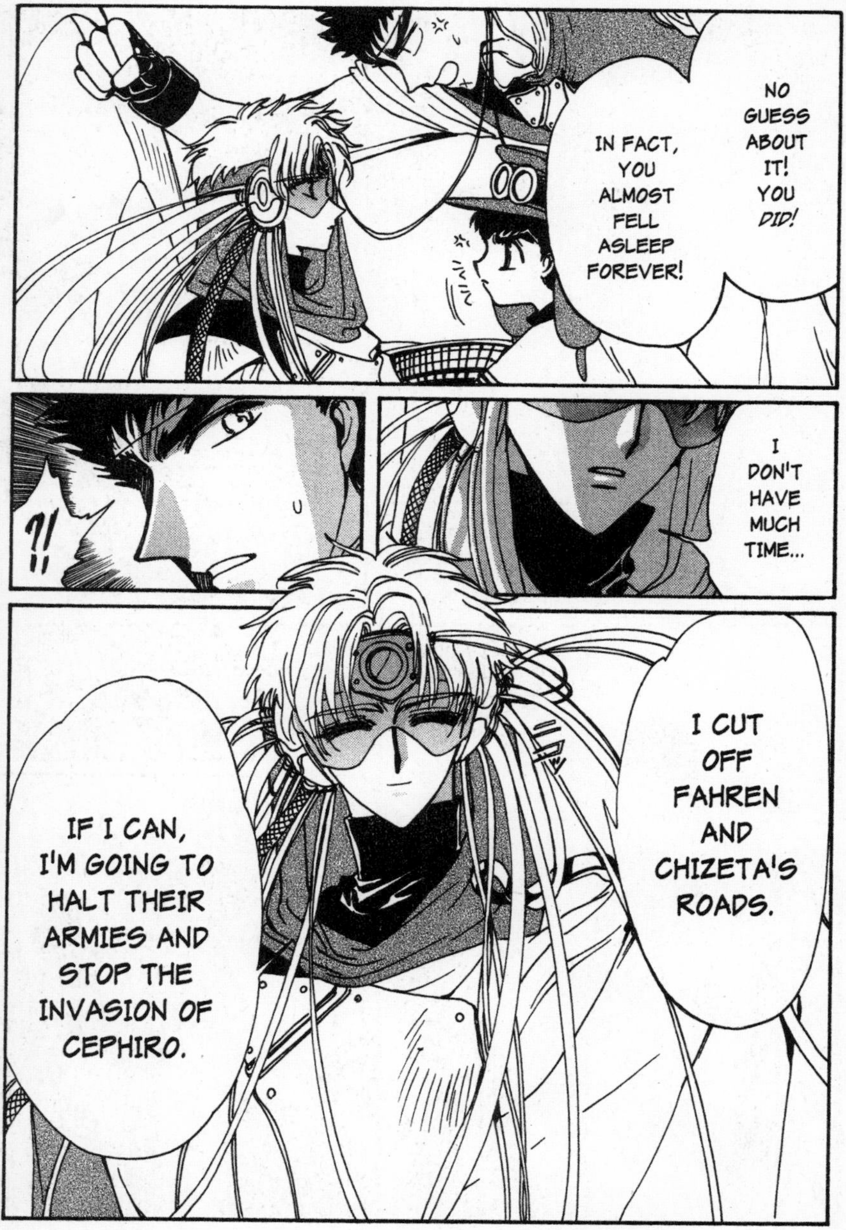
NO GUESS ABOUT IT! YOU *DID!*
IN FACT, YOU ALMOST FELL ASLEEP FOREVER!
I DON'T HAVE MUCH TIME...
?!
I CUT OFF FAHREN AND CHIZETA'S ROADS.
IF I CAN, I'M GOING TO HALT THEIR ARMIES AND STOP THE INVASION OF CEPHIRO.

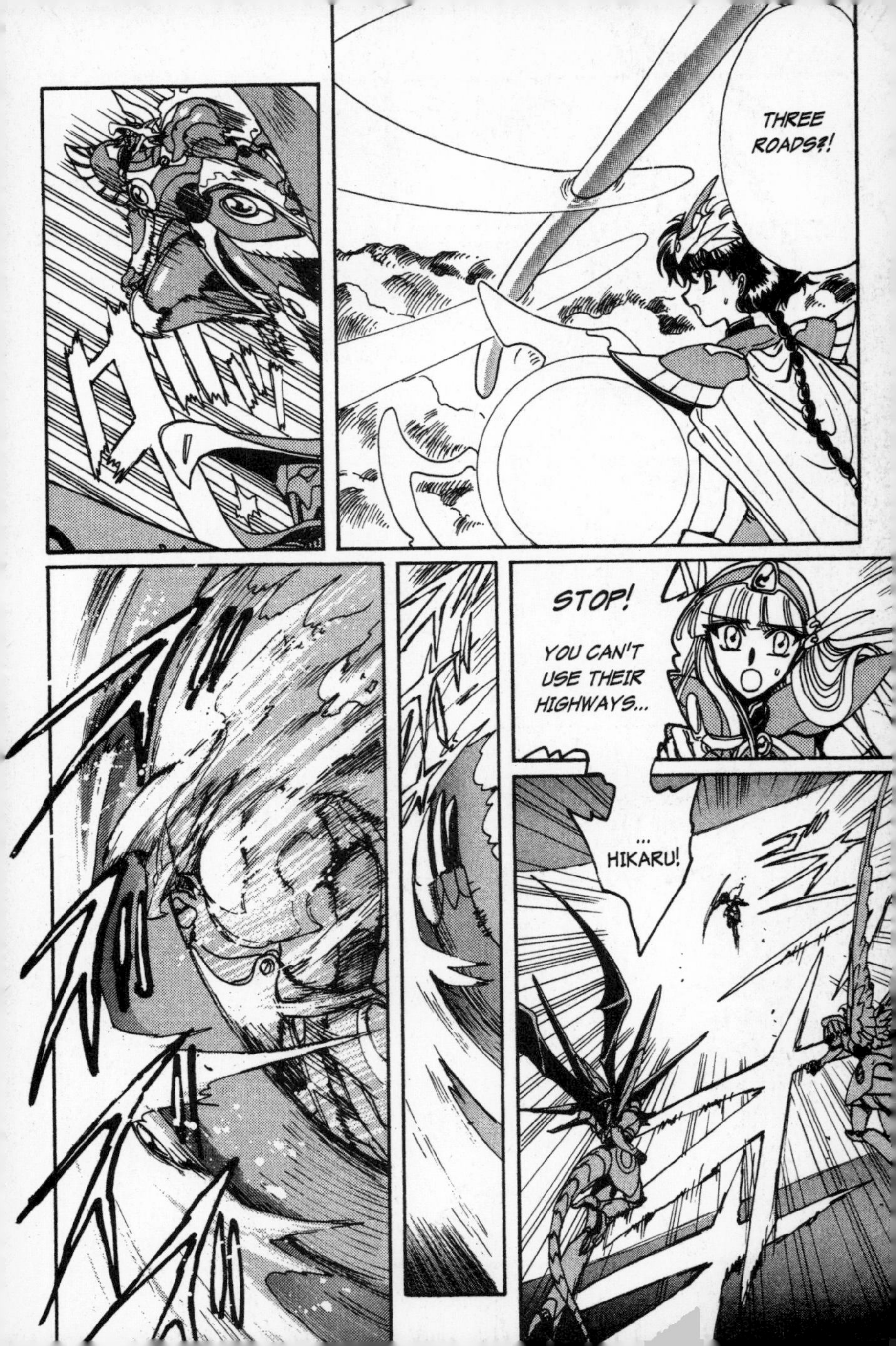
THREE ROADS?!
STOP!
YOU CAN'T USE THEIR HIGHWAYS...
... HIKARU!

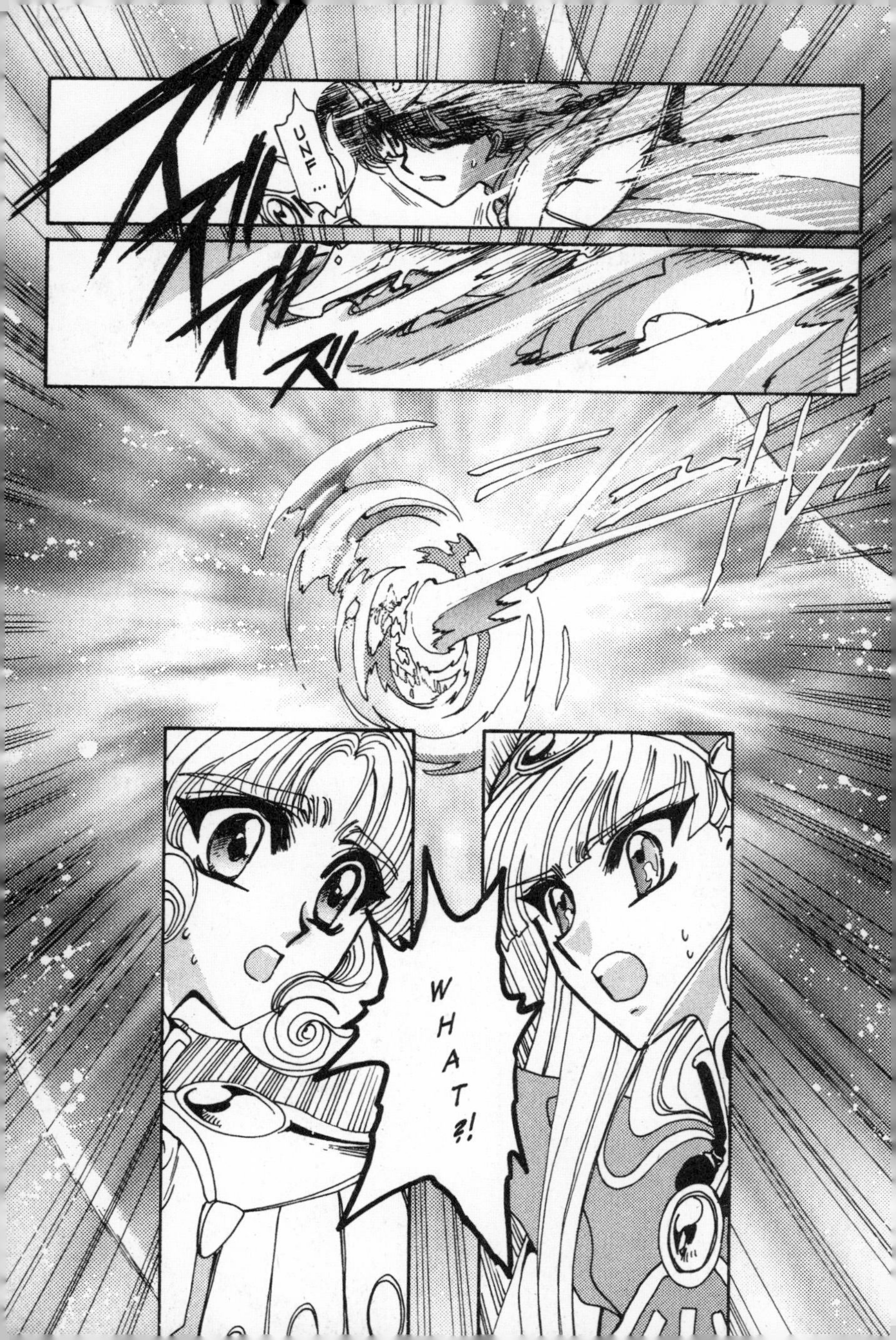
UNF...
WHAT?!

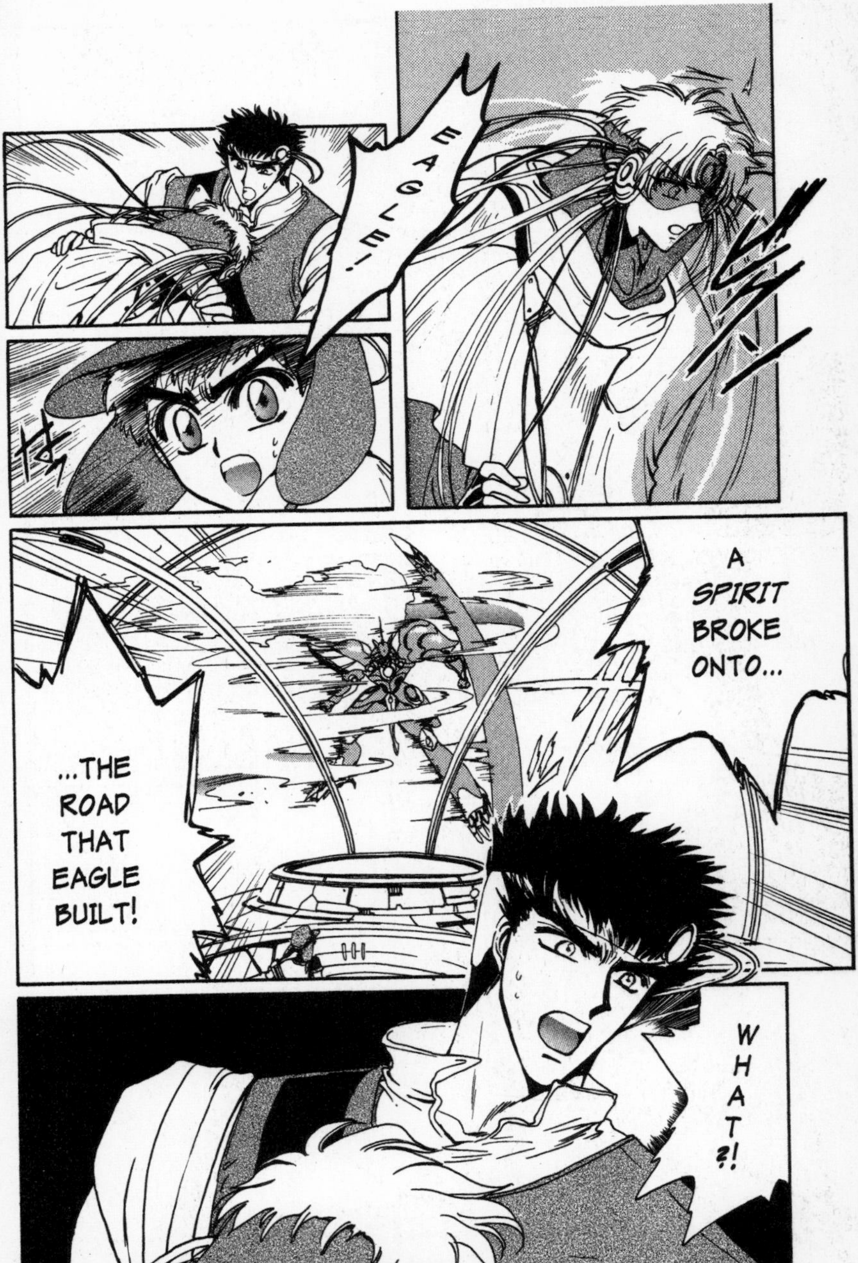
EAGLE!
A SPIRIT BROKE ONTO...
...THE ROAD THAT EAGLE BUILT!
WHAT?!

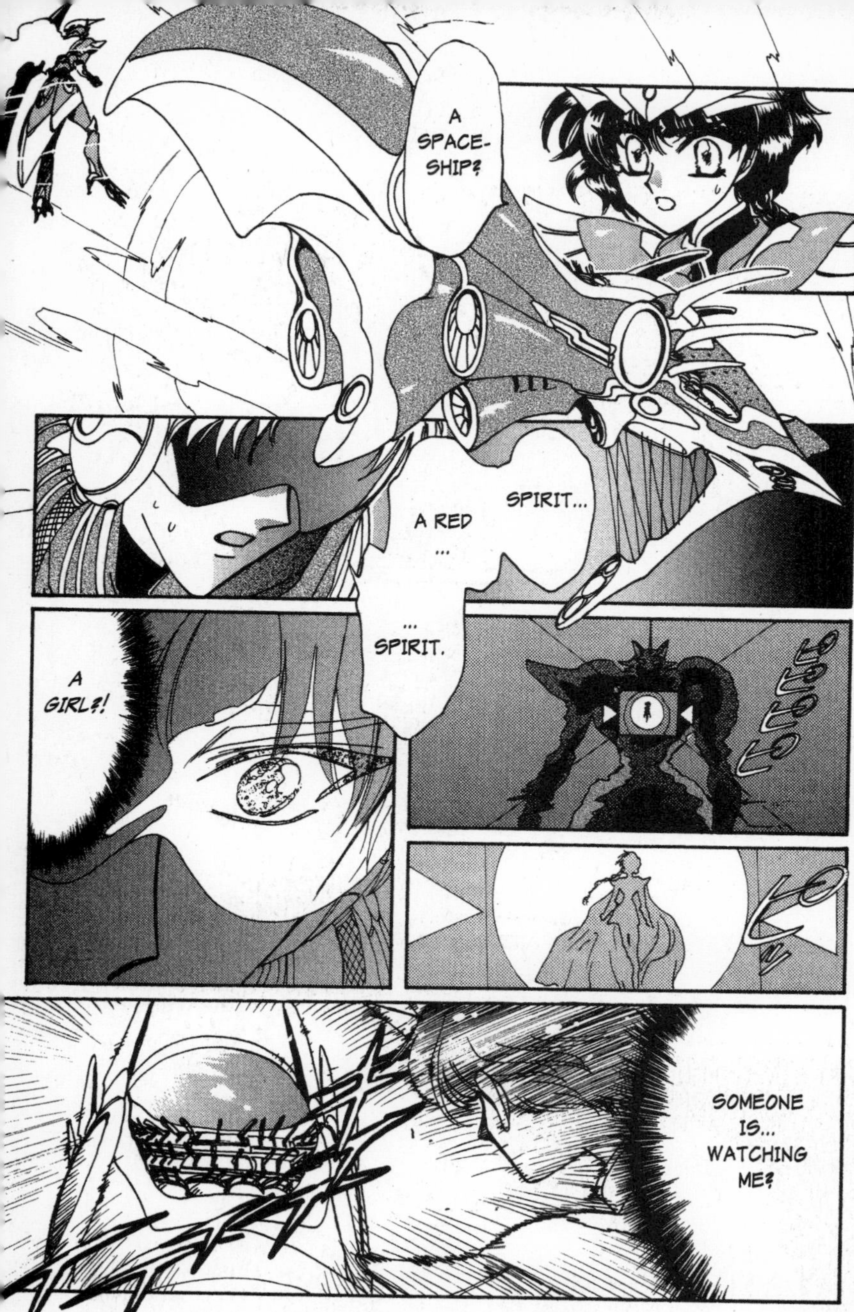
A SPACE-SHIP?
A RED ...
SPIRIT...
... SPIRIT.
A GIRL?!
SOMEONE IS... WATCHING ME?

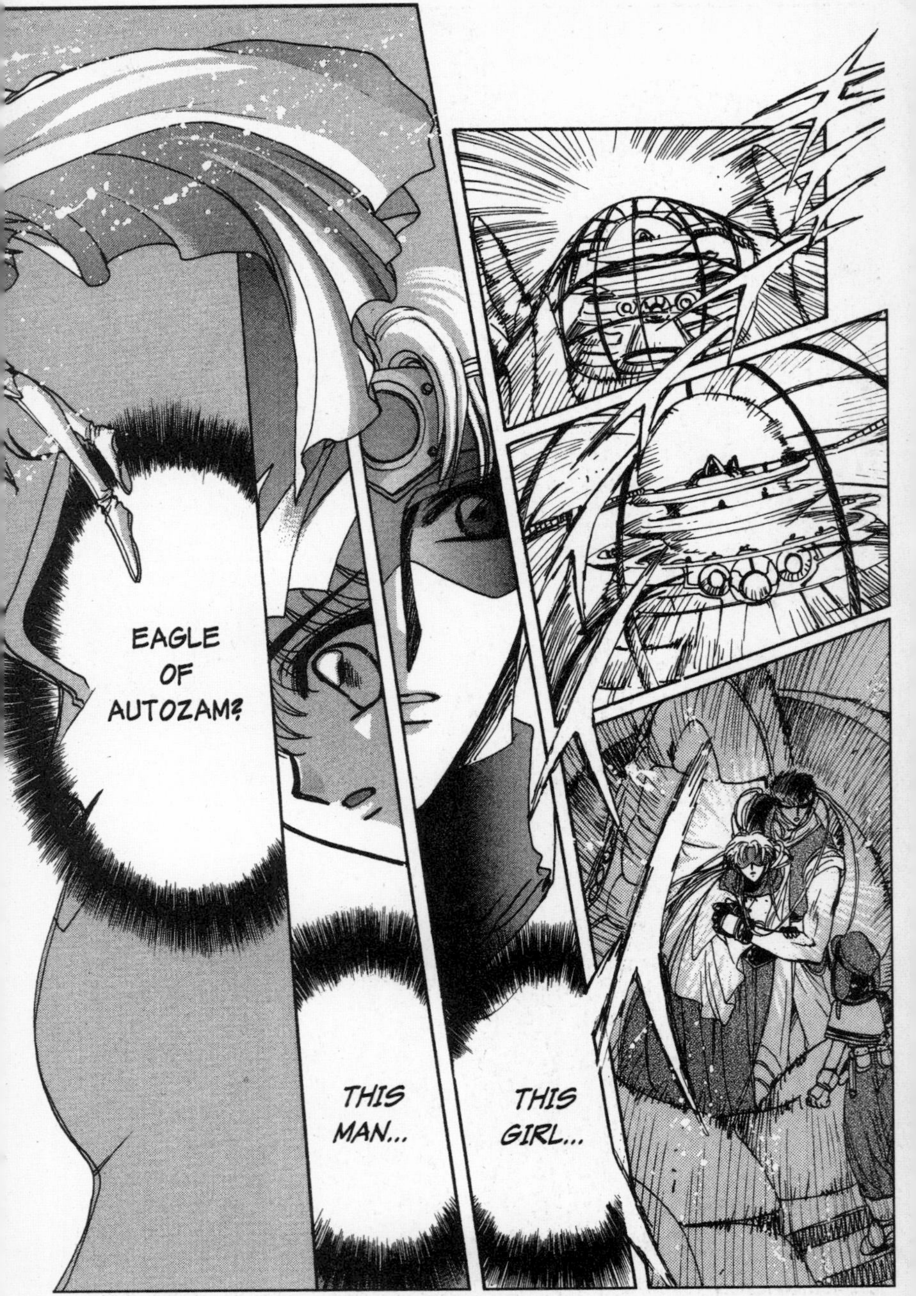
THIS GIRL...
THIS MAN...
EAGLE OF AUTOZAM?

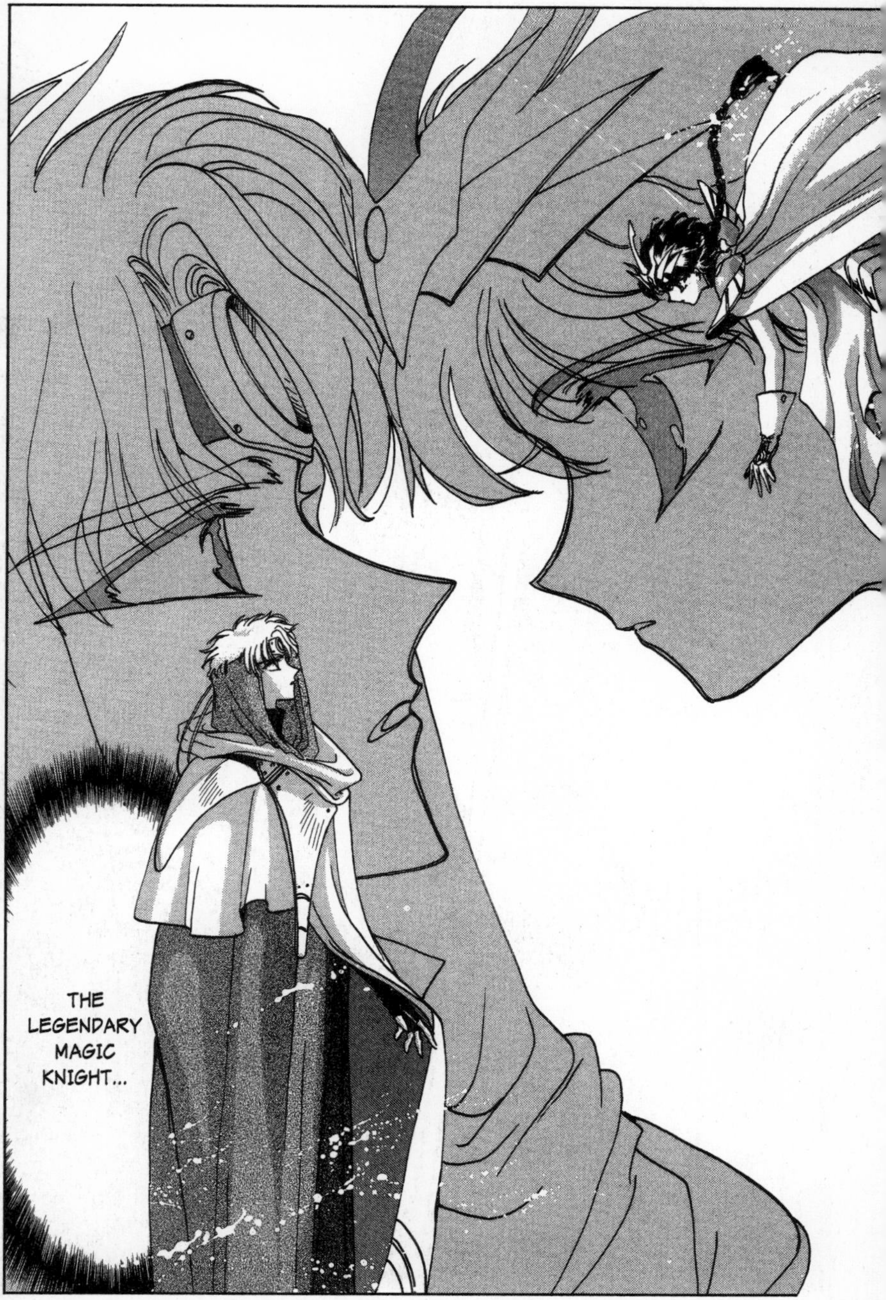
THE LEGENDARY MAGIC KNIGHT...

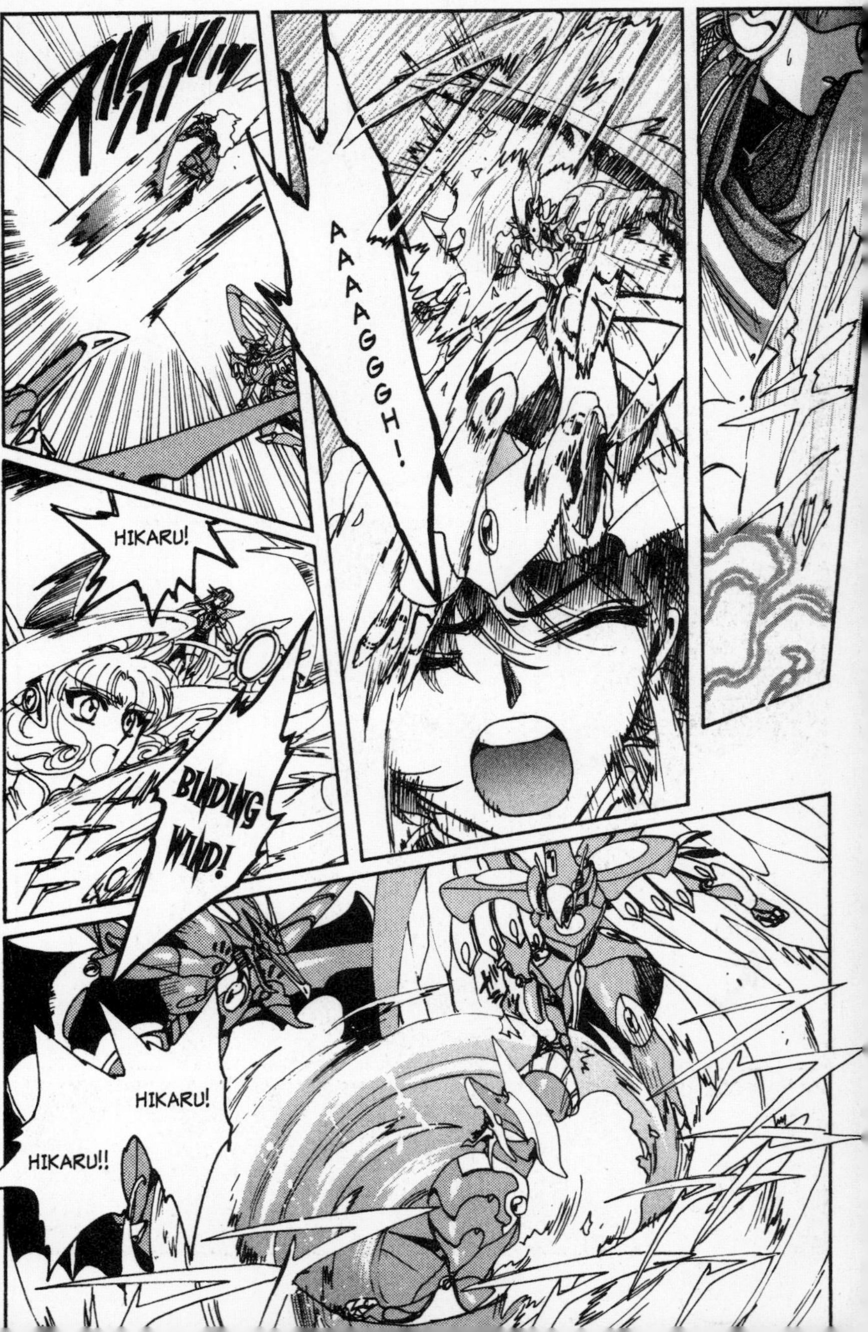
AAAAGGGH!
HIKARU!
BINDING WIND!
HIKARU!
HIKARU!!

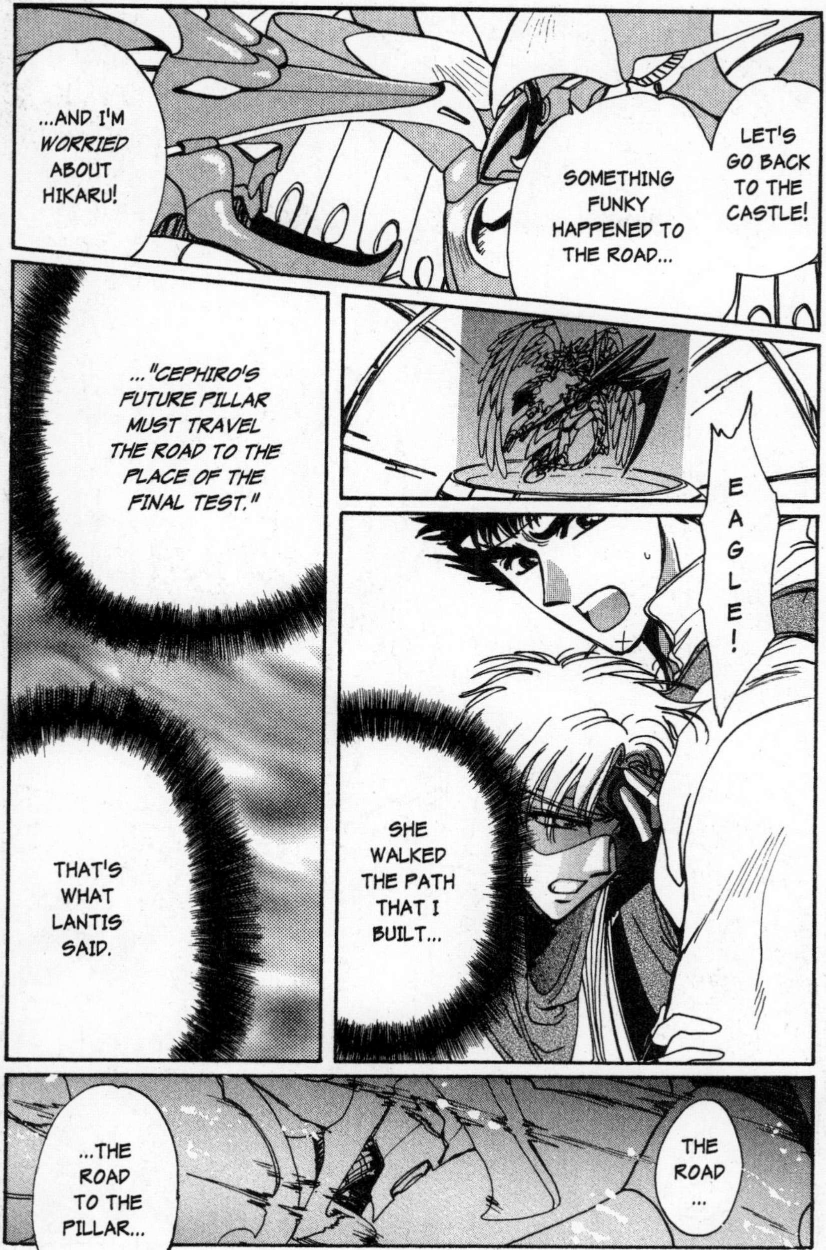
LET'S GO BACK TO THE CASTLE!
SOMETHING FUNKY HAPPENED TO THE ROAD...
...AND I'M *WORRIED* ABOUT HIKARU!
EAGLE!
SHE WALKED THE PATH THAT I BUILT...
..."CEPHIRO'S FUTURE PILLAR MUST TRAVEL THE ROAD TO THE PLACE OF THE FINAL TEST."
THAT'S WHAT LANTIS SAID.
THE ROAD ...
...THE ROAD TO THE PILLAR...

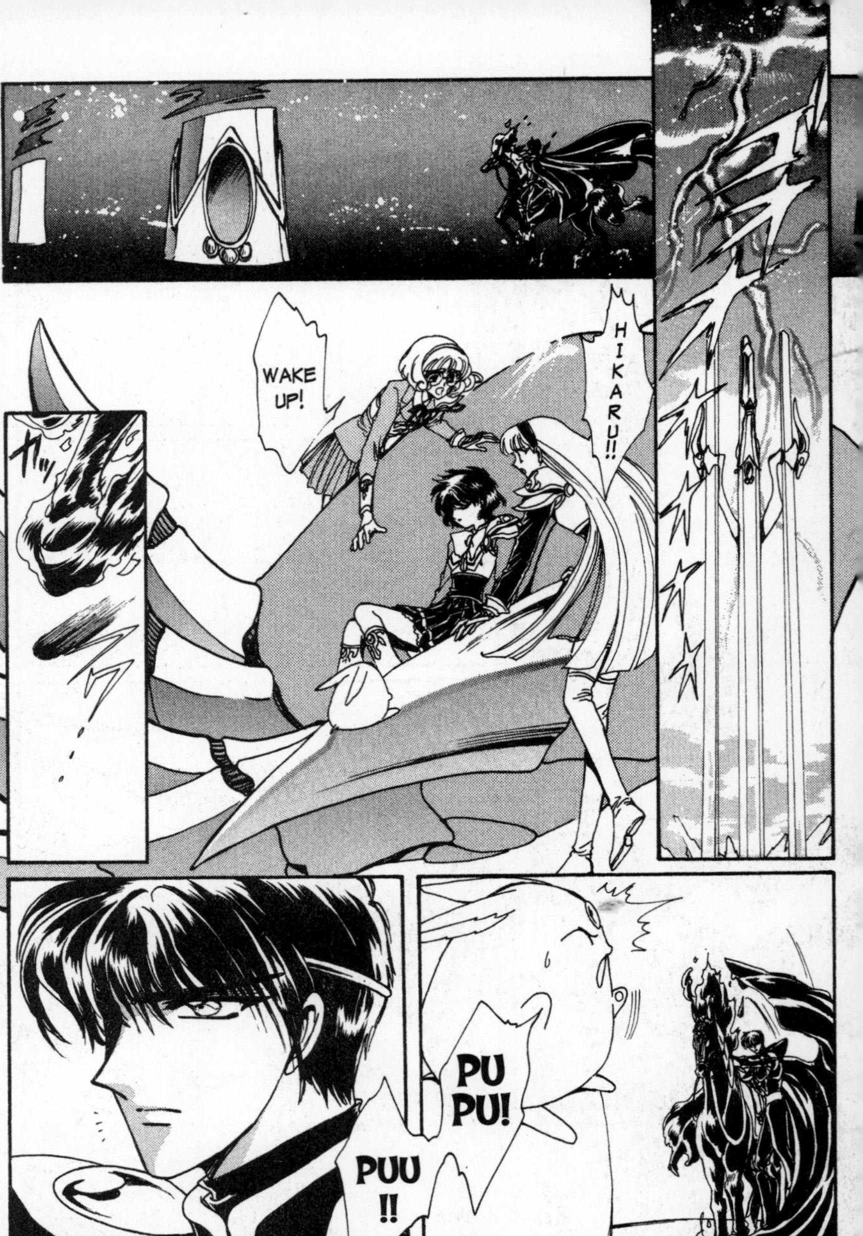
HIKARU!!
WAKE UP!
PU PU!
PUU !!

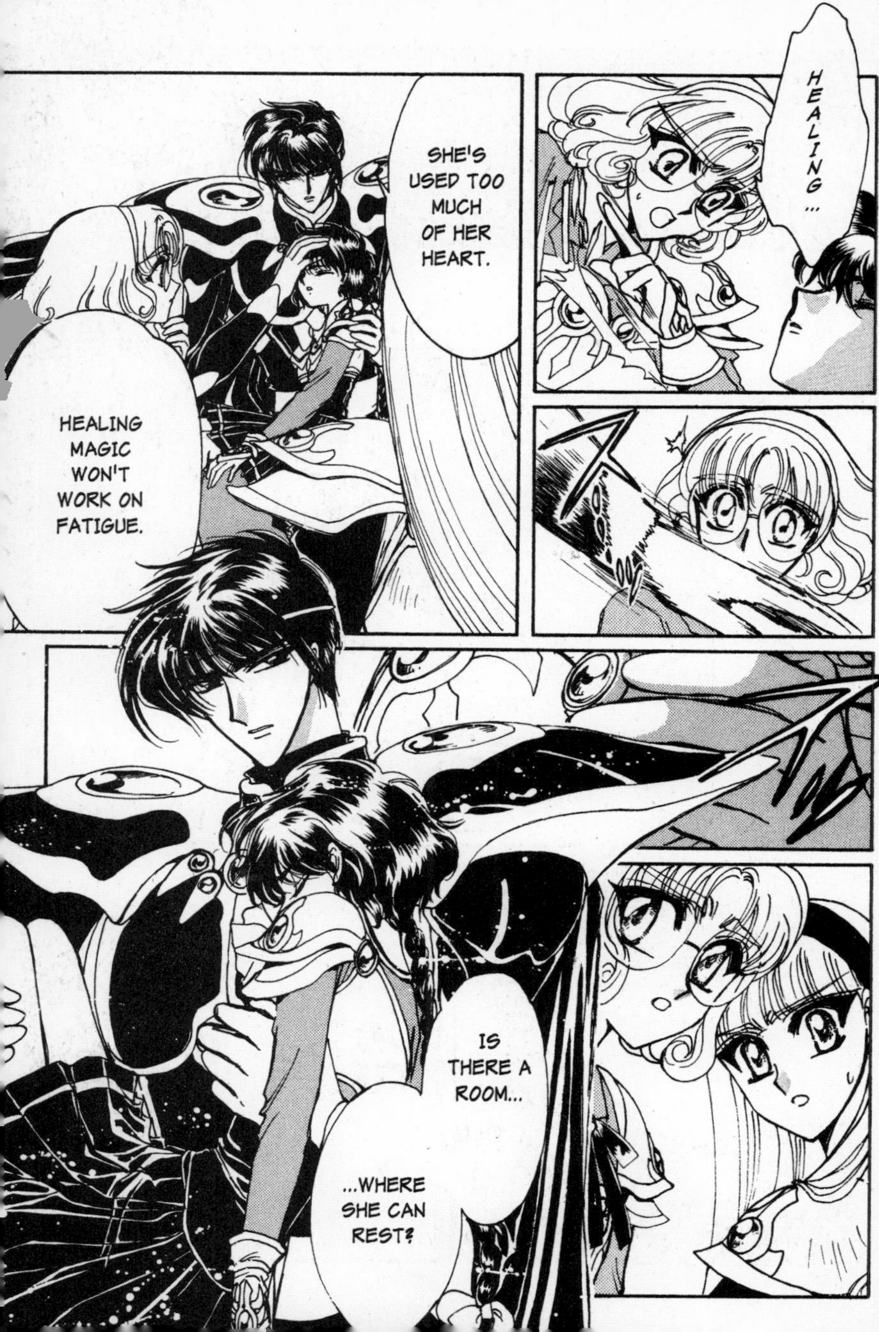
HEALING...
SHE'S USED TOO MUCH OF HER HEART.
HEALING MAGIC WON'T WORK ON FATIGUE.
IS THERE A ROOM...
...WHERE SHE CAN REST?

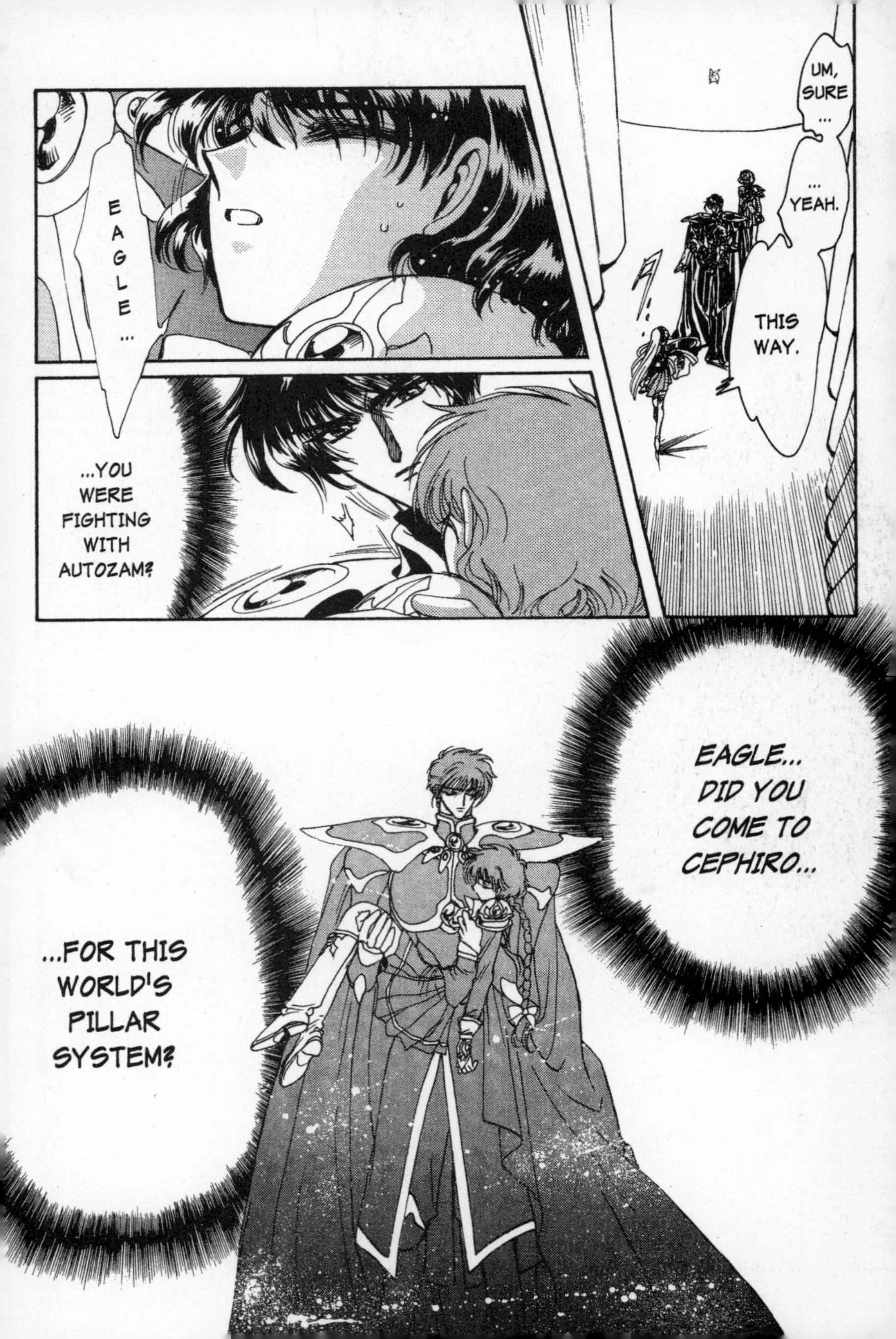
UM, SURE ...
... YEAH.
THIS WAY.
EAGLE ...
...YOU WERE FIGHTING WITH AUTOZAM?
EAGLE... DID YOU COME TO CEPHIRO...
...FOR THIS WORLD'S PILLAR SYSTEM?

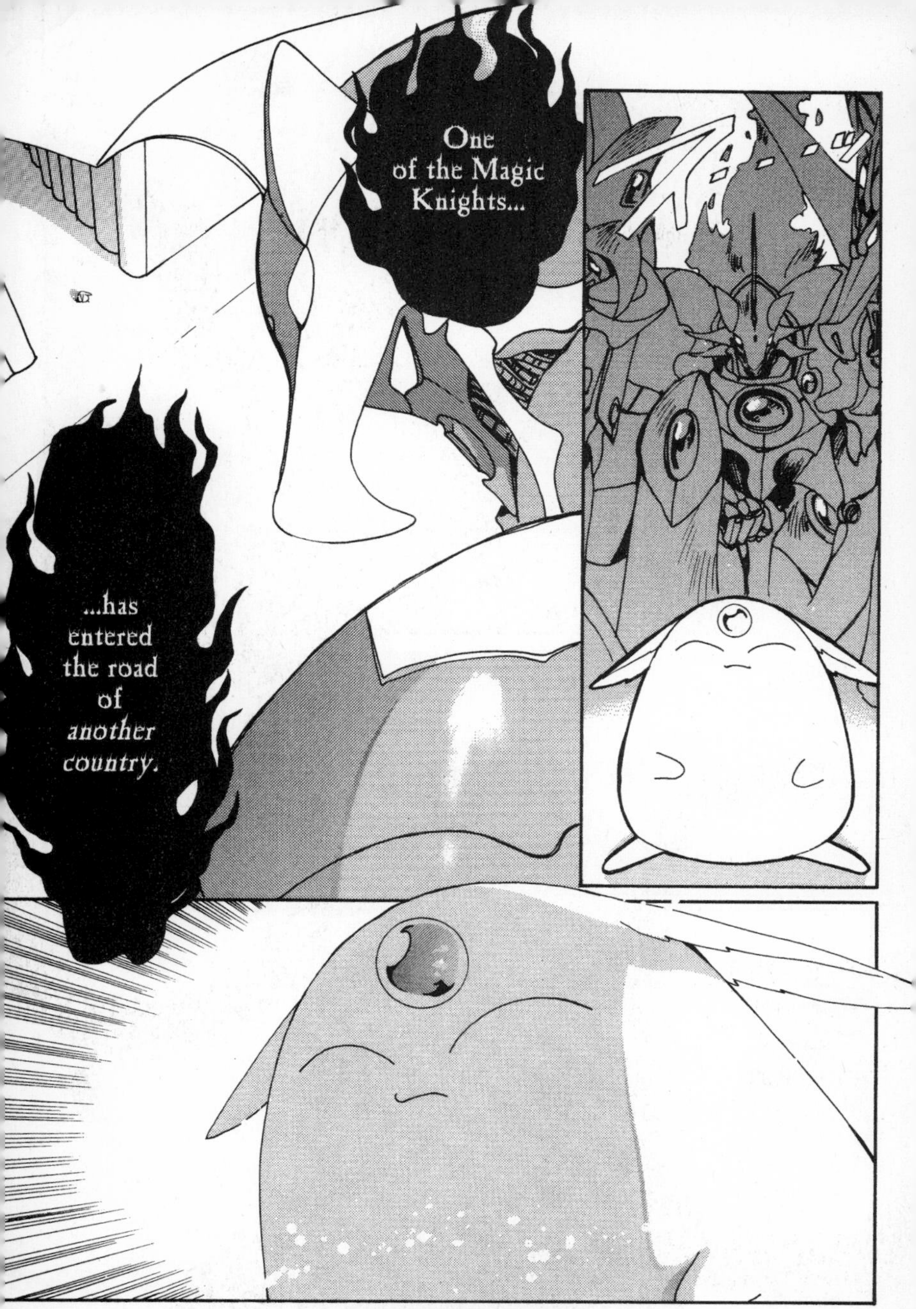
One of the Magic Knights...
...has entered the road of another country.

●TO NEXT STAGE●

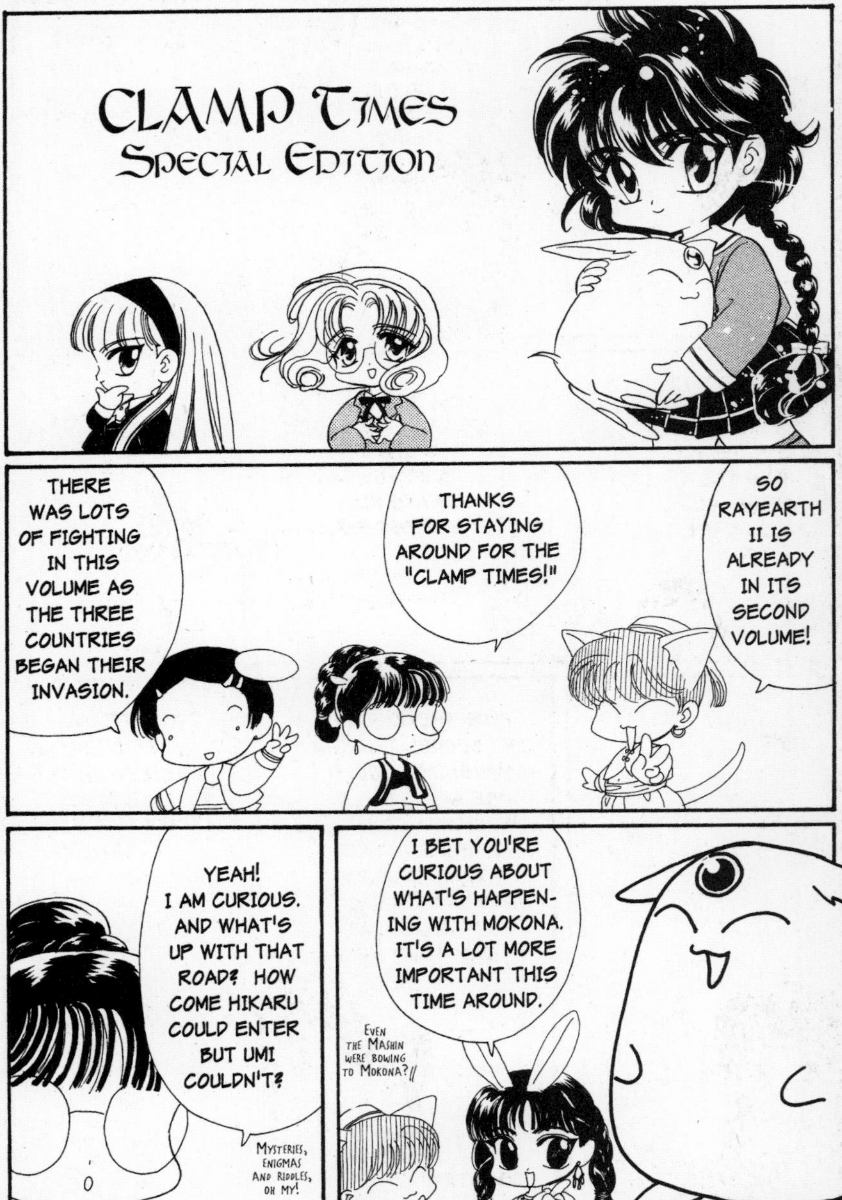
CLAMP TIMES
SPECIAL EDITION
SO RAYEARTH II IS ALREADY IN ITS SECOND VOLUME!
THANKS FOR STAYING AROUND FOR THE "CLAMP TIMES!"
THERE WAS LOTS OF FIGHTING IN THIS VOLUME AS THE THREE COUNTRIES BEGAN THEIR INVASION.
I BET YOU'RE CURIOUS ABOUT WHAT'S HAPPENING WITH MOKONA. IT'S A LOT MORE IMPORTANT THIS TIME AROUND.
EVEN THE MASHIN WERE BOWING TO MOKONA?//
YEAH! I AM CURIOUS. AND WHAT'S UP WITH THAT ROAD? HOW COME HIKARU COULD ENTER BUT UMI COULDN'T?
MYSTERIES, ENIGMAS AND RIDDLES, OH MY!

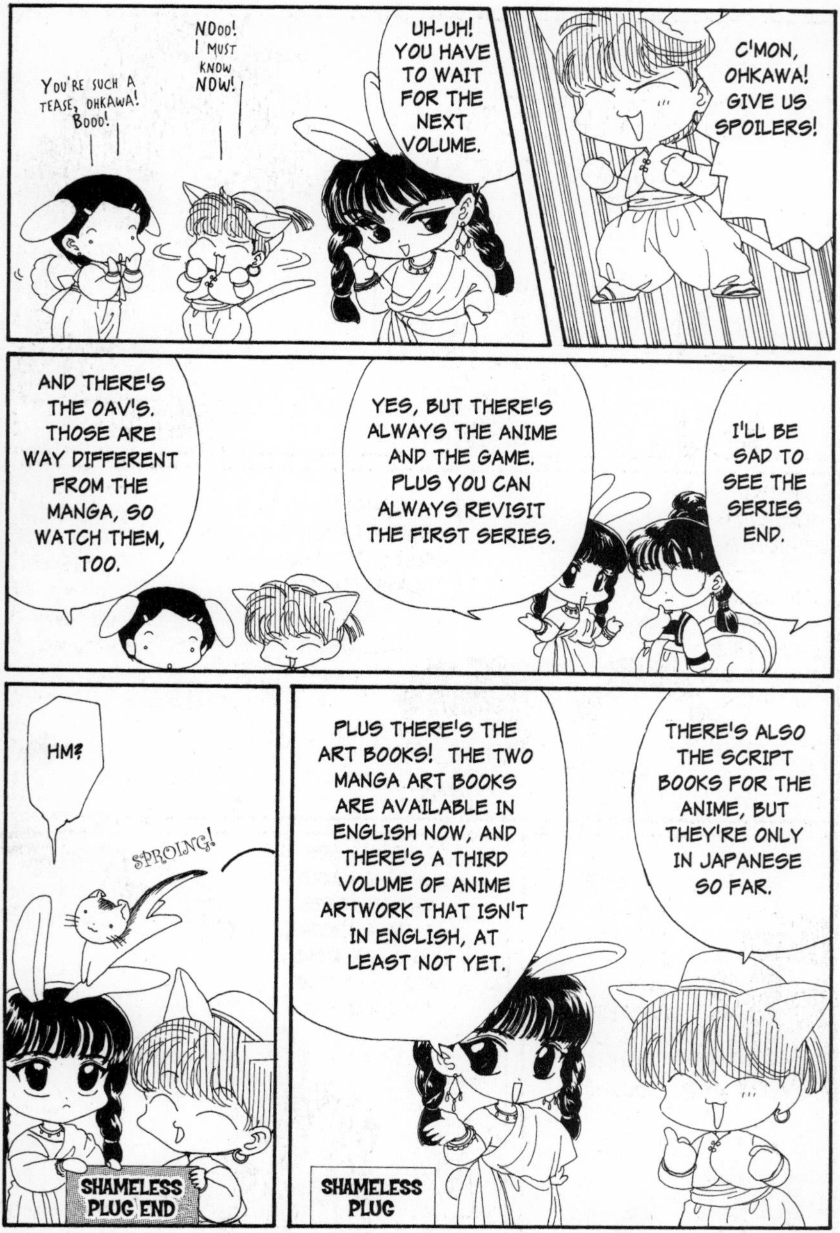
C'MON, OHKAWA! GIVE US SPOILERS!
UH-UH! YOU HAVE TO WAIT FOR THE NEXT VOLUME.
NOoo! I MUST KNOW NOW!
You're such a tease, Ohkawa! Booo!
I'LL BE SAD TO SEE THE SERIES END.
YES, BUT THERE'S ALWAYS THE ANIME AND THE GAME. PLUS YOU CAN ALWAYS REVISIT THE FIRST SERIES.
AND THERE'S THE OAV'S. THOSE ARE WAY DIFFERENT FROM THE MANGA, SO WATCH THEM, TOO.
THERE'S ALSO THE SCRIPT BOOKS FOR THE ANIME, BUT THEY'RE ONLY IN JAPANESE SO FAR.
PLUS THERE'S THE ART BOOKS! THE TWO MANGA ART BOOKS ARE AVAILABLE IN ENGLISH NOW, AND THERE'S A THIRD VOLUME OF ANIME ARTWORK THAT ISN'T IN ENGLISH, AT LEAST NOT YET.
SHAMELESS PLUG
HM?
SPROING!
SHAMELESS PLUG END

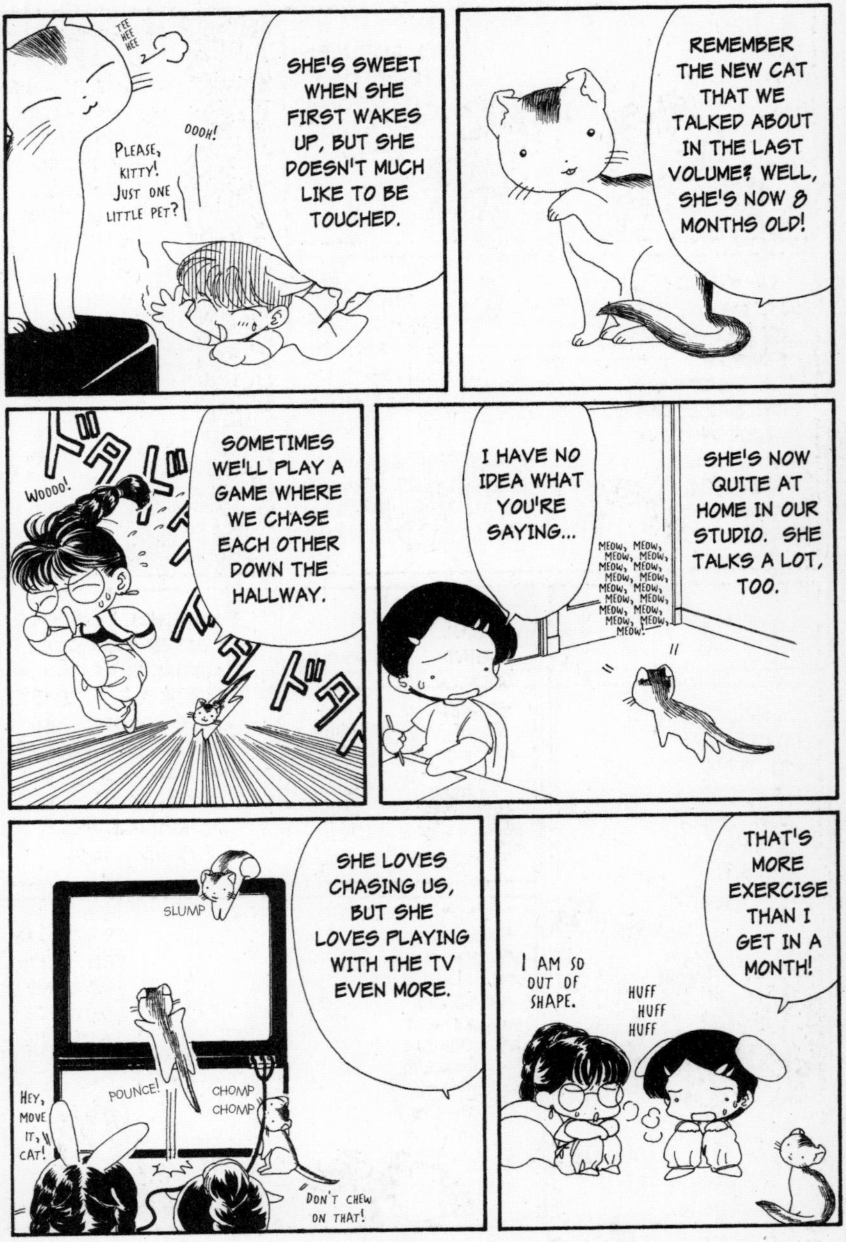

REMEMBER THE NEW CAT THAT WE TALKED ABOUT IN THE LAST VOLUME? WELL, SHE'S NOW 8 MONTHS OLD!
SHE'S SWEET WHEN SHE FIRST WAKES UP, BUT SHE DOESN'T MUCH LIKE TO BE TOUCHED.
TEE HEE HEE
OOOH!
PLEASE, KITTY! JUST ONE LITTLE PET?
SHE'S NOW QUITE AT HOME IN OUR STUDIO. SHE TALKS A LOT, TOO.
I HAVE NO IDEA WHAT YOU'RE SAYING...
MEOW, MEOW, MEOW, MEOW, MEOW, MEOW, MEOW, MEOW, MEOW, MEOW, MEOW, MEOW, MEOW, MEOW, MEOW, MEOW, MEOW!
SOMETIMES WE'LL PLAY A GAME WHERE WE CHASE EACH OTHER DOWN THE HALLWAY.
WOOOO!
THAT'S MORE EXERCISE THAN I GET IN A MONTH!
HUFF HUFF HUFF
I AM SO OUT OF SHAPE.
SHE LOVES CHASING US, BUT SHE LOVES PLAYING WITH THE TV EVEN MORE.
SLUMP
CHOMP CHOMP
POUNCE!
HEY, MOVE IT, CAT!
DON'T CHEW ON THAT!

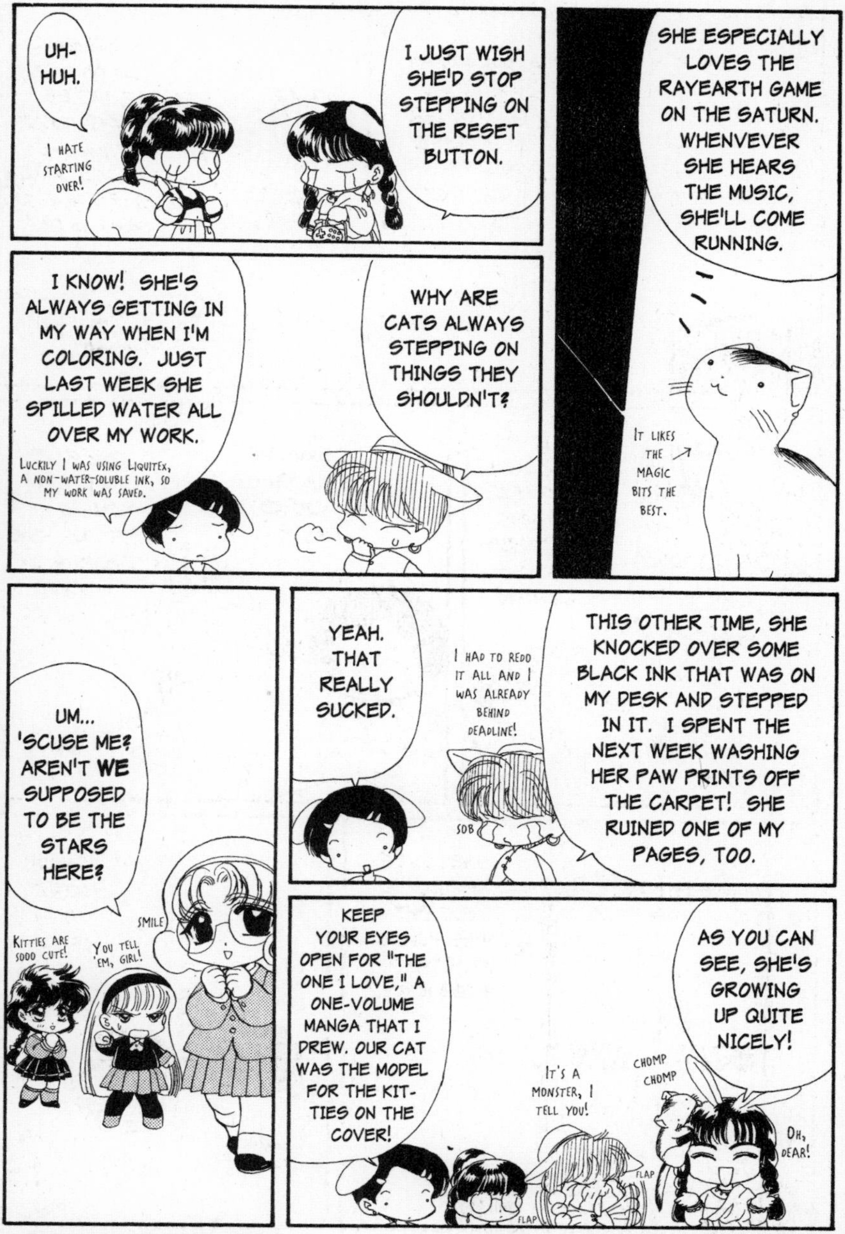
SHE ESPECIALLY LOVES THE RAYEARTH GAME ON THE SATURN. WHENVEVER SHE HEARS THE MUSIC, SHE'LL COME RUNNING.
It likes the magic bits the best.
I JUST WISH SHE'D STOP STEPPING ON THE RESET BUTTON.
UH-HUH.
I hate starting over!
WHY ARE CATS ALWAYS STEPPING ON THINGS THEY SHOULDN'T?
I KNOW! SHE'S ALWAYS GETTING IN MY WAY WHEN I'M COLORING. JUST LAST WEEK SHE SPILLED WATER ALL OVER MY WORK.
Luckily I was using Liquitex, a non-water-soluble ink, so my work was saved.
THIS OTHER TIME, SHE KNOCKED OVER SOME BLACK INK THAT WAS ON MY DESK AND STEPPED IN IT. I SPENT THE NEXT WEEK WASHING HER PAW PRINTS OFF THE CARPET! SHE RUINED ONE OF MY PAGES, TOO.
I had to redo it all and I was already behind deadline!
SOB
YEAH. THAT REALLY SUCKED.
AS YOU CAN SEE, SHE'S GROWING UP QUITE NICELY!
CHOMP CHOMP
Oh, dear!
FLAP
It's a monster, I tell you!
FLAP
KEEP YOUR EYES OPEN FOR "THE ONE I LOVE," A ONE-VOLUME MANGA THAT I DREW. OUR CAT WAS THE MODEL FOR THE KITTIES ON THE COVER!
UM... 'SCUSE ME? AREN'T WE SUPPOSED TO BE THE STARS HERE?
SMILE
You tell 'em, girl!
Kitties are sooo cute!

●TO NEXT STAGE●

Next time in Magic Knight Rayearth II...

Many battle to become Cephiro's new Pillar, but only two will be allowed to enter the road and take the test. Who will those two be, what will happen to them, and what will become of Cephiro's citizens when a new Pillar is chosen? Can Cephiro become "truly beautiful"? Come back for the shocking conclusion of Rayearth II!

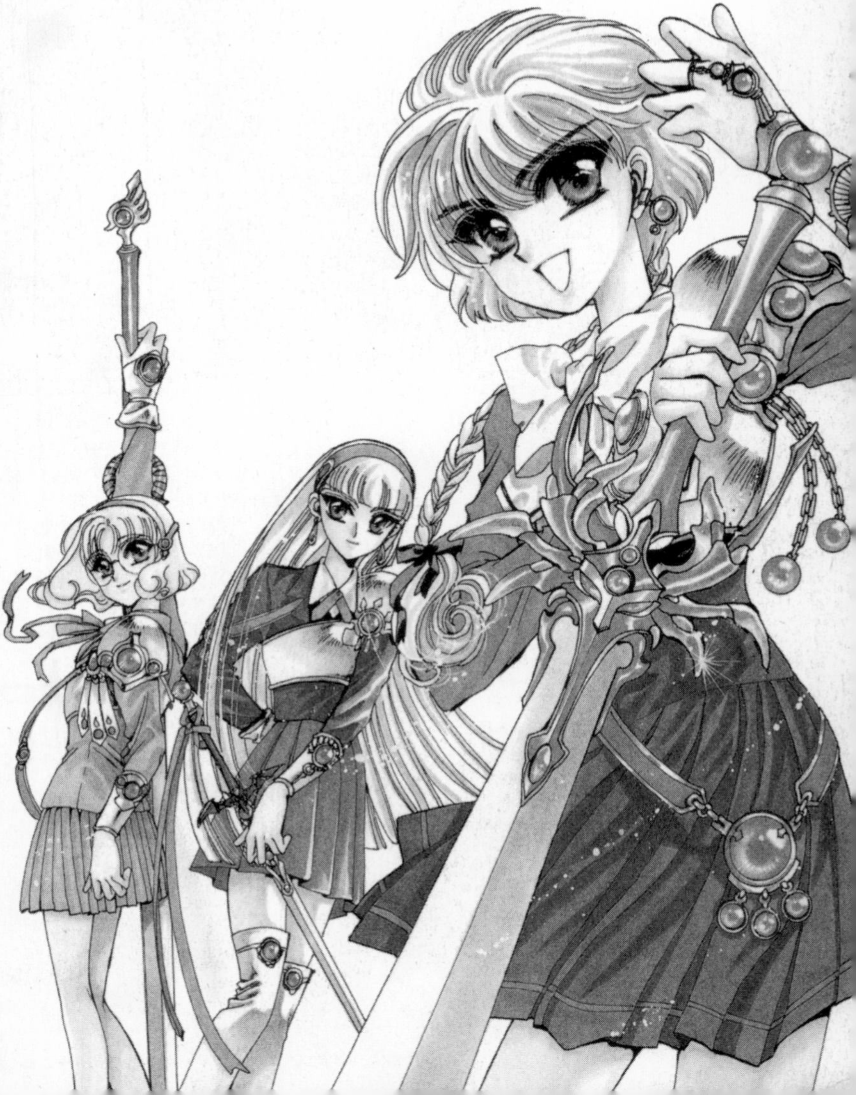

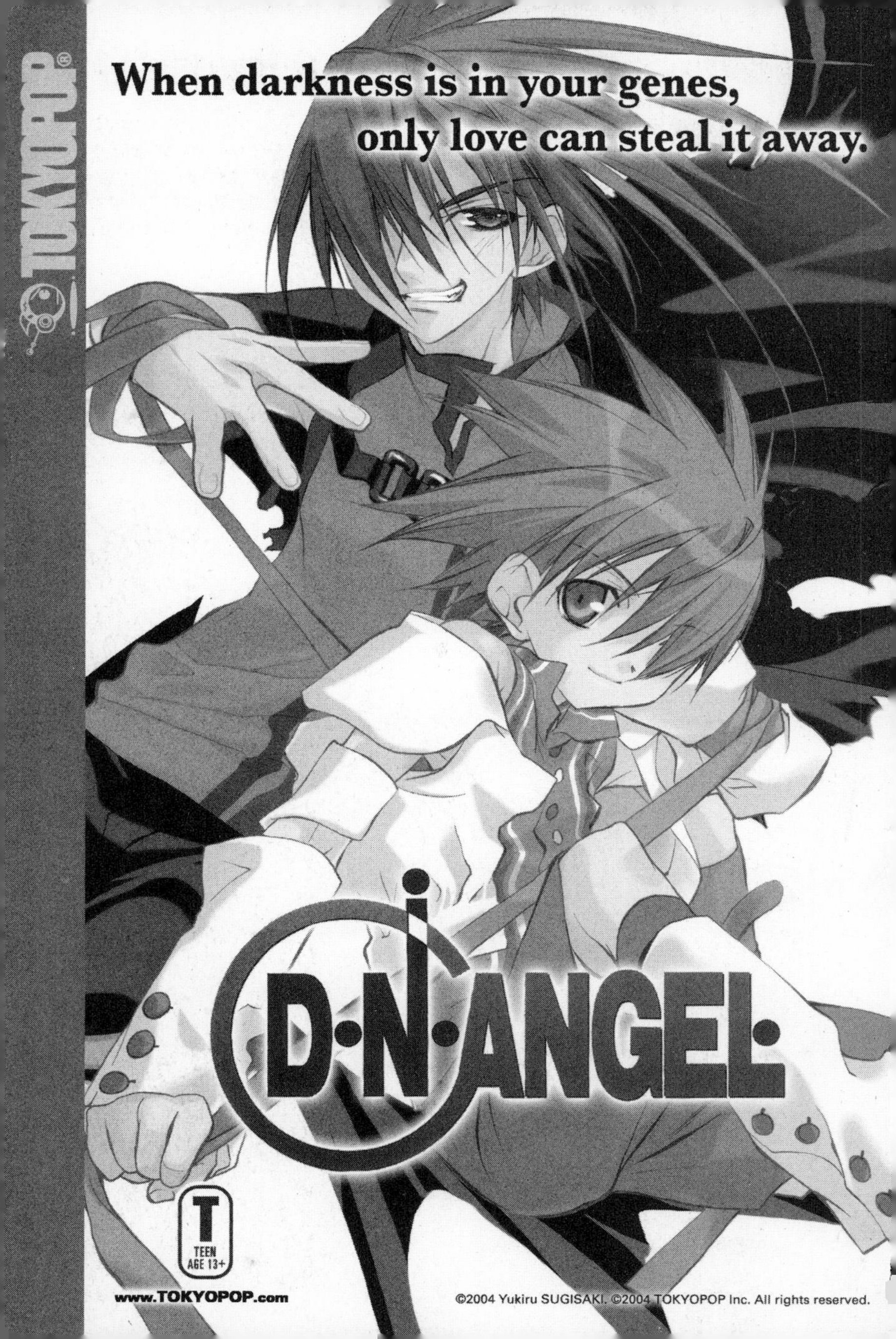
TOKYOPOP
When darkness is in your genes,
only love can steal it away.
D·N·ANGEL
T
TEEN
AGE 13+
www.TOKYOPOP.com
©2004 Yukiru SUGISAKI. ©2004 TOKYOPOP Inc. All rights reserved.

STOP!

This is the back of the book.
You wouldn't want to spoil a great ending!

This book is printed "manga-style," in the authentic Japanese right-to-left format. Since none of the artwork has been flipped or altered, readers get to experience the story just as the creator intended. You've been asking for it, so TOKYOPOP® delivered: authentic, hot-off-the-press, and far more fun!

DIRECTIONS

If this is your first time reading manga-style, here's a quick guide to help you understand how it works.

It's easy... just start in the top right panel and follow the numbers. Have fun, and look for more 100% authentic manga from TOKYOPOP®!